Introduction to Philosophy of Technology

Mark Coeckelbergh

New York   Oxford
OXFORD UNIVERSITY PRESS

Oxford University Press is a department of the University of Oxford.
It furthers the University's objective of excellence in research, scholarship,
and education by publishing worldwide. Oxford is a registered trade mark of
Oxford University Press in the UK and certain other countries.

Published in the United States of America by Oxford University Press
198 Madison Avenue, New York, NY 10016, United States of America.

© 2020 by Oxford University Press

Library of Congress Cataloging-in-Publication Data

CIP data is on file at the Library of Congress
978-0-19-093980-9

Printing number: 9 8 7 6 5 4 3 2 1
Printed by LSC Communications, Inc. United States of America

TABLE OF CONTENTS

PREFACE FOR TEACHERS

Before getting started, let me say more about the rationale for this textbook and its aims. This is mainly directed at fellow teachers and senior researchers, so if you are a student, you're welcome to skip this and go straight to the introduction.

As a *teacher*, my rationale for embarking on this journey was that I felt that an update was needed in terms of contemporary work and contemporary technologies. When developing a brand-new course that introduces students to philosophy of technology at the University of Vienna, I had to do a lot more work than I expected, since it turned out that I could not just use existing course books. Many existing course books and introductions to the field are good but by now outdated. I also noticed that many existing courses are not as comprehensive as they could be, often being focused on one particular approach. Some are also exclusively disciplinarily oriented. This book incrementally improves on these gaps and as such aims to contribute to higher education in this area—and, hopefully, to the ongoing growth and consolidation of philosophy of technology as a field on its own.

Moreover, while my main aim in this textbook is not to argue for a particular view or approach in philosophy of technology, as a *researcher*, I also have an agenda concerning the field, and this agenda has shaped the text as it stands. This is the case with any textbook. There is no such thing as an entirely "neutral" or "objective" textbook in philosophy, and I believe it is better to make one's stance explicit. This book is not only an update and an attempt to be slightly more comprehensive than previous textbooks. The way it is set up also contains a vision about how to do philosophy of technology. It is a vision that is inspired by, and critically responds to, what I see as some problematic views about doing philosophy of technology among philosophers inside and outside the field. Since philosophy of technology is a young field and therefore includes a lot of discussion on what philosophy of technology should be, let me say more about this here (and in the last part of this textbook).

First, I respond to a view that I believe is common among many philosophers outside the field: the view that philosophy of technology is applied philosophy. The usual way philosophers deal with topics such as technology is to conceive of technology as belonging to a field of application; that is, it is assumed that it is the role of philosophers to develop concepts and theories and then—if necessary at all—apply this to a particular field, whether it be technology or another one. Philosophy of technology, then, is conceived of as a branch of applied philosophy. According to this view, it seems, the "real" and "important" philosophy is going on elsewhere.

Second, philosophy of technology is sometimes seen by other philosophers as a branch of philosophy of science. It is assumed that technology is applied science, and that therefore the important philosophical questions that should be asked in this area really concern science (and therefore have already been asked by philosophers of science), or it is assumed that philosophy of technology is mainly about instruments used in science. According to this view, philosophy of technology is wrong in its claim to be a subdiscipline on its own.

Third, partly in response to more traditional views in philosophy and taking inspiration from science and technology studies, many contemporary philosophers of technology have taken an "empirical turn" (see later in this book), which focuses on material artifacts used in everyday life and analyzes these by developing and using its own conceptual tools rather than borrowing from philosophy of science or other philosophical subfields. Now sometimes this move has implied a turn away from the humanities and from traditional philosophy altogether, leading to a practice that is perhaps not "un-philosophical" but in any case risks to be divorced from traditional philosophical subfields and unrelated to (other) developments in the humanities. So here there is a danger that one takes the view that other subdisciplines in philosophy are really not needed.

In response to these developments, the vision of philosophy of technology that has influenced this book is the following. First, at its best, philosophy of technology is not merely "applied" philosophy but is philosophy proper, and this philosophical work can also start from *technology* rather than from concepts and theory. Second, technology is not merely applied science; technological practices (use, development/design, maintenance, etc., of technology) have their own kinds of knowledge, language, etc., and cannot be understood only by using philosophy of science: it needs its own concepts and theories. (And science is one of these technological practices.) Third, it is not only possible but also desirable (if not necessary) to develop one's own theories and even to take an empirical turn while at the same time engaging more with, learning more from, and even contributing to traditional subfields of philosophy and other fields in the humanities, which is itself transforming and changing. Finally, for all these purposes and for the further development of the field, philosophy is not enough: there is a need for interdisciplinarity and transdisciplinarity, and for reaching out beyond academia to artistic practices and policy, for instance—at local and global levels. Philosophy of technology is a discipline, but in my view it should be one that at the same time understands itself in a relational way and connects to other fields and reaches out beyond academia.

This vision has informed and shaped this textbook and the reader will notice it, especially in the final chapters, which reflect on methodology. But the main goal of this book is of course to introduce *students*—ideally upper-level undergraduates and graduate students who already have some background in philosophy or related academic fields—and *beginning researchers* to an exciting, relatively new, and growing field of philosophical and academic inquiry. I hope that for you, the teacher, this book may be a useful tool, a good teaching technology.

ACKNOWLEDGMENTS

Thanks are due to editor Robert Miller and the entire OUP editorial team, including Anna Deen, Sydney Keen, Alyssa Palazzo, Molly Zimetbaum, Leigh Ann Florek, and Patricia Berube for working on this book project. Deanna Hegle, and Wendy Walker also did a great job editing and proofreading, thanks.

I would like to thank the following reviewers for their helpful feedback during the later stages of this book:

Shannon Vallor, Santa Clara University
David Gunkel, Northern Illinois University
Glen Miller, Texas A&M University
Carl Mitcham, Colorado School of Mines/Renmin University of China
Anna Greenspan, NYU Shanghai
Kevin Stoehr, Boston University
Fred Gifford, Michigan State University
Diane Michelfelder, Macalester College

I also thank Zachary Storms and Isabel Walter from University of Vienna for helping with proofreading and images. I am also grateful to those who provided images, including roboticist Hiroshi Ishiguro, performance artist Stelarc, and philosophers Don Ihde, Bernard Stiegler, Andrew Feenberg, and Albert Borgmann.

Finally, I'd like to warmly thank all people who accompanied me during this journey in the past two years: family, friends, and colleagues. Special thanks go to my children, Lotte and Arno, for being patient when I worked on my book, and to my good friends, near and far, for being part of my life.

1 INTRODUCTION: PHILOSOPHY OF TECHNOLOGY

INTRODUCTION

CASE/TECHNOLOGY:
Nuclear Technology and the Atomic Bomb

Let's start with a bomb. Accidents and large disastrous events often draw attention to technology and the need to think about technology. An important event in 20th-century world history that made philosophers and others think about the potentially detrimental effects of technology was the use of nuclear weapons in the bombing of Hiroshima and Nagasaki by the United States in 1945 at the end of World War II. The bombs killed more than 129,000 people, most of them civilians. The bombs were the outcome of the so-called Manhattan Project, a research and development project in which theoretical physicist Robert Oppenheimer and other scientists played a key role. Nuclear science and technology is a good example of so-called dual use: it can be used for the generation of electricity but also for military purposes. But is responsibility for the development of such technologies only to be ascribed to the politicians and members of the military who deploy them (or not)? Or are the scientists and the people involved in the development of the technologies also responsible for its effects?

FIGURE 1.1 Atomic cloud over Nagasaki, August 9, 1945

1.1. Thinking about Technology?

Technology is not an obvious topic for philosophers. At first sight, it may seem that questions concerning the nature of reality and existence, the justification of our knowledge, our use of language, the right and the good, etc., have very little to do with technology. At best, thinking about technology seems to belong to an "applied" domain or to the philosophy of science; at worst, it may be seen as a non-philosophical preoccupation that is better dealt with by engineers and scientists. This view reflects the gap in academia between, on the one hand, humanities and, on the other hand, the sciences, engineering, and similar fields. Technology seems to belong to the latter domain. This gap is mirrored in wider society, for instance, in occupations: some professions deal with people, texts, culture, art, etc., whereas others deal with material things, technology, and infrastructure. Or so it is assumed.

Indeed, technology is not an obvious topic for anyone to reflect on. This is paradoxical since technology is part of our daily lives. But *usually* we are (literally) unaware of the technologies we use and indeed of our use of technologies. The technologies remain invisible. In his famous work *Being and Time*, Martin Heidegger (1927) made a distinction between ready-to-hand (*zuhanden*) and present-at-hand (*vorhanden*): in use, technologies are not visible, they are ready-to-hand; and we just use them without thinking. Only when something goes wrong or when we take a theoretical attitude do we become aware of them and they become present-at-hand as technological artifacts. But this is the exception, not the rule. Think of a computer program: we use it and do not attend to the technology as such; but when the program breaks down or the computer's operating system crashes, we become aware of the technology and our dependence on the technology. Or consider a nuclear power plant: we usually do not think about where our electricity comes from until there is a report about a nuclear accident or risk. And some people even freak out if there is no Wi-Fi connection available or if the person they just met is not on social media; this also makes us aware of how dependent we are on an internet connection and on specific social media, all of which are normally used mindlessly. We use technology but do not stand back and reflect on our use.

This situation is regrettable, since many of the things that go right and wrong in our world have to do with technology. Consider the wealth accumulated in Western countries, which was only possible by means of all kinds of technologies used in industry and in services; or consider climate change, which also depends on the use of technology. Think of how dependent our lives have become on smartphones, the internet, and related technologies; or of problems with technologies such as car accidents, nuclear disasters, environmental pollution, and so on. If we ignore technology, we do not only ignore material artifacts; we ignore our world. Not to think about technology at all, or leave that thinking to scientists and engineers, is both ignorant and irresponsible.

Philosophy of technology is a disciplined and systematic attempt to think through these kinds of issues, including the question of how we can best understand technology and the challenge to evaluate new technological developments. It is an academic discipline, but it can also take the form of a public philosophy, or it can take interdisciplinary and transdisciplinary routes. Perhaps it has to, if it aims to have impact on the issues it talks about.

Now thinking about technology can be done in many ways. What is philosophy of technology all about? What kind of approach can and does it take? What do philosophers of technology do? This book offers some answers to these questions. Let us start with conceptual analysis: one thing philosophers like to do, or should do, is to critically discuss the language we use to talk about technology. Philosophers often aim to define and discuss the central terms they use. Here that central term is technology. What is **technology**? Technology can be defined in different ways, and it is good in discussions about technology to always make explicit what we talk about. Technology can take the form of human-made things, artifacts, which can be material or immaterial. For example, a car is a technology in this sense (material), or a computer program (immaterial). It can also come in the form of infrastructure or a system; for example, roads for cars, a public transport system, or the internet and the hardware needed to run these cars, systems, and infrastructures. Technology can also be seen as a device, a more or less smart thing that we use to make life easier for us: for example, a thermostat. Yet often definitions in terms of artifacts or devices hide the infrastructure, hide everything that is needed to make the technology work. Human labor, for example. Technology can also be seen as an activity, or a skill, for instance the activity or skill of using, operating, inventing, making, maintaining, and so on. It can be a volition, for instance the will to power. (See also Mitcham [1994] for a number of conceptions of technology.) We can also encounter technology as an idea, which can be (partly) realized or not, such as the idea of the new human, enhanced by technologies, or the idea of the cyborg: a merger between humans and machines. These ideas can find their expression in nonfiction but also in fiction, for instance science fiction. The different chapters in this book will show various shapes of technologies. But let us start with discussing one very popular and common definition of technology: technology as a tool or instrument.

This definition of technology is often what we have in mind when we think of technologies: we think of a hammer, a phone, a car, or a computer as instruments for human purposes such as making furniture, communicating with a friend, getting to your holiday destination, or writing an essay. When we use such instrumental definitions, we assume that we humans set the goals; the technology is then the means to reach these goals. Seen from this perspective, our aim to engage in thinking, understanding, and critically evaluating technology is not really about technology: it is about what we want to do with technology, it is about our human aims, values, concerns, and projects. It is these aims, values, projects, and so on that need understanding and evaluation, not technology itself. Many people think that what matters is not the technology but what you (aim to) do with it. But is this view, which is often called the *instrumental* conception of technology, adequate?

Philosophers like to question our everyday intuitions, and this is also the case here. A central claim of contemporary philosophers of technology is that technology is *not* a mere instrument. This goes against the everyday understanding of technology as a tool, which we then can use for good or for bad—for whatever aim we humans give it. Technology, then, is not a mere means to human ends. The instrumental understanding is not "wrong" because, of course, technology is *also* a means; but it is misleading if it suggests that it is a mere means. The perhaps surprising claim is that the means also shape the ends. Philosophers of technology argue that technology shapes what we do, what we value, what it means to be human, and more generally what we think. We can only ignore this at our peril; if we want to gain a critical relation to what we do, we'd better take technology seriously as a philosophical problem on its own and gain a critical relation to *technology*.

However, to really understand this claim and its full implications is not easy. Perhaps it is so difficult to move beyond the instrumentalist understanding of technology because of the language we use. The way we talk about technology, for example, as a tool or as a means, often suggests its instrumentality, already includes it. And there is nothing "wrong" with using that language, since technology can also be a tool and an instrument. But technology is so much more than a tool; and even if it is a tool, maybe it is precisely *as* an instrument and a tool that it also influences our thinking.

Heidegger, for example, argued that modern technology is not only or not so much about instruments but rather about a way of revealing, a way of perceiving and constructing the world. He thought that modern technology lets nature appear as a standing-reserve (German: *Bestand*) that we can use, manipulate, and control (Heidegger 1977). For example, when we use a hydroelectric power plant, nature becomes a reserve of power for our use. Whether or not Heidegger was right about this, the point here is that technologies are about how we think about and relate to the world, and conversely, how the world appears to us, how we experience the world. This example does not only suggest the non-instrumentality of technology, that technology is more than just a tool: it also shows that technology is not only about "applied" matters if that would mean that thinking about specific technologies is not philosophically interesting; rather, it is about core, traditional concerns of philosophy, such as how we know, experience, and relate to the world. I will give more examples in the course of this book, such as questions concerning metaphysics and language.

Another approach does not so much argue *against* the instrumentality of technology as such but rather starts from it to then show that, as an instrument, it has these more-than-instrumental consequences and meanings. For instance, I have used Wittgenstein's view of language to argue that technology-in-use is always embedded in games and a form of life (Coeckelbergh 2017). And one of the influential approaches in contemporary philosophy of technology, Ihde's postphenomenology and related mediation theory, can also be interpreted and revised to emphasize that it is precisely in their use that technologies mediate and shape human–technology relations. Here, thinking about use helps us to think about how we relate to the world, which by itself is a classic philosophical question. Don't worry about this now; I will return to this in chapter 4 (Ihde) and chapter 11 (philosophy of language).

But philosophy of technology is not only a way to engage with perennial questions in philosophy. It may also help us to think through some problems we encounter with contemporary technologies. Today, when new technologies are being developed, thinking about technology gains a certain importance and urgency. We cannot wait until the climate and the ecosystem have drastically changed before rethinking our relation to nature and the role technology plays in this. We cannot wait until robotics and artificial intelligence are applied and embedded in all aspects of our lives before standing back and questioning if we really want these technologies—and, if so, how we want to integrate them into our lives and societies in a meaningful and ethical way. We cannot wait until our cities have radically changed because of the use of smart technologies before thinking about how new technologies can and should rechange urban environments and related ways of life. We cannot wait until we are forced to integrate digital technology into our bodies and brains before thinking about the possibilities, risks, and dependencies related to wearable and interface technologies. We need to better understand and evaluate technologies *now*. In this sense, philosophy of technology is not, and should not be, a luxury or extra but a much needed way to contribute to shaping and thinking about the future and about the human condition, *our* future and our condition and that of our descendants.

1.2. Approach, Structure of the Book, and Overview of Chapters

The guiding vision throughout this book is that (1) technology is more than an instrument, that it also changes us and our thinking, and that we should pay more attention to it in order to understand what we're doing and understand ourselves;

(2) there is an urgency to think about technology since new technologies are being developed now and may lead to significant and radical transformations of human lives, of societies, and of the planet; and (3) thinking about technology can also be philosophically interesting, and not *in spite* of starting from technologies but *because* of that. Philosophy of technology also deserves its own field, although its further growth will depend on maintaining or developing links with other subfields in philosophy, other academic disciplines, and practices outside academia such as policymaking and art.

The structure of this textbook follows this approach. I give an overview of concepts and theories used in the field, but previous introductions have been *updated* by adding contemporary theories and there is more emphasis on *technologies* and problems related to technology. It is argued that thinking about technology is fueled by technological developments themselves: that new technological developments are not merely the passive object of reflection (as in "a field or problems one applies one's preexisting concepts and theories *to*") but rather have led to *new ways of thinking*. It is shown that some of the most vibrant and exciting new conceptual developments in the field come from engagement with these technological developments (and of course also theory) and with fields and practices outside philosophy and academia. At the same time, the book also shows how philosophy of technology can benefit from making more connections with traditional subfields in philosophy, such as metaphysics or philosophy of language, and with other disciplines and practices. Hence, after the introductory chapters, there are 3 further parts in the book that reflect these different aims: one part focuses on philosophy of technology by starting from theory; one shows how philosophers of technology often start from technology; and another one emphasizes links with other philosophical subfields, other disciplines, and practices outside academia. Each chapter also includes "In focus" textboxes about specific authors, review questions and questions for further discussion, recommended reading, and a list of key terms. But to support the emphasis on how new technologies spark new thinking, there are also textboxes on new technologies and related cases.

Let me now provide a more detailed overview of the chapters. The next chapter, chapter 2, gives an overview of the history and landscape of the course. The emergence of philosophy of technology as a systematic and more or less autonomous subdiscipline is relatively recent, but there is a long cultural history of thinking and narrating about technology, including historical figures such as Kapp, Simmel, Weber, Benjamin, Jaspers, Ellul, Mumford, Husserl, Heidegger, and Wittgenstein; but also earlier modern thinkers such as Rousseau, and reaching back to the ancient past, for example, to Plato's dialogues. I comment on the distinction between humanities and engineering philosophy of technology (Mitcham 1994) and sketch the historical context and landscape of the discipline, including the current geographical situation and questions concerning cultural difference. I also raise the question that is already evident concerning transdisciplinarity, which will be further addressed in chapters 12 and 13.

Part 2 gives an overview of some influential theories in the field. Chapter 3 offers some sources for a phenomenological-hermeneutical approach—such as Heidegger, McLuhan, and Merleau-Ponty—and contemporary discussion of these sources. In particular, the chapter focuses on Heidegger's "The Question Concerning Technology" and gives a brief overview of work by McLuhan, Merleau-Ponty, and Dreyfus. Chapter 4 focuses on postphenomenology and mediation theory: the work of Don Ihde and authors such as Peter-Paul Verbeek and Evan Selinger, who are often seen as part of the postphenomenological "school" and who offer theories of how technologies mediate our relation with the world. The chapter gives an overview of, and critically discusses, the work of Ihde and Verbeek. Chapter 5 turns to critical theory and feminism to highlight the social and political dimension of our dealings with technology, including Andrew Feenberg and Donna Haraway. I start from Marx and contemporary applications of Marx (Fuchs), and then turn to the critical theory tradition that went beyond Marx: Marcuse, Foucault, Feenberg, and Winner. The chapter ends with a brief overview of feminist thinking about technology (Haraway and Wajcman) and some critical discussion. Chapter 6 then gives an overview of some other selected approaches: pragmatism, analytic philosophy of technology, and transcultural philosophy of technology. The focus is on Dewey, empirical turn-style and engineering-oriented analytic philosophy of artifacts, and the examples of Simondon (French philosophy of technology), Flusser (Brazil), and Confucianism (Chinese philosophy of technology).

Part 3, then, shows more clearly that philosophy of technology is not only about developing new theory and then applying it to technology but that it also often starts from *technology*. By focusing on specific themes linked to new technological developments, I show how philosophers have been inspired by technologies (and the problems they raise) when crafting their new concepts and theories. Chapter 7 offers a summary and discussion of how information technologies have led some to propose a philosophy of information, zooming in on Floridi's work. First, a summary of his philosophy of information and ethics of information is outlined, then a critical discussion is provided. The chapter invites thinking about how our current digital technologies transform (our perception of?) reality and raises moral-philosophical problems such as the questions whether artificial agents can be moral agents. The latter kind of question leads us to chapter 8. It shows how some philosophers have taken inspiration from developments in robotics to do work on moral standing and think about human relationships. The chapter offers an overview of some questions and answers in the discussion about moral agency and moral patiency, including work from Sullins, Floridi, Johnson, Bryson, Darling, Gunkel, and Coeckelbergh (the author of this book). It also links to the debate about sex robots (e.g., Levy and Richardson) and to posthumanism. In chapter 9, this line is continued, where the focus is on how developments in genetic engineering and "cyborg"-like technologies have led to transhumanist and posthumanist thinking. The chapter gives an overview of the discussion about human enhancement and transhumanism (featuring authors such as Bostrom and Kurzweil) and offers a critical discussion of transhumanism. It also says more about Haraway's and Latour's posthumanism. It is shown again how technological developments can be taken as a point of departure for raising interesting philosophical questions. Chapter 10 then turns to the implications of Latour's work for thinking about "nature" and to thinking in terms of the "Anthropocene," both of which are understood as responses to climate change and ideas about geoengineering. The first part explores what a non-modern approach to the environment could mean; the second part maps and constructs some philosophical responses to the question concerning the Anthropocene. This discussion invites us to rethink the relation(s) between technology and the natural environment, including revisiting the language we use to talk about humans, technology, and the environment.

Finally, part 4 introduces readers to ongoing discussions about the nature and future of the field—discussions that are very much part of what is going on in the field and hence cannot be omitted. It is argued that philosophers of technology should do, and that many are already partly doing, a kind of "philosophy of technology +": the field can and should reconnect to, and learn from, other subdisciplines in philosophy, including not only ethics but also, for example, philosophy of language (chapter 11); engage with other disciplines, and not only engineering and social sciences but also humanities (chapter 12); and also move into fields and practices outside academia, for instance technology development and innovation, policy, and art, which can reveal new risks and possibilities (chapter 13). Chapter 11 provides examples of crossovers to ethics (e.g., Vallor), philosophical anthropology (e.g., posthumanism), and philosophy of language (e.g., Coeckelbergh). Chapter 12 discusses the opportunities and challenges of transdisciplinarity for philosophers of technology and gives some examples of work that engages with engineering and computer science, social sciences (e.g., science and technology studies, also called science, technology, and society studies [STS]), and (other) humanities—all of which are themselves developing transdisciplinary clusters and offshoots. Chapter 13 outlines some possibilities for reaching out to practices beyond academia: responsible innovation and value-sensitive design, policy, public engagement, activism, and art. The chapter ends with a reflection on the role of philosophers (of technology) in society and the implications for education in the light of democratic change.

REVIEW QUESTIONS

1. What is technology?
2. Why is thinking about technology not an obvious topic?
3. Give an example of a technology that has sparked philosophical discussion.
4. What is philosophy of technology?

DISCUSSION QUESTIONS

1. Is technology an instrument for human purposes?
2. Who is responsible for the effects of technological developments?
3. What did you think philosophy of technology was about before you read this chapter? How does that compare to what you know now?
4. Do you think that philosophy of technology is a separate field and discipline?

KEY TERMS

Philosophy of technology   Technology

2 HISTORY AND LANDSCAPE

CASE/TECHNOLOGY:
Search Engines, Knowledge, and Memory

Today there is a lot of information on the internet, and we have powerful search engines like Google. Does this mean we have to memorize less information? Do we need less knowledge? Do we need a different kind of knowledge, such as the skill to search for information on the internet? Or do we still need a good base of knowledge? And will the availability of all this information and search possibilities have the result that our memory becomes less good?

FIGURE 2.1 Google search engine

2.1. Beginnings: Two Ancient Myths

While philosophy of technology is a relatively recent (sub)discipline, there is a long history of thinking about technology, starting already in ancient times. In Plato's writings, for instance, we can already find two myths that are directly relevant to philosophy of technology.

One can be found in the *Protagoras*: the creation myth of **Prometheus**. The god Zeus asks the Titans Prometheus and Epimetheus to distribute qualities and forces to the creatures, but Epimetheus forgets to give any to the humans (the mortals). It is said that whereas the animals were well provided for, the human race was "completely unequipped" and "naked" (Plato, *Protagoras*, 321c). Prometheus then steals the *technai* (the mechanical arts) and fire, which he gives to the mortals to compensate for their lack of qualities (321d–e). The myth thus portrays human beings as incomplete and subsequently completed by technology.

Much later in history, philosophers of technology have taken up this idea. For example, according to the French philosopher Bernard Stiegler, human beings are **prosthetic beings**: they lack something, and technology compensates for this. This implies that humans are constituted by technology and have to invent their existence. The human condition is a technological condition. Humans and technology originated and evolved together. We have exteriorized our organic

FIGURE 2.2 Zeus's eagle pecks at the exposed liver of Prometheus (Painting by unknown Italian artist, around 1600).

memory to the inorganic-technological, which enables us to go beyond the present—thus making possible time, society, and culture (Stiegler 1998, 2004).

IN FOCUS:
Bernard Stiegler

Bernard Stiegler is a French philosopher and author who has been thinking about new media and technologies for many decades. His best-known work in this area is the trilogy *La technique et le temps* (*Technics and Time*; e.g., Stiegler 1998). He is influenced by Heidegger and Simondon, among many others. He is head of the *Institut de recherche et d'innovation* at Centre Georges-Pompidou in Paris, founder of the political and cultural group *Ars Industrialis*, and founder of the online school Pharmakon.fr. He became interested in philosophy when he was in prison for armed robbery.

FIGURE 2.3 Bernhard Stiegler

Another theme this myth touches on is that of technology as **hybris**: the capacity to create and invent was supposed to be a divine one, but humans have stolen it and are hence doing something that is normally reserved for the gods. By developing technology, they are disrespectful, going too far, beyond what they are meant to do and to be. In modern times, this myth takes the form of the story of **Frankenstein**. In Mary Shelley's story *Frankenstein: Or, the Modern Prometheus* ([1818] 1992), the scientist Victor Frankenstein creates a new being by galvanizing an assemblage of dead body parts. The scientist is then horrified by what he created, and the "monster" turns against him. Again the message seems to be (at least this is how the novel is often read) that developing technology is something reserved for the gods; and if we play the sorcerer's apprentice (another metaphor), this is dangerous: technology may turn against us, we might be punished for the "sin" of making use of this stolen capacity. Today, some responses to technology are still inspired by this myth. Consider, for example, visions about artificial intelligence (AI): there is the nightmare of the machine that turns against us and dominates us, that becomes a *terminator*—to use a term from a famous science fiction film. Is this a real danger? How autonomous is technology? And is the question regarding mastery the most important question to ask regarding AI and robotics?

Another relevant myth can be found in Plato's *Phaedrus*, where we find a legend about the Egyptian gods Theuth and Thamus who discuss the use of letters. Theuth is said to be the inventor of many arts, including calculation and astronomy, but also the art of writing. Theuth goes to King **Thamus** to show his inventions, enumerating all the uses and benefits of the new technologies. About writing, he says that it will make the citizens wiser and give them better memories. But Thamus is less impressed than might be expected. He argues that inventors are not always the best judges of the utility of their inventions and that the technology of letter writing will create forgetfulness in learners since they will not trust

FIGURE 2.4 Boris Karloff as Frankenstein (1931)

their own memory but rely on the external written characters. Readers will appear to know everything but will have no knowledge of the truth and no wisdom:

> Theuth said: "O King, here is something that, once learned, will make the Egyptians wiser and will improve their memory;" . . . Thamus, however, replied: "O most expert Theuth, one man can give birth to the elements of an art, but only another can judge how they can benefit or harm those who will use them. And now, since you are the father of writing, your affection for it has made you describe its effects as the opposite of what they really are. In fact, it will introduce forgetfulness into the soul of those who learn it: they will not practice using their memory because they will put their trust in writing, which is external and depends on signs that belong to others. . . . they will imagine that they have come to know much while for the most part they will know nothing. And they will be difficult to get along with, since they will merely appear to be wise instead of really being so." (Plato, *Phaedrus*, 274e–275b)

Again we have an interesting point of departure for contemporary discussions about the effects of technology, including writing technologies and so-called digital technologies and new media. The history of writing, but also that of printing, for instance, is also a history of complaints against these technologies. For instance, in the 15th century, the Venetian editor Hieronimo Squarciafico was already concerned that books would make their readers less studious (Lowry 1979). In the 20th century, media theorist Walter Ong and his teacher Marshall McLuhan have famously written about the shift from an oral to a literacy culture, and how this changed human consciousness (Ong [1982] 2005). New technologies and media were thus not mere tools; they changed our thinking and our culture. This raises the question of what new digital technologies and media do to our consciousness and thinking, and indeed how they in turn are transforming our culture. According to McLuhan (1964), we are returning to a culture of orality. According to Stiegler, who in this work also comments on the *Phaedrus* (and the *Meno*), the new technologies create a new technological milieu for the mind, which is then exploited by capital as desire is commercialized (Stiegler 2004). Today we debate about new social media. Do they make us less social? Do they contribute to a new mass society? What do they do to our consciousness? Do they render our minds more fragmented? Is it more difficult to focus? And do the new media empower or disempower? Are we the product rather than the client, milked for our data, functioning as slaves in the attention economy?

There are of course more interesting elements in ancient philosophy for philosophers of technology, such as the figure of the **Demiurg** (creator of the world) in Plato who is compared with what craftsmen do; Aristotle's comments on slaves and tools in the *Nicomachean Ethics*; Aristotle's distinction in the *Physics* between natural things and artifacts (*physis* and *poiesis*) and the notion of craftsmanship as an imitation of nature; Aristotle's distinction in the *Nicomachean Ethics* between various kinds of knowledge (theoretical or scientific knowledge [*episteme*], art or craft knowledge [*techne*], prudence or practical knowledge [*phronesis*], intellect or intuitive apprehension [*nous*], and wisdom [*sophia*]—although how to translate these terms is not obvious and a matter of scholarly discussion); and Aristotle's doctrine of the four causes—the latter of which is taken up by Heidegger in his famous essay concerning technology (Heidegger 1977). For the purpose of continuing this brief history, let us jump to early modern times, to the English philosopher, statesman, and scientist Francis Bacon.

Bacon is best known for his work *Novum Organum* (*The New Organon*; [1620] 2000). It is usually read by philosophers of science, since it is important in the development of the experimental method. But it is also interesting for philosophers of technology. According to Bacon, knowledge is power: not so much in the sense of "power over people," but rather the power to change nature. Nature is to be understood and conquered. Against medieval scholars who read Aristotle, Bacon argued that we cannot gain knowledge of nature by merely reading books. We need to observe and experiment; we need "works." In these experiments and works, technologies play a key role. He writes, "Neither the bare hand nor the unaided intellect has much power; the work is done by tools and assistance, and the intellect needs them as much as the hand" (Bacon [1620] 2000, 33). But Bacon's aim is not only the advancement of natural philosophy (now we would say science) as such; there is also an important societal dimension to his project. In his novel *The New Atlantis* ([1627] 2000), in which a visitor explores the mythical island Bensalem, technology is assumed to play a key role in both natural philosophy *and* society: technical works are important not only to test our theories but also to improve the living conditions of people. In Solomon's House, Bensalem's place for scientific-technological innovation, technology is centrally important. The "preparations and instruments we have for our works" are explained to the visitor. There are many instruments and devices in the House, including flying machines and other technologies that did not yet exist at his time. Metals, medicines, and "a water" are used for prolongation of life; beasts are used to "make commixtures and copulations of different kinds." There are also instruments that generate heat, sound instruments, instruments that imitate the birds and can fly, and instruments that "deceive the senses." The "mechanical arts" and crafts are part of it. But the aim is not profit or serving private interests. The members of the House work for the benefit of the people and society. It is Bacon's vision that the power we gain over nature, the enlargement of "the bounds of human empire," is used for the benefit of humankind. Knowledge should be used in practice, to better the conditions of people (see also Reydon 2012). So here warnings for the danger of hybris are gone: humans can experiment, create, and study the works of God, who "might have the more glory in the workmanship of them."

Science and technological innovation are fine, even mandatory. We need "the sciences, arts, manufactures, and inventions of all the world" to improve human lives and human society. Today, this idea is relevant to discussions about science and technological innovation. Should technology benefit only particular people or society as a whole? And if it is society as a whole, *how* can we make sure this happens? How ethical is and should technology be? What are the political implications of new technologies? What is technology's societal role?

Later, at the end of the 18th century, Jean-Jacques Rousseau is less enthusiastic about science and related human pursuits. In his *Discours sur les sciences et les arts* ([1750] 2011), Rousseau argues that science and the arts corrupt human morality since they lead to people searching for prestige and honor in society, to "sophisticated wits" and "fashionable people"; we would be better off if we lived a simpler life. Enlightenment philosophy and science might be good for a few, for geniuses such as Bacon or Newton; for most of us it does not lead us to the virtue and piety that Rousseau imagined pervaded the cities of Sparta and Rome. In contrast to Bacon, Rousseau thus radically questions the use and moral benefit of having scientific knowledge:

> Answer me, then, illustrious philosophers, you thanks to whom we know the ratios in which bodies attract one another in a vacuum . . . Answer me, I say, you from whom we have received so much sublime knowledge;

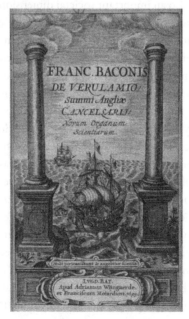

FIGURE 2.5 *Novum Organum*, 1645

if you had never thought us any of these things, would we therefore have been any less numerous, less well governed, less formidable, less flourishing or more perverse? (Rousseau [1750] 2011, 15)

Moreover, in Rousseau's book *Emile* ([1762] 1991), he questions the benefit of knowledge one can gain from books as opposed to one's own experience. He is not opposed to knowledge of nature as such, and he does not reject science and technology in general; rather, he is against knowledge and experimentation that is removed from our daily experience, and against technologies we do not need for living a simple and virtuous life. Following Rousseau, one could question the value and use of technological advancement if those are divorced from experience. Contrary to Bacon and certainly contrary to (other) **Enlightenment** philosophers and scientists, Rousseau thought that science and technology do not necessarily contribute to what is really valuable and good in society and in human beings. This remains an important question for today, when new advanced technologies are being developed. Do we really need them? Do we need them to lead a good life, a virtuous life, a meaningful life? Do we need technology to become wise? And are technologies still connected to our experience? The question of what *kind* of knowledge humankind needs and the question regarding the relation between technology and virtue remain highly relevant today—also, and

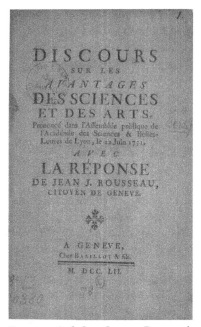

FIGURE 2.6 Jean-Jacques Rousseau's
Discours sur les sciences et les arts

perhaps especially in advanced technological societies. (Later in this book, I will say more about virtue and technology when I refer to Shannon Vallor's work.) Later in this chapter, I will also touch on the question of alienation.

Of course this is a very limited selection of historical thinking about technology before the 19th century; there are obviously many other writings that directly reflect on technology or that, directly or indirectly, are relevant to contemporary philosophy of technology. For instance, I have not said much about medieval thinking about technology and thinking about technology in other cultures and civilizations. This is not a coincidence: the history of ideas is often written from a Western perspective; and compared to the history of science, there is still a lot of work to do to reveal the history of thinking about technology since it is often not so visible (yet). Although in the past 50 years, for instance, science and technology and cultural studies scholars have made valuable contributions in this area, much of that history still needs to be written.

2.2. A Brief History of the Discipline

The "acknowledged" or "official" history of philosophy of technology as a discipline usually starts in the 19th century, when Ernst Kapp writes his *Grundlinien einer Philosophie der Technik* ([1877] 2015). Arguably, Karl Marx had earlier already considered technology: as a means of production. He understood that this production is related to social conditions and argued that the use of machines under **capitalism** is alienating, since workers do not have ownership of the means of production and also lack ownership of the products of their labor. However, Marx thought that under the right conditions, technology can also liberate us: when it ends scarcity.

CASE/TECHNOLOGY:
The Machine

Philosophers of technology often talk about "machines" or "the machine." However, the term can mean very different things, ranging from ancient Greek or Renaissance simple mechanical devices to more complex automata in the 18th century; industrial machines in the time of Marx and Engels; computers in the 1980s; to all kinds of robots, small and smart internet-connected devices, and so-called molecular machines or nanomachines today. Etymologically, the term machine is related to contrivance and plot. Machines have always fascinated philosophers and have played a role in reflections on the human. For example, Descartes regarded non-human animals and the human body as machines.

Later William Morris also saw the problematic consequences of machines; but, like Marx, he also noted possibilities for liberation: perhaps they could release us from labor (Morris [1884]). And one can try to interpret earlier philosophers such as Feuerbach as having implications for thinking about technology. He defended an anthropological materialism that, before Merleau-Ponty and (in philosophy of technology) Ihde, acknowledged the importance of the body (Feuerbach [1843] 1983). Attention to the body is also present in the philosophical anthropology of Plessner, who wrote about how the body mediates our relation to things, and about how tool use led to the development of intelligence and language ([1941] 2003). The relation between body and technology remains an important topic today. But Kapp's ([1877] 2015) work remains a milestone: for the first time in the history of philosophy, someone thought that technology was a worthy subject on its own and tried to (re-)conceptualize technology itself and its relation to humans.

In Kapp's thinking, philosophical anthropology and thinking about technology are closely interwoven. Technology is very much connected with our human condition. Like in the myth from the *Protagoras*, humans are seen as lacking something that technology supplies. Humans have the sciences and the arts instead of instincts; we (have to) create and enhance ourselves (Kapp [1877] 2015, 40). According to Kapp, tools are **organ projections**: the tools take over the shape of the human organs and their potential use and force (54). The mechanical is thus

FIGURE 2.7 Ernst Kapp

understood in organic terms. Tools are extensions of the human body, and language and institutions such as the state are extensions of the mental life. Humans used a stone axe instead of a hand and stone, a hammer instead of a hand (especially the fist) and arm. And technology is not only about simple tools but also about technological systems: the railroad is an extension of the circulatory system; telegraphy is an extension of the nervous system (132–144). Kapp already imagined a "universal telegraphics" (144) linking languages and inventions into a global transfiguration of the earth (see also Mitcham 1994, 23). He suggests a kind of Hegelian development in which the mechanical takes a less material, more transparent and spiritual form. The question of whether technology is an extension returns in contemporary debates about information technology and the internet, not in the least since some technologies are literally connected to the human body. In the 1960s, McLuhan (1964) saw technologies as extensions of the physical and nervous system. Today we could ask, Is the internet an extension of the human nervous system? Is there a development toward less material, more spiritual forms of technology and culture? And what is the link between technology and social institutions?

Subsequent philosophers of technology remain interested in the impact of technology on the mental and social life, which is often discussed in the context of a critique of modernity. In the beginning and middle of the 20th century, many philosophers—mainly in the German-speaking world but also in France, for instance—point to the less advantageous effects of technology in the context of modern life. They tend to emphasize the darker sides of modernity and see technology as playing at least an ambiguous role in this, if not the main force, problem, and danger. Georg Simmel, for instance, saw a tension between the individual's striving for independence and technology: "The deepest problems of modern life flow from the attempt of the individual to maintain the independence and individuality of his existence against the sovereign powers of society, against the weight of the historical heritage and the external culture and technique of life" (Simmel [1903] 2002, 11). In *The Philosophy of Money* ([1907] 2004), Simmel sees money as a tool that creates indifference, distance, and depersonalization. While he has a nuanced view and also sees that money can connect people, he mainly sees technologies such as money as contributing to processes of objectification and quantification of human life and culture. Max Weber argues in *Die protestantische Ethik und der Geist des Kapitalismus* (*The Protestant Ethic and the Spirit of Capitalism*; [1905] 1992) that the technical and economic conditions give us an order that becomes an "iron cage," imprisoning us in systems of rationalization, control, and bureaucracy. Moreover, as technical means and calculations replace the magic and mystery of the past, the world becomes **disenchanted** (Weber [1919] 2014). Not only the gods are gone, as Friedrich Schiller claimed; more generally, there is now no longer a place for magic and mystery in a rationalized and secularized Western society. Later, in "The Work of Art in the Age of Mechanical Reproduction" ([1935] 1969), Walter Benjamin argues that with mechanical reproduction, art loses its aura and spirituality.

Whereas Simmel, Weber, and Benjamin are still sensitive to the ambiguity of technology and modernity, writers such as Jaspers and Ellul defend a very dark view of modern technology. In *Man in the Modern Age* ([1931] 2010), Karl Jaspers sees technology as a demonic power that has been summoned by humans and now turns against them (consider again the Frankenstein myth). Like many other philosophers in the 20th century, such as Ortega y Gasset and later Herbert Marcuse, he complains about **mass society** and mass culture, brought about by machine technology that standardizes and mechanizes not only production but also social life. Jaspers argues that technology leads to mass life. Workers become part of the machinery, cogs in an "interlocking wheelwork" (Jaspers [1931] 2010, 39). Individuals merge in the mass. He sees a conflict between the technical "mass-order" and human life (44). Humans become alienated: they are "harnessed in an apparatus directed by an alien will" (55). They no longer have the possibility of self-realization and become disconnected from the world. Although Jaspers thinks that technology could maybe give us new access to the world, his view is largely pessimistic and focuses on the danger of being mastered by the machine.

Does this mean we can no longer make choices? In *Technics and Civilization* (1934), the American philosopher Lewis Mumford argues that to understand society and ourselves, and to master the machine, we first have to *understand* the machine. He links the invention of the clock to the need for an orderly routine, first in the monastery and then later in capitalism. Thus, technology interlocks with, and shapes, what we do. It supports and forms our routines. Yet he thinks that what matters are our moral and economic choices, not the technology itself. We should bring technology in harmony with our cultural and societal patterns; technology itself cannot be the whole answer (Mumford 1934, 434).

But can we still give an answer "outside" technology? Jacques Ellul supports what is often called **technological determinism**. Ellul argues in *La Technique ou l'Enjeu du siècle* (1964) that technology has become autonomous (14) and this **autonomous technology** now dominates humans, who have adapted to technology—or rather the technology has adapted them (6). It is no longer a mere means or a mediator, but has become a reality in itself with which we must reckon (63). Technology is itself a form of determinism (xxxiii); it has grown in power and has taken over our activities, creating conditions that are "less than human" (4). Against Marxists, Ellul (1964) argues that capitalism did not create that inhumane world; the machine did (5). In contrast to the Greeks, whose moderation and self-control enabled them to resist the force of technology, we submitted to it and played the role of "sorcerer's apprentice" (29). Technology leads to suffering and social problems (104), and in the end cultural breakdown (122). It absorbs everything and is totalitarian (125).

We become its slaves (138). We no longer feel at home in this world of technology (333), this "monolithic technical world" (428). Technology thus becomes a danger. Martin Heidegger argues in his essay "The Question Concerning Technology" (1977) that modern technology is an "enframing" (*Gestell*) and a danger, revealing and ordering nature as a standing-reserve for our use. Can we escape the danger? Or is there a saving power *in* the danger? (I will say more about Heidegger's view of technology in chapter 3.)

Today, while some of the answers these philosophers give may seem outdated, at the very least the questions they ask are still relevant and seem more important than ever, when new machines and devices are used and being developed that promise to (further) transform our (life)world. What is the impact of our new technologies on social and mental life? For example, are the new social media giving us new possibilities for self-realization, or are they turning us into attention addicts, creating a new mass society, and alienating us from each other? Is technology an autonomous force, and if so, does it determine us and our societies, or can we make decisions about technology, about how we want to live our lives, and how we want to live together? Will robotics and AI release us from unpleasant labor and liberate us, or will these technologies become so intelligent, autonomous, and powerful that they will enslave us? Is more automation part of the solution or is it the ultimate danger? Are we progressing toward total automation, and is this a dream or a nightmare? Should robots be designed to be our slaves or our partners? Do we live in a kind of new iron cage, a silicon cage perhaps? Do we live in a disenchanted world, or are there new ways of enchantment, perhaps also *with* technologies (Coeckelbergh 2017)? Are technologies still magic? What do we really want from technologies in the first place? Or will the new technologies shape what we want? And are there ways to think beyond these dichotomies? Or is our thinking itself trapped in a technological mode? The history of thinking about technology is an indispensable resource for philosophers of technology who want to think about the present and the future of new technologies and society.

Moreover, the history of philosophy does not only offer thoughts on technology; it can also help philosophers of technology to find and reflect on their approach and method. For example, today there are still some philosophers of technology who are inspired by Marx's political economy approach or by Jaspers's more existentialist approach. And in chapter 3, we will encounter Heidegger, who was writing in the tradition of phenomenology. Earlier, Edmund Husserl argued for doing a phenomenology of the "lifeworld," making room for the study of our daily world as opposed to the world constructed by mathematics and the sciences (Husserl [1936] 2012). Heidegger's writings on technology stand in that tradition. More generally, studying philosophers such as Husserl and Heidegger raises the question how close philosophers of technology should stay to the lifeworld, and how "empirical" and "material" philosophy of technology can be and should be.

In chapter 11, I will argue that Ludwig Wittgenstein, who is usually neglected in philosophy of technology, can also be used in philosophy of technology: in the *Philosophical Investigations* ([1953] 2009), he compares use of language to tool use, and he also may inspire us in terms of his method.

In the next chapters, I continue the history and zoom in on particular approaches. Let me now turn to the historical context and general landscape of the discipline.

2.3. Historical Context, Landscape of the Discipline, and Critical Questions

The birth of philosophy of technology must be put in the context of technological and societal changes in the past two centuries. The technological and industrial revolution of the 19th century and related scientific discoveries, which also produced entire new disciplines and made engineering very important, had an enormous impact on society. It created new urban environments, new working conditions, and new political movements.

CASE/TECHNOLOGY:
The Industrial Revolution

At the end of the 18th century and during the 19th century, new production technologies transformed manufacturing: machines such as steam-powered tools replaced production by hand and the use of more simple tools. This changed entire industries, such as iron production and the textile industry in Great Britain. There were also new advances in chemistry. But it was not only a technological, scientific, and economic revolution: the lives of many people changed. There was a growth in population. Factories and the railroad changed urban and rural landscapes. The cities grew as people migrated to the cities to find work. The so-called working class grew. There were new employment opportunities in the factories, but as Marx and Engels described, the working conditions were bad and the wages (too) low. Working hours were long, and there was pollution and depletion of natural resources. People lived and worked in dirty, unhealthy, and unsafe environments. There was unemployment and social and political tensions.

In the 20th century, there were the two world wars in which technology played a significant role. Consider again the atomic bomb. There was also the exploration of space. There were crises of meaning. People struggled to cope with the changes. In response to these technological developments, revolutions, and crises, then, it became increasingly important to think about technology, especially in a more critical and systematic way than anyone had ever done before.

As philosophy of technology grew and further developed into a discipline, it was rooted in various intellectual traditions and philosophical approaches. Sometimes it also started from disciplines or practices outside philosophy—social sciences, or engineering, for example. Technology can be approached from various angles, and it is important to take this into account to understand the current landscape of the discipline.

A useful starting point for this purpose is Carl Mitcham's distinction between "engineering" philosophy of technology and "humanities" philosophy of technology (Mitcham 1994). **Engineering philosophy of technology** starts with analyzing the nature of technology and uses technological terms to understand technology and human affairs. **Humanities philosophy of technology**, by contrast, relates the meaning of technology to what goes beyond technology: culture, ethics, politics, religion, and so on; reflection on technology is then done from a non-technological point of view. Ellul and Heidegger are examples of such an approach. Although these two approaches can and have been reconciled to some extent—for instance, my own writings and Ihde's postphenomenology, which combines hermeneutics (humanities) with a focus on material artifacts in science, can be considered as attempts at reconciliation—it is still the case that some philosophers of technology lean closer to engineering, science, design, and so on (e.g., information theory, engineering ethics, or philosophy of design), whereas others stay more within discourse about philosophers (e.g., Heidegger) and philosophical approaches (e.g., phenomenology). We should add to Mitcham's distinction that there are also researchers who start from the social sciences rather than from the humanities or from engineering and science. For example, there is also thinking about technology in science and technology studies (STS), sociology, cultural anthropology, and so on.

IN FOCUS:
Carl Mitcham

Carl Mitcham is a philosopher of technology and professor at the Colorado School of Mines and Renmin University, China. He is known for thinking about engineering and philosophy, thinking about interdisciplinarity, and engaging with non-Western philosophy—for example, in China and in Latin America. His book *Thinking Through Technology* (1994) has become a classic introductory text in the field.

This plurality and variety must be welcomed since it enriches the field, but it must be acknowledged that it also creates problems. When different perspectives and traditions meet, there can be friction and confusion due to use of different languages, discourses, and cultures. For example, in a discussion about AI, it may happen that one participant refers to empirical work in AI research, computer science, or experimental psychology, whereas another talks about mythology, science fiction, and Heidegger. In discussions about robotics, some stay close to discourses and vocabulary from robotics, psychology, computer science, and scientific theories; others are rooted in a specific philosophical tradition; for example, they might take a phenomenological or hermeneutic approach, or draw on Marx. And philosophers talking about the politics of technology from the perspective of political philosophy may not always know work in STS that is relevant to this theme and vice versa. It is often challenging to find *interfaces* and *mediators* that really enable meaningful communication, mutual learning, and setting up new research that combines approaches. That being said, some of the best work in the field manages this: it combines different approaches, or at least succeeds in making its own work relevant to others coming from different directions. Such work might also be interdisciplinary or transdisciplinary, or even go beyond academia; I will return to this issue at the end of this chapter and in part 4.

There may also be cultural differences in the sense of linguistic and geographical differences. But, perhaps unfortunately, this problem does not often occur. Geographically speaking, philosophy of technology is far from being a global affair, and like in academia in general, a rather limited number of languages and styles are dominant. There are more philosophers of technology in North America and Europe than anywhere else in the world, for example in the United States, Germany, and the Netherlands. And the language is often English, sometimes German or French. Of course there are philosophers of technology elsewhere too, for example in Brazil and in China. But the general picture is not very balanced, to say the least. Maybe such an uneven distribution is not uncommon in philosophy and in academia in general; but that does not mean that it should go unnoticed or that it must be seen as entirely unproblematic. It renders the practice not as inclusive as it could be. Moreover, it is especially odd to observe this since contemporary technologies are themselves rather global and distributed in character, pervading so many lives everywhere on the planet and supposedly drawing together people all over the world, endangering the world, etc.—whatever the claim in question is. Thus, the issue of geography raises the question of whether in different geographical areas there are different philosophy cultures drawing on their own traditions; and if so, if these differences are sufficiently taken into account in contemporary English-speaking philosophy of technology. Are some geographical areas, languages, and cultures systematically advantaged or neglected? In philosophy at large, there is certainly an advantage for English-language speakers and a disadvantage for those who speak different languages. For example, there are philosophers of technology in France and in the Spanish-speaking world, but they are not always read in the English-dominated areas. Which language dominates and should dominate in philosophy (if any)? And if English is currently the dominant language, is that fair and does it create problems for researchers and for the quality and diversity of the research? These questions are also relevant to philosophy of technology. In chapter 6, I will ask if, given cultural differences, there can be a "global" and/or intercultural philosophy of technology, for example, between "West" and "East." And the discussion concerning differences can also be extended to factors that are not necessarily related to different geographical places, such as gender or ethnicity. For example, are women sufficiently represented within philosophy? And if not, how is philosophy of technology doing in this area? Compared to philosophy in general, the situation for women in philosophy of technology seems slightly better, but that does not mean that all issues are solved.

Finally, in terms of approach, there is a difference between those philosophers of technology whose work remains within the boundaries of academia (usually, but not exclusively, in universities) and those who also practice philosophy beyond those boundaries: they may practice a form of public philosophy that intervenes in public debates and political issues, make contributions to the media (press, TV, social media, etc.), or offer policy advice. Many contemporary philosophers of technology also talk to, or collaborate with, engineers and scientists. This raises the question of what role philosophers of technology should take. Often issues concerning new technologies hit the public debates. Sometimes there is also the chance to advise companies that develop technologies. Are these opportunities to bring philosophy of technology to people outside academia? Is it risky, and if so, what are the risks? Is there perhaps a *duty* on the part of the philosopher of technology to offer advice, contribute to the debate, and so on? Should philosophers of technology take up the role of intellectuals? How much should they occupy themselves with, and respond to, issues in their society? How critical should they be and how critical can they be? Should they contribute to policymaking? Should they advise large corporations active in the technology field, or even work for them? Should they take funding from any government, from private companies, or even from the military? Should they go to the labs of designers and talk to artists? Should they even set up and participate in collaborative projects? Or should they focus on developing and discussing concepts and theory in the study room and seminar room?

This also relates to the question of how empirical or empirically oriented philosophers of technology should be: if they should be empirical or empirically oriented at all (a question that in turn is again related to the "engineering" vs. "humanities" issue). This is an important and ongoing debate within the field.

For example, philosophers of technology of the so-called empirical turn have argued that philosophy of technology should be empirical—although they tend to disagree about what the means in practice. Are philosophers of technology supposed to do conceptual work only, or does a focus on artifacts, for instance, imply that one should also take on board technological and designer approaches and collaborate with people in those fields? I will give an example of what "empirical" could mean in chapter 4 when I discuss postphenomenology. I will also raise the issue again when I comment on ethics of technology. And in part 4, I will further reflect on inter- or transdisciplinarity and on the public role of philosophers of technology.

REVIEW QUESTIONS

1. What can we learn from 19th- and 20th-century philosophy of technology, and from the history of thinking about technology in general?
2. What is meant when it is said that technologies are organ projections or extensions?
3. What is autonomous technology and technological determinism?
4. What is so dangerous about technology according to 19th- and 20th-century thinkers?
5. Does everyone benefit equally from technology?

DISCUSSION QUESTIONS

1. Is technology today autonomous, and in what sense? Is technological determinism true? Do we still control technology?
2. Do you think social media and other contemporary technologies change your mind and consciousness, and if so, how?
3. Does the internet and its search engines make your memory redundant and bad?
4. What kind of knowledge do we need to acquire in the digital age?
5. Do we live in a mass society?
6. Do you think that technology is dangerous?
7. Should technology benefit the public good, and if so, how can we make sure it does?
8. Do we live in an "iron cage"? Why (not)?
9. Do we need modern technology to lead a good life?
10. Is the world disenchanted?
11. Should philosophers of technology collaborate with the military? Should they contribute to public debates about technology? More generally, what should their role be in society?
12. Is there a gender balance in philosophy, and what do you think about this issue?
13. How should philosophers of technology deal with cultural differences?
14. How empirical should philosophy of technology be?

RECOMMENDED READING

Mitcham, Carl. 1994. *Thinking Through Technology: The Path Between Engineering and Philosophy*. Chicago: University of Chicago Press.

KEY TERMS

Autonomous technology
Capitalism
Demiurg
Disenchanted
Engineering philosophy
   of technology

Enlightenment
Frankenstein
Humanities philosophy
   of technology
Hybris
Mass society

Organ projection
Prometheus
Prosthetic beings
Technological determinism
Thamus

2 THINKING ABOUT TECHNOLOGY BY STARTING FROM THEORY

PHENOMENOLOGY AND HERMENEUTICS: HEIDEGGER, MCLUHAN, AND CONTEMPORARY WORK

CASE/TECHNOLOGY:
Robotics and Artificial Intelligence and the Question about Mastery

Recent advances in computing hardware, robotics, and artificial intelligence (AI) make some people believe that machines will sooner or later be smarter than us and that we will lose the mastery over technology. For some, this is a nightmare prospect, and they think that we should try to keep control. For others, that machines outsmart us could be of benefit to humanity, provided that we develop AI that is good for us. Are we still the masters of our tools today—indeed, are they still tools at all? Or did we already lose mastery long ago? And do we set the ends of technology, or does technology do that for us?

FIGURE 3.1 Female robot

3.1. Heidegger's Essay Concerning Technology: Beyond an Instrumental Understanding of Technology

A key text in philosophy of technology is Heidegger's '*Die Frage nach der Technik*' ('The Question Concerning Technology') (1977). It is an important text if we want to go beyond an instrumental understanding of technology and see technology not only as an object but also as a way of thinking.

IN FOCUS:
Martin Heidegger

Martin Heidegger was a 20th-century German philosopher who is well known in the continental philosophical tradition, especially in phenomenology and hermeneutics. His best-known philosophical work is *Being and Time* ([1927] 1996), which asks the question of being and reconceptualizes the human being in terms of *Dasein* and "being-in-the-world." In philosophy of technology, his later work on *The Question Concerning Technology* (1977), in which he sees modern technology as an "enframing" (German: *Gestell*) and a danger, is also well known. He is a controversial figure because of his affiliation with Nazism as rector of the University of Freiburg, his anti-Semitic views in the *Black Notebooks*, and the argument made by many scholars that his philosophical work is in agreement with his political views.

FIGURE 3.2 Martin Heidegger

In his essay, Heidegger (1977) starts with the question of what technology is: the question concerns the essence of technology. The common answer consists of two statements: technology is "a means to an end," and technology is "a human activity." The activity is setting ends and then producing and using the means to reach these ends (Heidegger 1977, 4). This is what Heidegger calls the instrumental and anthropological definition of technology (5). These definitions are "correct," even "uncannily correct." It is true for ancient technology and for modern technology. Heidegger gives the example of a power plant "with its turbines and generators" and the jet aircraft. Moreover, connected with this conception of technology is the idea that we master technology and should master technology, also and especially when it "threatens to slip from human control" (5). Think about the contemporary discussions about robotics and AI: many people argue that we should remain the masters of technology. The will to master technology manifests itself especially at the moment when control becomes more difficult.

Heidegger's aim in the 1977 essay, however, is to explore the idea that technology is *not* a mere means to human ends. To arrive at a non-instrumental definition, he interprets Aristotle's doctrine of the four causes and discusses the example of a silversmith making a chalice. Instead of focusing on what the silversmith does (working, making), Heidegger writes about a "bringing forth" (8). Something is brought into appearance (10). Both in nature and in crafts, something is brought into appearance: there is a bringing forth. But in crafts, the bringing forth happens in the craftsman or artist (11), not in itself. This "straying" enables Heidegger to move away from the instrumental and anthropological definition: technology is no longer a mere means to and end or something that humans do, but rather it is a "revealing" (11). Heidegger writes, "Technology is therefore no mere means. Technology is a way of **revealing**" (1977, 12). What does he mean by this?

It means, among other things, that technology is also a way of seeing the world and a way of thinking, or rather a way the world shows up for us and a way of thinking we become part of—and we are not in control of that. This becomes clear when we read what Heidegger (1977) says about modern technology. Modern technology is also a revealing (14), but a particular way of revealing: a "challenging" (German: *Herausfordern*). Whereas, according to Heidegger, older technology such as the wooden bridge, the windmill, and the work of the peasant does not challenge, modern technology does. He gives again the example of the hydroelectric plant that makes the river Rhine appear as if it is "something at our command" (16). It is there to be unlocked, transformed, stored, distributed, and so on. Modern technology thus enables a particular kind of revealing or unconcealment: one that orders everything to stand by, one that makes nature into a "standing-reserve" (17). Even the machine is ordered, is a standing-reserve; it is not autonomous. Heidegger gives the example of an airliner that stands ready on the runway, ordered to ensure transportation (17). And again, like in the example of the craftsman, humans are participants in this. They accomplish the challenging, participate in the ordering, but they do not have control over the unconcealment itself (18). We may think that we use technology and that therefore we have control over it; but at the same time, we do not control the way of revealing. This depends on the kind of technology used. Heidegger writes, "Man can indeed conceive, fashion, and carry through this or that in one way or another.

FIGURE 3.3 Hydroelectric plant on the Rhine River

But man does not have control over un-concealment itself, in which at any given time the real shows itself or withdraws" (1977, 18). And with modern technology, humans become *themselves* standing-reserve, human resource, "commanded by profit-making" (18).

This leads Heidegger (1977) to conclude that this understanding goes beyond the instrumental and anthropological definition of technology. It is no longer anthropological since "modern technology as an ordering revealing is . . . no merely human doing" (1977, 19). He calls the modern challenging that orders *us* as much as nature and everything else—that is, the essence of modern technology—the **enframing** (German: *Gestell*). Modern technology enframes (20). And it is no longer instrumental. There is an unconcealment that comes to pass (21). The real reveals itself in a particular way, for example, as standing-reserve (23). In this sense, the essence of technology is nothing technological (23), and it is not exclusively a human doing (24).

The question is then whether we can gain a free relation to technology, given this essence of modern technology. Heidegger writes that there is a "destining" and a revealing that "holds complete sway over man" (1977, 25). Yet he also writes that it is not "a fate that compels" (25). For Heidegger, freedom is not about "unfettered arbitrariness" but lies in "the realm of destining" (25). What does he mean by this? It seems that once we understand enframing and the essence of technology, then we are already more free. To gain a free relation to technology is to go beyond pushing on blindly with technology (25) or rebel against it (26).

Rather, "when we once open ourselves expressly to the *essence* of technology, we find ourselves unexpectedly taken into a freeing claim" (26).

However, in the revealing of modern technology, it becomes difficult to reach this freeing realm. There is a "danger" in modern technology, even a "supreme danger" (Heidegger 1977, 26), especially when everything is presented as standing-reserve for humans or as a "construct" (27) of humans. This gives us the "delusion" that "it seems as though man everywhere and always encounters only himself" (27). Thus, the three-fold problem is that when, with modern technology, the *destining* of enframing holds sway, humans have a problematic relationship to themselves; "it drives out every other possibility of revealing," and we become unaware of revealing as such: revealing itself is concealed (27). What is dangerous, then, is not technology but the rule of enframing, which makes it difficult if not impossible for us to "enter into a more original revealing" (28).

Nevertheless, Heidegger (1977) thinks that there is also the saving power where the danger is. We may consider a granting that makes us share in the revealing:

> On the one hand, Enframing challenges forth into the frenziedness of ordering that blocks every view into the coming-to-pass of revealing and so radically endangers the relation to the essence of truth. On the other hand, Enframing comes to pass for its part in the grating that lets men endure—as yet unexperienced, but perhaps more experienced in the future—that he may be the one who is needed and used for the safekeeping of the coming of the presence of truth. Thus does the arising of the saving power appear. (Heidegger 1977, 33)

We do not see this saving power as long as we stare at the technological (Heidegger 1977, 32). Instead, we have to reflect on the (non-technological) essence of technology that leads us to "the mystery of all revealing" (33). Moreover, Heidegger recommends to consider the arts, which are a similar yet different bringing forth.

> Because the essence of technology is nothing technological, essential reflection upon technology and decisive confrontation with it must happen in a realm that is, on the one hand, akin to the essence of technology and, on the other, fundamentally different from it. (Heidegger 1977, 35)

Heidegger imagines that in ancient Greece, art was also a *techne*, but one that was a revealing that yielded to "the safekeeping of truth" (1977, 34). He suggests that today the arts are "called to poetic revealing" and that this may "foster the growth of the saving power" (35). The realm of art may provide a realm in which we can reflect on technology.

Heidegger's view of technology has been criticized for being too deterministic, abstract, and monolithic about technology: we seem to be determined by the destiny Heidegger speaks about, and he looks at Technology with a big "T" rather than specific technologies and their use (see also postphenomenology's criticism in chapter 4). Many readers of Heidegger also find his texts obscure and difficult to understand. And he has been linked to Nazi ideology. There is some truth in these criticisms. Feenberg has rightly argued that Heidegger's abstract philosophy does not enable us to discriminate between technologies such as agricultural techniques and the Holocaust (Feenberg 1999, 187). (As we will see in chapter 4, postphenomenology therefore proposes a different, more empirically oriented approach.) And even if we accept Heidegger's epistemology of revealing, one could argue that his focus on technology or modern technology in general does not disclose the manifold revealings technology is capable of, apart from letting everything appear as standing-reserve and ordering. It also remains unclear what the mystery is we miss today; his nostalgic comments on ancient Greek thinking and practices suggest that ancient art and crafts can help us; but it is not clear, for example, why in that past there would have been a total absence of ordering or will to mastery, or why craft work would have been experienced in more mysterious terms than technology today. (Both kinds of technologies and technological practices might have been rather mundane, and/or both could have a "magic" or "mystery" aspect.) More generally, his rejection of pre-modern technology seems inconsistent, as Ihde and Verbeek have argued (Ihde 1993; Verbeek 2005, 60–76). Ihde has called Heidegger's view "romantic" (Ihde 1993, 106–107) and thinks that there is only a difference in degree between the technologies. Verbeek has argued that Heidegger measures tradition and modernity with "different scales" (Verbeek 2005, 75): historical for modern technology (the rule of enframing now in modernity) and ahistorical for ancient technology (making visible being itself). For example, the windmill also seems to use nature as a standing-reserve and can be seen in a historical way; his nostalgia for older technology seems not (always?) justified. And Heidegger seems so preoccupied with the question of "Being" and the life of the mind that it seems difficult to use his thoughts for what seems more urgent: to intervene in the world, to change the world, perhaps including to develop technologies that are less bad and degrading and support a different attitude toward the environment and toward others. If everything is enframing, then there seems little room for a more (pro) active, constructive, and positive approach to critical thinking about technology. Heidegger also wrote anti-Semitic texts and joined the Nazi party (NSDAP) after being elected as rector.

That being said, it is instructive to make comparisons between technologies that at first sight appear to be totally different; this may help us to criticize and discuss particular problems, technologies, and attitudes. Heidegger's notion of standing-reserve can do, and has done, some work in environmental philosophy, for example. It is also not clear if Heidegger's view is really against a more constructive approach (Pattison 2000, 73). Heidegger argues not against technology as such; as Pattison points out, enframing can be found in all kinds of areas of life (2000, 56); it seems that his criticism is more directed against a way of (modern) thinking than against what we commonly call science and technology. Moving toward a different attitude toward nature, for instance, does perhaps not exclude the development of new technologies (see also Coeckelbergh 2015). While there is certainly a lot of nostalgia for a pre-modern world in the text (like many other thinkers in the German-speaking world, especially in the 19th century, he idealized ancient Greece), Heidegger must have realized that we cannot return to the past—if such a place and time as he imagines it ever existed at all. It is also interesting to discuss if there are fundamental differences between ancient and modern technologies, or (one could add) between modern and contemporary technologies. And is his view really determinist about technology? That depends on how we interpret, for instance, the phrase that we participate in the ordering: while, abstractly speaking, humans certainly do not have full control over whatever comes to pass in the history of being, more concrete human decision-making and action, and indeed the kind of freedom we commonly speak about, are maybe not entirely excluded. It is also not clear why his anti-Semitism and his link with Nazism would entirely disqualify all aspects of his philosophy, including this text on technology. Suspicion and criticism are certainly justified; ignoring his entire work is probably not. Furthermore, Heidegger's writings show that philosophy can also use and create a different language; maybe we should also be more open and appreciative toward this than some commentators are in philosophy of technology. Thus, in general, there is more room for alternative interpretations than many of the criticisms suggest. But beyond issues in Heidegger scholarship, it is clear that, in spite of these objections, Heidegger has done a significant and interesting effort in thinking beyond the conception of technology as a mere instrument and as a human activity, which makes him a key figure in and for the field. This is also the case with the next thinker we discuss: Marshall McLuhan.

3.2. McLuhan's Understanding of Media

While McLuhan is not a phenomenologist in the usual sense of the word, his work can be linked to the phenomenological and hermeneutical tradition—including Heidegger—if we interpret his claims about technology's effects on human consciousness and society as saying something about our being-in-the-world and how we are shaped by technology (see, e.g., Nagel 2010). Moreover, although he is usually seen as a media theorist, he can be helpfully interpreted as a philosopher of technology (Van Den Eede 2013). Like Heidegger, McLuhan stresses the non-instrumental role of technology; and, like Heidegger, he thinks that technology and its impact on human lives is perhaps not deterministic but in any case not simply a matter of human control, will, and decision. Moreover, McLuhan's conceptualization of technology as extension stands in a tradition ranging from Kapp and Merleau-Ponty to contemporary thinking about technology; and his specific claims about electric technologies seem highly relevant to contemporary information technology, in particular the internet and related technologies. Let us take a closer look at his work, with a focus on *Understanding Media* (McLuhan [1964] 2001).

IN FOCUS:
Marshall McLuhan

Herbert Marshall McLuhan was a 20th-century Canadian professor who is well known in media theory and philosophy of media. His educational background was in language (English). He is famous for the phrase "the medium is the message" and for the term **global village**. The new medium of his day was TV, but he is seen as predicting the World Wide Web already in the 1960s. He is best known for his work *Understanding Media* ([1964] 2001) in which he argues that instead of focusing on the content, we should study the medium

FIGURE 3.4 Marshall McLuhan

and its impact on human consciousness and society. Often philosophers of technology ignore media theory and media studies, including McLuhan; but he and the field he shaped have a lot to say on technologies and their effects.

McLuhan argued that media are not just means to transfer a message but are themselves (part of) the message. With his famous claim that **"the medium is the message"** (McLuhan [1964] 2001, 7) he meant that new media and technologies are not mere means that are totally under our control, but they also shape our relation to ourselves and to others. Their personal and social consequences are much deeper than we think since they change our consciousness and our forms of association and action. They change what we do, how we do things, and the pace and scale of our actions. In the beginning of the book, he gives the examples of automation technology, electric light, the railway, and others. Automation technology does not only tend to eliminate jobs but also creates new roles for people and has integral and decentralist effects on forms of human association (McLuhan [1964] 2001, 7–8). The railway not only introduced a new way of transportation but also "accelerated and enlarged the scale of previous human functions, creating totally new kinds of cities and new kinds of work and leisure" (8). And with electricity, one can suddenly do things one could not do before, for example playing basketball games at night. Technologies thus change our patterns and processes. They are not mere means to help us with what we do and what we do together; they change what we do and what we do together. McLuhan thereby criticizes instrumental understandings of technology such as "Firearms are in themselves neither good nor bad; it is the way they are used that determines their value" since they totally ignore "the nature of the medium of any and all media" (12), which changes the form of our existence. Therefore, study of media and technologies should not focus on the "content" of media (what they are meant for, their function) but on the medium itself. Understanding technologies, then, means understanding their "grammar" (14): how they restructure and reconfigure our relations. Today, however, we are distracted and do not see that the medium is the message. We are usually unaware of the medium—for instance, when we write we do not realize that language, speech, and print are involved.

Putting this in practice, McLuhan ([1964] 2001) compares mechanical with electric media and technologies. Whereas mechanization fragments processes, electricity makes things instant and integral (12). They also extend in different ways. According to McLuhan, all technologies are extensions. But whereas mechanical technologies offered a limited extension of our bodies in space, "today, after more than a century of electric technology, we have extended our central nervous system itself in a global embrace, abolishing both space and time as far as our planet is concerned" (McLuhan [1964] 2001, 3).

Here it is instructive to compare Merleau-Ponty's examples in the *Phenomenology of Perception* ([1945] 1962) and Don Ihde's descriptions of the "embodiment" relation (see chapter 4). According to Merleau-Ponty, the body is not only something we "have"; we "are" also our body and it is a way of relating to the world. It is a condition of possibility of perception and movement. As such, the body organizes what we see and do; we know through the body. This is also applicable to using and handling technological artifacts. For example, we learn to handle objects, and these objects then become part of what Merleau-Ponty calls a **body schema**, one's awareness of the moving body in space. He gives the examples of a blind man's stick, a feathered hat, and the typewriter: in all cases, the technologies become part of the body. In particular, they become extensions of the body. Ihde calls this an "embodiment" relation: the technology becomes part of the body and mediates our perception. Technologies can thus be extensions and mediators that shape our perception and actions.

IN FOCUS:
Maurice Merleau-Ponty

Maurice Merleau-Ponty was a 20th century French philosopher in the tradition of phenomenology, influenced by Husserl and Heidegger. He is well known for his philosophy of perception, which stresses our embodied engagement with the world. In *Phenomenology of Perception* ([1945] 1962) he argued that we know the world through the body. In contemporary philosophy of technology, Don Ihde's post-phenomenology is very influenced by Merleau-Ponty.

FIGURE 3.5 Maurice Merleau-Ponty

McLuhan's conception of extension by electric technologies, however, goes beyond the immediate, nearby handling of technologies and its effects on our perception, action, and being-in-the-world. It takes on a social and global dimension. Instead of changes in the perception of one individual, McLuhan ([1945] 1962) is interested in "all of them together"; that is, in the "the whole psychic and social complex" (4) that now encompasses the entire planet. In this sense, "the globe is no more than a village" (5). McLuhan's point is not only that we became more interconnected; the point is that we are now involved with everyone and everything. The technological extension of bodies is replaced by the creation of one integral technological and psychic milieu. Technology thus realized the aspirations of McLuhan's contemporaries for "wholeness, empathy, and depth of awareness" (5). Individual separation is replaced by social involvement and awareness. Human existence becomes a global affair. He writes:

> If the work of the city is the remaking or translating of man into a more suitable form than his nomadic ancestors achieved, then might not our current translation of our entire lives into the spiritual form of information seem to make the entire globe, and of the human family, a single consciousness? (McLuhan [1964] 2001, 67)

And "In the electric age we wear all mankind as our skin" (52).

In this context, McLuhan ([1964] 2001) sees the emergence of "a faith that concerns the ultimate harmony of all being" (6). The new media and technologies did not only extend our bodies but changed our entire psychic-social environment. Moreover, the new awareness also creates an issue with regard to responsibility: if the globe becomes a village, and if no part of us remains untouched or unaltered by the changes (26), then this "sudden implosion" has also "heightened human awareness of responsibility to an intense degree," creating an "Age of Anxiety" (5).

CASE/TECHNOLOGY:
The Internet

McLuhan wrote long before the internet was developed. Are his views applicable to today's internet and related digital and electronic technologies? Is there a sense in which the internet has extended our consciousness and shaped our perception? Has the internet created a more integral awareness? Do we now live in a global village? And what are the consequences for responsibility, given that human existence has become a global affair? Do we live in an age of anxiety?

Whether or not we agree with McLuhan's specific claims about electric technologies—which seem very applicable to electronic technologies as well, if not to a higher degree—his non-instrumental understanding of technology, his conception of extension, and his attention for the social and the temporal and spatial changes brought about by new media and technologies remain very interesting and relevant today. The same is true for his claim about responsibility, which raises questions concerning potential barriers to this awareness and to taking up this global responsibility: if this is our condition, then do we want to know, what can we know, and what can we do (Coeckelbergh 2013)? With regard to current electronic devices, consider also his claim that, like **Narcissus**, the "gadget lover" becomes fascinated by an extension of himself, involving him in "a state of numbness" (McLuhan [1964] 2001, 46).

And is the internet "a live model of the central nervous system itself" (47)? In any case, our studies and understandings of the effects of new digital technologies on our consciousness and social relations have only begun, and McLuhan encourages us to go on. He especially seems to recommend a broad and historically sensitive approach to technology and media, ranging "from speech to computer" (47).

One could also do more work on the relation between language and technology. McLuhan sees language as a technology and an extension (e.g., [1964] 2001, 86). He and his student Walter Ong are also famous for analyzing the shift from orality to literacy (Ong [1982] 2002) and then, according to McLuhan, back to the integral awareness of orality. And in *Laws of Media*, McLuhan and his son Eric equate technology, metaphor, and language:

> It makes no difference whatever whether one considers as artifacts or as media things of a tangible "hardware" nature such as blows and clubs or forks and spoons or tools and devices and engines, railways, spacecraft, radios, computers, and so on, or things of a "software" nature such as theories or laws of science, philosophical systems, remedies or even the diseases in medicine, forms or styles in painting or poetry or drama or music, and so on. All are equally artifacts, all equally human. (M. McLuhan and E. McLuhan 1988, 3)

According to the McLuhans, both artifacts and words can be investigated grammatically (McLuhan & McLuhan 1988, 224); that is, how as extensions they change us, reconfigure our environments and us. Technologies transform "the user and his ground" (98). It would also be interesting to study further how contemporary technologies (re-)shape our lived time. And McLuhan takes an approach that suggests understanding the human, the human body, and human subjectivity not as a pre existing given but as something that is shaped by media and technology. The problem with the Narcissus attitude is that we regard the extensions "as really out there and really independent of us" (75), whereas humans and technologies are intimately connected. This view decenters the human, in the sense that the focus is now on the relation between human and machine, whereby both are mutually constituted, modified, and constructed. Humans and machines co-evolve:

> Physiologically, man in the normal use of technology (or his variously extended body) is perpetually modified by it and in turn finds ever new ways of modifying his technology. Man becomes, as it were, the sex organs of the machine world, as the bee of the plant world, enabling it to fecundate and to evolve ever new forms. (McLuhan [1964] 2001, 51)

This view is in line with more recent so-called **posthumanist** thinking about humans and technology, which questions boundaries between humans and technology. Finally, it is interesting that McLuhan suggests that artists can make us aware of the changes in sense perception ([1964] 2001, 19) brought about by new media and technologies. He writes that "the artist is indispensable in the shaping and analysis and understanding of the life of forms, and structures created by electric technology" (McLuhan [1964] 2001, 71). The artist is thus not only an expert perceiver of the changes at hand, but is also needed for finding out how to move on. He must "play and experiment with new means of arranging experience" (McLuhan [1964] 2001, 276). Note that this should not only happen in the field of "art" narrowly defined; for McLuhan, people in science or in the humanities can also be "artists" if they grasp what is going on and if they have an "integral awareness" (72), although it is difficult to keep up, since technology is also "ahead of its time" (71). McLuhan himself was of course a master in sensing and describing the transformative power of new media and technologies.

There have been many criticisms of McLuhan in media studies, for instance of his method and style or his distinction between **hot and cool media**, which is not very often used today. Here I would like to focus on three objections that are still relevant to philosophy of technology today. First, like Heidegger, McLuhan received the criticism that his view amounts to technological determinism. If media shape us, how much room for freedom do we have? In reply, one could interpret his view as not excluding freedom because technology is always connected to its use in a social context, and hence a variety of uses are possible. One could then discuss if this interpretation goes far beyond McLuhan, or if it can still be supported by the text. More importantly, however, as philosophers of technology, we should always ask what exactly it means to say that technologies shape us. Second, his view that technology is an extension can be criticized. Surely technology is not only an extension, it can also be a milieu, for example, or can be seen as being entangled with humans. The question is then if McLuhan's view excludes these other meanings. It seems to me that his view is not at all opposed to these other meanings but is connected to them. The electric technologies he talks about amount to an extension, but one that becomes an environment and one that constitutes us, thereby being intimately connected to what it means to be human. Third, one could ask if McLuhan was not too optimistic about the promises of the new technologies he discusses. He connects electric technologies with the hope of a more integral way of life and experience. But contemporary electronic technologies seem to divide rather than make whole, "**dividuating**" (Deleuze 1992) us into measurable parameters, divided up into data that are then sold. So one could object that the new media are used for commercial purposes and that people are exploited rather than integrated into a global consciousness and awareness. Furthermore, bombarded with an overload of information, we may not develop an attitude of global responsibility but rather one of apathy. Where is the new consciousness? Where is the new world promised by the technology and the (counter)culture of the 1960s?

3.3. Some Contemporary Work in Phenomenology and Hermeneutics of Technology

Many philosophers of technology continue the phenomenological and hermeneutical tradition, including but not necessarily taking the form of postphenomenology. Someone who certainly deserves mentioning here is Hubert Dreyfus,

---

CASE/TECHNOLOGY:
Artificial Intelligence

AI mimics cognitive functions we usually associate with humans such as learning and problem-solving. The current "explosion" in AI is made possible by developments in machine learning. Algorithms are getting increasingly better at identifying patterns in streams of data. Using so-called deep learning and neural networks, computers can now be trained to perform tasks rather than being programmed by a human being, as in classical AI. This has resulted in a range of new technologies: computers being able to play strategic games such as chess and Go, but also devices that can understand human speech, autonomous cars, intelligent robots, and so on. Yet it is highly doubtful that machines could ever have what is called "general intelligence" (that is, perform any cognitive task humans can do), let alone achieve consciousness ("strong AI"). Today there are discussions about the ethical and societal impact of AI.

FIGURE 3.6 Sculpture "Go" commemorating AlphaGo's victory over Lee Sedol, Vienna

who is known for his interpretations of Heidegger (and Husserl and Merleau-Ponty) and for his work on the philosophy of AI. He also did work on skill development, with his brother Stuart Dreyfus.

IN FOCUS:
Hubert Dreyfus

Hubert Lederer Dreyfus was an American philosopher and professor at the University of California, Berkeley. Influenced by phenomenology and existentialism (mainly Heidegger), he commented on *Being and Time* and wrote about technology, skill, and meaning. He is widely known for his critique of AI (Dreyfus 1972), which was influenced by the phenomenological work of Heidegger and Merleau-Ponty. Long before the so-called empirical turn (see chapter 4), Dreyfus had already had discussions with engineers at MIT and questioned the goals and assumptions of their AI research program. He also played a significant role in explaining and making available continental philosophy to philosophers in the English-speaking world.

FIGURE 3.7 Hubert Dreyfus

In *What Computers Can't Do* (1972 and subsequent editions), Dreyfus criticized what according to him are four assumptions made in AI research: (1) the assumption that the brain and mind are analogous to computer hardware and software, (2) the assumption that the mind works by performing computations on representations, (3) the assumption that all activity can be formalized, and (4) the assumption that reality consists of a set of facts. Inspired by Heidegger (in particular *Being and Time*), Dreyfus argued that instead we have a specific kind of being-in-the-world that is based on our embodiment and our being part of the social. If AI is supposed to be human-like intelligence, then it would also have to have bodies and live in societies. Against cognitivism, Dreyfus emphasized embodiment and knowing-how, instead of knowing-that. Dreyfus also used Heidegger's distinction in *Being and Time* ([1927] 1996) between tools being present-at-hand and ready-to-hand: when we use the tool, it is invisible, we are not aware of it; this is a kind of implicit knowledge. When we drive, for example, we do not usually think about what we do; our knowledge is implicit, unconscious, and embodied. Only when something goes wrong, or when we learn a new skill, are we aware of the tool (e.g., the gears of the car); then it becomes present-at-hand. In a report, the brothers Stuart and Hubert Dreyfus (S. Dreyfus and H. L. Dreyfus 1980) argued for a five-stage model of skill acquisition: when we are novices, we need rules; but as we move toward the highest, expert level of skill, we are not only able to plan and see the more situational and holistic aspects of a problem, we also gain a more intuitive grasp of situations and can improvise rather than relying on rules. Whether or not this model is empirically correct, it highlights the implicit and embodied dimension of knowledge. This direction of research remains interesting and relevant for philosophical thinking about our (use of) technologies, from simple tools to advanced robots.

While initially many AI researchers ignored his work, today AI research is no longer (only) about the manipulation of symbols and formal rules, and some researchers are also inspired by phenomenology—including Dreyfus's work. It also needs to be said that today, cognitive science, which is related to AI and robotics research, usually takes an embodied and **enactivist** direction (e.g., Varela, Thomson, and Rosch 1991). In any case, Dreyfus made an interesting connection between philosophical work in phenomenology (especially Heidegger) and technology development and science. His work has much to offer with regard to understanding how we handle technology as embodied beings, although his conceptualizations of technology and human–technology relations are limited, and more should be said about the social and about the link to virtue (Coeckelbergh 2018).

Today, many other philosophers are inspired by the phenomenological and hermeneutical tradition, including an interest in topics such as embodiment and Heidegger. For instance, inspired by phenomenology and hermeneutics, Bernhard Irrgang has discussed technological praxis and embodiment, focusing on how we handle technologies and on changes in the lifeworld (see, e.g., Irrgang 2010). Helena De Preester has written about technological embodiment. Responding to Ihde and referring to work by Merleau-Ponty, but also taking into account relevant empirical sciences, she has argued for a distinction between body extensions and incorporation of non-bodily objects into the body (De Preester 2011). And Jochem Zwier and others have argued for a phenomenology, rather than a postphenomenology, of technology. Inspired by Heidegger, they claim that postphenomenology and related mediation theory adheres to a theoretical attitude and enframing instead of paying attention to the ontological dimension (Zwier, Blok, and Lemmens 2016). Some of these discussions take place in response to Ihde and the empirical turn; I will say more about this turn and its critics in chapter 4.

Finally, some researchers in philosophy of technology engage with McLuhan's work. For example, in *Amor Technologiae* (2013), Yoni Van Den Eede has helpfully interpreted McLuhan as a philosopher of technology and has used McLuhan to frame the human–technology relation in terms of love. He also interpreted McLuhan's view of metaphor (Van Den Eede 2015). I have read McLuhan for thinking about responsibility (Coeckelbergh 2013) and for my work on language and technology (Coeckelbergh 2017). But there is still a lot of room for more work in this area, including building bridges between philosophy of technology and media studies. (With regard to the latter, philosophers working on the border between the two fields, such as David Gunkel and Charles Ess, should also be mentioned.)

In chapter 4, I will focus on how postphenomenology has taken up phenomenology and hermeneutics and has thereby made an influential, important, and ongoing contribution to thinking about technology.

REVIEW QUESTIONS

1. What is Heidegger's view of technology, and how can we make sense of it?
2. What could be potential criticisms of Heidegger's view of technology, and is it still relevant today?
3. What is the role of the arts in understanding technology?
4. What is McLuhan's view of media?
5. What does McLuhan's view mean for thinking about the human?
6. What could be potential criticisms of McLuhan's view?
7. How can and should we use phenomenology and hermeneutics for thinking about technology today?

DISCUSSION QUESTIONS

1. Does modern technology turn everything—including human beings—into a "standing-reserve"?
2. Do you agree with Heidegger's view of modern technology? Why (not)?
3. Are we still masters of contemporary technology? If so, will this change in the future, and is that to be welcomed or avoided?
4. Are advanced digital technologies such as the internet, computers, robots, etc., still tools, or are they more than tools? If so, in what sense are these media also the message?

5. Did the internet lead to a more integral and global consciousness? Could it, in principle? Explain why (not).
6. In what sense do contemporary technologies "extend" our minds and/or bodies, if at all?
7. Are we all gadget lovers today, and does this lead to a narcissistic state of numbness?

RECOMMENDED READING

Coeckelbergh, Mark. 2018. "Skillful Coping With and Through Technologies: Some Challenges and Avenues for a Dreyfus-Inspired Philosophy of Technology." *AI & Society* 1–19. (Online first)

Heidegger, Martin. 1977. "The Question Concerning Technology." In *Martin Heidegger, The Question Concerning Technology and Other Essays*, translated by William Lovitt, 3–35. New York: Harper Torchbooks.

McLuhan, Marshall. (1964) 2001. *Understanding Media: The Extensions of Man*. Reprint, London: Routledge.

KEY TERMS

Body schema

Dividuation

Enactivism

Enframing, Modern
   technology as

Global village

Hot and cool media

Narcissus

Posthumanism

Revealing or unconceal-
   ment, Technology as

The medium is the message

CASE/TECHNOLOGY:
Driving a Car

When thinking about a car, we may reflect about modern society and culture and about cars as modern technologies that fit a particular kind of society: a modern, individualist society. But we can also consider the car as an artifact, a designed and engineered artifact. We can then describe how it is made and how it works. And we can also describe how it is *used*, as a technological artifact. We then realize that usually (literally) we do not think about the car. The car does not appear to us as a separate technological artifact. When we drive, the car is part of us moving about. We do not see the car as a separate thing: we move in traffic with the car. The car

FIGURE 4.1 Self-driving car

is *embodied*. It is what Heidegger called ready-to-hand. Only when it breaks down or when, for example, we want to buy a new car does it become present-at-hand. It appears to us as an object. But usually (that is, when and during driving), it is part of us. Perhaps one could even say that it becomes part of our body: as we move about, we experience the edges of the cars as the frontier of our body. Similarly, usually when we wear glasses, the glasses are experienced as part of us, as embodied. We see the world through them. They themselves are not in view. Now for this description and analysis, we do not consider the whole of modern society and culture; instead, we zoom in on the artifact, in particular on how it is used and experienced. This is a form of phenomenology that is arguably more "empirical" than many earlier ones. It is called postphenomenology and is part of the "empirical turn" in philosophy of technology. This is the topic of chapter 4.

4.1. Introduction: The Empirical Turn

In the 1980s and 1990s, some philosophers of technology in the United States and in the Netherlands took what they called an **empirical turn** (Achterhuis 2001). Positioning themselves against classic philosophers of technology such as Heidegger, Ellul (see chapters 1 and 2), and Jonas, they claimed that they focus more on concrete artifacts and practices rather than on grand—and often dystopian—theories about "technology" in general. Often close to what Mitcham called "engineering" philosophy of technology and learning from STS, philosophers such as Ihde, Winner, Feenberg, and Verbeek addressed issues concerning concrete technological artifacts, their design, and their place in society. Instead of focusing on the study and interpretation of authors such as Heidegger, these philosophers—to use Achterhuis's words—"stand in the middle of the world of designers and users of technology" (Achterhuis 2001, 8).

This chapter gives an overview of some influential work by two prominent philosophers of technology of the empirical turn, who nevertheless kept a link with one of the classic approaches in philosophy of technology (phenomenology and, to some extent, pragmatism and hermeneutics): Don Ihde and Peter-Paul Verbeek. Then some objections are articulated, including references to recent literature in philosophy of technology.

4.2. Ihde's Postphenomenology and Material Hermeneutics

4.2.1. Postphenomenology and Human–Technology Relations

The American philosopher of technology Don Ihde proposed a new approach to philosophy of technology that he coined **postphenomenology** (Ihde 2009). Ihde endorses, and contributes to, criticisms of Heidegger and other classic philosophers of technology made by the empirical turn philosophers: he moves away from the concern with technology overall, rejects transcendental analysis (he assumes that this leads to a "high altitude" analysis) and the supposedly "romantic or nostalgic tastes" that led to dystopian views of technology; instead, he sets out to examine "technologies in their particularities" (Ihde 2009, 21–22). His approach to do this derives from engagement with phenomenology, pragmatism, and hermeneutics.

IN FOCUS:
Don Ihde

Don Ihde is an influential American philosopher of technology and professor at State University of New York, Stony Brook. He founded the so-called post-phenomenological school. He strongly rejected Heidegger's romanticism and focus on technology as enframing and instead focused on concrete artifacts and human–technology relations. He is known for his work on what he calls "technoscience," examining the "material hermeneutics" of the instruments of science. Influenced by Merleau-Ponty, Ihde emphasizes embodiment and rejects Cartesian dualism. He has always been a strong proponent of interdisciplinary research.

FIGURE 4.2 Don Ihde

Let us start with phenomenology and pragmatism. Unlike classic phenomenology of technology influenced by pragmatism (see chapter 6) and by Merleau-Ponty, postphenomenology studies concrete artifacts in their materiality, in their relation to bodily perception and bodily technique, and as used in practical and lifeworld contexts.

From pragmatism, Ihde adopts a focus on the *use* of technology and learns that experience is related to the physical and the material as well as to the cultural-social. He then borrows from Husserl's phenomenology variational theory and intentionality, but he reinterprets and uses these ideas for the purpose of thinking about technology. He interprets the phenomenological term "variation" (think about Gestalt switches) in a way that stresses active perceptual engagement and embodiment and applies that interpretation to technology: he argues that the "same" technology is used in very different ways, involving different bodily techniques. He gives the example of the bow and arrow and the related practice of archery and shows how very different practices emerged. Ihde calls this **multistability** (Ihde 2009, 16). With regard to intentionality, he argues that both classic phenomenology and pragmatism entailed an "interrelational ontology" according to which "the human experiencer is to be found ontologically related to an environment or a world, but the interrelation is such that both are transformed within this relationality" (Ihde 2009, 23). Ihde then once again enters *technology* into the picture. Technology is not seen as belonging to the domain of objects but as mediating consciousness itself (23).

What does it mean to say that technology mediates consciousness, mediates our experience of the world? To understand this, let us turn to Ihde's *Technology and the Lifeworld* (1990) in which he develops an account of what he calls "human-world relations" (Ihde 1990, 23) and in which he emphasizes the mediating role of technology (**technological mediation**). Phenomenology of human-world relations thus becomes the "phenomenology of human-technology-world relations or human-technology relations" (41). Ihde (1990) uses the following scheme (simplified for the purpose of this summary; see also Verbeek 2005, 125–128):

- Embodiment relation: (I–technology)–world
- Hermeneutic relations I–(technology–world)
- Alterity relations I–technology–(world)
- Background relations

When we have an *embodiment* relation to technology, we use the technology but are not aware of it: inspired by Heidegger's distinction between ready-to-hand and present-at-hand in *Being and Time* (see chapter 3), Ihde argues that there is a "withdrawal of technology from within direct experience" (Ihde 1990, 32). For example, when we are wearing glasses or driving a car, the glasses and the car are embodied in the sense that we use them without thinking about them. The relation can be expressed as "I–glasses–world" (73) or "I–car–world." Inspired by Merleau-Ponty's examples about a woman wearing a feather in her hat and the blind man's stick, Ihde argues that the experienced body can be extended with artifacts and that these artifacts then shape our perception and actions. When there is a *hermeneutic* relation, by contrast, the technology is visible and the world is interpreted ("read") by the user through the technology. But the technology is not a mere instrument: it once again changes our perception.

For example, a clock does not merely represent time; it already contributes to a particular interpretation of time. We have a relation to the "technology–world." In an *alterity* relation, we also have a relation to the technology, but here the technology does not mediate our perception or present the world; rather, it becomes itself a something else or even a someone else, a quasi-other. Ihde uses the term "alterity" (1990, 98). For example, a robot may become a quasi-other. We experience that we are interacting with something other. Here the technology is "focal" (107): it is in the foreground. By contrast, in *background* relations, the technology also structures and mediates our experience, but it remains in the background. Think of a thermostat, which is in the background but shapes our experience of heat and cold.

CASE/TECHNOLOGY:
Robot as Quasi-Other

Autonomous and intelligent robots, especially when they take human form (so-called humanoids), do not appear to us as mere tools, like a hammer or a knife. Instead, because of their appearance and behavior, we often perceive them as quasi-others: we see them in a similar way as we do when another human being or a pet moves about in our environment (e.g., home environment) and interacts with us. Sometimes they are especially designed to appear as social agents. So-called social robots are developed to interact with us in ways that are similar

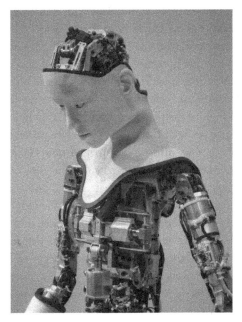

FIGURE 4.3 Humanoid robot

to human–human interaction. In these cases, the robot is neither a mere tool nor object that is part of the world, nor an embodied technology—but it is experienced as similar to human others, as "alters."

Ihde thus picks up work by Heidegger and Merleau-Ponty but puts much more focus on the *technology* as a concrete material artifact that mediates our experience in various ways. Moreover, Ihde's emphasis on multistability also enables him to pay attention to how the use of artifacts varies in and with different cultures. This idea of "varieties of technological experience" (Ihde 1990, 151) and use also applies to our own culture in which "a multiplicity of users can pick up and use technologies in such different ways" (164). Instead of enframing (Heidegger), Ihde (1990) sees a pluricultural lifeworld (158) with various technological experiences and uses. Again the emphasis is on the non-instrumentality of technology, but here there is more attention to particular artifacts and diversity of experience and use.

4.2.2. Material Hermeneutics

Another significant source of Ihde's thinking is hermeneutics. Already in *Technology and the Lifeworld* (1990), he writes about interpretation and uses textual metaphors. In *Expanding Hermeneutics* (1998), he shows how science in practice involves a "visual hermeneutics" (137) and that instruments enable new perceptions and interpretations. This leads him to engage with the tradition of hermeneutics. But instead of limiting analysis of hermeneutics—here construed broadly as "interpretative activity" (Ihde 1998, 2)—to texts, Ihde argues that scientists also interpret: science is a hermeneutic practice. Ihde shows this by giving the example of the greenhouse effect, which as a phenomenon is constructed by means of images and technologies that enable detection and measurement. For example, the state of the planet is shown as the "whole Earth" (Ihde 1998, 58–59). This "hermeneutic of things" (59) has always been practiced in the history of science. Ihde tells a semi-fictional story of how Galileo was "tinkering with his optical instruments" (154), in particular the telescope. In line with his postphenomenology, Ihde stresses the material and bodily aspects of scientific practice; it is a "perceptual-bodily activity." At the same time, it is also an interpretative activity, albeit one that does not only engage with texts but also with things: "an interpretative activity with the thingly" (159). This **material hermeneutics** leads to the view that things co-constitute and co-construct the world. According to Ihde's so-called strong program, new technologies create new worlds; and indeed, this means that we live in a different world today than in the past. Again the technology plays a non-instrumental or more-than-an-instrument role. Technology is not only a means or an object of hermeneutics, something that is read. One could interpret Ihde as implying that technology is not passively but actively hermeneutic.

Compared to classical hermeneutics, this is quite a step. Traditionally, in the Jewish-Christian biblical tradition, hermeneutics used to be limited to the world of words, the world of texts, which stood in need of interpretation (Ihde 1998, 10). This approach remained influential in modern and 20th-century philosophy, although the meaning of hermeneutics was generalized to the activity of inter-pretation. Ihde's contribution must be situated in this project: he broadened the meaning of hermeneutics to the material, technological sphere: artifacts now not only stand in need of interpretation but also actively mediate our interpretation of the world. But Ihde's material hermeneutics should not only be understood as an "expansion." As with his postphenomenology, this turn to the artifact implied a turn away from the language-and text-oriented philosophy of the hermeneutical tradition, in particular from the work of the French philosopher Paul Ricoeur. Ihde knows Ricoeur's work very well but takes distance. He does not directly use Ricoeur or the notion of narrative, for example, and links him to "postmodern sympathies" (85) and "poststructuralists and deconstructionists" (Ihde 1998, 126) obsessed with language. Ihde's focus on the hermeneutic function of material technologies and instruments is thus also a move away from the study of language. (See also my discussion of objections later in this chapter.)

4.3. Contemporary Postphenomenology and Mediation Theory

Today there are a number of philosophers belonging to the so-called postphe-nomenological school who work with this approach and have further developed it, such as Peter-Paul Verbeek, Evan Selinger, and Robert Rosenberger. To show the possibilities and vitality of postphenomenology with regard to thinking about contemporary technologies, let me zoom in on Verbeek's mediation theory and his claims about the morality of things.

Verbeek is a Dutch philosopher of technology who, situating himself in the empirical turn, has further popularized Ihde's scheme of human–technology relations, applied postphenomenology to the design of artifacts, and developed theory about how artifacts mediate *morality* and shape the *human*.

4.3.1. Verbeek's Version of Postphenomenology: Mediation and the Mutual Constitution of Subject and Object

A seminal and influential work in this direction, which endorses Ihde's project but also further develops it, has been Verbeek's *What Things Do* (2005). Turning against the *horror materiae* (intense fear of matter) of the philosophical tradition (Verbeek 2005, 1) and especially the linguistic turn of the 20th century, but also against philosophers of technology focusing on alienation such as Heidegger and Jaspers, Verbeek argues that we should take artifacts seriously by analyzing human–technology relations. He criticizes Jaspers for reducing technology to bureaucracy and mass production, to the conditions of possibility from which it arises (Verbeek 2005, 45). Heidegger is charged with being not only too much removed from technological practices, but also with having provided a biased, nostalgic view of technology. Echoing Feenberg, Heidegger's transcendentalism is seen as abstract and monolithic (Verbeek 2005, 61), and deterministic: we cannot alter anything, it seems. But Verbeek also argues that Heidegger treats modern and ancient technologies in a way that seems biased against modern technologies. He agrees with Ihde that Heidegger is selective: the modern power plant is seen as part of enframing, but why would an ancient temple not disclose the surrounding woods as raw material used for its building (Verbeek 2005, 69)? Verbeek adds that Heidegger seems to use two perspectives: a historical one for modern technologies and an ahistorical one for traditional ones (72). He also criticizes Heidegger for placing technology entirely in the context of the history of being, which means that it is no longer "viewed in terms of specific technological artefacts" (93).

IN FOCUS:
Peter-Paul Verbeek

Peter-Paul Verbeek is a contemporary Dutch philosopher of technology and a professor at the University of Twente in the Netherlands. He is part of the so-called empirical turn philosophers in the field, focusing on analysis of concrete artifacts. He is also a prominent member of the postphenomenological school. Influenced by Ihde and Achterhuis, he has further developed theory about how technology plays a role in human–world relations—in particular, how artifacts mediate what we see and do. One of his most influential writings is *What Things Do* (2005).

To remedy these shortcomings, Verbeek—like Ihde, picking up the tool analysis in *Being and Time* and turning away from Heidegger's later work—embarks on developing "a phenomenological philosophy of technology that takes actual technology seriously" (2005, 95). The basis of this work is Ihde's postphenomenology of human–technology–world relations, which Verbeek reads as relations of mediation and stresses that subject and object mutually constitute one another: the human is not given but is constituted by technology (129); there is a "mutual constitution of subject and object" (130). Technologies thus not only transform our perception; they also constitute us, make us what we are. Verbeek sees this as a way of expanding on Ihde's framework. Moreover, technologies are not necessarily alienating; there are various ways in which the world can manifest itself, and this does not necessarily entail alienation or "reduction," as some classical phenomenologists thought. He writes

The role of technology in human everyday life involves far more than calculative thinking. Technologies actively shape the relation between human beings and their world, and provide many varied and enriched ways in which that world can be encountered. (Verbeek 2005, 145)

Verbeek thus agrees with Ihde that (new) technologies constitute (a new) reality (2005, 135), but adds that the human is also constituted (anew). Moreover, Verbeek also stresses that technologies mediate what we *do*. Technologies do not only mediate our perception; they also shape our existence and action. To elaborate on this, Verbeek draws on the work of Bruno Latour (for more, see chapters 9 and 12), in particular *We Have Never Been Modern* (1993). Latour questions the modern subject–object dichotomy and, in Verbeek's (2005) words, sees humans and non-humans as being "bound up with each other in a network of relations" (149). For Latour, the social is made up of human and non-humans. Not only humans exist, but so-called **actants** also exist, and they mediate what we do in various ways; there are various kinds of "technical mediation." For example, a gun can change the "action program" of someone who wants to take revenge to the action program of "killing of the person" (Verbeek 2005, 156); a bulky key ring can be used to encourage hotel guests to return their keys when they leave the hotel (157); or a speed bump can be used to slow down drivers, which makes drivers slow down not because of the traffic regulation but because they want to avoid damage to their car (159). While Latour's perspective differs from (post) phenomenology, Verbeek uses his theory to show how technological mediation is structured and, more generally, to support his point that technological artifacts shape experience and action—and in this way shape human existence. Verbeek then further develops this point about existence by commenting on Borgmann, whose analysis of technological mediation he calls "somber" (179); instead of discouraging engagement, for Verbeek, new technologies can mediate the relation between humans and their world in various ways and contribute to the good life. The key question is then to change and design technologies in ways that "create new forms of contact between human beings and their world" (235) and shape our lives and existence in better ways.

His focus on the mediation of *action* as opposed to only the mediation experience, together with the concern about technology and the good life and the design angle, has led Verbeek to another contribution to the postphenomenology of technological artifacts: the view that technological artifacts mediate morality. At the end of *What Things Do* he writes

The design of technology thereby becomes no longer an internal technological affair, but appears to be a moral matter as well. Technologies are not merely functional objects but also have dimensions of style and meaning;

they mediate the relations between human beings and their world, and thereby shape human experiences and existence. Technologies help to determine how people act, so that it is not only people but also things who give answers to the classical moral question, "How to live?" It is time that we take the contributions of technology seriously and combine our forces to provide new answers to this ancient question that still applies to the technological world in which we live. (Verbeek 2005, 235–236)

In subsequent work such as *Moralizing Technology* (2011), Verbeek has further developed this point about **moral mediation**. If technology shapes our decisions and actions, then it is important to consider its moral role. He puts this in a strong way: not only do things have moral significance or moral consequences or a moral dimension (2011, 2); he argues for a **morality of things** (2011). While things do not have minds or consciousness, they mediate and shape moral decisions and actions.

Here I propose to focus on his article on ultrasound (2008b) in which he provides a postphenomenological analysis of a concrete case that formed the basis of this further work on the morality of things. Verbeek shows that the way parents see their unborn child, think about having the child, make decisions about the child, and in fact their entire experience of the pregnancy, is mediated and shaped by the ultrasound technology. In terms of the subject–object relation, both subject and object are constituted by the technology as mediator: the subjectivity of the parents and the child. Let me summarize how Verbeek unpacks this argument to show how he applies and expands Ihde's postphenomenological framework.

CASE/TECHNOLOGY:
Medical Sonography/Ultrasound

In the context of medicine, (ultra)sonography is a diagnostic medical imaging technique that uses ultrasound (sound waves with a frequency higher than what humans can hear) to visualize what happens in the body. For example, the technique is used a lot to visualize the fetus in the womb at various stages of pregnancy in real time (obstetric ultrasonography). The advantage is that it is a non-invasive and non-destructive technique to test and detect. In the case of obstetric ultrasonography, it gives information about the progress of the pregnancy, the development of the fetus, and the health of the mother. Since this enables detection of developmental defects and abnormalities before birth, the technique has made possible ethical discussions about decisions concerning abortion—for example, in the case of Down syndrome—and has affected the way pregnancy is experienced (by mothers and others involved) and conceptualized (e.g., medicalization of pregnancy).

4.3.2. Material Morality: Ultrasound Technology and Moral Decisions about Pregnancy as an Application of Verbeek's Postphenomenological Theory

Verbeek already stressed the mutual constitution of subject and object in *What Things Do*, as a way of expanding Ihde's framework, and repeats the point here:

> What the world "is" and what subjects "are," arises from the interplay between humans and reality; the world humans experience is "interpreted reality" and human existence is "situated subjectivity." Postphenomenology, then, consists in the philosophical analysis of human-world relations—including its technologically mediated character—and of the constitution of subjectivity and objectivity within these relations. It does not close the gap between subject and object stressing that subject and object are always linked via the bridge of intentionality but by claiming that they constitute each other. In the mutual relation between humans and reality, a specific "objectivity" of the world arises, as well as a specific "subjectivity" of human beings. (Verbeek 2008b, 13)

However, Verbeek now stresses the moral dimension of this mediation and mutual constitution. If the technology shapes the experience and interpretation of reality, then it also shapes the moral decisions made on the basis of these perceptions and interpretations (Verbeek 2008b, 14). He describes how ultrasound is used to calculate the risk that the child will have Down syndrome. This means that the unborn and the reality of the unborn are interpreted through the technology. The ultrasound imaging does not only constitute the unborn as an individual being, separate from the mother, which creates new relations (e.g., the father is more involved, the health care professionals now also have knowledge of the child); it also constitutes the fetus as a (possible) patient and turns the experience of pregnancy into a medical process and a process of choice:

> In fact, the very possibility to have sonograms made at all, and therefore to detect congenital defects before birth, irreversibly changes the character of what used to be called "expecting a child." It inevitably becomes a matter of choice now: also the choice not to have an ultrasound scan made is a choice, even a very deliberate one in a society in which the norm is to have these scans made—from the predominant idea that not scanning for diseases is irresponsible, because then you deliberately run the risk to have a disabled or sick child, causing suffering both for the child and for the expecting parents and their families. (Verbeek 2008b, 16)

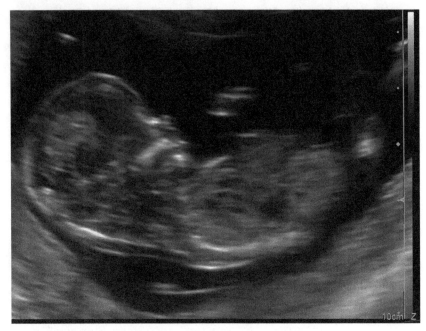

FIGURE 4.4 Scan of an ultrasound image of unborn child

The technology thus also "embodies morality" in the sense that moral decisions regarding the child are mediated by the technology and in the sense that the very situation of having to make a choice is created by the technology. This does not only constitute the unborn but also constitutes the expecting *parents* as decision-makers (Verbeek 2008b, 17). There may also be an increase in abortions. The technology is thus not at all morally neutral but has morally relevant implications. In this sense, Verbeek "moralizes technology."

For Verbeek, this "technologically mediated constitution of the subject" (2008b, 21), and indeed of morality, is not a reason to reject technology but to assess and experiment with its mediation to shape how we are and want to be today as subjects in our technological culture (21). We can make choices—in this case, for example, to use the ultrasound technology to only measure expected date of birth or by using different techniques. One could also want all tests. The point, Verbeek argues, is that we can choose our subjectivity and hence the mediations. Instead of rejecting technology, we then actively relate to its mediations. Influenced by Foucault, Verbeek argues that we need practices of the self that explicitly deal with technological mediations to arrive at a responsible use of technology and shape the kinds of beings we want to be (2008b, 23).

This leads us to the question regarding technology and the human and Verbeek's answer to that.

4.3.3. Mediation and the Future of the Human

According to Verbeek, many classic approaches to technology oppose the lifeworld to the system, and technology to the human. Instead, he proposes to take "the interwoven character of the human and the technological" (Verbeek 2008b, 19) as the point of departure for thinking about ethics and about the human. Against an "externalist approach," which opposes a human realm to a technological realm, Verbeek argues that humans are technological beings (Verbeek 2011, 4). In his non-humanist, posthumanist, and non-modern view influenced by Latour (Verbeek 2008a), humans are technological, and things have morality and intentionality as they transform our perception and action. Against the Enlightenment image of the autonomous subject, he places a heteronomous subject that is interwoven with, and shaped by, its material environment. Against a modern thinking that strictly separates subjects and objects, against a humanism that neglects the material aspect of the human, and in response to the German philosopher Sloterdijk who wrote a controversial essay on the "breeding" of humans by means of humanist and posthumanist "anthropotechnologies" (he wrote on biotechnologies that alter the biological constitution of the human being) (Sloterdijk 1999), Verbeek argues for taking into account artifacts as a material and non-human reality that shapes human actions and decisions—and indeed shapes humans and their "coming-in-the-world" as they are bred and tamed by lots of artifacts that function as anthropotechnologies: not only texts (the focus of humanists and humanities scholars) but also material technologies such as ultrasound are means by which we are tamed and tame ourselves. Not only biotechnologies but all kinds of technologies play this role. Influenced by Foucault, Verbeek argues that by our designing and mediating technologies (objects), we also at the same time design, style, and cultivate the human (subjects), although we are not totally in control: the artifact itself can give rise to unintended mediations, such as when a revolving door prevents wheelchair users from entering a building. His **posthumanist** view thus crosses boundaries between humans and non-humans. In what we could call the making of morality and the making of the human, there are what Verbeek calls "alliances" between humans and non-human entities. The human can only exist in and through its relations to the non-human; and in his sense, the human is always the more-than-human (Verbeek 2008a).

Verbeek's posthumanist position must be put in the context of the discussion of posthumanism and transhumanism and its significance for philosophy of technology, which I will outline in chapter 9.

4.4. Critical Discussion

There are a number of criticisms that could be, and often have been, presented in response to postphenomenology. Let me cluster and discuss some of these here.

First, given that postphenomenology claims to look at concrete artifacts, and that phenomenology in the Husserlian tradition is supposed to describe the features of experience, going to the "things themselves"—which is interpreted by Verbeek as literally going to the material artifacts—the approach is surprisingly theory driven. It appears that the starting point for philosophical investigation is not descriptions of the experience of technology but rather a scheme of human–technology relations (including an abstract picture of subjects and objects) and more generally mediation theory, which is then applied to concrete cases. This approach has proven to be fruitful but also bears the danger that some experiences of technology might be missed, if they fall outside the theory or scheme of human–technology relations. Moreover, there is also the danger of generalization. For instance, by lumping together all kinds of experiences into the category of embodiment, one risks missing differences between experiences; for example, between experiences of body extensions and experiences related to incorporation of non-bodily objects into the body (De Preester 2011; see also chapter 3). Researchers in phenomenology could reply to this objection that their approach does not rule out doing more specific investigations and that some work really starts from specific cases such as ultrasound. However, the question is then still how heavily the theory weighs on these investigations and whether it only opens up or also closes some investigations in the postphenomenological spirit.

Second, one may also question how *phenomenological* postphenomenology still is if it rejects transcendental ontology. Zwier, Blok, and Lemmens (2016) have argued that the specific way postphenomenology has executed the empirical turn forfeits phenomenological questioning. They accuse postphenomenology of taking a theoretical attitude and of creating a mediation theory about ontic beings (technologies) rather than engaging in an ontological mode of questioning à la Heidegger, thereby contributing to what Heidegger calls enframing. Indeed, one may ask if postphenomenology, at least in the form of mediation theory, investigates the structures of experience or rather presents a quasi-mechanistic model of things that "do things." Furthermore, Dominic Smith has argued that postphenomenology was wrong to reject a transcendental approach, and that the latter has far more potential than postphenomenology suggests and is not necessarily incompatible with the empirical turn (Smith 2015; see also Coeckelbergh 2017b). While some philosophers present the transcendental in a way that invites the criticism of Ihde, Feenberg, and Verbeek, according to Smith, the transcendental can be a useful form of argument. Smith proposes a "transcendental empiricism" (2015, 546) inspired by Deleuze. Like Zwier et al. (2016), Smith thinks that without a transcendental approach, we remain at the ontic level, for example, when we talk about "agents" constituting one another (Smith 2015, 538). According to Smith, part of the problem is that postphenomenology entirely rejected postmodernism and poststructuralism, which we may learn from for thinking about technology. An opponent may submit that it is not (yet) clear how this transcendental empiricism works. But there is a lot of room for various approaches in this direction, which are not necessarily Deleuzian. In my book *Using Words and Things* (Coeckelbergh 2017b) and in other publications on using Wittgenstein for philosophy of technology, I have defended the inclusion of a transcendental approach to understanding using and performing with words and things.

Third, these criticisms lead me to my objection about the neglect of language in postphenomenology. By rejecting postmodernism and classic thinkers such as Heidegger altogether, postphenomenology has neglected the role of language in our experiences and actions with technology (Coeckelbergh 2015, 2017b). I have argued that, in their effort to distance themselves from postmodernism and Heidegger, Ihde and Verbeek have unduly turned away from language. To remedy this, I have proposed two routes. One remains within postphenomenology: here the aim is to integrate the role of language in the theory of human–technology relations and mediation theory by revising these theories. The key idea is not only to insert technology as mediator between humans and their world but also to see language as mediator. This revision (Coeckelbergh 2017b, 170–174) then enables us to expand rather than reject Ihde's and Verbeek's framework. Another route is to develop an alternative view, which replaces theory of human–technology relations by a different approach: for instance, a Wittgensteinian or transcendental approach that focuses on the structures or "grammar" of technological experience, use, and action (Coeckelbergh 2017a, 2017b). This goes beyond postphenomenology, or at least beyond postphenomenology as it has been theorized by Ihde and Verbeek.

Fourth, related to the points that postphenomenology is not phenomenological enough and that language is neglected is also the objection that (Ihde's) expanded hermeneutics is not hermeneutical enough, and is certainly uninformed by Ricoeur. Indeed, while earlier in his career Ihde engaged with Ricoeur's work, later Ihde does not make good use of his work, in the name of turning away from postmodernism and other language-oriented philosophy. This is to be regretted since the notion of narrativity and other work from hermeneutics could enrich the postphenomenological framework (Coeckelbergh 2017b, 211–214). In response, Wessel Reijers and I have tried to construct a framework centered around the notion of **narrative technologies** (Coeckelbergh and Reijers 2016, and subsequent work). We have argued that narrative theory can not only be used to theorize how humans interpret—read—technology, as in Ihde or Kaplan (2006, 49), but also to study how technologies actively shape and reconfigure our narratives, in particular by configuring lived and narrative time into a plot, organizing characters and events (Coeckelbergh and Reijers 2016; see also Coeckelbergh 2017b, 217). By applying our framework to blockchain technology (Reijers and Coeckelbergh 2016), we have shown that this more narrative and ontological approach does not lead to less empirically sensitive investigations.

Fifth, our work on narrative technologies also developed in response to another, in my view important, objection to postphenomenology: it is insufficiently sensitive to the social dimension of human experience, use, and action with technology. While postphenomenologists say that they are interested in the link between technology and society and sometimes connect to STS, if we zoom in on the central theoretical framework of human–technology relations, social relations are absent. The focus is on human subjectivity and how that is mediated by technology. But social relations, or, for that matter, intersubjectivity, is not part of the picture. Although, for instance, Verbeek says in his article on ultrasound technology (2008b) that the technology impacts social relations, these social relations are not theorized or centrally connected to the mediation framework; the focus is on relations to material things, not other humans. But just as in the case of language, it would be interesting and helpful, even necessary, to pay more attention to not only how technologies have consequences for society but also to how social relations themselves shape and *mediate* our relations to technology. And here too one could either revise mediation theory or go beyond it. In my work on Wittgenstein and technology, and influenced by Winner, I have chosen the latter option: I conceptualized this relation in terms of how technology is embedded in, and structured by, games and a form of life (Coeckelbergh 2017a). But it would also be interesting to theorize social relations as mediators, next to language and technology, and to further conceptualize, within a postphenomenological framework, how the social relates to technology.

Sixth, Ihde acknowledges and uses pragmatism in his work. The focus on use contexts (and of course experience) especially is borrowed from pragmatism. Like Husserl, it is one of the philosophies Ihde starts from. However, he then very quickly moves on, after, for instance, lamenting that Husserl and Dewey did not make technology thematic to their philosophies (Ihde 2009, 22). Verbeek largely borrows this attitude. The result is that the relation with pragmatism is not extensively discussed; and once the theory of human–technology relations is developed, it disappears from the radar. But pragmatism—including Dewey's pragmatism—is a richer potential source for thinking about technology than is suggested in Ihde and Verbeek. Dewey was very interested in tools and techniques, and he has a complex view of relations among science, technology, and aesthetic experience that can be interpreted and used for thinking about technology (Hickman 2015; see also Coeckelbergh 2017b). In chapter 6, I will give a brief overview of Hickman's use of Dewey.

Seventh, Verbeek's posthumanism and focus on the "the morality of things" has given rise to confusion and objections. Some translate the question to "Do things have **moral agency**?" This is not surprising, since Verbeek himself speaks of "moral agency" being distributed over humans and artifacts (Verbeek 2008b). Peterson and Spahn (2011) have argued that technological artifacts cannot be moral agents. While they acknowledge that artifacts sometimes affect the moral evaluation of actions, they claim that they are not moral agents. Technologies have no intentionality and, cannot be responsible for their effects, and humans and technologies still have a separate existence. Against Verbeek, they defend the common view that artifacts are neutral tools (Peterson and Spahn 2011, 411). Perhaps some of these objections could be avoided if Verbeek would not use terms and phrases such as the "morality of things" and the "moral agency of things" but stay with the claim that technologies mediate morality. On the other hand, Verbeek wants to defend a posthumanist view that challenges our common understandings of technology; and, influenced by Latour, he radically questions our modern insistence on the separation of subjects and objects, things and people, culture and nature.

Eighth, another objection that can be raised is directed against the notion of mediation, or at least against using this notion instead of a more refined (post) phenomenological analysis. By narrowing down all possible roles of technology in human experience and action to mediation, other roles may remain out of sight; I already suggested this. But even if we stay within the language of mediation, one could object that Verbeek's use of the term "mediation" employs the meaning of medium as an in-between but does not consider another sense of medium: that of medium as milieu. (See again McLuhan and especially media ecology.) Looking at the metaphor, Verbeek's medium often appears as a quasi-thing that "sits" or "stands" in between subject and object. This is so since Verbeek focuses on things, on artifacts. But the metaphor of a milieu, water, etc., could reveal another way technology can function and appear. And there are more possibilities. For instance, technology can appear as infrastructure. By focusing so much on things and on things-as-in-betweens, these additional ways in which technologies can appear and can shape what we see, think, and do remain invisible.

Finally, one could ask if Ihde's and Verbeek's views, and postphenomenology in general, are critical enough. "Critical" can refer here, on the one hand, to "being critical of one's own language and discourse." One effect of the neglect of language is that there is a tendency to the naïve use of terms as metaphors. Central terms such as "use," "mediation," and "subject" are often not sufficiently discussed. "Critical" can also refer to "critical theory" and "being critical of society." Ihde and Verbeek tend to limit their analysis to individual subjectivity (see previously) and do not generally engage with critical theory. An exception is Verbeek when he rejects Habermas's distinction between lifeworld and system and the reduction of technology to an instrumental form of rationality (e.g., in Verbeek 2011, 82). More generally, Verbeek rejects dialectical approaches and rather sees technology as constitutive of human beings and as itself political (Verbeek 2016). While I am sympathetic to this criticism and acknowledge that Verbeek tends to take some kind of critical perspective by using Foucault, it might be interesting to explore ways of combining postphenomenology and critical theory rather than closing off this route of inquiry entirely. Now themes such as exploitation, capitalism, gender problems, etc., remain largely out of sight. While Verbeek, in his response to Lemmens, is right that a macro-level approach is not enough and that a micro-level analysis is also needed, and that the political significance of technologies cannot be reduced to its origins in systems of production and social organization (Verbeek 2016), neither can the political significance of technologies be reduced to what things do: a macroanalysis is also needed. Moreover, in recent thinking about the political economy of new media, for instance, in the work of Fuchs, micro- and macroanalysis are connected. This takes us to the next chapter on critical theory and feminism.

REVIEW QUESTIONS

1. What is the empirical turn?
2. What is postphenomenology and material hermeneutics?
3. What is mediation theory?
4. How do Ihde and Verbeek conceptualize human–technology relations?
5. What is multistability?
6. What is technological mediation?
7. What does Verbeek mean by the claim that things have morality?
8. What view of the human emerges from Verbeek's work?
9. What criticisms can be raised against Ihde's and Verbeek's postphenomenology?

DISCUSSION QUESTIONS

1. Do you think the empirical turn in philosophy of technology is and was a good change of direction?
2. Is postphenomenology still phenomenology?

3. Are the approaches of Ihde and Verbeek helpful to analyze technology (or better: technologies)? If not, what are the revisions or alternative view you propose?
4. Do artifacts shape morality? *Are* they "moral," and if so, in which sense? Can things have morality?

RECOMMENDED READING

Ihde, Don. 1990. *Technology and the Lifeworld: From Garden to Earth*. Bloomington: Indiana University Press.

Ihde, Don. 2009. "What is Postphenomenology?" In *Postphenomenology and Technoscience: The Peking Lectures*. Albany: State University of New York Press.

Latour, Bruno. 1993. *We Have Never Been Modern*. Translated by Catherine Porter. Cambridge, MA: Harvard University Press.

Verbeek, Peter-Paul. 2005. *What Things Do: Philosophical Reflections on Technology, Agency, and Design*. University Park: The Pennsylvania State University Press.

Verbeek, Peter-Paul. 2008. "Obstetric Ultrasound and the Technological Mediation of Morality: A Postphenomenological Analysis." *Human Studies* 31(1): 11–26.

KEY TERMS

Actants

Empirical turn

Human–technology relations

Material hermeneutics

Morality of things

Moral agency

Moral mediation

Multistability

Narrative technologies

Posthumanist

Postphenomenology

Technological mediation

CRITICAL THEORY AND FEMINISM

CASE/TECHNOLOGY:
Digital Technologies in a Corporate and Capitalist Context

Digital technologies are not developed in a vacuum but often in the context of a private corporation and a more or less capitalist socioeconomic system. The electronic gadgets we use are produced somewhere, sometimes in circumstances that have been described as exploitative. Their production also uses natural resources. Moreover, today much of the hardware and software is in the hands of a few companies, which gives them a lot of power to make decisions about the technology and its use. And in industry, the development of more intelligent and autonomous machines means that there is the possibility of unemployment if these machines replace workers. Critical theory asks questions about the nature and fairness of these systems, about sustainability, about the mode of production, about labor, and about power and agency. Are we in the hands of large corporations such as Google, Facebook, and Amazon? Can we resist or do we (have to) follow how they script our use and actions? Are mobile phones generally produced by means of capitalist exploitation? What is the relation between power and technological innovation? What is the political economy of social media? Will robotics and AI lead to massive unemployment, a new proletariat—maybe one that now also includes many middle-class people? Are machines necessarily an instrument for exploitation? How democratic is technology? Feminism also asks many critical questions: Is there such a thing as gendered technology? Do current technologies reinforce inequality between men and women? In what ways can algorithms be biased (e.g., gender bias, racism, etc.), and (how) can we avoid such biases?

5.1. Marx: Political Economy and Technology

Next to postphenomenology, critical theory is an important and influential approach in contemporary philosophy of technology. Here not Heidegger but Marx and his followers are the main source. Like in the case of Heidegger, there is of course a lot to say about Marx's work, but here I focus on articulating his view of technology on the basis of my reading of the first volume of *Capital* ([1867] 1976).

IN FOCUS:
Karl Marx

Karl Marx was a philosopher and transdisciplinary thinker *avant la lettre*, engaging in philosophy, economics, political theory, journalism, and of course revolutionary socialism. Philosophically, his work is influenced by Hegel. Marx argued that in a capitalist context, there is a class struggle between those who own the means of production and the proletariat (working classes) that sell their labor power and get exploited. He

FIGURE 5.1 Portrait of Karl Marx

thought that eventually the working class would become aware of this (develop class consciousness), and this would lead to revolution and the establishment of a communist, classless society that brings about universal emancipation. His most known works are *Capital* ([1867] 1976) and *The Communist Manifesto* (written with Friedrich Engels). Marx has been very influential on politics and history. His view(s) of technology are less well known and studied.

For Marx, technology—in the form of machinery—is mainly seen as a means of production. Yet Marx's *Capital* does not so much analyze (industrial) production processes but rather a particular mode of social relation and social organization: **capitalism**. Whereas "pure" economic theory abstracts from social structure, his political economy reveals that social structure and—influenced by Hegel but taking a materialist turn rather than an idealist one—its dialectical logic. In the first volume of *Capital*, Marx responds to the (bourgeois, capitalist) view that workers freely sell their labor to capitalists in exchange for a wage. According to Marx, this is misleading, since capital appropriates the **surplus value** from the workers: the value created that exceeds their own "labour-power" and what it costs to hire them. Whereas formally speaking they are "free" to sell their labor, in practice they are forced to sell it under these conditions. Whereas in earlier times, brute force was used, capitalism is a force that is hidden below the appearance of free exchange; we did not progress much beyond feudal societies. Now in the Industrial Revolution, machines enable the capitalist to increase productivity. Increases in productivity then lead to profit and capital accumulation. For the workers, they actually lead to longer working days and misery for them and their families. Work becomes alienated as "living labour" is subordinated to the rhythm needs of the machine, instead of the needs of human beings, and more generally to capital ("dead labour"). Marx says that capital is like a **vampire** that "lives only by sucking living labour, and lives the more, the more labour it sucks" (Marx [1867] 1976, 342). Moreover, the horrors only increase once capitalists sell export (345). This exploitation then leads to class struggle: the workers demand a reduction of the working day and an increase in wages; they do not accept that the fruits of the increased productivity are appropriated by the capitalist. This struggle is then transformed into "a struggle for the overthrow of the capitalist system," as Mandel puts it in his introduction (Marx [1867] 1976, 35). **Let us look at the argument** in more detail and focus on the role of technology.

In chapter 10 of *Capital* (Vol. 1), Marx discusses the role of machinery in the logic of political economy, in particular in the context of the factory. The problem he sees is that the machine increases productivity but at the same time also increases surplus value (Marx [1867] 1976, 492) This is made possible by the machine, which is not a simple tool but performs with tools (495). Moreover, by doing this it does not simply replace workers (497); the entire production process changes as the size of the machine increases and many machines are used; a "complex system of machinery" (499) is the result. Workers then get the role of assisting the machine. Furthermore, the transformation of the mode of production in one sphere (e.g., textile industry) also transforms other spheres (e.g., transport). For the workers, this implies that their work, lives, and environment change. First, if and when only little strength is required to assist the machines, women and children are incorporated in the system (517), and they also suffer "physical deterioration" (520); they too become "mere machines for the production of surplus-value" (523). Second, the use of machines also enables, and leads to, the prolongation of the working day (526). Fewer workers are needed (they are "set free"), but they have to work longer. Third, even if the working day is limited by law, labor is intensified: more work has to be done within a given period of time. Looking at the factory as a whole, the worker effectively becomes part of the machines.

The worker is no longer the "dominant subject" who tends the machines as "object." Instead, under use by capital, "the automaton itself is the subject, and the workers are merely conscious organs, co-ordinated with the unconscious organs of the automaton" (544). The worker adapts his movements to the motion of the machine, and workers become replaceable (546). From his childhood, the worker is transformed "into a part of a specialized machine" and is helplessly dependent on the capitalist (547). Marx compares factory work with craft work:

> In handicrafts and manufacture, the worker makes use of a tool; in the factory, the machine makes use of him. There the movements of the instrument of labour proceed from him, here it is the movements of the machine that he must follow. In manufacture the workers are the parts of a living mechanism. (Marx [1867] 1976, 548)

Humans become tools, and workers become entirely exhausted and unfree. Work becomes meaningless. Marx compares it to the torture of **Sisyphus**. This is why he thinks it is torture and unfree:

> Factory work exhausts the nervous system to the uttermost; at the same time, it does away with the many-sided play of the muscles, and confiscates every atom of freedom, both in bodily and in intellectual activity. Even the lightening of labour becomes an instrument of torture, since the machine does not free the worker from the work, but rather deprives the work itself of all content. (Marx [1867] 1976, 548)

This is why Marx ([1867] 1976), using a vampire metaphor, thinks that capital, "dead labour" sucks up "living labour-power" (548). It is mainly a metaphor for the capitalist taking surplus value from the worker, but Marx also thinks that capital is literally doing damage to the mental and physical health of human beings. Workers have to do meaningless routine tasks and have to perform their labor under bad material conditions with high temperatures, a lot of dust and noise, and "danger to life and limb" (552). The methods for raising the productivity of labor thus lead to the exploitation of the worker, who is damaged in a bodily but also a mental way. As Marx puts it in his chapter on capitalist accumulation, they turn the worker into "a fragment of a man," "an appendage of a machine," and alienate him from "the intellectual potentialities of the labour process": the result is a mean "despotism" (799). The machine plays a key role in this transformation of the methods of production and thereby also in the new kind of enslavement workers are subjected to.

Naturally, Marx argues, this has led to revolt against the machine. The machine becomes a competitor when the machine takes over jobs; this change and the misery it produces are acutely felt by the masses (Marx [1867] 1976, 557). It is not true, he argues, what the bourgeois political economists say: that "setting free" workers leads now to new or better employment, since new capital becomes available. What happens instead, he argues, is that a reserve army of workers is created "at the disposal of capitalist exploitation" (567). But it is not the machine as such that is the problem. Commenting on the **Luddite movement**, he writes

> It took both time and experience before the workers learned to distinguish between machinery and its employment by capital, and therefore to transfer their attacks from the material instruments of production to the form of society which utilizes those instruments. (Marx [1867] 1976, 555)

Thus, Marx is not against technology or against machines. His argument is much more subtle. While the machine plays a role in the transformations he describes, it is not the machine itself that is to blame—and indeed not even specific individuals (capitalists). Capitalism is the problem; that is, a specific form of social relation and organization that makes humans the slaves of machines rather than using the machines to liberate them. If machines were to serve a different, socialist form of social organization, Marx suggests, they would be emancipatory. Consider, for instance, his argument that the inclusion of women and children in the "collective working group," in spite of all its bad effects (e.g., on the health and well-being of children), also provides the foundation for "a higher form of the family"; he thinks that this group can be developed into a more human direction if liberated from the brutal capitalist system in which "the worker exists for the process of production, and not the process of production for the worker" (Marx [1867] 1976, 621). Or consider his argument that capitalism brings together agriculture and manufacture and thereby "creates the material conditions for a new and higher synthesis, a union of agriculture and industry" (637). Getting rid of the capitalist mode of production, Marx suggests, would also help us to end robbing and ruining the soil and end robbing and ruining the worker; after all, "the soil and the worker" are the sources of wealth (638).

What does this analysis of 19th-century political economy and machines imply for thinking about technology today? This is of course a big question. There are at least two routes by which I propose to explore answers to this question within the confines of this introductory text. One runs through 20th-century critical theory and culminates in the work of empirically oriented philosopher of technology Andrew Feenberg, who combines Marcuse's critical theory, science and technology studies (STS), and Heidegger. Langdon Winner also connects with STS and the "empirical turn." Another route makes a more direct link with Marx and even *Capital* by applying his method of political economy analysis to contemporary technologies, in particular social media. Let me start with the latter.

5.2. Marx 2.0: Social Media and Exploitation

At first sight, in many so-called advanced Western countries, the use of technology today has little in common with the dusty and noisy factories of Marx's time and the wild capitalist environment in which workers were exploited. Many

---

CASE/TECHNOLOGY:
Social Media and Web 2.0

Social media are web-based applications and websites that enable the creation and exchange of information via networks. Examples are WhatsApp, Facebook, Twitter, Instagram, Pinterest, Snapchat, and YouTube—just to mention a few popular ones. They belong to what is often referred to as Web 2.0: WWW-based sites and applications that have a focus on users that actively generate content, are easy to use, and work well together with other systems, products, and devices—in contrast with Web 1.0 passive viewing of content on websites. These kinds of technologies offer a lot of opportunities for communication, interaction, networking, discussion, participation, and collaboration, but they also raise ethical and political questions; for example, with regard to privacy and data protection, spamming, trolling, harassment, and hate speech, and the question of who should make and decide the rules and control the specific medium. I say more on social media in the textbox in chapter 11. Here the question is, How can we use Marx to critically analyze social media?

FIGURE 5.2 Smartphone social media icons

people today spend their working time in clean offices using technologies that seem to serve them well; and since Marx's time, labor laws have limited the possibilities for capitalist exploitation. But this is only at first sight: there is much more going on—or so it has been argued by Christian Fuchs and others inspired by Marx, who take seriously Marx's analysis of **political economy** and apply it to today's media and technologies. Let me zoom in on Fuchs's analysis of the political economy of **social media** as an example of such an analysis and its potential benefits for thinking about contemporary technologies.

In *Social Media: A Critical Introduction* (2014), Fuchs proposes to apply critical theory approaches to social media. He starts with a defense of the relevance of Marx today: the financial crisis of 2008 and responses such as the **Occupy movement**, he argues, have made people aware not only that there are huge gaps between rich and poor but also that capitalism itself is in crisis. According to Fuchs, the right tool to analyze the problem—and, more generally, to understand our world and our struggles for a better world today—is the work of Marx. Marx teaches us that technological phenomena are the outcome of social relations, and Marxian critical theory and its method of dialectical reasoning helps us to question all kinds of forms of domination and exploitation (Fuchs 2014, 12–13). Here I propose to focus on how Fuchs uses Marx's critique of political economy for questioning contemporary social media.

Fuchs argues that social media are not as participatory, liberating, democratic, and public sphere facilitating tools they seem, but are colonized by capitalism and dominated by big corporate actors (Fuchs 2014, 102). To create surplus value and accumulate capital, the working day has to be prolonged and productivity has to be increased. And this is what is happening with social media use, which Fuchs and others interpret in terms of production and labor. The social media user and its labor are sold to advertising companies. Users who upload content produce content (**data commodity**) and are themselves a commodity sold to advertisers (Fuchs 2014, 107). Users invest a certain amount of labor time. Corporations then sell the data commodity. The surplus value is created by the users and the employees of the company. But the users are unpaid; they work for free. Users get access, but this is not a salary because it cannot be converted, for instance, into food. All online time is surplus labor time. Therefore, the users are "infinitely exploited" (110–111). It is in the interest of the company then that the user spends a lot of time online, since then more data can be transformed into profit. And just as the 19th-century capitalist is dependent on the workers, 21st-century social media capitalists are dependent on the users doing their labor. Thus, Fuchs understands social media use as a new form of labor and a new form of exploitation. It also involves surveillance and a new kind of factory, for example "the Internet factory" (118). This factory is not at one location; the exploitation takes place everywhere (118). We think that we play, for instance, in our so-called free time. But in fact we are engaged in digital labor: we are producing data, turning our content and ourselves into a commodity that is then sold by the capitalist. Moreover, devices such as iPhones are connected to exploitative forms of labor that produce them. The joy provided by Western phones is made possible by "the blood and sweat of Africans and Asians" needed to extract the minerals needed for the phone and to produce it (120). In those countries, sometimes "slave-like conditions" exist (120). Thus, "the exploitation of play workers in the West is based on the pain, sweat, blood, and death of workers in developing countries" (Fuchs 2014, 121). Ideological mystifications of social media detract us from seeing these new forms of exploitation and its class character (122).

Fuchs also gives concrete examples. For instance, he claims that **Google**, which has become ubiquitous, also involves exploitation of users and, more generally, the same kind of political economy just described:

> Google's users and employees produce its surplus value and have made it into the powerful company that it is today. The people using Google or working for Google are permanently exploited and dispossessed of the profit that they create. The contemporary proletariat does not so much work at conveyor belts in industrial firms. To a certain degree it creates surplus value for Google (and other social media companies) by using and producing its services. The factory is today not only in spaces of waged employment, but also in the living room, the bedroom, the kitchen and the public spaces—the factory is everywhere. (Fuchs 2014, 130)

In more detail, the commodification and exploitation happen because (1) the company's search algorithm indexes content produced by all users—unpaid users—and (2) when users employ the algorithm and use other services, they are also doing unpaid labor for the company since this generates data that are then sold to advertising companies. More users of Google means more data. And—this is often overlooked—since the whole internet is used as a resource (a resource Google does not pay for), more users of the World Wide Web and its growth also means profit, since it means more and better search results and hence more users of Google. Therefore, Fuchs (2014) calls Google "the ultimate user-exploitation machine" because it instrumentalizes all users and their data for generating profit (131). In the end, the aim seems to be a commodification of all knowledge. And with its powerful search engine, it is also at the same time the ultimate surveillance machine. Moreover, Fuchs also argues that Google employees are exploited, having to work long hours and do overtime (145).

Like Marx, however, Fuchs (2014) does not oppose the technology as such. In principle, the technology could be transformed into a public search engine (148) and be used for the benefit of humanity:

> Google stands at the same time for the universal and the particular interests on the Internet. It represents the idea of the advancement of an Internet that benefits humanity and the reality of the absolute exploitation of humanity for business purposes. Google is the universal exploiter and has created technologies that can advance a universal humanity if, in an act of universal appropriation, humans act as a universal subject and free themselves and these technologies from exploitative class relations. (Fuchs 2014, 149)

5.3. Critical Theory about Technology beyond Marx: From Marcuse and Foucault to Feenberg and Winner

5.3.1. Introduction

The term "critical theory" usually refers to work by the so-called **Frankfurt School** (*Frankfurter Schule*), although the term can also be used more broadly, as in this section. The philosophy of the Frankfurt School draws on Marx and Freud and combines philosophy and social sciences. The term refers to work by Marcuse, Adorno, Horkheimer, Benjamin, and Fromm. Other critical theory scholars include Lukács, Gramsci, and Habermas. The Frankfurt School observed the rise of totalitarianism and other new forms of social domination; instead of the end of capitalism predicted by Marx, it seemed that modernity was on its way to more enslavement rather than liberation. In *Dialectic of Enlightenment* ([1944] 2002), Adorno and Horkheimer argued that the project of the Enlightenment failed: instead of reason, the Frankfurt School observed everywhere the domination of what they called **instrumental rationality.** In the words of Habermas, the lifeworld was colonized by the system (Habermas 1981). According to Marcuse, both capitalism and Soviet communism involved social repression, and advanced industrial societies create false needs. In *One-Dimensional Man* ([1964] 2007), Marcuse argues against consumerism. Habermas, however, was more optimistic than, say, Adorno or Horkheimer, and worked around the concept of "communicative reason"; he is still a very influential thinker. Later, Michel Foucault, often classified as belonging to a postmodern version of critical theory, points to specific historical and cultural contexts rather than generalizing about capitalism or modernity or "the system." And in the 1980s and 1990s, scholars in philosophy of technology such as Feenberg and Winner took an "empirical turn" and started to develop their own version of critical theory by learning from STS. To introduce some of this work and explore what it means for thinking about *technology*, let me zoom in on Marcuse, Foucault, and Feenberg (and Winner), who each developed their own unique response to Marx and earlier critical theory.

5.3.2. Marcuse

In (early) critical theory, technology is often linked to the "system" that oppresses, with the "instrumental reason" that it enables total control. In his famous *One-Dimensional Man*, Marcuse also argues that technology is used for domination and social control. Industrial society itself becomes totalitarian by manipulating the needs of people (Marcuse [1964] 2007, 5). The machine is an instrument for political control:

> Today political power asserts itself through its power over the machine process and over the technical organization of the apparatus. The government of advanced and advancing industrial societies can maintain and secure itself only when it succeeds in mobilizing, organizing, and exploiting the technical, scientific, and mechanical productivity available to industrial civilization. (Marcuse [1964] 2007, 5)

While the machine can potentially lead to freedom (Marcuse [1964] 2007, 6), it is now used to control us and give us **false needs** (7). We have to behave in

FIGURE 5.3 Herbert Marcuse

accordance with advertisements and the prevailing, particular interests. We have "free choice between brands and gadgets" (9) but this is not real freedom. We are "cogs in a culture-machine" (68). Marcuse argues that while technology has always been used for control during the modern period, it is now used in a new sense: "in the contemporary period, the technological controls appear to be the very embodiment of Reason for the benefit of all social groups and interests—to such an extent that all contradiction seems irrational and all counteraction impossible" ([1964] 2007, 11) The private sphere of the individual is invaded. We identify with our society, and hence there is no longer a basis for resistance (12). People identify with the existence that is imposed on them (13). But this alienation is difficult to recognize; it even feels pleasant. We are entertained:

> The means of mass transportation and communication, the commodities of lodging, food, and clothing, the irresistible output of the entertainment and information industry carry with them prescribed attitudes and habits, certain intellectual and emotional reactions which bind the consumers more or less pleasantly to the producers and, through the latter, to the whole. The products indoctrinate and manipulate; they promote a false consciousness which is immune against its falsehood. (Marcuse [1964] 2007, 14)

Pleasantly bound, we do not want change. But we become one-dimensional in thought and behavior (Marcuse [1964] 2007, 14). Resistance appears unreasonable. Again Marcuse points to the role of technology in creating these conditions when he suggests that change is only possible if we change the technological basis: "Qualitative change also involves a change in the technical basis on which this society rests. . . . The techniques of industrialization are political techniques; as such, they prejudge the possibilities of Reason and Freedom" (20). Yet real change becomes difficult if not impossible in a totalitarian universe:

> Technological rationality reveals its political character as it becomes the great vehicle of better domination, creating a truly totalitarian universe in which society and nature, mind and body are kept in a state of permanent mobilization for the defense of this universe. (Marcuse [1964] 2007, 20)

All opposition is integrated in this totality. Marx thought that a political revolution would bring about change, but he assumed that we could keep the same technology—now used for the end of liberation. But this technology, Marcuse suggests, is part of the problem. Technical rationality is embodied in "the productive apparatus" (Marcuse [1964] 2007, 25). A change would be needed in "the technological structure itself" (25). But we cannot imagine a different universe since, as consumers, we (literally) buy the promise of a comfortable life. And for the workers, this means that they become part of a machine in a more radical way than Marx imagined. In Marx, surplus value is still created by the workers, by living labor. But now, Marcuse argues, productivity is determined by the machine. The output of individuals cannot even be measured any longer (31) There is total integration into the machine, the plant, and the system. Moreover, when capitalist bosses become bureaucrats, "the tangible source of exploitation disappears behind the facade of objective rationality. Hatred and frustration are deprived of their specific target, and the technological veil conceals the reproduction of inequality and enslavement" (35). The organizers and administrators are themselves dependent on the system. Master and servant are trapped in a vicious circle (36).

Technology plays the role here of supporting a system of total control and administration, which deprives potential resistance of its basis by invading into our private needs and thoughts. When we consume and are entertained, we no longer want change and we do not see the exploitation. However, ultimately, what is wrong with all this is not technology but the rationality of the system itself, or more precisely, the way labor is organized (Marcuse [1964] 2007, 148). In the end, like Marx, Marcuse focuses on this social organization and on the **false consciousness** related to it, not on technology itself (technology embodies the false consciousness; 149). On the other hand, Marcuse rejects the idea that technology is politically neutral, for instance the claim that a computer can be used for capitalism or for socialism. Although he seems to endorse Marx's focus on the (social) mode of production rather than the technology, he also says that when technology becomes the universal form of production, this changes: "when technics becomes the universal form of material production, it circumscribes an entire culture; it projects a historical totality—a 'world'" (Marcuse [1964] 2007, 158). (Here Marcuse is closer to Heidegger and postphenomenology: technology is not just an instrument but reveals and shapes a world.) Thus, in this particular historical stage, when modern technology becomes the dominant mode of production, technology and society come closer. In this new "universe," to speak with Marcuse, domination comes in the form of technology:

> In this universe, technology also provides the great rationalization of the unfreedom of man and demonstrates the "technical" impossibility of being autonomous, of determining one's own life. For this unfreedom appears neither as irrational nor as political, but rather as submission to the technical apparatus which enlarges the comforts of life and increases the productivity of labor. Technological rationality thus protects rather than cancels the legitimacy of domination, and the instrumentalist horizon of reason opens on a rationally totalitarian society. (Marcuse [1964] 2007, 162)

Marcuse concludes: "The liberating force of technology—the instrumentalization of things—turns into a fetter of liberation; the **instrumentalization** of man"
(Marcuse [1964] 2007, 163)

In the medium of technology, both humans and nature become the object
of organization; they are reified, caught in the web of Reason (Marcuse [1964]
2007, 172). Is there a way out? Perhaps the artist can articulate values alien to
established society, Marcuse suggests (251), and he seems to regret the cancel-
ling of the "romantic space of imagination" (253). But, he argues, imagination is
itself not immune to processes of reification; we have to liberate the imagination
(254). This requires politics, but how can the vicious circle be broken? Dialectical
theory cannot offer the remedy (257). "The critical theory of society possesses no
concepts which could bridge the gap between the present and its future; holding
no promise and showing no success, it remains negative" (261).

But although Marcuse takes technology very seriously here, it mainly appears
in the form of "technological rationality": it is a kind of rationality. What remains
out of sight are material artifacts and concrete material forms of organization.
What remains excluded is concepts that, in a more positive spirit, try to bridge
the gap between present and future. Like Hegel's narrative about the Spirit and
Heidegger's narrative about Being, we find ourselves here in a narrative about
Reason that unfolds itself; and Marcuse is its secretary.

5.3.3. Foucault

Like Marcuse, Michel Foucault did not make technology the center of his work.
Yet technology can be highlighted and (for the most part) read into his thoughts
on power. Foucault responded to Marx's conception of power. Whereas Marx
and the neo-Marxists of critical theory focus on domination on the level of
the system, on capitalism as a form of social relations and social organization,
Foucault turns to the **micro-mechanisms of power** and subjection in specific
modern institutions such as the prison and the hospital. Moreover, he has an interest in techniques for the positive constitution of the self, the "technologies" of
the self. Let us look in more detail at Foucault's views and interpret them in a way
that focuses on the role of technology.

Whereas for Marx legal freedom hides exploitation, for Foucault it is disciplines, systems of micro-power that are to be found behind the veil of formal
liberties. He does not analyze the production of commodities but the production of knowledge and the production and mechanisms of power and control
everywhere—not only in the factory but also in the prison, in the hospital, in
the family. According to Foucault ([1976] 1998, 93), power is everywhere;
everywhere there are "micro-relations of power" (Foucault 1980, 199) that

IN FOCUS:
Michel Foucault

Michel Foucault was a French 20th-century philosopher and social theorist, often linked to post-structuralism and postmodernism. He is well known in philosophy of technology and beyond for his focus on power in relation to knowledge, subjectivity, and bodies in the context of modern societal institutions such as the prison and the hospital, but also so-called technologies of the self. He historically investigated the production of truth and the disciplining of people. Foucault has influenced many critical theorists, including feminists, and the contemporary humanities in general.

FIGURE 5.4 Michel Foucault, painted portrait

pervade the social. Relations of power are interwoven with other relations such as production, kinship, and sexuality; and there are not only economic interests but all kinds of strategies (142). Moreover, power also involves resistance. He rejects a binary structure of dominators versus domination. Instead of looking only at official political forms of power, power exercised from above, he focuses on the "capillary level of power" (38), "the point where power reaches into the very grain of individuals, touches their bodies and inserts itself into their actions and attitudes, their discourses, learning processes and everyday lives" (39).

CASE/TECHNOLOGY:
Surveillance: The Panopticon and Airport Security

The panopticon is a type of architecture or technology designed by the English philosopher Jeremy Bentham in the 18th century. It was used in prisons to enable the monitoring of many persons, as the prisoners could not see those who watched them or even know *if* they were watched. Foucault referred to the panopticon in his description of disciplining in the prison. Today the panopticon metaphor is often used to describe contemporary forms of surveillance such as surveillance on the internet and surveillance involved in airport security. In the airport, technologies are used to monitor everyone for the sake of security and to maintain nation-state borders. Technologies used include CCTV cameras, biometric passports, and body scanners. The technologies are used to exercise power in various ways. It is often claimed that after 9/11, we live in surveillance societies, which implies that in the airport, everyone is seen as a potential threat to security and therefore everyone is subject to a constant gaze and various security procedures involve disciplining of persons and control of human bodies. Is this a contemporary panopticon? And can we resist at all?

FIGURE 5.5 Inside one of the prison buildings at Presidio Modelo, Isla de la Juventud, Cuba

For example, in *Discipline and Punish* (1975), Foucault looks at the prison and sees there a particular mechanism of power, which we could interpret as an architecture and indeed a technology of power: the **panopticon**. Bentham designed the building in such way that prisoners can be observed but the observer remains hidden. This makes possible the exercise of power, control, and surveillance at a micro level. In an interview about geography, Foucault himself uses the term technology:

> By the term "Panoptism," I have in mind an ensemble of mechanisms brought into play in all the clusters of procedures used by power. Panoptism was a technological invention in the order of power, comparable with the steam engine in the order of production. (Foucault 1980, 71)

This technology comprised, or was combined with, technologies of record-keeping, which were already used in economy and taxation. But then these methods were used for permanent surveillance of people everywhere: the formula of "power through transparency" worked (Foucault 1980, 154). It was also used by the state, but this was based on what already happened at smaller scale (72). But it is not the case that the one in the central tower is free or outside the system. As Foucault puts it, "it's a machine in which everyone is caught, those who exercise power just as much as those over whom it is exercised" (1980, 156). Power, then, is not something that one individual or one class possesses; instead, there are many more forms of domination than one class dominating another one. And power circulates and is "exercised through a net-like organisation," which means that individuals are always "simultaneously undergoing and exercising this power" (98). For Foucault, individuals do not "have" power but are the effects of power (98).

We can use this panopticon concept to think about technologies today, for instance to critically discuss social media (Fuchs et al. 2012, 1–8): Do new social media constitute a kind of panopticon? The tentative answer is yes. Instead of centralized surveillance, it has a more horizontal structure. Everyone watches everyone. But it embodies the same surveillance and control idea: we are watched without knowing who is watching. Power is gained by means of transparency. The internet and social media seem to constitute a machine in which everyone is caught. And we may add that through the use of digital technologies, we are undergoing and exercising power, and are thereby produced and constituted as subjects and individuals. Of course, we may resist; but this resistance happens *within* "the machine," within the meshwork of power. Instead of talking about production, dialectical processes, and class struggle, Foucault urges us to engage in the "unravelling of actual processes" (1980, 164) of power and control, and suggests that Marxist concepts are not sufficient for this.

In his later work, Foucault focuses more on the constitution of the self. He speaks of "the hermeneutics of technologies of the self in pagan and early Christian practice" (Foucault 1988, 17). Here the focus is not so much on disciplining and repression, as for instance in his work on the prison (Foucault 1975) or his history of sexuality ([1976] 1998), but rather on practices of the self. Although he uses the term "technologies," in line with the postmodernism of his day, which was all about discourse and signs, the focus is not so much on the material dimension, understood in the sense of material artifacts rather than, say, means of production or techniques. Earlier Foucault wrote about "the order of things" or "words and things" (*Les mots et les choses*) ([1966] 1994); but in this analysis of *episteme*, the focus was on the conditions of discourse. We can of course try to interpret him in a way that brings out the material dimension and combine his thinking with postphenomenology (Dorrestijn 2011); but this takes us already beyond Foucault and to the next section.

5.3.4. Feenberg and Winner

Foucault already shows that a more empirical orientation can be very fruitful for critical theory; however, the material-artifactual dimension remains undertheorized. Can we combine critical theory with an empirical turn, understood as a turn to

---

CASE/TECHNOLOGY:
Biased Algorithms and Algorithms Not in the Interest of Consumers: Job Selection, Criminal Justice, and Online Stores

Imagine that an employer uses an algorithm to make decisions about job applications, and that it turns out that the algorithm systematically favors white males. Is this unfair? And if so, (1) why is it, and (2) what could be done to make the algorithm more fair, if anything? What if a similar problem turns up in the use of algorithms in the legal system? For example, should we let algorithms make questions about parole? Another question: Do smart algorithms employed by online stores such as Amazon work against the interests of consumers or is the picture more complex? Do they mislead people or just nudge them? Are some ways of getting people to buy things (e.g., showing items that "other people also bought" or even adding an item when going to checkout) acceptable, and if not, why and could it be avoided? Is it a problem with the technology or a problem with the capitalist system, or neither? And should the development of these technologies be more democratic-participative? Could it be, given the socioeconomic system we currently have? Is that system just and fair, according to you, and why (not)? Should we ask about the system or about the specific technologies and artifacts, or both? Should there be more regulation of these technologies? And what do citizens and consumers know about these technologies anyway? Is there too little knowledge? What kind of knowledge is there? What kind of knowledge *should* we all have of these technologies? Should users/consumers/citizens have a say in the development of technology, and what would be the advantages and justification for this?

material artifacts? This brings us to the work of two interesting contemporary philosophers of technology in the critical theory tradition: Feenberg and Winner, who, in contrast to most of their forerunners in classical critical theory, explicitly thematize *technology* and take a more empirical approach and connect with STS. Both also defend moving toward a more democratic and participative politics of technology.

Andrew Feenberg was influenced by Marcuse and Foucault (and through Marcuse by Heidegger) but made his own contribution to critical thinking about technology. To outline his approach, let me focus on Feenberg's *Between Reason and Experience* (2010) in which various threads of this work come together.

IN FOCUS:
Andrew Feenberg

Andrew Feenberg is a philosopher of technology and a professor in Canada. A well-known figure in critical theory of technology, he is influenced by his teacher Marcuse. He was active in the New Left movement and participated in the May 1968 events in Paris. In his work, he argues for a democratic transformation of technology. He developed what he calls instrumentalization theory, which combines technological rationality ideas from critical theory with a Heideggerian focus on the lifeworld and an empirical orientation borrowed from STS. The latter led to his case studies, for example, on Minitel. He also has an interest in Japanese philosophy.

FIGURE 5.6 Andrew Feenberg

Feenberg's project addresses a central problem in philosophy of technology: What is technology? More specifically, he starts with the question, How can we understand technology development and design? His answer is that there is a rational side to technology since knowledge of nature is required to make it, but that experience is needed to make sure that the device functions in the social world

(Feenberg 2010, xvii). The focus on rationalization is borrowed from earlier critical theory. But Feenberg then makes a bridge to STS, which has shown how design is never a merely technical matter but the outcome of a social process in which various actors and interests play a role. The technical disciplines present technology in terms of rational specifications, but these are the outcome of "past social influences" that remain hidden (xviii). He writes with regard to environmental problems: "Existing technology is not the result of purely rational decisions about the most efficient way to do things but depends on social choices between alternative paths with different environmental consequences" (Feenberg 2010, 3).

In this way, Feenberg remains loyal to a central Marxist idea: social relations always feed into our things and our formal rules, although they are hidden; and it is these social relations that need to be revealed and analyzed to arrive at a genuinely critical theory. Moreover, Feenberg borrows from Marcuse and others the idea that we have become alienated from experience. Here this means technology is alienated from experience (xvii). But now an "empirical turn" is taken: the focus is on concrete material technologies and their design. This questions the strict distinction between technology and experience made by previous critical theorists. Against Habermas's idea that the system colonizes the lifeworld, Feenberg (2010) sees complex interactions between system and lifeworld (59). Thus, although Feenberg does not abandon these kinds of distinctions as such and keeps terms such as system and alienation (60), he is more interested in how **system and lifeworld** are connected—indeed, how reason and experience are connected. The internet, for example, is not separate from the lifeworld but belongs to it (59). Both classic critical theorists and transhumanists do not sufficiently recognize the role of meaning and human relations in modern technological systems (60–61), including the social tensions that are unleashed by new technologies.

Feenberg's (2010) stress on the social character of technology and what technology studies call the **co-construction of society and technology** (xxi) also enables him to argue against the idea that technology is autonomous or that there is a determinism when it comes to technological development (xviii–xix). There is feedback from users, there is the possibility of resistance, and new social and political groups emerge in response to new technologies. For example, the environmental movement has given rise to democratic interventions. "Social groups form around the technologies that mediate their relations, make possible their common identity, and shape their experience" (xxii). Feenberg mentions a famous example analyzed by Trevor Pinch and Wiebe Bijker (1989). In the late 19th century, when the design of the bicycle was not yet fixed, there were different interpretations by social groups that led to different solutions. With their constructivist approach, Pinch and Bijker show that alternative versions are possible, depending on different interests of various actors (Feenberg 2010, 67). This variability, which Pinch and Bijker (1989) call "interpretative flexibility," implies that there is no determinism and that social groups co-shape what the technology becomes. The social meaning and cultural horizon of technical objects is important; technology is not just about "function" (Feenberg 2010, 14). Afterward, the conflicts are quickly forgotten (23), but that does not mean they are not there. To show this, it is insufficient, as Marxists do, to focus on capitalism; the critique must extend "down into the technical base, the forces of production" (17), where social meaning and functional rationality are intertwined (18). Technical design standards, for instance, are not just technical but frame a way of life.

Conceptually, Feenberg (2010) brings together philosophy of technology and STS by means of his proposal to analyze technology at two levels: a primary, technical level at which people and things are decontextualized; and a secondary level at which they are recontextualized as the technology is realized in a social context in which the code is influenced by interests and might be challenged (65). In his **instrumentalization theory,** Feenberg calls these two aspects "primary" and "secondary instrumentalization":

> Critical theory of technology distinguishes analytically between the aspect of technology stemming from the functional relation to reality, which I call the "primary instrumentalization," and the aspect stemming from its social involvements and implementation, which I call the "secondary instrumentalization." Together these two aspects of technology constitute the "world" in something like the sense Heidegger gives the term. (Feenberg 2010, 72)

Feenberg (2010) uses Heidegger here to explain how in the development of technologies first objects are *de-worlded*: they are removed from their context to be analyzed and manipulated (72). But then they are re-worlded in the sense that they re-enter the social environment, which means they gain meaning that feeds back into the design, and they contribute to meaning as they become part of the lifeworld. They form the cultural horizon (73). A car, for instance, does not only have the function of automotive transportation; it is of course a means of transportation, but it also "signifies the freedom of the individual in a world where residence is separated from work, the distribution of goods, and most other destinations. In sum, the meaning of 'transportation' and therefore of 'means of transportation' is relative to the lifeworld that determines the spatial distribution of things" (Feenberg 2010, 177).

From the Heidegger of *Being and Time*, Feenberg borrows the idea that meaning is not separate from the tools but emerges out of their use and knowledge of them. *Dasein* lives in a world of ready-to-hand things, worlds "emerge in the human encounter with reality," as Feenberg puts it (2010, 187). But contrary to Heidegger, Feenberg sees this not as a revealing but as a construction. It is a practical encounter (209) with reality. We thus construct worlds by means of technology. Meaning is not something separate. We enact meanings in everyday practice (193). Worlds must be understood as "realms of practice" (217).

Against existentialists who see a loss of meaning in a technological age, Feenberg (2010) argues that "the world is still meaningful in the age of technology, although the meanings have certainly changed" (75). If we only study technology at the level of primary instrumentalization, we overlook its second, meaning-receiving and meaning-giving instrumentalization. Instead, a critical theory must make explicit these meanings and thus adopts also a hermeneutical perspective: "A hermeneutics of technology must make explicit the meanings implicit in the devices we use and the rituals they script. . . . As a world, technologies shape their inhabitants" (Feenberg 2010, 79).

Yet in spite of this Heideggerian angle, Feenberg does not abandon Marxist concerns. In secondary instrumentalization, interests and "ideology" play a role; Feenberg also speaks of "bias": "Technical codes are always biased to some extent by the values of the dominant actors. The critical theory of technology aims to uncover these biases" (Feenberg 2010, 68). Past biases and values have been translated into code, but we do not see this anymore and therefore falsely believe that technology and values are opposed (77). We ignore "the social forces behind technical functions" (78). But tension and conflicts are related to the social life and its meanings: they emerge "where the abstraction leaves behind essential aspects of social life" (178). The hermeneutic and the critical aspects are thus connected for Feenberg, as are the technological and the political. There are processes of "translation" between technical and political discourses (179). But the overall framework remains antagonistic. It is about tensions and struggles: "Tensions between design and lifeworld contexts give rise to demands that are eventually translated into new codes and designs" (180). There is even a sense in which limits emerge from the lifeworld itself, such as threats to health, which then leads to a technical response (214). But there are always struggles and interests at play in these struggles, and science itself cannot tell us what to do (216). Contrary to Latour, Feenberg does not see nature or science itself as political; he retains modern dichotomies. But struggles concerning technology and nature *are* political.

Indeed, struggles over technology must be seen as "political" struggles (Feenberg 2010, 80). We therefore need to recognize that there is such a thing as a politics of technology. Once we are aware of this political aspect of technology, we can change things. We can open up technology to "a wider range of interests and concerns" (82). By involving the users, we can make technology more participative and connected to human values: "Design would be consciously oriented toward politically legitimated human values rather than subject to the whims of profit-making organizations and military bureaucracies" (Feenberg 2010, 81).

According to Feenberg, user involvement is especially present in the design of information technologies such as the internet (2010, xxiii). He discusses cases of information technology such as the French **Minitel** to show how technology is socially shaped. This implies that the design of industrial society is not determined but contingent (3), and we can try to create a more democratic technology. We can overcome alienation and recontextualize technology, indeed move toward an **alternative modernity** (77), if we democratize technology. In contrast to Fuchs, Feenberg (2010) is more optimistic with regard to the internet: he thinks the internet "supports interaction and participation to an unprecedented degree" (3), and this improves the prospects for what he calls "democratic rationalization" (3). With this term, he means that more actors must be given access to the design process (77); that a broader range of human needs must be considered (179); and ultimately that *democracy* must be extended not only into the world of work, as Marx argued, but also into the world(s) of technology in all kinds of domains—in fact every domain since technology is everywhere. Democracy thus must be extended "beyond its traditional bounds into the technically mediated domains of social life" (6). With regard to democratic values and principles, Feenberg especially thinks of equal distribution but rejects state socialism: "Technology has beneficial potentialities that are suppressed under capitalism and state socialism. These potentialities could be realized along a different developmental path were power more equally distributed" (Feenberg 2010, 71).

Feenberg thus leaves more room for agency than (he thinks) Heidegger does. He criticizes Heidegger for being too abstract, which implies that he "cannot discriminate between electricity and atom bombs" (Feenberg 2010, 25). He suggests that by seeing modern technology as something separate from society, Heidegger contributes to, instead of critiquing, the decontextualization of technology and its design (26). He also rejects what he sees as Heidegger's despair: the idea that only a god can save us (194). Instead, inspired by Marcuse, Feenberg thinks technological reform is possible and shows that there is democratic initiative, participation, and resistance. There are new forms of agency (55). Technologies can be "hacked" (27). We can design different technologies, potentially leading to a different, more democratic society. Feenberg thus rejects dystopian visions: human beings can change the system that dominates them (61). However, he also rejects utopian visions; instead of a radical and disruptive break, he sees a democratic transformation "from below" (82), involving "smaller social and technological changes" (55).

Feenberg (2010) gives the example of this "from below" changes and user "hacks." Teletel, which was designed as an information system, was employed for anonymous human communication (97). Feenberg writes that "users invented a new form of human communication to suit the need for social play and encounter in an impersonal, bureaucratic society" (104). Minitel, meant to be a vehicle for rationalistic technical codes, was also subverted from its intended purpose and was transformed into a communication device (102–103). The human dimension gradually won. This is possible since technology is anyway always already at the intersection with the human and the cultural. It is not purely functional but "condenses technical and social aspects" (123). In the context of a global world, this also means that when technology is transferred between cultures, it requires new interpretations and adaptations. Technology transfer also reveals how cultural technology is, as Feenberg shows in his discussion of Western technology in Japan.

This shows how empirical studies can enrich our thinking. However, Feenberg does not think we can replace critical thinking about technology with technology studies that stress social and cultural embeddedness of technology. In particular, he argues that we should not drop the emphasis on rationality and rationalization; we should also explain technology in terms of its rational form (Feenberg 2010, 130–131) More generally, Feenberg argues that we still need modernity theory. He criticizes Latour for his "symmetry of humans and non-humans," accusing him of conservatism: Feenberg worries that the definition of terms such as "culture," "nature," and "society" seems then a matter of the definition established by the stronger party (143). His proposal is to use the concept of interpretation to link modernity theory and technology studies (146–147). Trying to reconcile different traditions, he returns to his instrumentalization theory, formulated in terms of de-worlding and re-worlding:

> On the one hand, the evolution of technologies depends on the interpretative practices of their users. On the other hand, human beings are essentially interpreters shaped by world-disclosing technologies. Human beings and their technologies are involved in a co-construction without origin. (Feenberg 2010, 149)

Thus, using a hermeneutic perspective, Feenberg (2010) tries to achieve the double aims of his program "to explain the social and cultural impact of technical rationality without losing track of its concrete social embodiment in actual devices and systems" (150). Modernity theorists overlook the latter, but posthumanists, according to Feenberg, miss a sense of how users transform technologies (153). And they perhaps also miss "the economic forces that dominate technical development, design, and the media" (156). Feenberg is looking for (conceptualizing) an alternative modernity; and for him, this still involves what critical theorists have traditionally done: a discussion and critique of reason and rationality. Marx criticized the way his society implemented the rational principle of equal exchange. Feenberg speaks of "formal bias" (2010, 163) and focuses more on technology than many readers of Marx have done in the past. He follows Marcuse, not in his pessimism, but in his hope that we may redesign technology and society to serve humanity rather than dominate it (166). Feenberg (2010) recovers Marcuse's hope that we can change the "technical apparatus in accordance with the needs of free men" (200). But contrary to Marcuse, who only hints at a solution and projects a future where art and reason come together (206), Feenberg offers a concrete conceptual tool: his instrumentalization theory, which explains how technologies are part of both a technical context and a lifeworld context of meaning (168), and which he gives a hermeneutical twist by adding the concept of lifeworld (207). This tool opens up the possibility of transformation through changing simultaneously our technologies and our societies: the promise of a democratic rationalization. Philosophically, it is the promise of bridging the modern gap between reason and experience, and between science/technology and the lifeworld.

As Callon remarks in his afterword, Feenberg (2010) comes "surprisingly close" to STS (219). This is also true for work by Langdon Winner, who, like Feenberg, recognizes the political aspect of technologies and makes a bridge to STS.

IN FOCUS:
Langdon Winner

Langdon Winner is an American philosopher of technology famous for his claim that artifacts have politics. He is also known in science and technology studies. In his seminal paper "Do Artifacts Have Politics?," Winner (1980) argued that artifacts embody

FIGURE 5.7 Langdon Winner in Madrid

social relations and hence power and politics, and are sometimes even linked to particular political relationships and sociological systems. He is part of the empirical turn in philosophy of technology; but in contrast to, for example, Ihde and Verbeek, he stresses the political dimension of technology. He is influenced by critical theory but also, for example, by Wittgenstein; and his approach is compatible with STS and other social sciences, which can help to reveal the interests and biases linked to specific artifacts. Winner suggested that Wittgenstein's term "forms of life" can be used to argue that technologies are always embedded in culturally and socially established patterns—an idea that I have taken up in my recent work (e.g., Coeckelbergh 2017a, 2017b). Winner's interest in Wittgenstein has also made him sensitive to use of language in the discourse about technology. (See also chapters 10 and 11 in this book.)

Let us take a brief look at Winner's famous article "Do Artifacts Have Politics?" (1980). Winner claims that artifacts "embody specific forms of power and authority" (121). Against the view that what matters is not the technologies themselves but the social and economic system in which they are embedded (122), Winner argues that technical things *do* matter and that we should take technical artifacts seriously; he defends the view that they have political properties: "rather than insist that we immediately reduce everything to the interplay of social forces, it suggests that we pay attention to the characteristics of technical objects and the meaning of those characteristics" (Winner 1980, 123).

To understand what this idea that **artifacts have politics** means, Winner (1980) provides the example of low-hanging overpasses on Long Island, which prevent busses and therefore, Winner suggests, also exclude poor people and black people (123–124). While this example has been criticized, it forcefully shows how politics can enter the design of things. Hence, as Feenberg also suggested, the process of technology development itself can be very biased in its effect (Winner 1980, 125), whether intended or not. Winner argues that technologies build order in our world, and different people have different power to influence what kind of order is built:

> From such examples I would offer the following general conclusions. The things we call "technologies" are ways of building order in our world. Many technical devices and systems important in everyday life contain possibilities for many different ways of ordering human activity. Consciously or not, deliberately or inadvertently, societies choose structures for technologies that influence how people are going to work, communicate, travel, consume, and so forth over a very long time. In the processes by which structuring decisions are made, different people are differently situated and possess unequal degrees of power as well as unequal levels of awareness. (Winner 1980, 127)

Features in the design of things are thus political in the sense that they establish and support particular power patterns, in a particular context. Since our choices are "fixed" in material equipment, we'd better give attention to these design and structuring choices, as much as we give attention to the making of laws.

> The issues that divide or unite people in society are settled not only in the institutions and practices of politics proper, but also, and less obviously, in tangible arrangements of steel and concrete, wires and transistors, nuts and bolts. (Winner 1980, 128)

Marx, Winner suggests, took seriously technology. He made us think about what technology makes possible or necessary in political life (Winner 1980, 130).

We'd also better recognize that technology is inherently political. It can be biased, or at least strongly compatible with certain forms of social organization or system rather than others.

Winner's view is compatible with Feenberg's view and with STS studies of specific artifacts, and is also an important voice in the empirical turn in philosophy of technology. Compared with the social constructivism found in STS, however, both Feenberg and Winner do not hesitate to make evaluative, normative claims. They do not only aim to show *that* and *how* technology is political; they also openly defend a particular political direction, one that endorses a more democratic and participative model. The next and last example of a critical theory approach is also not allergic to taking a more evaluative course.

5.4. Feminist Thinking about Technology

5.4.1. Feminism

Still largely missing in the previous pages when it comes to critical thinking, however, is feminist theory and its concerns. While often influenced by critical theory (Marx and Foucault), this is not necessarily the case, and there is much more to say about feminism. There are many sources of inspiration, and it cannot be reduced to critical theory: it has its own unique angle(s). Often feminism calls attention to the gender dimension of social relations and power, although its spectrum of topics and relevance is not at all limited to this, and its contributions are also an attempt to change not only society but also philosophy. Before zooming in on examples of feminist thinking about technology, let me give a brief and—like other theories featured in this introductory book—necessarily incomplete and simplified summary of what feminism is about.

Feminist thinking about technology must be put in the context of feminist thinking in general. There are many varieties of feminism, and some connect with critical theory. Whereas Marxism is traditionally concerned with the oppression and emancipation of (male and female) workers by the capitalist system, **feminism** focuses on the oppression and emancipation of women—in ways not limited to their oppression by capitalism. **Patriarchy**, not capitalism, has been the main target of many feminists. So-called first-generation feminists argued for women's rights. Some were what Marx would call "bourgeois" liberals; others were more left and radical. Later, when women received more formal rights (in the so-called West at least), feminists have pointed out various forms of **sexism** in society. Like Marx, they pointed out that behind formal rights and arrangements, there are hidden forms of bias and oppression. Some took inspiration from Foucault's view that power is not only or not necessarily centralized or a matter of a struggle between classes, but that it is rather everywhere, dispersed in social relations and present in institutions such as the family. So-called second-wave feminists drew attention to the social construction of women's identities, arguing against the tendency to reduce women to their biological identity. Some feminists argued for valuing the specificity of women's identity; women are different from men, and women and men do not have to become the same. Postcolonial theory questioned the idea of a universal women subject, calling attention to the experiences of non-Western women. Others have criticized that subject by pointing out that not everyone fits or has to fit in the binary male/female category. Today an influential view is that gender is performatively created, as Judith Butler (1988) has argued. But feminism is and was not only about a focus on women and gender issues; it has also changed philosophy: it led to the recognition of the role of women in the history of philosophy *and* to the development of different epistemologies, political philosophy, and ethics: for instance, care ethics, ecofeminism, and feminist posthumanism. Feminism is also about men and about the question of how we (men and women) should do *philosophy*.

CASE/TECHNOLOGY:
Design of Household Robots

Imagine an engineer who designs a service robot, in particular a robot that does household work, in such a way that its shape looks like that of a woman. What do you think may be problematic about this design and why?

FIGURE 5.8 Artist impression of a household robot with a female shape

5.4.2. Feminist Philosophy of Technology

In philosophy of technology, feminist concerns include the contribution women have made to science and technology, the effect of technology on women, and criticisms of gendered technology. For instance, with regard to the effects of technology on women, it has been argued that the introduction of household technology has not really improved the social position of women and that modern reproductive technologies such as the contraceptive pill and the ultrasound have not liberated women but put them under the control of medical specialists (Dusek 2006). Some of these arguments already consider concrete technologies; philosophers of technology put them in a more central position in their analysis. With the empirical turn in philosophy of technology, scholars have started to pay attention to specific technological artifacts and their gendered design and social-technological construction. For instance, in my work on robotics, I often draw attention to gendered humanoid robots to show how artifacts are embedded in, and co-constitute, our cultural games and form of life. Gender issues may arise in our use of language but also in the design and use of technology, since that use is always connected to wider social contexts (Coeckelbergh 2017, 13). With Feenberg, one could say that they are also always connected to social experience, as they are part of the lifeworld as much as they are part of rational design. (However, I question his dualistic thinking in terms of rationality and experience.) Furthermore, there is continuing interest in the intersection between posthumanist thinking and feminist thinking, and its application to technology. The same is true for so-called ecofeminism, which takes a more ecological approach. Is feminism only about women, or is it also about non-humans? Let me zoom in on two famous feminist texts on technology: one by Haraway ([1991] 2000), which represents feminist and posthumanist thinking on technology, and one by Judy Wajcman (2004), which is influenced by STS.

IN FOCUS:
Donna Haraway

Donna Jeanne Haraway is a prominent American scholar in feminism and women's studies, posthumanist studies, postmodernist theory and literature, and science and technology studies. She was a professor at the University of California, Santa Cruz. She is famous for her "A Cyborg Manifesto" ([1991] 2000) but also studied human–animal relations, offered a critique of the science of primatology (arguing that

FIGURE 5.9 Donna Haraway, 2010

their stories tend to be masculinized and questioning Western human nature narratives), and is generally interested in political and social issues. She studied zoology, philosophy, and literature.

Donna Haraway's "Cyborg Manifesto" ([1991] 2000) is by now a classic in posthumanist philosophy of technology, but it is also an important feminist text. It is influenced by the socialist tradition but moves beyond the modern human by means of the figure of the **cyborg**. The cyborg is a "hybrid of machine and organism, a creature of social reality as well as a creature of fiction" (Haraway [1991] 2000, 291). This is a "blasphemy" compared to, say, traditional Marxism since it already crosses two boundaries that were always implicitly present in critical thinking: one is the boundary between humans and non-humans, in particular between humans and machines; the other is the boundary between reality and fiction. She then argues that this cyborg is meant to change "what counts as women's experience" (291) and to question "the tradition of racist, male-dominated capitalism," moving us to a "post-gender world" (292). How does this work?

Haraway questions the nature–culture duality, which leads to domination of nature and women (which is seen as natural). Instead, she wants to cross that nature–culture boundary and other boundaries: she proposes that we not only take pleasure in connecting to other living creatures but also transgress the human–machine boundary (Haraway [1991] 2000, 293). Our machines have become "disturbingly lively," and it is no longer clear what is nature and what is culture (294). For Haraway, this is not a problem but something we should embrace and celebrate, and something that should transform our conception of politics and indeed our thinking about technology. The problem is no longer that "man" may be destroyed by "the machine" (294). Against these kind of dualisms—she explicitly mentions Marcuse (295)—Haraway presents the transgression of boundaries as the basis for a better, radical politics. For thinking about technology and women, it means that myths about technology that controls us and fantasies about the appropriation of women's bodies (and domination of nature) are replaced by a vision of the world in which people are not afraid of their "kinship with animals and machines" and in which there is room for partial and fractured identities and for "witches, engineers, elders, perverts, Christians, mothers, and Leninists" (295).

Instead of grounding feminism on a female essence, Haraway argues, we should assume "contradictory, partial and strategic" identities ([1991] 2000, 295). "Being female" is constructed in scientific discourses and social practices (295). "We" or "us" is a political myth; there is no unity, only affinity. Haraway affirms a **postmodern identity**, which is about difference. She thinks that "previous Marxism and feminism" assumed a totalizing and naturalizing "woman" (296). "Woman" is not an innocent category (297). Haraway argues against Marxist feminists: for her the problem is not alienated labor but "to be constituted by another's desire," to not exist as a subject (299).

Thus, Haraway's socialist-feminist politics does what critical theory should do in response to transformations in technology and society. It addresses "the social relations of science and technology" and sees communication technologies and biotechnologies as tools that change social relations, including "enforce new social relations for women worldwide" ([1991] 2000, 302). She sees how electronics implies "fundamental transformations" (303). But instead of using the classic Marxist toolkit, she takes a posthumanist and difference-thinking turn; she draws attention to how boundaries between humans and machines are blurred: "mind, body, and tool are on very intimate terms" (303). To understand what happens, dualisms such as base and superstructure or material and ideal no longer work. And to understand what happens to women, we have to avoid totalizing categories, including perhaps the category "women" itself. Haraway discusses what happens to work when the new technologies transform our societies. She points to the medical visualization of women's bodies. So the point remains that technology creates new social relations. But Haraway searches for a non-totalizing way of talking about this, and finds it in the figure of the cyborg: we can learn from our fusions with animals and machines "how not to be Man" (310); that is, how to escape the domination and the dualist thinking. She sees not a threat but possibilities in the breakdown of distinctions. The cyborg myth is meant to subvert and displace "hierarchical dualisms and naturalized identities" (Haraway [1991] 2000, 311). She presents a view of the self and the body that does not end at the skin (314); but more generally, she presents the transgression of all boundaries as a new way forward for feminist thinking. The cyborg offers new political possibilities. For philosophy, it offers "a way out of the maze of dualisms" (316). For thinking about women, "cyborg gender" (316) offers a way to escape totalization: not only the goddess but also the cyborg is now an option. For thinking about technology, her posthumanist view means that we can move beyond the idea that technology dominates us: if we are the machine and if the machine is us, then we can be responsible for machines (315).

Haraway's ([1991] 2000) posthumanist version of feminism and thinking about technology is interesting and continues its influence generally, and also in philosophy of technology. However, through its close link with postmodern critical theory, Haraway's cyborg is still rather cultural and textual, not so material and practically engaged with technologies. It can be questioned if she really managed to move beyond the dualisms she criticized. It is supposed to be material-semiotic, but the emphasis is still on **semiotics**. Philosophers of the empirical turn and the STS scholars they liaise with are interested in a more material version of technofeminism.

Judy Wajcman's work can be seen in this light, although she remains close to Haraway. In her book *TechnoFeminism* (2004), Wajcman brings together feminist studies of technoscience and STS to show how artifacts themselves are shaped by gender relations, gender meanings, and gender identities. The starting point is that there is a mutual shaping of gender and technology: "technology is both a source and a consequence of gender relations" (7). Like Bijker and others in STS, Wajcman stresses the contingency of technological change. But now the focus is on gender. Under the influence of STS, **technofeminism** studies the material realities of technology production and use (Wajcman 2004, 122) and connects this with gender issues. For example, Wajcman makes a link between the production of mobile phones and rape of women: the mineral coltan needed for the phones is mined in Central Africa, where exploitation and conflict has consequences for women (122). And according to Wajcman, the smart house, focused on things such as lighting, security, and information, is a male fantasy, as it ignores housework and is symptomatic for the neglect of women's experience in the design of technology. While here Wajcman mainly summarizes other people's work and does not provide more detailed analysis of the production and use of artifacts, the general direction she takes in this work is promising and also opens up possibilities of bringing together STS-style technofeminism and what could be further developed into a feminist postphenomenology: both share attention to "the things themselves."

Note, however, that this is only one possible way of combining feminist thinking and philosophy of technology. As is clear from my summary of feminism and indeed from the theories presented in this book, both feminism and philosophy of technology offer many potential intellectual sources and strands that we can use for thinking about technology from a feminist angle.

5.5. Critical Discussion

This chapter shows that Marx and critical theory are not at all outdated or irrelevant for understanding technology today but instead, like (post)phenomenology, provide a fruitful and influential approach. Of course, like (post)phenomenology, it has its own problems and challenges. In the course of presenting these various approaches within critical theory, I have already indicated some objections. Let me end this chapter by presenting and discussing some of these objections and adding some more.

First, from the perspective of phenomenology, Marxist thinking seems to neglect first-person experience by focusing on the general socioeconomic conditions and ideologies. For philosophy of technology, this implies that the concrete experience of people using and designing technologies seems to be missing. A Marxist could reply that phenomenology neglects how our concrete experience is not just a matter of individual or mental consciousness and experience but is always connected to social relations and conditions, which need critical scrutiny and tend to be neglected or insufficiently addressed by phenomenology.

Second, from the side of postphenomenology, Marxism and critical theory have been accused of only focusing on technologies of production and general categories such as "the system" or "capitalism" involving dualism between lifeworld and system. Postphenomenology, by contrast, promises to look at specific technologies and brings together lifeworld and system (Feenberg) or radically questions the very dualist categories on which critical theory's analysis is based (Haraway, Latour, Verbeek). For example, in *Moralizing Technology*, Verbeek (2011) argues against Habermas's view that the lifeworld is colonized by the system: according to him, technology should not be reduced to a form of instrumental rationality, and technological objects are "interwoven with the various forms of the lifeworld" (Verbeek 2011, 82). Influenced by the later Foucault (and Dorrestijn's work on this), Verbeek argues that we should study how technological mediations shape the subject; there are moral self-practices, and technology plays a role in this. A critical theory opponent—Habermasian or not—could reply that by stressing the role of technology in the shaping of the subject in this way, the social context in which this self-shaping is embedded remains invisible and that postphenomenology is blind for the ways in which technology is an instrument for domination and reification. By stressing Foucaultian practices of the self, postphenomenology risks to support an individualist neoliberal or even conservative social-political position, just like Heidegger did.

Third, Feenberg seems to offer a solution to these problems by combining critical theory with (Heideggerian) phenomenology. He shows how system and lifeworld interact, but he retains a critical perspective. He manages to combine discourse about struggle and discourse about meaning; this is not a small accomplishment. He also rightly criticizes STS for rejecting engagement with modernity theory altogether. That being said, it remains a challenge to combine Marx and Heidegger, critical theory and phenomenology, discourse about "technology" and an empirical turn in the form of STS-style research. From both sides, one may question if Feenberg's philosophical project has succeeded. For example, from the side of critical theory, one may ask if Feenberg's language of "worlding," borrowed from Heidegger, is sufficiently connected to praxis; and if critical theory and socialism can and should be reduced to the ideals of democracy and participation. Is Feenberg radical enough? Moreover, in spite of Feenberg's repeated insistence on democratizing technology, he does not engage much with contemporary political theory related to these topics (Coeckelbergh 2012). From the side of postphenomenology and STS, one may question Feenberg's instrumentalization theory: his hanging on to rationalization theory and, more generally, the dualist distinction he makes between rational technology and technology as experienced in the lifeworld. And influenced by Latour, Verbeek (2012) has argued that we need an a-modern way of thinking, rather than an alternative modernity and Feenberg's dualist distinctions.

Finally, by questioning modern distinctions, Haraway's contribution to critical theory goes in a non-modern direction but remains postmodern in her close affinity with signs, texts, and fiction. Postphenomenology, influenced by Latour, offers a more material and arguably more straightforwardly non-modern perspective. But this criticism also opens up the potential for working toward a synthesis of, or merging of, Haraway, Ihde, and Latour—and more generally a synthesis of feminist critical theory and postphenomenology. Moreover, while Haraway understandably wanted to break with other, earlier critical theory, perhaps both approaches are more complementary than Haraway suggests. For example, we could try to read the cyborgs into Marx, who already noted how humans become part of the machine. And perhaps Haraway's postmodernism is in danger of losing its critical function when in her cyborg world, literally everything is embraced and included, and nothing and no one can escape; in some ways, this total lack of boundaries and distinctions may also be interpreted as a totalizing perspective. In any case, this issue raises the broader question of if, for critical thinking and indeed for non-modern thinking, we need boundaries and distinctions at all: and if so, which ones, and if it can be done without implying the dualisms and dominations Haraway opposes. Finally, a recurring problem with feminist approaches is that they often remain relatively isolated from (other approaches in) philosophy, including philosophy of technology. Whether this is so because feminism continues to be marginalized by other approaches or whether feminists themselves insufficiently engage with other approaches (perhaps both are true), it is worth trying to combine feminist and non-feminist approaches in contemporary thinking about technology. Otherwise feminist approaches are doomed to remain a footnote to the history of philosophy of technology; given feminism's critical and hermeneutical potential and success, this would be a pity, both for the further development of feminism and for thinking about technology.

REVIEW QUESTIONS

1. Briefly outline Marx's theory of political economy.
2. Use Marx's analysis of political economy to arrive at an understanding of social media.
3. Explain Marcuse's theory and its relevance for thinking about technology.
4. Explain how we can use Foucault in understanding contemporary surveillance.
5. Outline Feenberg's philosophy of technology.
6. Why are artifacts political according to Winner?
7. What is feminism and what does a feminist approach imply for understanding and evaluating technology? Give examples of such an approach.
8. What criticisms can be raised against these various versions of critical theory?

DISCUSSION QUESTIONS

1. Is it helpful and relevant to use Marx's analysis of political economy in understanding contemporary digital technologies?
2. How can we combine critical theory with (post)phenomenology in our thinking about technology?
3. How can Marcuse's and Foucault's insights be made fruitful for contemporary thinking about technology?
4. Is Feenberg's and Winner's project to combine critical theory with STS successful, and how can it inform other approaches in philosophy of technology?
5. Should philosophers of technology always use or collaborate with STS, and why (not)?
6. Should contemporary philosophy of technology be(come) feminist, and why (not)?
7. How can various versions of critical theory be integrated, and what are the problems doing so?
8. How can critical theory inform, or be integrated with, other approaches to understanding and evaluating technology? Give an example of how such an integration can be done according to you.
9. How can bias in, and discrimination by, algorithms be avoided, if at all?

RECOMMENDED READING

Feenberg, Andrew. 2010. *Between Reason and Experience: Essays in Technology and Modernity*. Cambridge, MA: MIT Press.

Haraway, Donna. (1991) 2000. "A Cyborg Manifesto." In *The Cybercultures Reader*, edited by David Bell and Barbara M. Kennedy, 291–324. London: Routledge.

Marx, Karl. (1867) 1976. "Machinery and Large-Scale Industry." In *Capital: A Critique of Political Economy*. Vol. 1. Translated by B. Fowkes, 492–639. Reprint, London: Penguin. (Reprinted 1990).

KEY TERMS

Alternative modernity

Artifacts have politics

Capitalism

Co-construction of society and technology

Cyborg

Data commodity

False consciousness

False needs

Feminism

Frankfurt School (*Frankfurter Schule*)

Google

Instrumentalization (of humans)

Instrumentalization theory

Instrumental rationality

Luddite movement

Micro-mechanisms of power

Minitel

Occupy movement

Panopticon

Patriarchy

Political economy

Postmodern identity

Semiotics

Sexism

Sisyphus

Social media

Surplus value

System and lifeworld

Technofeminism

Vampire

PRAGMATISM, ANALYTIC APPROACHES, AND TRANSCULTURAL PHILOSOPHY

CASE/TECHNOLOGY:
Neonatal Care Technology

Contemporary neonatal care technologies increase the chance of survival for prematurely born children; for example, by means of better incubators and ventilation. But children born very early (e.g., 25 weeks) are still in a critical medical condition; and often hard, morally relevant decisions have to be made. Sometimes it is decided to stop treatment since prolonging treatment by means of the technology may prolong or even increase suffering without giving the child a sufficiently high chance of survival. Such decisions are very difficult to make. In such situations, general moral principles are often of little help. Of course moral dignity is important, for example, but what does that mean in these cases? And one can have a general rule such as "If the child will suffer from severe handicaps, then treatment should be stopped." But does the child fall into

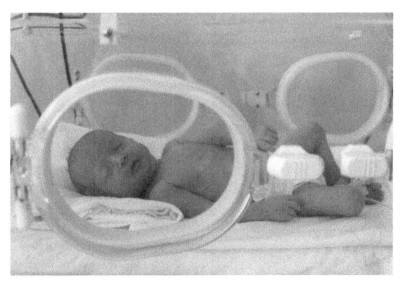

FIGURE 6.1 Neonatal care technology

that category? That is the hard question, one that is both medical-technical and ethical at the same time. Here it helps to look at the details of cases, at the experience and practices involved. These show that an important part of decision-making in this area relies on moral imagination and moral improvisation when assessing situations: practitioners imagine the future of the child and project future scenarios, parents put themselves in the shoes of their child and imagine if they would be able to live with themselves after a particular decision, and the question whether a child falls into a particular category (say a choice between two options) is sometimes transcended by means of moral-medical improvisation that imaginatively and creatively creates new options. Moreover, the decision is a social matter: it takes place in a social context and many parties are involved (Coeckelbergh & Mesman 2007). This way to approach ethics of technology is inspired by a pragmatist approach, in particular John Dewey's work, which questions the role moral principles and rules usually get in ethics. Of course such principles can be helpful; but when it comes to moral deliberation in practice, the emphasis is on moral experience itself and imaginative coping with situations by those involved (see also Fesmire 2003). In this chapter, I will say more about Deweyan pragmatism and how it can be used for thinking about technology.

This chapter outlines a selection of other approaches to philosophy of technology that are also significant and interesting but were missing in the previous chapters: pragmatism, analytic philosophy of technology, and intercultural or transcultural approaches.

6.1. Pragmatism

Pragmatism as a philosophical tradition began in the United States in the second half of the 19th century and is usually associated with the names of William James, John Dewey, and Charles Sanders Peirce. Later pragmatists include Richard Rorty and (in his later work) Hilary Putnam. Pragmatists consider thinking and concepts as tools to solve problems rather than representations of reality. Whether ideas are valuable depends on how they are used; it depends on human experience, which involves trial and error. They also reject Platonic and idealist views that oppose the real to appearance, and the absolute to the world of senses, experience, and time. For them, experience and inquiry are connected and are to be seen in relation to a specific and concrete situation. And like Marxists, pragmatists are concerned with changing the world rather than representing it. For example, Dewey criticized inconsequential armchair philosophy and the reification of concepts: concepts are often presented as if they existed independent from human experience and practice. Instead, they must be seen as ways in which we deal with social problems; social intelligence is about **experimentation** and explorations, and concepts play a role in that. And there is no such thing as fixed ends (for which technologies would then be the means). Dewey rejected the gap between ends and means, created by traditional philosophy. He was opposed to the idea that we need metaphysical foundations for morality and that we can solve moral problems a priori, apart from their practical and social situation. As Steven Fesmire (2003) has argued, moral deliberation rather requires the dramatic rehearsal of possibilities in a way that is responsive to the situation. Moral rules and theories are tools (Hickman [1990] 1992, 114). Pragmatists also reject Cartesian dualism and all kinds of metaphysical dualisms. Richard Rorty, influenced by Dewey and others, has famously argued against (Cartesian and other modern) epistemology, in particular against **representationalism**: knowledge is not about mentally mirroring external reality (Rorty 1979). Instead, Rorty proposed that thinkers exercise irony and empathy: we should become aware of the contingency of our philosophical vocabulary and try to understand others' suffering. Moreover, institutions should not embody universal principles but should be seen as social experiments. Like Dewey, Rorty rejected **foundationalism** and metaphysical philosophies.

In philosophy of technology, pragmatism has been rendered useful for thinking about technology by Larry Hickman, among others. In particular, Hickman has interpreted John Dewey's work in the context of contemporary questions regarding science and technology. Dewey is not known for his views on technology, but they are both interesting and relevant for thinking about technology today. Let me summarize Hickman's interpretation of Dewey and then indicate and suggest some contemporary uses of pragmatism in philosophy of technology.

IN FOCUS:
John Dewey

John Dewey was an American philosopher and educational reformer who wrote in the first half of the 20th century and is considered one of the key figures in pragmatism. He replaced dualist modern epistemology about passive minds responding to the world with a naturalistic view that sees knowledge as arising from active adaptation to, and manipulation of, the environment. His ethics is more social and experimentally oriented (although Dewey did not see a gap between the natural and the social). He rejected dogmatic, simplistic, and detached moral principles, which in his view cannot deal with the moral and social problems that arise in dynamic environments. Instead, his views on ethics and education start from the assumption that human beings are social beings and can achieve personal growth only by means of social habits and institutions. He argued that social problems need to be solved by means of imagination, creativity, and experimentation. He believed in the ideal of democracy, and was interested in how social reform can take place.

FIGURE 6.2 Portrait of John Dewey

In *John Dewey's Pragmatic Technology* ([1990] 1992), Hickman has outlined what according to him is Dewey's unique critique of technology. Dewey criticized Aristotle's emphasis on theoretical knowledge, foundations, and essences; instead, the construction of theories is itself a case of "the use of productive skill" (Hickman [1990] 1992, 18). In Dewey's instrumentalist account of inquiry, technology is not just about artifacts but also involves ideas: both are tools of inquiry, which is not directed at certainty but at dealing with new problems. In *Experience and Nature* (1929), Dewey claims that the idea is a work of art. Hickman ([1990] 1992) explains that Dewey criticizes the divisions between fine arts and practical arts (crafts) (62) and, related to this, objects to the divorce of ends from means (66). Plato and Aristotle demeaned the activities of craftsmen (96); *theoria* was seen as the highest form of knowledge, which according to Dewey is the reason why the Greeks failed to develop an experimental science (109). Turning Aristotle's order "on its head" (Hickman [1990] 1992, 107), Dewey instead connects theory with practice, and the physical with the metaphysical. Tools are not value neutral and also shape our intelligent selection of ends; both goals and ends are to be tested in practice: they are not fixed and should not be fixed (119). This view implies that science is to be seen as a matter of instrumentation and experiment, in contrast to what the ancient Greek philosophers thought (36). More generally, knowledge should not be reified or abstracted from **experience** and practice, and does not only take place inside the cortex (38), "in your head." In Dewey's "Copernican revolution," knowing is connected to the world; it takes place "inside experienced situations" (37). This **instrumentalist** view of knowledge also implies, Hickman argues, that for Dewey the problems of philosophy and the problems of technology are inseparable (1). Philosophical tools and other tools are no longer seen as belonging to entirely different spheres; there is one world of inquiry and experience, and inquiry uses tools to deal with a problem in a situation, which then produces further meanings. This means that according to Dewey, we need a broader, non–dualistic view of tools. Hickman writes

> While there may be good grounds elsewhere for distinguishing extra-organic tools from those that are interorganic—a hammer from a "therefore," for example—such a distinction is not appropriate to Dewey's technologized theory of inquiry. Controlled thinking is technological insofar as it utilizes tools and instruments: some of those tools are conceptual; some, physical; some, the hardware that extends our limbs and senses. For the purposes of Dewey's theory of inquiry, tools of all types come into play; where they are distinguished into various kinds, such distinctions are made chiefly in terms of the various materials on which they operate and to which they are appropriate, and of the degree of precision required for the task at hand. ([1990] 1992, 36)

Thus, goals and ideals are also tools as they are part of human inquiry. Even speech and written language are artifacts, shaped for a purpose (Hickman [1990] 1992, 115). And arguing against "faculty" philosophy and "faculty" psychology, Dewey thinks that we should not reify human intelligence in terms of intellect or will. Instead, Dewey argues, humans rely on habits, which are the result of previous inquiry (16). New problems then require new inquiry and experimentation. Of course technology is not always about inquiry. There is also routine, there are **habits**. There is tradition and novelty (60). But note that habits themselves are also like tools: they only have their meaning in use (16). Furthermore, Hickman uses Dewey to argue against all kinds of forms of technological determinism, including the view that means of production determine patterns of social organization, which Hickman associates with Marx (142). Dewey thinks that we can change society through **public deliberation**. Instead of the abstract laws of history (Marx) and reified systems (critical theory; Ellul), Dewey draws our attention to concrete decisions made by human beings. Abstract intuitions are replaced by concrete situations (Hickman [1990] 1992, 154). There is no abstract problem of freedom, but there are concrete choices to be made. For Dewey, the social is not to be abstractly reconstructed, as in social contract theory; the social should not be conceptualized in terms of individuals versus society (170) since we are always already associated with others. What matters is public and **democratic deliberation** and education in specific situations and faced with concrete problems, using the method of "experimentation"—this is in line with his "instrumentalism" (195)—and accepting responsibility for the consequences of human action (197). Experience will tell whether our solutions are good. In contrast to two other major figures of 20th-century philosophy—Heidegger and Wittgenstein—Hickman argues that "only Dewey took it as his responsibility to enter into the rough and tumble of public affairs" ([1990] 1992, xv; see also 197). In contrast to this, Hickman argues, Heidegger and Wittgenstein took a rather mystical attitude (199), refusing to engage in the political life. Thus, Hickman places Dewey's view of technology within Dewey's broader view of inquiry—the "instrumentalist" view that inquiry itself is about using tools and about production—and its responsiveness to social and public problems. Concepts and ideas are also tools, including moral rules and theories (114). We use them to cope with problems, and this "we" is important since ideally we should have public and democratic deliberation about these problems and take responsibility for the consequences for our actions. Individual armchair philosophy abstracted from social and practical contexts may not be very helpful, and indeed not very instrumental.

What does this view, that inquiry is itself technological and that it is about making responsible choices and needs to be public, imply for technology? Hickman ([1990] 1992) concludes that responsible technology then means that we test it, adapt it to changing situations. Technology is not a thing but "the sum of concrete activities and products of men and women who engage in inquiry in its manifold forms: in the sciences, in the fine and useful arts, in business, in engineering, and in the arts we call political" (202). Instead of the pessimism of technological determinism, we thus arrive at a view that centers on productive, social inquiry and constructive experiments. If there are problems, such as the destruction of the environment, it is not technology that is to blame; instead, it is "the failure to sharpen and use the technological tools required for intelligent social planning" (203).

Some people would object, and have objected, to Dewey's "lumping together" of tools. Hickman defends Dewey by saying that such criticisms presuppose that we draw a sharp line between organism and environment. But, we may ask—aided by both Dewey and, for example, Merleau-Ponty—why should the skin be the relevant border (Hickman [1990] 19692, 43)? Moreover, keeping in mind the phenomenological philosophical traditions that are featured in the beginning of this book, we may also ask, with Hickman, was Dewey a naturalist or is he close to phenomenology? There are various Dewey interpretations (Hickman [1990] 1992, 30). In any case, and this is interesting with a view to trying to connect various approaches to philosophy of technology, Hickman has argued that *post-phenomenology* and pragmatism are closer than one might think; in particular, Ihde and Dewey are close. According to Hickman, both reject the dystopian writers of the Frankfurt school, oppose Heideggerian romanticism and a transcendental approach, move seamlessly between art and technology, and recognize the multivalence of technology. However, Hickman also notes some differences: it is not just that artifacts have different meanings under different conditions; meanings also bring forth new meanings. Moreover, while Ihde embraces some parts of the pragmatic program such as its anti-foundationalism, in contrast to pragmatism, he does not sufficiently develop the social and political implications of his work and implicitly endorses a split between material technology and culture and organism/environment dualism. For Ihde, sometimes there is just perception, without use of instruments. This assumes that instruments are necessarily material. For Dewey, logical entities are also tools. Conceptual tools are also instruments. For example, when Pacific navigators use wave patterns, this is also use of instruments: it involves the "deployment of conceptual tools and techniques" (Hickman 2008). Pragmatism thus offers both a *broader* and a more *social* definition of technology than postphenomenology.

This leads us to the more general question of how pragmatism may be used today for understanding and evaluating technology. Postphenomenology has adopted an interest in the concrete use of technology, but has not really done much more with the approach. Can more be done? When it comes to Dewey, his work offers a way to bring in a social and political dimension without use of Marx and critical theory; for some, this may be an attractive route. For postphenomenology in particular, it offers a convenient way out of what otherwise remains an approach that is too insensitive to social and political questions. Moreover, Dewey's broad understanding of the use of instruments also enables us to move beyond the culture versus materiality discussion. Postphenomenology has taken an empirical turn and understood this as a material turn against a postmodern focus on language and text. This makes it appear as if one has to choose between (material) technology and (non-material) language. But as Hickman (2008) already suggested, this dichotomy is misleading once one takes seriously Dewey's instrumentalism. In recent work, I have used Dewey and Wittgenstein to connect language and technology (Coeckelbergh 2017). In *Experience and Nature* (1929), Dewey argues that language is a tool, an "instrument of social cooperation and mutual participation" (vi). Like Wittgenstein, Dewey rejected the idea that meaning is something merely mental or "psychic" (1929, 179) and defended a use-oriented view of language. For Dewey, signs such as "H_2O" are meaningless unless one connects them to use and experience (1929, 194). We use language and other tools, and both are bound up with the social life; they are social instruments (Coeckelbergh 2017, 35). To suggest that we have to choose between a material and a cultural approach to technology, or between studying technology and studying language, is entirely ignorant of this insight and creates unnecessary tension. Hence Hickman rightly suggests that postphenomenology can learn more from pragmatism than it already has done. Furthermore, for pragmatists, it might also be interesting to further explore similarities with Wittgenstein's views. Hickman reminds us that before Wittgenstein, Dewey already made similar claims about language. For instance, Dewey already argued against the "picture theory" of language (Hickman [1990] 1992, 39) and against one-to-one correspondence between objects and names (57). Wittgenstein and Dewey could both be used to develop theory about the use of, and performance with, technology (Coeckelbergh 2017). That being said, of course pragmatism has its own drawbacks if viewed from the other approaches we discussed. For example, compared to Ihde, it seems not sufficiently appreciative of the precise phenomenology of technological experience; and compared to recent critical theory, there is no immediate attention to the political economy of technology use.

To conclude, Dewey's pragmatism turns out to be a fruitful and productive approach that deserves its place next to (post)phenomenology and critical theory. Pragmatism is a rich resource for philosophers of technology, even for those who do not want to totally embrace the approach in all its claims and implications. For instance, one could further think about how to combine postphenomenology and pragmatism (in new ways). Furthermore, whereas Hickman's ([1990] 1992) book has very little to say about contemporary technologies, Dewey's approach seems a promising one for doing that. For example, Dewey's criticism of Plato's metaphysics (according to Dewey, the distinction of real vs. unreal is only about the effects of technology and has no foundation in a reality outside of experience and practice) could be used to discuss the (apparent) problem of the real versus the virtual in computer games. And the neonatal care case in the beginning of this chapter shows how Dewey can inspire novel analysis of moral practices. Finally, pragmatism is not at all restricted to Dewey; this is only a selection. There is still a lot of work to do on James, Peirce, and Rorty, for instance, and some authors draw inspiration from (one of) them rather than Dewey. For example, Joseph Pitt has advocated an approach in the spirit of Peirce (Pitt 2011); Ciano Aydin (2015) has used Peirce to criticize the inside–outside distinction assumed in the extended mind thesis; and Ihde is sympathetic to Rorty.

6.2. Analytic philosophy of technology

While there is no unified subfield "analytic philosophy of technology" (Franssen 2009, 184), and while the distinction between "analytic" and "continental" is often criticized, some approaches in philosophy of technology are more informed by a philosophical tradition generally known as "analytic." Like other approaches, some limit themselves to conceptual work, whereas others are more empirically oriented and focus, for instance, on design. But in terms of method, they share an analytic approach that Franssen (2009) describes as follows:

> What characterizes analytic philosophy is an abhorrence of system-building and speculation, a preference for a detailed treatment of clearly delineated problems, an emphasis on clear definitions of the concepts used to put a problem and to answer it, an emphasis on language, conceptualization and formalization, a general acknowledgment of the relevance of empirical facts, and a great respect for the findings of science—to such an extent, even, that science and philosophy are considered to merge into each other or to form in some sense a continuum. (184)

Whether or not this definition clearly delineates the approach from others, it gives a good idea of the general orientation. Whereas in the past, analytic philosophers have often seen technology as applied science, and hence thought that questions regarding technology could be handled by philosophy of science, today at least *some* philosophers with an analytic orientation have started to work on philosophy of technology. Themes include, but are in no way limited to, questions regarding the nature of artifacts, the knowledge involved in technology use and innovation, the functions of artifacts from an engineering perspective, the design of technologies, artificial intelligence, and information.

Let me give an example of analytic work in philosophy of technology, which is part of the empirical turn in philosophy of technology and is often informed by what Mitcham (1994) called an "engineering" approach to philosophy of technology: work on the ontology of artifacts by Peter Kroes, Anthonie Meijers, and other analytic philosophers in the Netherlands. The central question of their research program is, what is the nature of technological artifacts? Their answer is the so-called **dual nature of artifacts thesis** (Kroes and Meijers 2006). Let me focus on Kroes's more developed formulation (Kroes 2010) and further work that links this thesis to the notion of sociotechnical systems and more generally "social factors" and ethics, expanding the thesis to an approach to philosophy of technology (Vermaas et al. 2011).

The central questions these authors started from are what distinguish technical artifacts from objects in the natural world, and how we can think about them in a way that does justice to the fact that they are not just "found" (like objects in nature) but designed and used to achieve goals (Kroes 2010, 51–52; see also Vermaas et al. 2011, 1). As Kroes (2010) puts it, we must ask

> Questions about whether technical artefacts are mere physical constructions, about what it means for a technical artefact to function properly or

to be used properly, about how technical artefacts are related to human intentions or human goals, or whether there is a clear demarcation line between technical artefacts and natural objects. (52)

When looking for an answer to this question, Kroes—as an "engineering philosopher of technology" (to use Mitcham's term)—turns to engineers, who, according to him, see technical artifacts as "physical objects with a function" (2010, 52). This leads him to develop the thesis that technical artifacts have a dual nature (55): they have physical, structural properties, but also intention-related, functional properties. This dual nature is related to two ways of conceptualizing our world: a physical view, according to which the world consists of objects that interact causally, and an intentional view, according to which the world consists of agents that act on the basis of reasons (55). The dual nature of artifacts thesis combines these views: "technical artefacts have a dual nature because they are, on the one hand, physical structures that realize, on the other hand, functions, which refer to human intentionality" (Kroes 2010, 55). If the artifact were only a physical object, it would not be an artifact that is made by human beings for a specific purpose. But, Kroes argues, we should also not black box its physical structure. We need both conceptualizations, including the physical (56). Moreover, according to Kroes, technical objects are different from "social objects" like money, since, as Searle has shown, the function of money is not performed on the basis of its physical properties. According to Searle, what matters is that we collectively declare something to have a particular function; it does not matter what it is physically (Searle 1995; 2006). For example, money can take the form of coins, but also of paper or even electronic money. For Kroes, technical objects are not like Searle's social objects: they need to have this link to physical properties, there needs to be an "intimate relationship between the function of a technical artefact and its physical structure" (Kroes 2010, 57).

CASE/TECHNOLOGY:
Money and Contemporary Financial Technologies
(Cryptocurrencies and Blockchain)

Money is an interesting case for philosophers of technology (and indeed for all philosophers). What is money? Is it a thing or can it also be immaterial? Is it social or physical, or both at the same time? Is it a medium of exchange or something else? How does money relate to the social? Is money itself a medium and a technology? In the past, commodities such as precious metals or conch shells could be money. And we still have paper money and coins. But today, with the development of digital technologies, there is electronic money (e.g., on a bank account), and there are so-called cryptocurrencies such as bitcoin. Cryptocurrencies are forms of digital currencies but, in contrast to most currencies we use today, they are not dependent on centralized control (e.g., by a central bank). This is made possible by blockchain technology. Blockchain is a list of records (blocks) that are linked and secured by cryptography and that grows each time a transaction is made. The blockchain is managed by a peer-to-peer network. Currently there is discussion about the ethical aspects of these technologies and their potentialy transformative influence on society. (For some discussion of financial technologies, see Coeckelbergh 2015.)

FIGURE 6.3   Gold and silver bitcoins

One could object that this view leaves out the social. But this is not necessarily so. The existence of something like the social is acknowledged. But it is conceived of in terms of (mostly human) agents that have intentions; according to this view, the technical artifact *itself* does not have a social nature. While Vermaas et al. (2011) admit that it is not always possible in practice to classify objects as either technical or social, they make a strict distinction between technical and social artifacts. Influenced by Searle's social ontology and analysis of money, which also assumes a strict distinction between the physical and the social, they write the following:

> Technical artefacts fulfil their function by virtue of their physical properties whilst social objects depend for their function upon their social/collective acceptation. In the case of social objects, such as money, the actual physical form taken is really immaterial which is why money may take very many different forms (from salt to digital information, e.g., "zeros" and "ones" printed on a chip card). In the case of a social object, such as money, the question "Of what does it consist?" does not really make sense if one bears in mind that it does not depend for its function on a given physical manifestation. The foregoing explains why, when it comes to designing social objects (laws, institutes, rules, et cetera), it is vital to possess knowledge of people's social behaviour (including matters such as: what gives rise to social acceptation and how can that be promoted). By contrast, when it comes to designing new technical artefacts, knowledge of the physical phenomena is required. (Vermaas et al. 2011, 12)

John Searle's Social Ontology

John Searle argued that social objects such as money or wedding rings get their social function by means of declaration, in particular collective declaration: there is a collective intentionality, which gives the object—regardless of its physical properties—its social function. Searle thus sharply distinguished between the physical object and the social function. For him, the materiality of the artifact does not matter; the collective intention is what gives meaning to the object (Searle 1995; 2006). (For more on Searle, see chapter 11.)

Moreover, the focus remains on the individual. Even if in further work it is acknowledged that artifacts are part of wider "sociotechnical systems"—for example, an airplane is part of the "world civil aviation system" on which the functioning of the artifact depends (Vermaas et al. 2011, 68)—these systems are seen as factors that help agents achieve their goals. Consider this formulation of the embeddedness of artifacts in sociotechnical systems:

> Naturally, all technical artefacts are embedded in human action, but in the case of many technical artefacts, they are also allied to wider systems

where the proper functioning of the artefacts not only depends on the technology in question but also on social factors. Those kinds of systems are sociotechnical systems. . . . For the individual user, technical artefacts embedded in sociotechnical systems are often difficult or impossible to use. However, with the help of all the individuals and legislation that constitute parts of such sociotechnical systems, users are often able to achieve their desired goals with these particular technical artefacts. (Vermaas et al. 2011, 2)

Thus, in this view, the link to the social always goes via human goals and intention, and is seen in terms of systems and individuals.

This focus on intentions leads to another objection: What if artifacts have unintended consequences? How can this view account for that? Vermaas et al. of course acknowledge that there are unintended consequences that cannot be avoided, and discuss the problems they raise: for instance, for dealing with risk, responsibility, and design (Vermaas et al. 2011, 103–115). However, it remains unclear how unintended consequences and their implications can be sufficiently conceptualized within an intention-centered view of the nature of artifacts. More "continental" approaches, which tend to conceptualize artifacts by understanding them as *already* intimately linked to the human and the social in ways that are not necessarily related to their physical structure or to the intentions and goals of those who design and use them, and which tend to acknowledge that artifacts have social consequences regardless of the designers' intentions, seem to shed more light on this. Moreover, one could develop the notion of "sociotechnical system" by borrowing from STS; but then there remains a tension between that more social-sciences-inspired approach—which is not necessarily interested in human individuals or their intentions and tends to conceptualize people as social "actors" with interests—and the analytic-philosophical approach, which focuses on individual "agents" with intentions and reasons. Finally, it may be asked if the development of specific views and arguments, such as the dual nature of artifacts thesis, into a larger, all-encompassing theory of technology as attempted in Vermaas et al. (2011) does not go against the idea that analytic philosophy was not supposed to develop grand systems.

6.3. Intercultural and Transcultural Philosophy of Technology?

One criticism of contemporary philosophy of technology is that it is centered too much on what is called "Western" culture. Indeed, the philosophical approaches discussed so far originate mainly in places in Europe and

North America. And even within Europe, usually overviews of philosophy of technology predominantly consider philosophers from the English-speaking and German-speaking worlds, only sometimes considering those from the French-speaking world; and neglecting entirely those from the Spanish-, Portuguese-, Danish-, etc., speaking worlds. To partly remedy this, there have been efforts to bridge between different "worlds." For example, some philosophers of technology in the West have turned to "Eastern" and "Asian" philosophy for inspiration(that is, philosophy from China and Japan), while some scholars in countries such as China, Japan, and South Korea have actively looked for collaboration with and have studied Western philosophers of technology. This raises questions such as, Is philosophy of technology mainly a Western practice? What can Western philosophers learn from non-Western philosophers? Is there such a thing as a "Chinese" philosophy of technology, given that there are the traditions of Confucianism, Daoism, and Marxism? Are there indeed differences between Japan and "the West" in attitudes toward technology, or are these differences exaggerated? Can there be a "global" philosophy of technology? In the West, philosophers such as Carl Mitcham, Andrew Feenberg, Charles Ess, and Rafael Capurro have addressed some of these questions and/or have tried to learn from non-Western philosophy.

Let me focus here on three examples of strands of thinking that go beyond Anglophone philosophy of technology or took place in a context outside Europe or North America: one European (French: Simondon), one Latin American (Flusser in Brazil), and one Asian (Confucianism).

6.3.1. French Philosophy of Technology: Simondon

First, as noted, there are asymmetries and borders even within philosophy of technology in Europe. For example, French philosophy of technology is still relatively marginalized in the English-speaking world. Often language functions as a barrier. But that is changing. For instance, in Anglophone writings, there is now more interest in the work of Gilbert Simondon. It helps that his study of the genesis of technical objects in *On the Mode of Existence of Technical Objects* (written in 1958) has now seen a first complete English translation (Simondon 2017). While I cannot do justice to all aspects of his work here—for example, there is much more to say about his theory of **individuation**, which is very central to his work—let me offer a brief summary of his general approach to the question concerning technology. I will focus on his view of the relation between technology and culture as expressed in the *Mode of Existence*.

IN FOCUS:
Gilbert Simondon

Gilbert Simondon was a French 20th-century philosopher of technology who is known for his theory of individuation and technology. Individuals are not the starting point but the effect of processes of individuation. Technical objects also come into being. Simondon argued against the dualisms of culture and technology, subjects and objects, theoretical and practical. Philosophy of technology is itself a way of overcoming these dualisms. Humans are seen as participants in processes of technical mediation; they are necessary for the machine's functioning and regulation.

FIGURE 6.4 Gilbert Simondon

Simondon (2017) argues against the view that culture and technology are opposed and that culture must defend itself against technology. According to him, culture must be expanded by incorporating technology. Instead of opposing the world of things to the world of meanings, we should see the reality of technology and machines as a human reality. Technology is a stranger perhaps, but strangers are humans (Simondon 2017, 16):

> We would like to show that culture ignores a human reality within technical reality and that, in order to fully play its role, culture must incorporate technical beings in the form of knowledge and in the form of a sense of values. (Simondon 2017, 15)

Simondon studies the relations between machines, and between humans and machines, and the values involved. He writes that the relation between humans and machines should neither be one of superiority nor of inferiority; instead, if we want to incorporate them into culture, we should see them in terms of a "relation of equality" (Simondon 2017, 105). He argues that self-regulation of the machine cannot be achieved by the machine alone but needs humans, who are necessary to take into account "the whole of the milieu" (140). Technical objects cannot be understood as existing by themselves; "their technicity can be understood only through the integration of the activity of a human user or the functioning of a technical ensemble" (245). Humans have to help by organizing the technical mediation between humans and nature (247–248). They are participants.

Moreover, by focusing on the *genesis* of technical objects, Simondon argues against seeing a technical as something that "is"; rather, it "becomes." The object is not "this or that thing"; instead, there is "coming-into-being" (Simondon 2017, 26). Technical structures evolve. Giving examples of technologies such as airplanes, boilers, and (other) machines, he describes processes of differentiation, concretization, adaptation to the technical milieu, and individualization as opposed to remaining a technical element. Concretized, technical objects are not simply the application of scientific principles but can be studied as if they were natural objects; yet they are not the same (Simondon 2017, 50)—even "automata are not a species" (51). Simondon sees the study of technical objects "as viewed by a spectator" as unscientific (51). For Simondon, the individualization of technical objects is about causality in a milieu (62–63). But humans enable the machine to function (151), indeed to regulate. This interest in regulation is similar to that of **cybernetics**. Simondon discusses Wiener's ([1948] 1960) work. But philosophically, he focuses on genesis, on coming-into-being, and he continues to link technology to culture when he describes successive stages of thought. For example, he sees technicity and religiosity as "the heirs of magic" (186), writes that human activity resonates "throughout technical realities," and claims that we can respect technical realities on the basis of our knowledge of them (229). Thus, for Simondon, ethics and politics are not to be divorced from technical realities. Philosophical thought must maintain "the continuity that exists between the successive stages of technical thought and religious thought, all the way to social and political thinking" (233).

One could interpret Simondon's thinking about technology as belonging to what Mitcham calls "engineering" philosophy of technology and to the empirical turn, understood as a turn to the material artifact. But the technical object is always understood as an artifact linked to humans, meaning, and culture—including ethics and politics, and even magical and religious thinking. Instead of seeing technology only as a threat or as alienating, Simondon suggests that humans and machines are kind of equals: there are liaisons and couplings between humans, machines, and the world; humans are not only directing the machine but also participate in its regulation. To conceptualize this, we need to go beyond the technology/culture dichotomy: we need a technical culture. Culture needs to recognize its material conditions; we need to recognize that technology is not neutral but has a mediating and normative role. We need to overcome the alienating division and conflict between technology and culture—not by imposing culture on technology, like some critical theory, or by appealing to poetry, like Heidegger, but by linking the two. Simondon (2017) writes, "it is culture, considered as a lived totality, that must incorporate the technical ensembles by knowing their nature, in order to be able to regulate human life according to these technical ensembles" (234). This sounds like technocracy, but for Simondon, technocracy is precisely due to the split between technology and culture. As Simon Mills puts it in his study of Simondon

> For Simondon the problem of industrial modernity was due to an extreme imbalance between the phases of technology and culture, which led to a dangerous technocratic attitude. What was required was the rebalancing of cultural values in response to the new technological reality they now operated with. This didn't mean the imposition of pre-existing humanist values upon technological inventions as those in the Frankfurt school proposed, but rather the need to understand how the dynamic interplay of technological development with culture was productive of new values and desires that required acknowledgement. (Mills 2016, 2)

According to Simondon, we must become aware that we participate in actions and processes, "in the technical network" (2017, 236). Philosophy and art can help in raising awareness. However, here Simondon warns again of understanding technical reality only from the outside, as a spectacle; instead, it must be known "through participation in its schemas of action" by "integration into the technical ensemble" (236). At the end of his book, he suggests that the notions of object and subject must be overcome (243), like the dualism theoretical versus practical, and that philosophy of technology (Simondon: technics) can play a key role in this:

> It is permissible to think that the dualism inherent in philosophical thought, a dualism of principles and attitudes because of the double reference to the theoretical and the practical, will be profoundly modified by

the introduction of technical activity considered as an area of reflection within philosophical thought. (Simondon 2017, 260)

Thus, it is philosophy of technology itself that can play a role in overcoming dualism:

> It seems that this opposition between action and contemplation, between the immutable and the moving, must cease in the face of the introduction of the technical operation within philosophical thought as area of reflection and even as paradigm. (Simondon 2017, 261)

This approach to the relation between culture and technology sounds very contemporary, and this part of Simondon's work may well be compatible with work from the so-called empirical turn—for instance, work by Verbeek and by Feenberg (who was influenced by Simondon)—or even with some posthumanist thoughts about "couplings" between humans and machines and embracing the machine.

More generally, making further links between French philosophy of technology and Anglophone philosophy of technology seems promising. Next to Simondon, there are many other French philosophers highly relevant to thinking about technology, such as Gilles Deleuze, Bernard Stiegler, and Bruno Latour, who were all inspired by Simondon. And there are other, non-Simondonian, French philosophers relevant to thinking about technology such as Michel Foucault, Jacques Derrida, and Jean-Luc Nancy. I already used Stiegler in the beginning of this book and presented Foucault; later, when I discuss moral status, I will also refer to Derrida; and in my chapter on different disciplines (chapter. 12), I will return to Latour (who influenced Verbeek).

6.3.2. Philosophy of Technology in Brazil: Flusser

Second, an interesting example of how to make bridges between different "language worlds" is provided by Vilém Flusser, a 20th-century thinker who was born in Prague but lived also in São Paulo (Brazil)—where he wrote in Portuguese, taught philosophy, and worked as a journalist—and Rio de Janeiro. Flusser's writings are not only an example of interculturality but are also interesting for philosophy of technology.

For Flusser, digital technologies make possible a new society, a **telematic society**. They are part of a history of increasing abstraction and immateriality, which ultimately leads to the creation of a second nature, a fusion of the natural and cultural. Flusser sees the same structures in technology (computers) and in nature, a networked ecosystem. But he thinks that this also enables the creation

FIGURE 6.5 Vilém Flusser, 1940

of new meaning. With art and science (and the breakdown of barriers between them) we can give meaning to our lives.

For example, in his essays on design, Flusser (1999) argues that our environment is no longer mainly made up of things: "Non-things now flood our environment from all directions, displacing things. These non-things are called information" (86). We feed information into machines that spew out "junk" at no cost (87), and all values will be transformed into information (88). According to Flusser, we must try to imagine this new life with non-things (89). We no longer handle things; we only use the tip of our fingers to tap on keys for the purpose of symbolic operations. What counts now is play, experience, and performance—not things (89). Flusser imagines the factory of the future as a place where robots become central (46). This leads not only to an adaptable factory but also to new human–technology relations. He argues that human beings and robots can function together, and sees space for learning and creative potential (46–47). But he also remarks that while the robot does what the human being wants it to do, "the human being can only want what the robot can do" (Flusser 1999, 48). Furthermore, the new society, the new machines, and the new design also create problems for responsibility: since the design process is organized cooperatively, it becomes unclear who is responsible. "No one person can be held responsible for a product anymore"; and if industrial processes are carried out by machines, it is not clear who is responsible. And who is responsible for a robot killing someone (67)? Flusser thus already asked questions that are still very relevant today, if not more relevant given current developments in robotics and AI.

6.3.3. East and West: Confucianism and Ethics of Technology

Third, let me give an example of an attempt to build a bridge between Western and non-Western philosophy of technology (apologies for the Western-centered formulation): Confucianism and ethics of technology. Pak-Hang Wong (2012)

CASE/TECHNOLOGY:
Digital Communication Technologies
and the Good Life

Have the internet and related digital communication and information technologies contributed to virtue and the good life? Some critics say that the technologies have not fostered better social relationships. According to the American psychologist Sherry Turkle, internet, social media, and robots have made us turn away from real life and have led to less interaction in the family. We are more connected but also more alone. People talk less. Children empathize less. Machines pretend to care but don't. Doctors look at a screen, not at you. We are addicted to the technologies; there is too little conversation. (See, for example, this interview with Turkle at https://www.theguardian.com/science/2015/oct/18/sherry-turkle-not-anti-technology-pro-conversation.) Is there sufficient evidence for these claims? And if what Turkle says is true, then how shall we deal with those effects? Shall we ban the technology? Develop different, more ethical technology? Or is the challenge rather the art of using the technology differently?

---

has proposed to use the **Confucian** tradition to thinking about ethics of technology. Responding to what he calls the "marginality of non-Western philosophical traditions" (Wong 2012, 67) in philosophy, including in debates about ethics of technology, Wong argues that the notions Dao, harmony, and personhood can provide an alternative account of ethics of technology.

Wong starts with outlining and interpreting a Confucian approach to ethics. First, he shows that the notion of Dao is not restricted to Daoism but is also important to Confucianism. **Dao** has various meanings and connotations, but the most relevant meaning for ethics is one that sees it as "the organising and governing principles for human and social affairs" (Wong 2012, 70). It is thus (also) a normative notion. As an instantiation of the Heavenly Dao (Heaven is understood as the source of all meaning and value), Human Dao "refers to the way human beings *should* live" (70). This is not understood in terms of norms and principles, but, Wong argues, as a virtue ethics, which asks us to follow and cultivate our nature, which is to realize Dao (71). Second, in Confucianism, harmony is emphasized. There should be harmony between human beings and Heaven, but also between humans and within the person: "it is an ideal relationship for within an individual and between individuals at the level of family, society, and the world" and hence not only intrapersonal but also interpersonal harmony is very important (72). But what does harmony mean? It does not mean sameness, maintaining the status quo, complete agreement, or oppression of difference; rather, it means balancing and coordination. One element should not dominate the others, as, for instance, in cooking (73). Moreover, in a way that reminds us of Deweyan ethics, Wong writes that what is good or bad can only be determined in a specific situation:

> For Confucians, what is good or bad, and what is right or wrong, can only be determined in a concrete situation, in which particularities become salient. Harmony is achieved by taking into account various possibilities in that situation. In other words, harmony involves contextualised and holistic thinking. (Wong 2012, 73–74)

Harmony, Wong argues, is more a process than a state. Third, the Confucian notion of a person is not the Western independent, rational, and self-determining being but rather a social, cultural, historical, and indeed ethical one (74). Human beings are inherently social and interdependent, and this has ethical implications:

> Confucians think that human beings are inescapably born into a web of social relationships, and that they can only mature within the web of social relationships. This is exactly why harmonisation, which involves a continuous negotiation and adjustment of interpersonal relationship for the sake of mutual enrichment, is seen as an ideal in Confucianism. (Wong 2012, 75)

This means that the family and the social roles one occupies are very important for ethical, indeed virtuous, living, flourishing, and developing. Each role has a set of proper conduct and attitudes (Wong 2012, 78), and the development of the person within and through these roles and relations is "an ongoing process" (75). Hence, virtue does not mean so much "having" virtue but rather realizing virtue as one develops self and personhood, understood in a relational way: self-cultivation is about "learning and [the] practice of relating to and interacting with others appropriately" (76). Personhood and virtue have to be practiced. And this is done in the complex situations of everyday life, where one has to make decisions that take into account the particulars of the situation. In this sense, Confucian ethics is a kind of skill (79). One needs know-how. This social, developmental, and skill-oriented approach is different from Western ethics, which emphasizes having properties such as autonomy and knowing rules and principles, and which distinguishes between private and public. According to the Confucian view, others coauthor one's personhood as one is part of a "web of relationships" and roles, and one's conduct in private life will carry over to public life; hence, transformation can take place in both self-modification and self (79–80).

Then Wong asks what this means for (thinking about) ethics of technology. He sees a link between a Confucianist approach and a turn toward thinking about **the good life** in (Western) ethics of technology, although the former differs from the latter since it bridges between the right and the good. I would also add that the former is more relational, whereas the latter is often formulated as an individual(ist?) ethics, focused on the well-being of the individual. Moreover, Wong argues that with its emphasis on harmony, Confucianism may not only inspire a more situational, contextualized, and holistic ethics but also help us to resist looking for a final answer. Instead, Confucianist thinking about ethics in terms of the ideal of harmony must be understood as a process of harmonization that "calls for a *continuous* negotiation and adjustment of relationships between human beings, society and technology" and that involves processes of learning and practice, especially the learning of know-how (Wong 2012, 81). Wong sees here a link to Borgmann's notion of focal practices (82). He also proposes more attention to roles, in particular how technology may transfer social roles and the associated responsibilities (82). Finally, Wong stresses practice:

> In order to perform a social role properly, Confucians have stressed that a person must learn and practise it. Translating it into a Confucian ethics of technology, it promotes an investigation of the kinds of actual and/ or potential practices engendered by technology and a study of whether those practices are conducive or detrimental to our performance of the social roles. (Wong 2012, 83)

This seems to bring Confucianism close to (Western) **virtue ethics**, which can also be interpreted as being about ethical practice. It also provides a link with approaches in philosophy of technology that focus on the ways we live our lives with technology—privately and publicly—and on the way we use technology to transform ourselves (Wong 2012, 83).

In this way, Wong (2012) suggests an attractive bridge between Confucianist and Western ethics of technology. However, it is not an easy bridge; and especially for those Western philosophers of technology focused on individual uses of technology—including individual virtue and well-being—it may be a bridge too far: in the form presented by Wong, a Confucianist turn seems to require the acceptance of, if not a different metaphysics (e.g., the notion of Heaven), and at least a "strong" or "deeply" relational, social, and holistic approach to ethics, which remains in tension with Western individualism and indeed with Western modernity. Is this our destiny, or can we escape this condition and do we need more efforts like Wong's? And is the study of philosophical traditions sufficient? Can and should we learn more from the "alternative modernities" (to use a term by Feenberg) that are being lived in the non-Western world, from the ways people *everywhere* on the planet *live* the bridges that philosophers seek? Are we too much focused on our concepts and theories, blind to the lived bridges between cultures that already exist? The pragmatist approach outlined earlier in this chapter would certainly urge us to attend to the ethical and technological practices and coping with situations in everyday life, and to the wisdom those practices and copings yield.

REVIEW QUESTIONS

1. What is the pragmatist, in particular Deweyan, approach to philosophy of technology? How does it differ from Ihde's approach?
2. Give an example of an analytic approach to thinking about technology.
3. How can Simondon's work be used in contemporary thinking about technology?
4. Who was Vilém Flusser?
5. What is a Confucian approach to ethics of technology?

DISCUSSION QUESTIONS

1. Is the pragmatist approach more helpful than postphenomenology or not? Or is this the wrong question? Why (not)?
2. Do you endorse the dual nature of artifacts thesis? Why (not)?
3. Is current (Anglophone) philosophy of technology too Western-centered and biased against philosophy of technology in other languages? If so, how could this be remedied?
4. Do current digital communication technologies create more distance between us, rather than connecting us more?

RECOMMENDED READING

Hickman, Larry A. (1990) 1992. *John Dewey's Pragmatic Technology*. Reprint, Bloomington: Indiana University Press.

Kroes, Peter. 2010. "Engineering and the Dual Nature of Technical Artefacts." *Cambridge Journal of Economics* 34(1): 51–62.

Wong, Pak-Hang. 2012. "Dao, Harmony, and Personhood: Towards a Confucian Ethics of Technology." *Philosophy & Technology* 25(1): 67–86.

KEY TERMS

Confucianism

Cybernetics

Dao (or Tao)

Democratic deliberation

Dual nature of artifacts
    thesis

Experience

Experimentation

Foundationalism

The good life

Habits

Individuation

Instrumentalism

Public deliberation

Representationalism

Telematic society

Virtue ethics

3 THINKING ABOUT TECHNOLOGY BY STARTING FROM TECHNOLOGY

7 FROM INFORMATION TECHNOLOGIES TO PHILOSOPHY AND ETHICS OF INFORMATION

CASE/TECHNOLOGY:
Digital and Virtual Worlds, *The Matrix*, and Beyond

In the 1990s, the internet and the World Wide Web promised a different, online, and digital world, cyberspace, which could be explored and conquered, and which would constitute a liberation from the offline world. In the context of computer gaming, so-called virtual worlds were created populated by avatars (digital representations of players) and often involving 3D graphical representations of a fictional world or universe. Science-fiction films such as *The Matrix* (1999) popularized the concept of living in a simulated reality, different from the real world. After the turn of the millennium, however, the pervasive presence and use of the internet and the massive use of new place-independent technologies such

FIGURE 7.1 Green data matrix

as smartphones and their applications make us question whether terms such as "cyberspace" and a "digital" sphere, and even offline versus online, are still appropriate terms to characterize our experience of technology today. While of course we may still desire to escape to a fictional world and use virtual worlds or technologies such as Virtual reality (VR), we increasingly experience our lives not as split between two different worlds but as immersed in one hybrid analogue/digital, online/offline lifeworld. Philosophers of technology can contribute to conceptualizing this new situation and experience. For example, Luciano Floridi proposed the terms "infosphere" and "onlife" to capture these phenomena.

7.1. Introduction

New electronic technologies such as the computer, internet, and smartphones are often discussed in terms of information: they are called new **information technologies** since these tools and processes store, transmit, and manipulate information. The use, study, and engineering of such systems is then called "informatics" or "information science." They concern *new* information technologies because cave drawings, alphabets, numbers, writing, and so on can also be considered information technologies.

As Rafael Capurro (2003) shows, the term "information" has roots in Latin (*informatio*) and Greek. Moreover, thinking about information technology must be put in its historical context: the recent history of thinking about information, the history of computer science, and what used to be called **cybernetics**. Figures such as John von Neumann, Alan Turing, Claude Shannon, and Norbert Wiener played key roles in that history. Wiener, for instance, thought that information was a third metaphysical principle, which could not be reduced to other principles: "information is information, not matter or energy" (Wiener [1948] 1961, 132).

IN FOCUS:
Norbert Wiener

Norbert Wiener was an American mathematician, philosopher, and professor at MIT in the first half of the 20th century. He is seen as the father of cybernetics (Wiener [1948] 1961), a transdisciplinary approach that tries to understand control and communication in animals and machines. Computer science applies concepts from cybernetics for the control of devices, and cybernetics played an important role in the development of the fields of robotics and automation. After the Second World War, Wiener warned that scientists should consider the ethical implications of their work.

Today, the development of personal computers and especially the internet has inspired some philosophers to propose the concept of "information" as the central concern of, and central concept for, a *philosophy of technology*. For these philosophers, conceptualizing our time and our technologies means conceptualizing information and its "revolution." In this chapter, I summarize and discuss Luciano Floridi's *The Philosophy of Information* (2011) and *The Ethics of Information* (2013) as examples of such an approach, including concepts such as the "infosphere" and "onlife." More generally, this chapter argues that technologies such as the internet and digital or virtual worlds raise metaphysical questions concerning the real and life. Is the real to be defined in terms of information? Is virtual reality real, and if so, what kind of reality is it? And what is life, given that both are now described in terms of information and that we have synthetic biology and autonomous intelligent machines that appear alive? What is the human? Are we informational beings? Are we information processing machines? Throughout this and the following chapters, I will emphasize that it is especially the new *technologies* that have inspired new ways of thinking about reality and about ourselves and show how thinking about technology can be an interesting *philosophical* project.

7.2. All about Information: Floridi's Philosophy and Ethics of Information

The rapid development of new electronic technologies and their transformative power have led some to understand what is happening as a *revolution*. Floridi has argued that we witness "the information revolution," which he understands as a **fourth revolution** after the Copernican, the Darwinian, and the Freudian (Floridi 2014). Previous revolutions already displaced humans from the center of the universe, from the center of the biological world, and from the center of pure rationality. According to Floridi, the fourth revolution is, and should be, once again profoundly altering our view of reality and of ourselves: of the self, identity, and the human. Our ontology and our philosophical anthropology are changing. Being has an information nature, and our selves are also informational (Floridi 2013, 210). In his hands, then, philosophy of technology—and any other philosophy, for that matter—becomes a "philosophy of information" (Floridi 2011), which he sees as an autonomous field like other branches of philosophy. His ambition is much more all-encompassing than saying something about technology: it is no less than providing a "comprehensive approach to philosophical investigations" (Floridi 2011, 24) through an "information turn" (24). Let me go into more detail now about Floridi's philosophy and ethics of information.

First, while Floridi does not endorse technological determinism and emphasizes that we can steer our boat like a sailor does (Floridi 2013, 1), he argues that there is a revolution happening that we can only grasp by means of the concept of information and that changes everything and everyone. Interestingly, he suggests that *the technologies themselves* alter the world. According to Floridi, new technologies and forms of engineering are an "ontologically powerful" force (Floridi 2011, 26): technologies "re-ontologize" in the sense that they fundamentally transform the intrinsic nature of the world (Floridi 2013, 6). This includes changing our thinking:

> Technology unveils, transforms, and controls the world, often designing and creating new realities in the process. It tends to prompt original ideas, to shape new concepts, and to cause unprecedented problems. It usually embeds, but also challenges, ethical values and perspectives. (Floridi 2011, 26)

To conceptualize this change and this reality, Floridi proposes an informational ontology, which sees reality or Being as synonymous with information—he writes that *reality is the totality of information* (Floridi 2011, xiii), which he also calls the **infosphere**: our lives, our technologies, indeed all entities must be understood as informational and as being part of an ecology of information. Digital data and digital technologies, then, change the infosphere and increase the informational space.

The new technologies and new metaphysics that unfold themselves here also blur the line between, on the one hand, offline and analogue, and on the other hand, digital and online. Our experience becomes **onlife** experience. The space of information is not something we can log in to or log out from, but an ecosystem on which we depend. Instead of Newtonian metaphysics, we need an informational and environmental one. Instead of a *Matrix*-like virtual sphere, "behind" which there is a "hard," material reality, we will soon see one infosphere:

> It will be the world itself that will be increasingly interpreted and understood informationally, as part of the infosphere. At the end of this shift, the infosphere will have moved from being a way to refer to the space of information to being synonymous with Being itself. (Floridi 2013, 10)

Figure 7.2 *Infosphäre* (infosphere), artwork by Matthias Zimmermann, 2016

Indeed, Floridi (2013) writes, "the infosphere is the totality of Being, hence the environment constituted by the totality of informational entities, including all agents, along with their processes, properties, and mutual relations" (65). With his informational ontology, he avoids and argues against digital ontology, "according to which the ultimate nature of reality is digital, and the universe is a computational system" (Floridi 2011, 317). Digital and analogue are merely ways in which reality is experienced; reality, according to Floridi, is informational.

Second, the change (therefore) also concerns us. If the nature of Being is informational, then we are and become also informational; we are what Floridi calls **inforgs**: "informationally embodied organisms" that are embedded in the infosphere (Floridi 2013, 14). As entities and agents that are part of the infosphere, our nature as human beings and as selves is also informational and environmental. Once again, it is shown that we are not in the center. We are part of the infosphere in which there are also other inforgs, for instance artificial agents. Floridi argues that we should not, and in the near future will no longer, see an ontological difference between the infosphere and the physical world. Moreover, disconnection and disruption will be experienced as highly problematic and even traumatic:

> When the migration is complete, we shall increasingly feel deprived, excluded, handicapped, or impoverished to the point of paralysis and psychological trauma whenever we are disconnected from the infosphere, like fish out of water. One day, being an inforg will be so natural that any disruption in our normal flow of information will make us sick. (Floridi 2013, 16)

The infosphere also enables us to develop our identities and selves. Floridi argues that information and communication technologies (**ICTs**) are very powerful technologies of the self (2013, 221). Think, for example, about social media, which young people use to shape their identity. But this also constitutes some dangers. For instance, since the self tries to see how others see itself by relying on ICTs (what Floridi calls the "digital gaze"), there is the danger that "one may be lost in one's own perception of oneself as attributed by others in the infosphere" (Floridi 2013, 225). Since they re-ontologize the infosphere (which we could understand as transforming everything and everyone into information), these new ICTs can also alter the nature of privacy and our understanding of privacy (235). But according to Floridi, this does not necessarily lead to disempowerment: whereas there is "a huge expansion in the flow of personal information being recorded, processes and exploited," there is also an increase in the control that agents may exercise to protect their data and life-cycle (2013, 236). We can adapt ourselves to a "glassy infosphere" (238), and it can also make us more accountable.

Third, once we accept this informational and environmental nature of the world and of ourselves, we need an adequate ethics in line with these insights: an **information ethics** (sometimes abbreviated as IE), understood as an environmental ethics. For this purpose, Floridi (2013) conceptualizes human moral agents as informational agents, systems, and objects that are embedded in an informational environment (27). All reality and all entities are considered "at an informational level of abstraction" (27). **Level of abstraction** refers to the method of abstraction Floridi (2013) uses, analogous to modeling in science, where only a limited number of variables are considered, all others being abstracted (30). In particular, it is inspired by so-called formal methods in theoretical computer science, which are mathematical modeling techniques in which only some observables are selected for a particular analysis. He gives the example of wine: to evaluate a wine, the tasting level of abstraction is relevant; whereas to purchase wine, observables like maker, region, price, etc., constitute the relevant level of abstraction (Floridi 2011, 52). Based on this method, he then sets up an information ethics and ethical discourse that is not human-centered but concerns "information as such" (Floridi 2013, 65) and thus—keeping in mind his information ontology—concerns everything that exists. Entities, then, are defined as "a consistent packet of information," and some entities are agents. Once again, it is stressed that all agents (human and non-human) are part of the infosphere as informational entities. Being is information, and non-Being is the absence of information or "entropy" (Floridi 2013, 65).

The moral question, according to Floridi, concerns then what is good for an informational entity in the infosphere. He answers this question by defining ethical principles, which demand that one avoids **entropy** (lack of order): it ought not to be caused, it ought to be prevented, it ought to be removed. And last but not least, "the flourishing of informational entities as well as of the whole infosphere ought to be promoted by preserving, cultivating, and enriching their well-being" (Floridi 2013, 71). Floridi's ontocentric ethics is thus concerned with Being and its flourishing (11), understood in an informational way, rather than with life, human beings, sentient beings, and so on. As an environmental ethics, it extends moral respect to all entities in the infosphere (similar to a biocentric ethics that might extend moral respect to all living entities). There is good in everything, understood as in everything informational. The infosphere has intrinsic value, and all entities in it have intrinsic value. Floridi's approach is thus similar to a deep ecology, where the land, earth, and the biosphere are replaced by the infosphere (2013, 133). It is an environmental ethics, conceptualized as an informational ethics (and vice versa). It includes not only living organisms and their habitats but also inanimate things (133). It is not biocentric but ontocentric, "where the latter is expressed in terms of an informational metaphysics" (307). Ontocentric ethics is thus understood as infocentric. Human moral agents are not central but are "guests in the house of Being" (133).

Furthermore, human beings are not the only ones that can act morally; there are also **artificial agents** that can do so. Not all artificial agents are moral agents. Floridi argues that this depends on the goodness of the action of the agent, which in turn is defined in terms of what it does to entropy in the infosphere: "an action is said to be morally qualifiable if and only if it can cause moral good or evil, that is, if it decreases or increases the degree of metaphysical entropy in the infosphere" (2013, 147). There can be artificial good but also artificial evil, evil actions done by artificial agents. Both artificial agents and human agents may be accountable for their actions, good or evil (191). Thus, Floridi's informational ontology enables him to formulate not only moral principles with regard to moral patiency (how entities should be treated) but also with regard to moral agency: what entities do and its moral relevance. (More on moral patiency and moral agency in chapter 8.) Both kinds of principles are connected: they all concern the well-being of the infosphere and its entities. This ethics is not based on the "mind" of agents or patients, on mental states, emotions, etc.; it is hence a **mindless morality** approach (Floridi 2013, 160), which can concern also artificial agents and, when it comes to patients, everything that exists. Moreover, morality can also be *distributed* in multi-agent systems (261), which may comprise artificial agents: there could be human, artificial, or hybrid multi-agent systems (265). A mindless morality then means that actions are evaluated with regard to their impact on the (informational) environment and its (informational) inhabitants (266), regardless of the naturalness or artificiality of the agents.

Finally, particularly relevant to philosophy of technology is what Floridi calls the **constructionist** dimension of his ethics: he defines humans as poietic creatures, who have the drive to construct—to build physical and conceptual objects and to exercise control and stewardship over them (Floridi 2013, 175). Many people may agree with this claim. But in Floridi, this capacity and drive, too, are redefined in onto-informational terms. Construction is understood as "a struggle against entropy" and is connected with the ethical demand to make the infosphere flourish: "Homo poieticus is a **demiurge**, who takes care of reality, today conceptualized as the infosphere, to protect it and make it flourish" (175). The infosphere is an ideal environment for the demiurge since it can easily be altered; the ethical question is then how this can be done "in a patient-friendly way" (176). We are stewards of nature (305), but here "nature" is reconceptualized as the infosphere. We are both within that nature and have a role in reshaping it and being responsible for its future (305). Thus, while in Floridi's philosophy humans are not the center of the universe, they seem to have a special, ethical role as responsible demiurges and stewards.

CASE/TECHNOLOGY:
Fake News and the Internet

A popular term in public discourse since 2017, **fake news** is false information mainly distributed by online social media and further spread by traditional media. It is intended to mislead and manipulate; for example, to damage someone or for political gain. Fake news is widely seen as a threat to democracy. Floridi interprets fake news as misinformation and as the deterioration and pollution of the infosphere. While there have always been lies, gossip, and misinformation, now the internet allows a bottomless supply of it. The role of ethics and philosophy is then to assist in the restoration of the infosphere and to create a blueprint for a better infosphere (see his article at https://www.theguardian.com/technology/2016/nov/29/fake-news-echo-chamber-ethics-infosphere-internet-digital). In other words, in line with his information ethics (2013) and philosophy of information (2011), Floridi sees fake news as an environmental problem: a pollution of the informational environment, the infosphere.

7.3. Critical Discussion

Floridi's approach attracts and has attracted a number of criticisms, some of which are discussed by Floridi (e.g., 2013). Let me present and discuss some of these objections and add some of my own, which are relevant for thinking about technology.

First, Floridi's *metaphysics* is not clear: at times it seems that he endorses "is" claims about reality (e.g., in his book on the philosophy of information; 2011), whereas at other times he embraces a metaphysics of *becoming* (often in his ethics of information; 2013). Has reality always been informational, or is Being changing in that direction because of our technologies? And if the latter is the case, then does this contradict the "is" claims? This question is relevant for thinking about technology since if Being is indeed changing because of technology, then technology gets a very important metaphysical role: as we have seen, it then is a "re-ontologizer," which changes not only our thinking about but also transforms the nature of Being itself.

Second, Floridi is often accused of *reductivism*, with regard to reality and especially with regard to humans. Does he reduce everything and everyone to information? Floridi denies that his approach is reductivist: he argues that the approach only considers humans at a specific level of abstraction, an information level of abstraction. His view is that "entities can be analysed by focusing on their lowest common denominator, represented by an informational ontology"

(Floridi 2013, 309); and he claims that this does not exclude other perspectives. He argues that just as the naturalization of human beings by Darwin helped us to see ourselves as part of the natural environment, an informatization of human beings helps us to see ourselves as inforgs part of the infosphere.

One could respond to this view in different ways. First, one may simply reject that humans, other entities, and reality can helpfully be understood in terms of information at all and instead propose to talk about humans, reality, etc., in other terms. This objection is weak since Floridi shows that talking about information adds some insights about humans and technology. Compare with Darwinism: the study of humans in the light of their biological evolution is clearly helpful and meaningful, regardless of whatever else humans are or may become. Second, even if one accepts including the informational level of abstraction, one may question if information is necessarily the *best* level of abstraction for understanding human beings, technologies, or other entities (one needs to specify which one). It is not clear, for instance, why the common denominator is always the most helpful level of abstraction. To say, like pre-Socratic philosophers, that everything is "x" (water, air, time, information, etc.) may be true or not; but how relevant is such an approach to, for instance, questions regarding specific technologies or even for an ethics of so-called information technologies in general? This level of abstraction *may* be useful for certain purposes, but not for others and not for most. Compare this to studying humans in terms of their bodies containing 60% water: this can be meaningful in some contexts or for some purposes (e.g., in medicine and biology), but in many contexts it is irrelevant. Third, even if Floridi's perspective is not *necessarily* reductivist and not in *principle* reductivist, one could argue that in *practice*, the discourse of philosophy of information excludes other perspectives on human beings, on reality, and so on. Compare this again to biology: it is absolutely acceptable to talk about human beings in biological terms in many contexts; but even if one rejects reductivism, clearly if one *always* and in all contexts talks about human beings in biological terms, this is problematic. Fourth, someone defending a traditional kind of humanism may take issue with what is arguably a posthumanist position: for many relevant questions such as moral agency, Floridi crosses the line between humans and non-humans. For some (posthumanists), this is a contribution to an exciting new line of inquiry. For others, it is a horror. The latter may frame their question in terms of reductivism, but what they really worry about is the crossing of that line that divides humans from non-humans. Finally, one may grant that the approach is not reductivist in its claims but question the *method* of levels of abstraction (on other grounds). This leads me to the next objection.

Third, regardless of the content of Floridi's claims (that all reality is information, etc.), one may question *the method of levels of abstraction*. First, one may defend the position that this method is fine for computer science, mathematics, and so on, but should not be used in the humanities and social sciences, which has other and perhaps better methods to talk about human beings, reality, and so on. The success of this objection would then depend on the specific objections and how well the alternative method is defended. Second, one may also argue that regardless of the field of application, there is something problematic with the method per se, with the "interface" (Floridi 2013, 326), regardless of its field of application. One could argue that *abstracting* is not epistemically and morally neutral but has problematic consequences. Here is my argument: by its nature, the method amounts to making a selection of variables; it always leaves out others. This has moral consequences. As I argued in my book *Growing Moral Relations* (Coeckelbergh 2012), when we ascribe a moral status to entities on the basis of a set of properties, this very epistemological operation already puts the entity at a distance and abstracts it from concrete relations and contexts. If the study of human beings and other beings is in practice limited to the informational level of abstraction and indeed to *any* level of abstraction, Floridi's approach seems to create an immense moral distance, like the scientific approaches (e.g., mathematical modeling) he takes inspiration from. If everything and everyone is abstracted into information, if there are only informational entities, then concrete living beings and lived relations are out of view. It may be that, theoretically speaking, it is acknowledged that this is only a model and a level of abstraction, like Floridi does. But the point is that this theoretical way of speaking itself is problematic. It is the very philosophical and scientific procedures, technologies, and interfaces that show only a small selection of reality (an epistemological problem) and that create distance between subject-observers and object-observables (a moral problem). And related to this, it is also the language use, such as "information objects" and "inforgs," which already creates the distance. (Note that this is not only a question about Floridi's approach. All media and interfaces used by philosophers [of technology and others] already have moral significance, regardless of the message. Further discussion is needed about what exactly the moral significance is. It may also be interesting to further discuss whether science and philosophy in general are already abstracting; and if so, what their moral significance is: if abstraction and distance are always bad or if some *degree* of abstraction might be acceptable or beneficial *under certain conditions or in specific contexts*. These are relevant questions for all philosophers, including philosophers of technology.)

Fourth, the abstraction of the theory has raised the question of if this approach works as an *ethics*. On the one hand, Floridi is right to say that for all philosophical ethics, there is always work needed to apply it (Floridi 2013, 314) and that **phronesis** is needed (317). And in fact, not only Floridi but also others, such as Herman Tavani, have applied the approach, for instance, to privacy. I have also offered the case of fake news as interpreted by Floridi. On the other hand, one may object that if *too much* work is needed to bridge the gap, then that gap is too wide. For example, to define fake news as pollution of the infosphere gives some normative direction but not practical guidance as to what to do about it. Of course, practical measures have been proposed, also by Floridi; but it is not clear how they are derived from, or depend on, his metaphysics and ethics.

One barrier to application as an ethics may well be that the approach does not enable us to distinguish between the moral status of diverse information objects: for instance, between living and non-living beings. This is Philip Brey's objection:

> Within IE, it seems, no difference in value exists between different kinds of information objects: every information object, qua information object, is intrinsically valuable and therefore equally deserving of respect. This apparent egalitarianism has the undesirable consequence that, from the point of view of IE, a work of Shakespeare is as valuable as a piece of pulp fiction, and a human being as valuable as a vat of toxic waste. Floridi will no doubt want to reply that differentiation is possible because some objects have additional worth beyond their status as information objects. But note that any such sources of additional worth lie beyond the scope of IE, because IE only assigns worth to things qua information objects. IE tells us that we should be equally protective of human beings and vats of toxic waste, or of any other information object, and that we have an (albeit overridable) duty to contribute to the improvement and flourishing of pieces of lint and human excrement. At best, this suggests that IE gives us very little guidance in making moral choices. At worst, it suggests that IE gives us the wrong kind of guidance. (Brey 2008, 112)

Again, Floridi could respond that at another level of abstraction, one can consider these differences. But this is indeed beyond the scope of his ethics. *If we stay within his approach*, his information ethics favors one level of abstraction over others, the informational one, from which such distinctions cannot be made.

Fifth, Floridi's ethics is based on a particular metaphysics; and whether or not one accepts the theory depends on the acceptance of this metaphysical, ontological foundation. What if someone rejects the premise? Does Floridi do enough to engage with people who disagree with the premises? As Bernd Stahl has argued (2008), Floridi follows a specific strategy of (not) dealing with *disagreement*:

> IE does not aim to show that there are implicit signs of agreement with its body of theory. Instead, it confronts the agent with a fairly complex argument, which essentially goes back to its ontological foundations. The agent who wants to engage with IE will at some stage come to the point where she needs to make a decision as to whether she accepts the

> intrinsic moral value of information entities qua information entities or not. In my mind it is one of the major shortcomings of IE that it offers little support for this choice and that it cannot convince agents who, for whatever reason, do not want to follow its ontological foundation. (Stahl 2008, 106)

Thus, Stahl suggests that it is a matter of "either you are with us or not": those who agree can use the theory, whereas others are excluded from the discourse. On the one hand, it is of course always the case that a theory or approach has certain premises, which may or may not be accepted. On the other hand, if an author wants his or her theory or approach to find wide application and be used widely, then it is important to have premises many people can accept—or at least put in more effort to convince people of the premises. (See also the objection concerning cultural differences following.)

Sixth, one may question if we still need *metaphysics and foundationalism* at all today. In the course of the development of his thinking (e.g., as represented in his ethics), Floridi clearly takes the metaphysical route (Floridi 2011, 1) and claims that his philosophy might be considered "a new kind of first philosophy"; in other words, a metaphysics. But there is an entire recent (20th-century) history of philosophy that questions metaphysics and foundationalism: for instance, pragmatism and poststructuralism. Now Floridi *does* respond to an earlier, 19th-century claim about the death of God: he argues there is and should be a "demiurgic turn" (2011, 23): after the death of God, we have to accept our destiny and responsibility as a creator and steward of reality. His approach includes this constructionist perspective. But Floridi ignores much of 20th-century philosophy that has questioned metaphysics, including creational metaphysics. The objection here is not that he should adopt an anti-metaphysical or anti-foundationalist perspective but rather that to support his view, he should do more to engage with work that questions his general philosophical approach.

Seventh, as a naturalist and realist, Floridi leaves little room for the insights of phenomenology, hermeneutics, and so on, which have questioned the idea of a "mind-independent reality" (Floridi 2011, 340). This includes ignoring insights from philosophy of language about the *mediation of language* in thinking about technology (for work on this, see, e.g., Coeckelbergh 2017). I can see no reason why such insights would be entirely irrelevant to thinking about information. Like many scientists, Floridi ignores how language mediates our view of reality. At best, to propose a metaphysics without considering this mediation of language runs the risk of being perceived as too philosophically naïve. At worst, it invites a dogmatic project in which the ultimate truth about reality is so clear that there is no place for interpretation and dialogue—a project I am sure Floridi would like to avoid.

In the light of the previous two objections regarding metaphysics and mediation, it may be instructive to consider the work of Rafael Capurro, who has
also proposed an information ethics and has even also proposed an ontological
foundation of information ethics, but has a very different approach as compared to Floridi and is in fact one of the latter's critics. Offering a different
reading of "ontological," Capurro has taken a more existentialist, Heideggerian
route and has criticized what he takes to be Floridi's abstraction from bodily
and space-time conditions. He has proposed to decenter metaphysics and
recognize what he calls the "unmarked space": the body and its *existential dimension* cannot be reduced to our body as data (Capurro 2006). While this
approach may be less clear and is less well developed and systematic than Floridi's, invites again discussion of the reductivism objection, and is vulnerable
to Floridi's criticism of talk about "digital" sphere and digital ontology, it il-
lustrates that even within the discourse on information ethics and philosophy
of information, one can also draw on other intellectual sources, sources that
enable a different take on the very project of a metaphysics and that point to
the danger of neglecting the body and human existence. Capurro's approach
also enables more attention for an intercultural information ethics, which includes addressing questions such as how the internet impacts on local cultural
values and transforms traditional cultures, and how an intercultural dialogue
on information ethics could take place.

Indeed, Floridi's information ethics—as outlined in the two books (2011,
2013) discussed—is not very sensitive to *cultural differences*. But again this
does not need to be a necessary feature of an information ethics. For instance,
Charles Ess has argued that a global information ethics must conjoin shared
norms but also preserve irreducible differences between cultures and peoples
(Ess 2006). According to him, a global information ethics must be pluralist,
and this pluralism can be found in both Western and Eastern thinking. Floridi's
information ethics, by contrast, seems monist and universalist (see also Stahl
2008) and, perhaps due to its metaphysical approach and scientific method,
seems unable to enter into a discourse on ethics and culture in a way that takes
into account the many discussions in the humanities and the social sciences
about this topic. Ess is more sympathetic to Floridi on this point and argues
that Floridi's philosophy and ethics of information has the advantage that it has
a "thin" or "light" ontology that can be shared globally (Ess 2008) while preserving the "thick" local ontologies. But it seems to me that the very opposite
can also be argued: Floridi's universalist ontology and his method of levels of
abstraction approach are rooted in a particular tradition of Western metaphysical and scientific thinking (the **prima philosophia** tradition, scientific modeling, etc.) and rest on a particular and "thick" claim (that ultimate reality is
informational); his ethics is hence "thicker" than Ess assumes. To suppose that

everyone and all cultures and peoples on earth could embrace this approach and are ready to accept that information as the ultimate reality is at best ignorant and at worst arrogant and imperialistic. Elsewhere, Floridi (2016) has discussed toleration, a concept that is highly relevant to the discussion about information ethics in a global world with cultural differences; but it is unclear how his views about toleration and design go together with the fundamental orientations of his philosophy of information.

Eighth, on the one hand, Floridi distinguishes between facts and norms and asks us not to confuse the two (Floridi 2013, 251); but, on the other hand, his ontological ethics does precisely that: it says that reality is informational and derives all kinds of "oughts" from this. Now it may be that it is fine to confuse the two. Floridi's answer to the objection that his approach commits a **naturalistic fallacy** goes this route: he argues that to insist on the danger of the naturalistic fallacy is to presuppose a value-empty reality; but, he argues, there is already Being overflowing with Goodness (Floridi 2013, 324). More generally, Floridi moves from an "is" (reality is informational) to an "ought" (his information ethics based on his metaphysics). But all this contradicts his claim about keeping facts and norms apart.

Ninth, this and similar claims are sometimes interpreted as entailing a *religious* perspective. Now whether or not this is problematic depends on whether or not one thinks religion in general is problematic and whether or not one believes that this particular religious perspective is problematic. Floridi admits that his approach can be seen as spiritual or is at least compatible with religions; he says, for instance, that "IE is based on an immanent, if perhaps rather spiritual, philosophy" (Floridi 2013, 329). If this is the case, what exactly does this immanent spirituality entail, and does this spiritual orientation contradict the more naturalist dimension of his philosophy or not? At the least, more needs to be said about this.

Finally, the question must be raised if the philosophy of information as proposed by Floridi can serve as a philosophy of *technology*. On the one hand, technologies clearly play an important role in his metaphysics of information: they re-ontologize the world and help to bring about the informationalization of the world. Furthermore, Floridi has made *applications* of this theory to technologies in many contexts. On the other hand, the *scope* of his approach is much wider than a philosophy of technology: it is meant to be a new, separate branch of philosophy (Floridi 2011, 1). His project is not about philosophy of technology as such; it is, after all, a philosophy of information. Hence, technology is only conceptualized in terms of information. Is this the best way of conceptualizing technology? Should it be the only way? At the very least, it must be admitted that there are many different ways of conceptualizing technology and that technology is a multifaceted phenomenon. Floridi may acknowledge this, but the framework he sketches for a philosophy of information suggests at least that these other conceptualizations and approaches are a lot less relevant, if not irrelevant. Even if one were sympathetic to considering technology from the angle of information, one could object that his philosophy and ethics of information is a helpful but only *one* perspective, next to others, which may be equally helpful. It is not clear how **pluralist** Floridi is when it comes to his approach. As is often the case with theory development, there is a danger of imperialism and even "colonialism" in terms of approach: other perspectives are either rejected or (and this is the colonialism) reinterpreted in one's own terms (i.e., information) without leaving conceptual space for other approaches. For instance, in Floridi's conceptual universe (imperium?), privacy can then only be discussed in terms of a problem with information; other approaches disappear from view. As I already suggested, perhaps it is his metaphysical and foundationalist approach that creates this danger: in a foundationalist framework, there seems to be no room for pluralism. (Now one may object that a pluralist approach involves the danger of relativism. But is a pluralist approach necessarily relativist? Are some approaches better than others, and how can we provide proof for that? What would such proof consist of? And are some versions of relativism acceptable? I will leave these questions unanswered here; the point is that philosophy of technology, like other subdisciplines in philosophy such as moral philosophy, is confronted with similar philosophical questions with regard to its methods and approaches. Philosophers always discuss a particular topic *and* what philosophy is and how it should be done.)

7.4. Conclusions for Philosophy of Technology

In this chapter, I have presented and critically discussed Luciano Floridi's philosophy and ethics of information. It is good to know something about his philosophy, given the influence it has had during the past decade. However, it is not only my purpose here to offer theory as such; I also wanted to show more about *how* philosophy of technology is being done and how it can be done. In this part of the book, I aim to show how some philosophers start from *technology* to develop their view. Of course Floridi also starts from theory, for instance, from formal methods, modeling, previous theory of information, a metaphysics, and so on. In many ways, his ethics is a kind of "applied philosophy," in particular applied metaphysics. But what really got his philosophical project going are the new technologies and the related sciences that "forced" him to rethink the nature of reality. In his case, it led to the conceptualization of reality as the totality of information and to the claim that new technologies re-ontologize the world: they radically transform our thinking and our reality.

His approach thus presents a particularly strong version of the claim in contemporary philosophy of technology that technologies are more than instruments: the idea that technology reshapes *everything*, transforms all Being and all beings. Furthermore, this chapter has also illustrated that taking seriously technology does not mean that one leaves philosophy or does *only* "applied" philosophy or "applied" ethics," which is no longer concerned with the "core business" of philosophy such as epistemology, metaphysics, etc. On the contrary, it has been shown that one can ask interesting *philosophical* questions and develop an original philosophical approach if one engages with new technological developments.

Beyond Floridi's particular view and approach, then, lies an interesting field of questions that at once (a) are about technology and (b) touch on the perennial questions in philosophy, including metaphysics and moral philosophy. What is the nature of reality, given that there seems to be something like a "digital" sphere? Or is this the wrong name, as Floridi argues? How can we conceptualize our experience of using the internet and related technologies today? Can we do this in ways that do not rely on the decades-long obsession with the term *information*? And given that there are "artificial agents" such as robots, does it make sense to sharply distinguish between humans and non-humans? How morally relevant is the life/non-life distinction? What is life anyway? What is intelligence? What is the human? I will return to some of these questions in chapter 11, where I further discuss how philosophy of technology is connected, and can connect, with other philosophical subdisciplines.

During the critical discussion, it has also become clear that doing philosophy of technology involves discussing questions about approach and method, just like other subdisciplines in philosophy. To the extent that this happens, it suggests that philosophy of technology is becoming a more mature and arguably more vital (sub)discipline. But once again, in this chapter, I wish to draw your attention to the role of technology in the process of reflection and conceptual work. They "force" us to ask again the big perennial philosophical questions, in the sense that they confront us with both theoretical and *practical* challenges. The point is that there is a *need* for asking these questions as we are confronted with intellectually stimulating advances in science *and* with the pervasive influence of the new technologies on our lives. Whatever one may think of Floridi's views and approach, it is hard to disagree with the intuition and experience that technology is thoroughly reshaping our world and us. In the light of these considerations, philosophy of technology should not be reduced to a marginal academic occupation or a leisure-time luxury. It may well have to be part of what we *have* to do, as philosophers and as human beings. Thinking about technology in more thorough and systematic ways than ever before may have to be part of humanity's survival package and coping strategies for the decades to come.

In the next chapters, I further stress this urgency and say more about the challenges raised by new technologies for our thinking and our lives.

REVIEW QUESTIONS

1. Briefly outline Floridi's philosophy of information. What is his metaphysics, and what is the role of technology in his metaphysics?
2. What does Floridi mean by the term "infosphere"?
3. What is does Floridi mean by "onlife"?
4. Briefly outline Floridi's ethics of information, and show how this ethics derives from his metaphysics.
5. What does "mindless morality" mean?
6. What method does Floridi use in his ethics?
7. What is "level of abstraction" as used by Floridi?
8. What is Floridi's view of the human being?
9. Present and discuss at least 3 objections against Floridi's view (e.g., against his metaphysics, ethics, method).

DISCUSSION QUESTIONS

1. How do you respond to Floridi's metaphysics and ethics of information? Argue why you (do not) endorse his views.
2. Is the ultimate nature of reality information? Is it reductivist to say so? And what does it mean for the understanding of technology?
3. Should philosophy of technology adopt a metaphysics at all, or should it reject *any* metaphysical perspective?
4. Should philosophy of technology be humanist or posthumanist? Why?
5. When it comes to our daily experience of the world and of technology, does it still make sense to distinguish between online and offline, according to you? If not, then how would you conceptualize this?
6. Are human beings inforgs? And is it reductivist to say so? Why (not)?
7. What do you think about Floridi's method "level of abstraction"?
8. Should philosophy of technology take inspiration from mathematics and the natural and engineering sciences when it comes to its method(s)? Or are other methods more appropriate?
9. Do current technological developments create an urgent need to think about technology? Does and should our thinking about technology respond to, or even depend on, technological developments? If so, in what way? Why (not)? What role should technology play in conceptualizing technology?
10. Can there be such a thing as a pluralist information ethics?
11. Should philosophers of technology be monist or pluralist when it comes to their approach(es)? (And does the latter imply relativism? If so, are there some forms of relativism that are acceptable?)

RECOMMENDED READING

Capurro, Rafael, and Birger Hjørland. 2003. "The Concept of Information." *Annual Review of Information Science and Technology* 37(1): 343–411.

Ess, Charles. 2006. "Ethical Pluralism and Global Information Ethics." *Ethics and Information Technology* 8(4): 215–226.

Floridi, Luciano. 2013. *The Ethics of Information*. Oxford, UK: Oxford University Press.

KEY TERMS

Artificial agents

Constructionism

Cybernetics

Demiurge

Entropy

Fake news

Fourth revolution

ICTs

Inforgs

Information ethics (IE)

Information technologies

Infosphere

Level of abstraction

Mindless morality

Naturalistic fallacy

Onlife

Phronesis

Pluralism

Prima philosophia

FROM ROBOTICS AND AI TO THINKING ABOUT MORAL STATUS AND HUMAN RELATIONSHIPS

CASE/TECHNOLOGY: Self-Driving Cars

Today many car companies are working on cars that do not need a human driver. Such self-driving cars (also called "autonomous cars") raise ethical questions. For example, if there is a situation in which the car has to choose between saving the life of the driver or saving the life of a pedestrian, what choice should it make and how should it make that choice? Should engineers and computer scientists make "moral machines" that have their own morality? And if so, what kind of morality? And self-driving cars also raise another very practical moral problem: Who is responsible when something goes wrong; for example, when the car runs over a pedestrian? The car company? The people who programmed the car? The driver, who is not really a driver? The pedestrian? As cars are becoming more autonomous, these questions will become urgent.

FIGURE 8.1 Self-driving car

8.1. Introduction

New developments in robotics and artificial intelligence (AI) raise philosophical questions with regard to the moral standing of these machines—or are they more than machines? Think about computers or robots that can win difficult games, can automatically trade or even execute lethal military actions, are able to engage in a conversation with you, can drive you to work, invite you to have sex with them, or can serve as personal assistants or artificial pets in the family. These robots or AI systems already exist, or are expected to be there in the near future. But, from an ethical point of view, do we want them? What if the decisions and actions they take are unethical? Can robots be held responsible? Can machines have a morality? And what if *our* interaction with them is unethical? What kind of ethics do we need to interact with them?

One way to order and select some of the questions is to use the moral agency versus moral patiency distinction (see, e.g., Floridi 2013, 135–136): one can consider the capacities of an entity to act and comport morally toward other entities, and one can consider the capacity of the entity to be the object of such moral acts or comportments. In so-called **machine ethics**, ethics of robotics, ethics of AI, and related fields, there are hence at least two kinds of philosophical questions with regard to the status of more autonomous intelligent and/ or human-like machines such as this: we can consider these machines (or any entity for that matter) as moral agents and as moral patients, and for each discuss their status.

On the one hand, as machines become smarter and more autonomous, they become capable of taking over tasks usually done by humans, such as driving a car (self-driving cars) or using a weapon to kill (autonomous lethal weapons). But should we delegate these tasks to them, given that they seem to lack full moral agency? Or is this a bias against machines? Can they have **moral agency**? Are our criteria of moral agency too human-like? Can these machines be developed with a built-in morality—a "**machine morality**"—or is this impossible? What does "machine morality" mean? Is it a morality similar to that of humans, or are there non-human kinds of morality? What does *morality* mean? These are questions regarding the moral agency of machines.

On the other hand, there are questions regarding **moral patiency**. As machines become more lifelike, often human-like or animal-like in their appearance and behavior, do we do anything wrong when we "mistreat" them, "abuse" them? Do they have a moral status at all, and if so, which one? For example, is it OK to kick a robot? Is it fine to do whatever one wants with a sex robot? Are they "mere machines" or are they more machines? And even if we would decide that they deserve some moral consideration, should we give them rights? And if so, under what conditions or according to what criteria? How do we decide on *moral* *status* anyway? Why do humans have (a high) moral status? How can our (mis) treatment of animals be justified, if at all?

The next sections offer an overview of some of the questions and answers in discussions about moral agency and moral patiency of machines. This will include approaches by David Gunkel and myself that try to change the very question(s) regarding moral status—whether that is the status of moral agency or moral patiency. In the last section, I will add a discussion about gendered robots and human relationships. Related to the moral agency and patiency issues are also ethical questions such as the following: Should robots be gendered? In what ways can this be problematic? Are relationships with machines acceptable and good? Is prostitution with robots morally better or worse than prostitution with humans? What is prostitution anyway: Is it a kind of labor? Is a sex robot different from (other) sex toys, morally speaking? Sex robots invite feminist and emancipatory concerns and make us think about the ethics of human relationships.

Like chapter 7, this chapter shows that new *technological* developments stimulate philosophical thinking, and that this is not only relevant to thinking about these specific technologies—robots and AI—but is also interesting and valuable as a *philosophical* exercise, since the discussion makes us rethink perennial philosophical questions regarding moral agency and patiency and concerning the ethics of human–human relationships. Again, the point is that philosophy of technology is always more than just thinking about technology; and that, paradoxically, this wider relevance is best exemplified by work that focuses on technology and starts from technology.

8.2. Moral Machines? The Discussion about Moral Agency

If self-driving cars, autonomous lethal weapons, financial algorithms, algorithms used in courtrooms, but also humanoid robots, take over tasks from humans, they invite the question of whether robots can and should be moral agents. This is

CASE/TECHNOLOGY:
Biased Algorithms

Some algorithms are used to make decisions, including, for example, legal decisions or decisions about job applications. Consider the following case. In 2013, a man in Wisconsin was denied probation by a judge who cited his risk of recidivism. That risk was predicted by a computer program (Correctional Offender Management Profiling for Alternative Sanctions [COMPAS]), used across the United States to forecast which criminals are likely to reoffend (for more about the case, see https://www.nytimes.com/2017/10/26/opinion/algorithm-compas-sentencing-bias.html). To what extent do we want to let algorithms decide such important things? What if we don't even know how the algorithm works, as was the case here? And what if the algorithm is biased? According to nonprofit news organization ProPublica, COMPAS was biased against black people: "black defendants were far more likely than white defendants to be incorrectly judged to be at a higher risk of recidivism, while white defendants were more likely than black defendants to be incorrectly flagged as low risk" (see https://www.propublica.org/article/how-we-analyzed-the-compas-recidivism-algorithm). Or consider the case of job applications: what if the algorithm is biased against women or older people? Of course humans also discriminate. Is it then the fault of the algorithm, or is the real problem the biases that are present in society? And is discrimination always unjustified? Is it avoidable at all? If not, then which discriminations are justified? Which should be avoided? And what does this imply for using algorithms in decision-making?

already a first distinction, between "can" and "should," which, similar to the question regarding robot rights (Gunkel 2018), can help us to order the discussion. In terms of positions, various combinations of "can" and "should" are possible. A common position is that regardless of whether robots *can* be moral agents, they *should* not be moral agents. Humans, and humans only, should make moral decisions. Robots should not be moral agents. The problem with this position, however, is that *if* not only robots but more generally machines do certain tasks autonomously, and if in practice machines already do morally relevant things, then we need to at least think of giving them *some* kind of "machine morality." Positions differ widely, however, on what such machine morality means. At least the following positions are possible and have been defended:

1. Machines can be full moral agents in the same way as humans are full moral agents.
2. Machines cannot be full moral agents, but we can give them a limited kind of morality or "functional" morality.
3. Machines can be full moral agents, but not in the same way as humans are full moral agents.
4. Machines can never be moral agents at all.

The first position claims that we can build artificial agents that are moral agents in the same way as humans are. The assumption is that we can know what human morality is, formalize it, and build it into the machine; or that we can build an artificial system that will itself learn human morality. This position often goes together with the idea that morality is a matter of rule following. An example is the so-called Laws of Robotics, introduced in Isaac Asimov's science fiction stories and often referred to in discussions about machine morality:

> First Law: A robot may not injure a human being or, through inaction, allow a human being to come to harm.
> Second Law: A robot must obey any orders given to it by human beings, except where such orders would conflict with the First Law.
> Third Law: A robot must protect its own existence as long as such protection does not conflict with the First or Second Law. (Asimov 1942)

In the stories, the worry was mainly that robots would turn against their creators or against humans in general. Today, this is still a concern in the public debate about robotics and AI. But there are also more practical and urgent ethical problems, which—like Asimov's stories—also show the difficulty of creating rules and applying them to specific situations. For example, in the case of a self-driving car, the issue is not whether the car turns against you as such but rather how it would deal with dilemmas such as this: If the rule is "a robot may not injure a human being," should the car avoid a child crossing the road and drive into a wall, killing the driver, or rather kill the child? This is an example of what philosophers call **trolley dilemma** issues, named after thought experiments that present a choice between options that all have morally bad consequences. In the original version, a trolley barrels down a railway track and you can choose between doing nothing and letting the trolley kill five people tied to the track, or

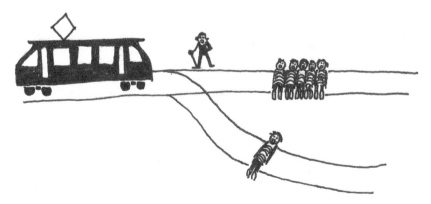

FIGURE 8.2 A trolley dilemma.
Source: Drawing courtesy of Christina Ernst.

pulling a lever and send the trolley to another track on which one person is tied (in one version: your child). What if the protagonist of this story is a robot or an AI? What kind of moral rules and artificial intelligence can help here? What would a human do? What should a human do?

In contemporary robotics, there are researchers who try to build moral principles and moral reasoning into robots to deal with ethical problems. Often these problems are framed in terms of dilemmas. While they admit that morality cannot be reduced to a couple of simple rules, and that not all ethicists agree on everything, they claim that *in principle*, it is possible to give machines a human kind of morality. An example of this approach is work by Michael and Susan Anderson (Anderson and Anderson 2011). They think that it is the ultimate aim of machine ethics to create what James Moor called "explicit ethical agents" (Moor 2006): perhaps not full ethical agents in the metaphysical sense (they lack certain ontological features humans have, such as consciousness), but they come close enough to how humans make ethical decisions. They assume that "ethics can be made computable" (Anderson and Anderson 2011, 9): we can give machines a set of principles. And given that for them ethics is a matter of rationality, Anderson and Anderson note that machines may even be superior when it comes to ethics, since human beings often "get carried away by their emotions" (9).

There are, however, severe problems with this kind of approach. The issue is not only that principles and laws often conflict and create difficult dilemmas, as Asimov's stories show (see, e.g., Clark 2011) and as trolley dilemma situations show. The main objection is that its assumptions about ethics and morality are fundamentally flawed. Ethics cannot and should not be reduced to following rules and principles and is not entirely a matter of rationality but also involves emotions and should involve emotions. The point is that even if a *human* being would be that kind of moral agent, she or he would not be a full moral agent at all. An example of this kind of objection can be found in Coeckelbergh (2010a): taking into account work that sees emotions as indispensable for moral judgment, I argue that when it comes to ethics, such rule-following robots would be "psychopathic" robots, which would be dangerous since they would lack full moral agency.

For these reasons, one could opt for the second position, which tries to build ethical considerations into machines but does not claim that this amounts to full moral agency (Moor's so-called implicit ethical agents). This is a direction Wallach and Allen (2009) have taken. They have argued that whereas artificial systems with "complete human moral capacities may perhaps remain forever in the realm of science fiction," more limited systems with "some capacity to evaluate the ethical ramifications of their actions" will soon be built (Wallach and Allen 2009, 8). They call this **functional morality**: the machines "have the capacity for assessing and responding to moral challenges" (9) and some ethical sensitivity, but they are not full moral agents. The authors give the example of autopilots, which have significant autonomy but still little ethical sensitivity (26); but also ethical decision support systems, which have limited autonomy but some degree of ethical sensitivity. Wallach and Allen give a system built by Anderson and Anderson as an example: there is some "rudimentary moral reasoning" (Wallach and Allen 2009, 27). The point is that it is still better to have systems like this than no built-in ethics at all. We need to build systems that can behave as ethically as possible. Another, related view is that if the human social and moral life depends on appearances (we do not know the real intentions of others, and we do not even know for sure if they have the necessary ontological proper-ties), then perhaps it is sufficient that a machine acts *as if* it is moral and even as if it has emotions; this may be sufficient to draw robots into our moral and social world (Coeckelbergh 2010a). It may be questioned, however, if machines will ever be able to create these appearances in a totally convincing and sustainable way.

However, these positions still hold on to the idea that, ideally, morality needs to be human-like and start from human morality. An alternative response to the problem with regard to the gap between machine moral agency and human moral agency is to argue that one can, and should, use different criteria for moral agency. Floridi and Sanders (2004) have argued that moral agents do not neces-sarily have to exhibit free will, mental states, or responsibility: they focus on what they call a "mindless morality." Whether an entity is an agent depends on the level of abstraction we set; for agency, we need to choose a level of abstraction in which there is sufficient interactivity, autonomy, and adaptability. For most entities there is no level of abstraction at which they can be considered an agent. But *if* we have a sufficiently interactive, autonomous, and adaptive entity, in other words an agent, then moral agency depends on whether the agent is capable of morally qualifiable action. For example, according to this approach, a dog can be an agent playing a key role in a moral situation such as search and rescue and is therefore a moral agent, even if it is not morally responsible. And a web bot can also be a moral agent if it correctly filters out many messages. Ethics, Floridi and Sanders argue, lies not exclusively within the human domain. They thus propose to analyze the behavior of entities in what they claim to be a non-anthropocentric way, and extend the class of agents and moral agents (Floridi and Sanders 2004).

Building on this account, John Sullins (2006) has argued that it is not nec-essary for robots to have personhood to qualify as moral agents. He sees three requirements for (full) moral agency and even moral responsibility:

1. Autonomy: the robot is significantly autonomous from any programmers or operators.
2. Intention: one can analyze or explain the robot's behavior only by ascrib-ing some predisposition or "intention" to do good or harm.
3. Responsibility: the robot behaves in a way that shows an understanding of responsibility to some other moral agent.

Sullins gives the example of a robot used in elderly care: if the machine carries out the same duties as a human nurse, is autonomous, behaves in an intentional way, and understands "its role in the responsibility of the health care system that it is operating in has towards the patient under its direct care," then that machine is a full moral agent (Sullins 2006, 29). In contrast to Floridi and Sanders (2004), Sullins assumes that moral agency and moral responsibility go hand in hand. And like Floridi and Sanders, the focus is on behavior of the entity, not on its mental states.

Against this approach, it could be argued that these arguments confuse moral *relevance* of actions with moral agency. It is one thing to recognize that such animals and robots do morally relevant things; it is another to say that they therefore have moral agency, which—so this argument goes—only persons or humans can have. For example, Deborah Johnson (2006) has argued that computer systems can be moral entities but not moral agents. They are produced and used by humans; and while they have intentionality, this intentionality is always linked to those of humans, and they do not have moral agency of their own. That is impossible since they do not have mental states; and if they did, they do not have "intendings" to act (Johnson 2006, 195), which arise from an agent's freedom. Computer systems like robots are components in human moral action. Floridi and Sullins could reply then that this definition of moral agency is too anthropocentric, that such a metaphysical freedom is not needed for moral agency, or that its conditions are already fulfilled in the relevant cases of artificial agents such as the rescue dogs: and that the objection confuses moral status with personhood or being a member of the human species. Ultimately, this debate seems to depend on whether one believes that moral agency is intrinsically connected to personhood or humanness.

8.3. The Discussion about Moral Patiency

Robots, or any other entity for that matter, cannot only be seen as (potentially) doing something in a moral situation (they can be the *agent*); they can also be on the receiving end of such an action: they can be the *patient*. How should we morally respond to robots? Do they deserve our moral consideration, especially those that interact with us in a human-like way? Should we perhaps even give rights to robots? These questions are especially relevant with regard to so-called social robotics, which aims at building "social" and interactive robots that live and work with humans in everyday contexts such as the household or the workplace. Such robots are intentionally designed to act in a human-like way such that "interacting with it is like interacting with another person" (Breazeal 2002, 1). The questions may also be relevant in cases where the robot looks like a human or an animal.

FIGURE 8.3 Woman and robot and binary code

The starting point of this kind of investigation is the perhaps puzzling fact that many people respond to robots in ways that go beyond seeing the robot as a mere machine. They empathize with the robot, care about the robot, and care for the robot. This is already the case for robotic vacuum cleaners, and even more for humanoid robots or zoomorphic robots (robots that look like animals). Consider, for instance, the case of a robot dog called "Spot" that was kicked by its designers to test its capabilities to stabilize itself (see http://edition.cnn.com/2015/02/13/tech/spot-robot-dog-google/index.html). Some people reacted with moral disapproval or even indignation, exclaiming phrases such as "Poor Spot!"; "Seriously Boston Dynamics stop kicking those poor robots what did they ever do to you?"; "Kicking a dog, even a robot dog, just seems wrong"; etc. Another case is HitchBOT (see http://mir1.hitchbot.me/), a hitchhiking robot that was vandalized and evoked similar reactions. Apparently some robots are sometimes perceived as more than a machine.

This has also been confirmed by empirical psychological research, for example, on empathy with robots. Suzuki et al. (2015) have shown that in response to pictures of painful situations involving human hands and robot hands that were threatened to be cut with a knife, people empathized also with the (humanoid) robots. And in experiments involving the "torture" of robots, Kate Darling has also shown that under certain conditions (e.g., people were first told a story that personalized the robots), people hesitate to smash robots (Darling et al. 2015). Hence, it seems that we treat at least some robots in some situations different from technological objects such as toasters; there is a notable difference in how we interact with them (Darling 2012).

FIGURE 8.4 HitchBOT at the bar

How can we understand these intuitions and responses? How can we address this issue from a philosophical perspective? One way to start doing this is to ask the question concerning moral standing. There are again a number of positions available:

1. Robots have no moral standing. Our intuitions and responses that suggest the robot is more than a thing are entirely wrong; robots are just machines, and we do not owe any moral consideration to them.
2. Robots have a weak form of moral standing: we do not have direct duties to robots but indirect duties (Kantian argument), or we should treat robots well if we want to be virtuous (virtue ethics argument; indirect arguments for moral standing).
3. Strong version: (Current) robots have moral standing, including perhaps rights—or at least, in principle (and maybe in the future) they *can* have moral standing, provided that certain conditions are fulfilled.
4. We are asking the wrong kind of questions and should approach the question of moral patiency differently and more critically.

The first position is that it is wrong or even *nonsensical* to even consider ascribing any moral standing to machines. They are things, not people. No matter how automated and interactive they may be (Johnson 2006, 197), they are tools. Or as Bryson has argued, robots are property, and we are not obligated by them (Bryson 2016, 6). They are not moral patients in any sense. The difference with the outright rejection of even the possibility of moral patiency, however, is that Bryson leaves open the possibility that in the future, robots may be created that meet requirements for having moral standing as a moral patient. In this sense, she affirms the third position, but the threshold is high—far too high for contemporary robots. This response is similar to the position with regard to moral agency that says that *if* robots were to have mental states, consciousness, etc., then we would have to grant them moral standing as moral agents; but current robots have none of that.

The difficulty with this position is that it neither explains nor justifies moral intuitions that there may be something wrong with, say, torturing a robot. An attempt to justify this intuition is offered by Kantian and virtue ethics arguments. While there is nothing wrong with kicking a robot from a deontological point of view (there is no moral law that forbids this) or from a consequentialist point of view (there is no pain or suffering, and more generally no harm, on the part of the machine), Kantian ethics and virtue ethics give us a different picture. They offer us "indirect" arguments for moral standing (Coeckelbergh 2010b).

Let us start with Kant's argument about indirect duties to animals. Kant held that humans are "altogether different in rank and dignity from things, such as irrational animals, with which one may deal and dispose at one's discretion" (Kant 2012, 127). Hence we do not have duties toward them. But, Kant argued, we have *indirect* duties since mistreating them makes us unkind and hard toward humans:

> So if a man has his dog shot, because it can no longer earn a living for him, he is by no means in breach of any duty to the dog, since the latter is incapable of judgment, but he thereby damages the kindly and humane qualities in himself, which he ought to exercise in virtue of his duties to mankind . . . for a person who already displays such cruelty to animals is also no less hardened towards men. (Kant 1997, 212)

Now this argument can and has been applied to robots. As Darling has argued, its logic extends to robotic companions (Darling 2012): if we treat robots in "inhumane" ways, we become inhumane persons. In similar ways, a virtue ethics argument may be constructed (as I have done in my talks on this topic). According to this argument, mistreating a robot is not morally wrong because of the robot being harmed but because doing so repeatedly and habitually shapes the wrong kind of moral character. The problem then is not a violation of duty or morally bad consequences for the robot but a problem of human character and virtue. Thus, treating robots well is a virtue; not doing so is a vice.

The problem with this approach, however, is that the full load of moral concern is on the humans, which those who defend at least some moral standing of robots find objectionable. But, with regard to the third position(s), what could be arguments for giving them moral standing as patients? There are at least three possibilities:

1. Traditional arguments for moral standing.
2. Non-anthropocentric argument (e.g., Floridi).
3. Social-relational arguments.

Traditional arguments for moral patiency require that entities have sentience, personhood, consciousness, the ability to suffer, or other features we usually associate with humans as moral patients. Someone using this kind of argument could argue that today's robots do not meet the criteria, but that in principle, *if* a robot were to have them, we would have to give them (high) moral standing, similar to the moral standing we give to humans. A problem with this argument is that we can never be entirely sure if and what an entity experiences. This is already a problem with regard to the moral standing of animals; it would also be a problem in case we find ourselves in doubt about a machine. For example, who knows what goes on "in the head" of a fish? A similar skeptical response may be used for the case of a highly intelligent machine in the future. Even the human case is not straightforward. Do we really know what is "in the head" of another person? Moreover, it is not entirely clear what sentience, consciousness, etc., is—if a unified concept makes sense at all. As Gunkel (2018) notes, philosophers and scientists tend to disagree on these questions. Another problem is that this approach does not seem to help with thinking about current robots. It only focuses on hypothetical machines in the future—it is highly doubtful if such machines can be developed at all (personally I'm very skeptical about this). Finally, this argument is entirely anthropocentric: it takes human features as the only sufficient condition(s) for moral standing.

In response, one could construct a non-anthropocentric argument with a lower threshold and non-anthropocentric criteria that *can* be measured such as autonomy and interactivity—similar to Floridi and Sanders's (2004) argument about moral agency. Or, like some approaches in animal ethics, one could give some *degree* of moral patiency to machines. Maybe fish have a lower moral standing than humans, but that does not mean they have no moral standing as moral patients whatsoever. Similarly, one could argue that now or in the future we may recognize some robots as having a specific degree of moral patiency, which is likely to be lower than that of humans. However, to support this argument, one would have to then identify suitable criteria for this, criteria that do not rely on sentience and that are still sufficient to give some degree of moral patiency status. But it is difficult to imagine such criteria.

An entirely different way of approaching the issue concerning moral patiency (and moral agency), however, is to deconstruct and change the question(ing) of moral standing itself.

8.4. Changing the Question: Toward More Relational Thinking

In my work on moral status (Coeckelbergh 2010a, 2010b, 2011a, 2011b, 2012, 2014), in particular but not exclusively the moral status of robots, I have deconstructed the question regarding moral status and proposed a more social, relational, phenomenological, and critical approach.

The starting point of my inquiries was the observation and intuition that most philosophical and scientific arguments about moral status do not sufficiently take seriously the experience and *phenomenology* of human–robot interactions and imaginations. I have argued that when it comes to that phenomenology, there is no such thing as a robot-in-itself (an object-in-itself) that can be defined independently from the observer or user (subject-in-itself), but rather a process in which object, subject, and indeed the "moral standing" or "moral status" of the robot are all outcomes—*emerge* from the process, relation, and interaction—rather than being given beforehand. Discussions in robot ethics still seem to assume an outdated, (early) modern epistemology and metaphysics. Inspired by the phenomenological tradition and other 20th-century philosophy, I have tried to bring in a more relational and less dualist way of thinking. Moreover, the usual philosophical arguments and scientific work generally neglect the intrinsically *social-*relational dimension (Coeckelbergh 2010b): the question regarding moral status is reduced to a psychological phenomenon (e.g., anthropomorphism; see again Darling 2017) or is discussed by philosophers and scientists in a rather abstract and detached way, their method excluding concrete humans and non-humans, the concrete relation between humans and non-humans, and indeed the (potential) moral patients themselves. Furthermore, moral standing and moral status are often discussed as if critical philosophy from Kant until today, including 20th-century philosophy of language, does not exist. In response, I changed the question to one concerning moral status *ascription* and its conditions of possibility, including language, social relations, and technology. I have argued that moral status is not independent from our use of language, our already existing social relations and encounters, and the technologies we use—all of which shape our thinking about the moral standing and moral patiency of "robots" and other entities, including our often problematic categorizations and generalizations such as "robot" and "animal." This enabled a more critical perspective on moral status, indeed a critique of moral status ascription *itself.* I have argued that the very project of determining moral standing of entities is problematic (Coeckelbergh 2012).

Let me give a brief summary of my main argument. I started by looking at the method used by those thinking about moral standing. Usually, philosophers use the following procedure: first, the question regarding the moral status of a particular entity is asked (and it is assumed that this is the question to ask and that there is nothing wrong with asking the question in this way); then the ontological status of the entity is determined; and finally, the moral status is inferred from this ontological status. The reasoning of what I have called the "properties approach" (Coeckelbergh 2012) goes as follows:

1. All entities of type A with properties P, Q, R, . . . have moral standing S.
2. Entity X is of type A (and has properties P, Q, R, . . .).
3. Therefore, entity X has moral standing S.

For example,

- All conscious entities have moral rights.
- This entity is conscious.
- Therefore, this entity has moral rights.

Or in the negative,

- All conscious entities have moral rights.
- This entity (e.g., this robot) is not conscious.
- Therefore, this entity (this robot) has no moral rights.

For example, sentience is taken to be a prerequisite for rights, a robot is said to lack sentience, thus it is concluded that it cannot have moral rights. However, this reasoning raises some epistemological problems. Starting with the first premise, how can we be sure that all entities of a particular type have a particular kind of moral status? The history of morals shows that we were often mistaken about this, for example, in the case of animals. Moreover, with regard to the second premise, and as I already noted previously, how can we be sure that a particular entity has the morally relevant property in question? We cannot "look into the head" of an animal, we cannot really know what it experiences. This is a problem, at least from a Cartesian, modern perspective. A deeper problem, however, is with *the procedure as such*. It creates distance from the concrete entity and relation to that entity. By performing a kind of moral-scientific dissection on the entity to reveal its ontological and moral properties, we (moral reasoners, moral philosophers, observers and commentators) distance ourselves from the entity. We detach ourselves from the entity, from our relation to that entity, and from the situation. We also proceed as if the entity can be defined in itself, independently of our thinking about the entity, the language we use to talk about the entity, and our current and/or previous experiences with the entity, the relevant encounters, situations, interactions, and narratives. We reason as if our reasoning itself is not shaped by our relational experience. We think of ourselves as isolated from that relation and from the entity in question. But our subjectivity is constituted by it, and the object is also shaped by the subject. What does this mean?

Consider robots again. If I have a personal opinion about the moral status of robots, or even if I construct *philosophical arguments* about them, then this opinion is shaped by my experience of particular robots. It is also shaped by a language that uses the lump category "robots" and does not differentiate between different kinds of robots. If I "meet" a robot, then this language of "meeting" already suggests human-like status, or at least a "social" status. If we use an "it" to speak "about" a robot or a "you" to "address" "it" ("her"? "him"?), then this language shapes the status of the robot; that status depends not only on what the robot technically "is" but is also linguistically constructed in the sense that our relation to it is always mediated by language (Coeckelbergh 2011b). In experiments like the ones Darling et al. (2015) conducted, moral status is also a matter of ascription and construction; that is, the status depends on, and is shaped by, how people talk about the robots. And how the robots were treated depends on that talking/thinking and on what kind of narratives were created before the encounter with the robot. For example, for your behavior toward robots, it matters if you are first told a personal friendship narrative or a terminator narrative about robots. And scientists who build the robots may have had different experiences in different situations. There are already relations and experiences before and while we ascribe moral status, and this influences the status. The relations and experiences come first and already give us knowledge of other entities before there is a "moral standing" procedure or tribunal, and indeed before there is a Cartesian procedure of doubt or so-called **problem of other minds** (Coeckelbergh 2014, 72).

This perspective is compatible with Gunkel's attempt to think "otherwise" (Gunkel 2012; Coeckelbergh and Gunkel 2014; Gunkel 2018), which also changes the question and, with its other-directed approach, gives a more social twist to it. As Ihde already argued, robots may appear to humans as quasi-others (Coeckelbergh 2011a). What would it mean to see them as others at all? Gunkel has used Levinas (1969) to say more about **alterity** and its implications for thinking about moral standing. Instead of assuming that we have to start from ontology and then move to ethics, as the procedure I criticized does, Levinas argued that ethics precedes ontology. We are first obliged to respond to the other. There is first the encounter and interaction with others, there is first the situated other; then we respond. To extend rights or moral standing to another entity, then, is not the right kind of moral gesture. Following Levinas (1969), we have to start from the other, not from ourselves (Gunkel 2018). Based on this *otherwise* thinking,

Gunkel sees robots also as others (in contrast to Levinas, who only considered humans as others), others to which/whom we have to respond. I write "which/whom" since language is important here. Gunkel and I have used Derrida to say more about this. For example, when making the difference between "who" is part of the moral community and "what" remains excluded, words are part of the act of inclusion/exclusion; they are not morally neutral (Coeckelbergh and Gunkel 2014). Hence, deciding and thinking about our moral language means deciding and thinking about moral standing itself.

IN FOCUS:
Emmanuel Levinas

Emmanuel Levinas was an important 20th-century philosopher. He was born in Lithuania and lived in France for most of his life. He is known for his view that ethics, not ontology, is primary and that this is the ethics of the "Other": in the encounter with the Other, the Other reveals himself in his alterity, and the face of the Other makes a demand on us. I am infinitely responsible to the other. His best-known book is *Totality and Infinity* ([1961] 1969). During World War II, he was a prisoner of war in Germany.

FIGURE 8.5 Emmanuel Levinas

In response to Gunkel, however, one may ask if a relational approach necessarily needs to be other-directed in the sense of referring to the (potential) alterity of the robot, or if we can also (or instead?) construe a relational kind of virtue ethics, which is more open to relations with non-humans than traditional Aristotelian virtue ethics and does not nail down the status of an entity beforehand, but which has a less dualist view. Instead of *either* starting from self and then going to the other *or* starting from the other and then going to the self, could we imagine an ethics that starts from the *relation* between self and other and defines virtue not in terms of character of the self but in terms of the shaping of that relation? Would that be a truly relational ethics, which even changes the question of Gunkel's alterity thinking? This remains to be further developed and discussed.

For researchers in the field of social robotics, the approach proposed implies that to address the problem of moral status, one should study how subject and object are entangled in various ways in the phenomenology and hermeneutics of moral status ascription and other activities and performances. For normative thinking about moral status, the approach means that it should be acknowledged that the "ought" depends on the "is," at least in the sense that our reasoning about moral standing is always shaped by previous and current relational experience. It also means that the exercise of ascribing moral status itself should be questioned; and that, at the very least, we should be more cautious and critical about how we think about robots, how we talk about robots and treat robots, rather than assuming and fixing their moral status beforehand (i.e., before experience) or in the abstract, in a dogmatic way. It means that instead of hurrying to the tribunal of moral status and pronouncing our moral verdict on the entity, one should first study and better understand the structure and grammar of how we think about moral status. This requires the epistemic virtue of patience and self-critical reflection. Moreover, if language plays such an important role in the construction and emergence of "moral status" or "moral standing"—indeed, in the construction, production, and emergence of "moral patients"—then we'd better use and integrate critical thinking about language in thinking about technology (e.g., Coeckelbergh 2017; see also chapter 11). What robots "are" and how we should treat them depends on how we talk and write about them: as individuals, but also as participants in a practice, a society, and a culture. Moral standing is part of how "we" do things—with "we" defined in various ways—that is, it is part of what Wittgenstein called a form of life (Coeckelbergh 2017). Our moral stance with regard to robots depends on larger patterns in our culture that encourage certain ways of interpretation and action rather than others (Coeckelbergh 2014, 73). Making normative claims about the moral status of robots may well be necessary in practice. But if we are keen to change the game, we'd better first understand it.

To conclude, by paying more attention to the phenomenology of how we perceive robots and interact with them (Coeckelbergh 2010a, 2011a), but also by studying this in a way that brings in the social, this relational approach may enable us to better understand our intuitions about, and behavior toward, robots. Hopefully, as a critical, non-dogmatic approach it will also help us to develop more adequate normative positions and make better decisions, enabling a critical stance toward our own thinking and perhaps also more respect for, and at the same time a more critical attitude toward, the thinking of others. For example, it may help to better understand where someone else's thinking may come from.

Moral standing, then, is not only about robots or animals as such, but also about humans—not only about *them* but also about *us*. And it is not only a philosophical but also a social-relational and political question.

This also becomes clear when we consider ethical questions regarding sex robots.

8.5. The Debate about Sex Robots and Human Relationships: Feminist (or Egalitarian) Questions

The development of human-like robots raises ethical concerns that link to gender issues. For example, is it ethically acceptable to design cleaning robots in the shape of a woman? Is the creation of humanoid robots a male obsession? And

---

CASE/TECHNOLOGY:
Sex Robots

Sex robots are human-looking (often but not exclusively female-looking) animated dolls used for sex. They mimic human movements, and some also react to human touch and movements and talk. As their appearance gets more realistic, and with the development of artificial intelligence, their range of capacities increases. Like other so-called social robots, they especially get better in language and communication. Some inventors of sex robots such as David Levy, claim that you can also have relationships with sex robots and that in the future, men will marry them. An example of a sex robot that is available today is Solana (RealDoll), which makes head movements and facial expressions, can talk, and is claimed to be capable of having "personality" and "moods."

FIGURE 8.6 Sex robots

what does the introduction of social robots at home imply for relationships between men and women (and in families)? In this section, I briefly zoom in on a discussion about one kind of human-like robots—robots used for sex—and one way of framing this issue: sex robots, in particular **robot prostitutes**.

In his book *Love and Sex with Robots* (2007), Levy emphasizes that using technologies for sex is nothing new: people have always been using sex toys, and the line between sophisticated sex dolls and sex robots is thin. In an article on robot prostitutes (2012), Levy also argues that if the purpose of sex robots is for men to achieve orgasm, this aim is not different from the purpose of vibrators for women (227). And as Sullins (2012) has argued, "since using a sex doll with only limited mechatronics and low level AI is just a very elaborate act of masturbation, the ethics of their use will depend on the ethics of self-gratification" (401). Levy (2012) also notes that (female) partners may not necessarily be upset by men using a sex robot: it may be seen as a form of masturbation, as a way of improving love-making skills, or as introducing a third participant in a threesome—it all depends on "the sexual ethics of the relationship itself" (228). And in response to those who see human prostitution as degrading, it may be argued that sex robots should be welcomed since they may liberate women from having to do this kind of work.

Against this positive view, there are also counterarguments. Many of these objections assume that there needs to be a link between sex and a relationship: an erotic relationship and/or a love relationship. An erotic relationship or a love relationship involve more than what can be achieved with sex robots. And even from a less relational, more user-centered perspective, it is doubtful if the latter can truly satisfy its users' physical and emotional needs instead of merely manipulating their users (Sullins 2012, 408). The argument that sex robots are not really capable of creating an erotic relationship is convincing. Sullins writes about the erotic:

> The kind of relationships that are evolving are not philosophically erotic, that is, challenging and compassionate, but rather one-sided affairs overburdened by fleeting passions and the desire to erase everything in the beloved that is not a complete reflection of the lover's preconceived notions of what he or she thinks they want out of a partner. Remember the main lesson Socrates was trying to give us in the Symposium is that we come into a relationship impoverished, only half knowing what we need; we can only find the philosophically erotic through the encounter with the complexity of the beloved, complexity that not only includes passion, but may include a little pain and rejection from which we learn and grow. (Sullins 2012, 208)

Defenders of sex robots could reply, however, that this argument confuses sex with an erotic relationship or with love, and that it is only an argument against "love robots" or "erotic robots" but not against sex robots. But even then, one could try to argue that *good* sex involves more than what interaction with a "sex" robot can do. Moreover, one may wonder if the use of sex robots does not influence the image users have of women and human relationships (see also following). *If*, and to the extent that, users choose sex robots as a *replacement* of a human partner or an alternative for a human-human relationship, then this seems highly problematic because it remains a one-sided, asymmetrical "relationship" and indeed invites the objection that the robot is used as a way to avoid difficult relationships and to have complete control over one's partner. The latter certainly makes a truly erotic relationship impossible and amounts to avoidance of *human relationships as such*—relationships that are always difficult and never enable total control. Note, however, that this is not necessarily an objection against the use of sex robots as a kind of add-on to a human relationship or tool for masturbation; it is an objection against replacement or avoidance of a human partner.

Another, less philosophical and more economic and societal objection against robot *prostitutes* in particular is that, as Levy (2012) acknowledges, robot prostitutes may put human prostitutes out of work, and hence the former may not at all be welcomed by the latter. To the extent that this happens or would happen, sex robots are also problematic, although this problem is then not different from, say, robots used in (other) services such as retail or cleaning.

A further potential objection is the following: those defending robot rights may argue that if sex robots become more advanced, they might have feelings of their own and therefore they should not be abused. This could be linked to one of the views on moral patiency (see section 8.4): current robots do not have rights, but future robots may. Whether or not this argument should be taken seriously depends on one's view of the future of robotics and artificial intelligence. Levy (2007) seems to think that robots will have feelings and that love can be engineered; others may argue that this is science fiction and symptomatic of a dangerous illusion that everything human can be fully understood by science and engineered.

Furthermore, from a feminist (or egalitarian) perspective, it has been claimed that robot prostitution is degrading for women and problematic in other ways, since it projects a problematic image of human relationships and of women (as sex robots, i.e., as things) and promotes morally problematic relationships and practices. For example, Richardson (2016), who heads a campaign against sex robots,[1] has argued that Levy's views and his use of prostitution work as a model for human–robot relations assume a problematic conception of prostitution, invite gendered notions of sexuality, and promote the idea of using a person as a thing. Richardson criticizes the conception of prostitution as something

---

1. The "Campaign Against Sex Robots" argues for a ban against sex robots, especially sex robots and sex dolls in the form of women and girls; see https://campaignagainstsexrobots.org/

positive and as "sexual labour" involving "sex workers"; in other words, that it is framed as a service. She notes that prostitution does not always involve consent, is often connected to violence and human trafficking, and often involves non-adults (Richardson 2016, 290). Moreover, Richardson doubts if sex robots would help to reduce prostitution, noting that the growth of the internet has not done this. She also points out that the use of non-humanlike tools such as vibrators by women is different from purchasing an adult or child for sex since in the latter case, "the subjectivity of the seller of sex is diminished and the subjectivity of the buyer is the only privileged perspective and viewpoint"; and the buyer of sex is at liberty to ignore the feelings of the other person, who is "turned into a thing" (Richardson 2016, 291). Empathy is "'turned-off'" (292). Sex robots seem to promote this way of dealing with others (especially women). Moreover, anthropologically speaking, robots are more than things: they are things to which "human constructs of gender, class, race or sexuality" are transferred (291). Sex robot fantasies, Richardson (2016) argues, are not separate from the real but are rooted in "human relations at work"; humans extend their lifeworlds and their culture and ethics into things such as robots (292) and sex robot fantasies. She concludes that sex robots will further "reinforce relations of power that do not recognise both parties as human subjects" (292).

In response to Richardson (2016), one could argue that prostitution is often done under consent. However, from a critical theory perspective, it may be replied that this ignores the unequal power relationships and that prostitution often involves exploitation and abuse. It is also doubtful if Richardson's claim that prostitution does not involve empathy *at all* is plausible. She seems to assume a too one-dimensional view of the buyer of sex and indeed of the prostitution practice, which is portrayed as being *entirely* devoid of feelings and empathy. One could submit that where humans are involved, feelings and empathy are at least always a *possibility* and are not excluded by definition. That being said, Richardson rightly points to the problematic aspects of prostitution and the problematic assumptions in Levy's all-too-positive and naïve view. And the point that sex robots are not mere tools but invite, promote, and perpetuate all kinds of meanings borrowed from human relationships—including many problematic aspects—is a helpful contribution to the discussion about sex robots. Richardson's approach is also in line with insights in philosophy of technology, including relational thinking and, for example, critical theory perspectives, and is relevant to thinking about robots in general. It shows, for example, why it can be problematic to formulate an argument about robots in terms of "slaves," as Bryson (2010) did: robots and their meanings are always tied to social relations. It directs us to societal questions that go beyond robotics. Finally, it suggests that we need to take seriously science fiction and fantasies, since and at least insofar as they are connected to real societal problems and influence real developments in robotics and elsewhere.

To conclude, the discussion about sex robots invites us to reflect on the ethics of human relationships and encourages doing philosophy of technology in a way that engages with societal problems, including gender issues but also thinking about human relationships. It is not only a discussion about robots, and not even only a philosophical debate about the meaning of sex, the erotic, and love. It is also a discussion about how we should (re)shape human–human relationships and society. Philosophers of technology can contribute to this discussion.

8.6. Humans, Non-Humans, and the More-Than-Human

This chapter shows again how a focus on technology, here social and humanoid robots, not only leads us to asking fundamental and perennial philosophical questions but also encourages us to develop new and original approaches to these questions; for instance, a more relational approach to moral status or an approach to technology that learns from anthropology. It shows that robotics is all about humans, and that technology is also about culture and society. It is also about non-humans, and not only robots but also, for example, animals. And if we consider again Floridi's position, questioning the moral status of robots is all about our relation to the world around us. It leads to *environmental* questions, understood as how we do and should relate to our environment. In the next chapters, I will introduce approaches to philosophy of technology that are more concerned with the non-human or the more-than-human: in chapter 9, the posthuman and the transhuman, then the natural environment and the planet. Again, the starting point will be technological possibilities and technological developments.

REVIEW QUESTIONS

1. Give an example of a case that raises concerns about moral agency.
2. Give an example of a case that raises concerns about moral patiency.
3. What is a moral agent? Can some robots be considered as moral agents, and why? Give an overview of the main positions and arguments in this discussion.
4. What is a moral patient? Can some robots be considered as moral patients, and why? Give an overview of the main positions and arguments in this discussion.
5. What does it mean to take a "relational" perspective on the question regarding moral patiency?
6. What does a virtue perspective imply for thinking about moral patiency?
7. What does a Levinasian perspective imply for thinking about moral patiency?
8. Do sex robots raise questions about human relationships and societal problems? And if so, why?
9. Give an overview of arguments for and against robot prostitutes.

DISCUSSION QUESTIONS

1. Are (some?) robots moral agents, according to you? Why (not)?
2. Do robots have moral status, according to you? Why (not)? What kind of moral status?
3. What do you think about the relational perspective on the question regarding moral patiency, as presented here?
4. Are sex robots morally problematic, according to you? Why (not)?
5. Are robot prostitutes morally problematic, according to you? Why (not)?

RECOMMENDED READING

Coeckelbergh, Mark. 2014. "The Moral Standing of Machines: Towards a Relational and Non-Cartesian Moral Hermeneutics." *Philosophy & Technology* 27(1): 61–77.

Floridi, Luciano, and J. W. Sanders. 2004. "On the Morality of Artificial Agents." *Minds and Machines* 14(3): 349–379.

Gunkel, David. 2018. "The Other Question: Can and Should Robots Have Rights?" *Ethics and Information Technology* 20(2): 87–99.

Levy, David. 2012. "The Ethics of Robot Prostitutes." In *Robot Ethics: The Ethical and Social Implications of Robotics*, edited by Patrick Lin, Keith Abney, and George A. Bekey, 223–232. Cambridge, MA: MIT Press.

Richardson, Kathleen. 2016. "The Asymmetrical 'Relationship': Parallels between Prostitution and the Development of Sex Robots." *ACM SIGCAS Computers and Society—Special Issue on Ethicomp* 45(3): 290–293.

Wallach, Wendell, and Colin Allen. 2009. *Moral Machines: Teaching Robots Right from Wrong.* Oxford, UK: Oxford University Press.

KEY TERMS

Alterity	Moral agency	Trolley dilemma (or trolley problem)
Functional morality	Moral patiency	
Machine ethics	Problem of other minds	
Machine morality	Robot prostitutes	

9 FROM GENETIC ENGINEERING AND CYBORGS TO TRANSHUMANISM AND POSTHUMANISM

CASE/TECHNOLOGY:
Gene Editing

Gene editing or genome editing is a type of genetic engineering that can modify the DNA sequence (genotype) of an organism. Common methods use engineered nucleases ("molecular scissors") to insert, delete, change, or replace DNA in the genome of a living organism. A known gene editing tool is CRISPR-Cas9, which uses an enzyme (Cas9) and a piece of RNA (gRNA) to introduce a mutation (change) into the DNA. The RNA finds the specific targeted sequence; Cas9 makes a cut. The cut is then repaired by the cell, which introduces a mutation. Transhumanists see gene editing as a technology for human enhancement, for example, to create children who are healthier or have other desired features (so-called designer babies). Gene editing is controversial, for example, because if it is used for human enhancement, it may have unintended consequences for the children and their future children (which perhaps we do not understand yet); or because it may be used by so-called biohackers or bioterrorists to modify organisms such as bugs.

FIGURE 9.1 Scientist with test tube and DNA molecule

9.1. Introduction

In the history of philosophy, there have always been discussions about what the human is. Often these discussions were framed as being about the nature or essence of the human. But whatever answer was given, there was more or less a consensus that the human, especially the human body, was unchangeable. Those who argued for educating human minds assumed that there was a human nature or essence, which may then be expressed or perfected, but would not itself alter. And even those who argued that human beings are not created but the outcome of evolution assumed that, at this moment in time, we have to take that body-as-evolved as given and fixed. Until today, it was assumed that we cannot change, or at least not *significantly* or *radically* change, the human body and life form that God or nature have given us, not as individuals and not as a species.

Moreover, even in modern times, when technology started to play a larger role in human societies, technology was understood in terms of tools; that is, in terms of instruments for realizing human ends. Humans and technology were supposed to be entirely separate entities: the former belonged to the sphere of spirit, ends, subjects, meaning, speech, and value, whereas the latter belonged to the domain of matter, means, objects, meaninglessness, muteness, and amorality. There was also always the assumption that there is a strict distinction between the living and the non-living, between human bodies, for example, and technological devices. It was thought that these domains could not merge and they should not merge: human subjects use technology as objects for their purposes, and living beings and dead objects are not to be mixed. Crossovers between these domains were seen as unacceptable, if not impossible.

Contemporary technologies, however, seem to challenge these assumptions. It is increasingly possible to alter the human genome through techniques of **genetic engineering** (or genetic modification). Biotechnology can and has been used to change the genetic makeup of all kinds of organisms, so-called **genetically modified organisms** (GMOs). Humans are no exception. There is plenty of research on gene therapies, which aim at replacing defective genes with better ones. Germline therapy can lead to inheritable changes, not only changes in individuals. A recent breakthrough technology is **gene editing** or **genome editing** (see "Case/ Technology: Gene Editing"): DNA of human embryos can now be *edited*. DNA is inserted, deleted, or replaced in the genome of a living organism using nucleases (a kind of enzyme) as "molecular scissors" that introduce breaks in the genome. All of these techniques can be used not only for therapy but also for *enhancement*. When this is done for humans, it is a form of **human enhancement**. There is the prospect of altering the appearance and abilities of individuals and even of the entire species to improve or "enhance" the human. In addition, there are all kinds of technologies—developed inside or outside the medical sphere—that lead to other changes to the human body and close couplings between humans and technologies. Technological artifacts are used as prostheses or as implants, for instance leg prostheses or cochlear implants. Pacemakers, devices implanted under the skin that control heart rhythm, have already been in use for many decades; and many technologies used in medicine involve a close coupling between humans and machines. Consider, for instance, the heart-lung machine, which made possible huge advances in cardiac surgery, or kidney dialysis machines. There is also the domain of synthetic biology, which applies engineering principles and knowledge from computer science to biology to redesign and fabricate biological "material" and "components"—which may or may not already exist in the biological world. The idea is to "build" new life forms. For example, one can try to make artificial tissue (e.g., artificial skin) and even entire organs, but also entirely new "systems" such as a network of cells that perform specific functions that do not exist in nature and display computing-like behavior. But there is also engineering at a smaller, molecular level: consider also again gene editing, which can be seen as a form of genetic engineering and synthetic biology. And all kinds of medicines and drugs have always been used to alter the human mind and consciousness. Again it seems that humans can be changed, even "enhanced" (improved), and that the borders between humans and technology, and between living organisms and "dead" technological objects, are thinner than previously assumed or have already been crossed in various ways. Furthermore, in the domain of robotics, some researchers attempt to create more lifelike, sometimes more humanlike, machines, which are not only more intelligent but also more humanlike in appearance and behavior, including social behavior (social robotics). Finally, scientists such as Kevin Warwick and artists such as Stelarc have been experimenting with **cyborg** modes of perception and behavior, involving implants and artificial extensions of their bodies and senses. The nexus between science and art includes experiments that involve biological organisms (e.g., bacteria) and technology, or performances that use virtual reality (VR) and augmented reality (AR) technologies to explore different, unusual experiences of the relation between self and non-self, humans and media, body and world. These technologies and practices do not only raise questions regarding the moral status of non-human entities (see chapter 8); they also raise questions concerning the relation between the human and the technological and between the living and the non-living; and they make us question once again what the human is and what the human should be and should become.

In this chapter, I show how technological advances have raised at least two kinds of philosophical (sub)questions regarding what the human is and what it should become: (1) should we enhance human beings and humanity, and (2) what is the relation between the human and the non-human? I present two kinds of answers to these questions that go beyond the answers of traditional philosophical anthropology, or, more precisely, two kinds of approaches and movements that define themselves as going beyond classical humanism: **transhumanism** and **posthumanism**. These approaches to the human are interesting for philosophers of technology since they redefine the relation between humans and technology in radical ways.

In the first section, I give an overview of transhumanist thinking, summarizing and discussing views from authors such as Bostrom, Kurzweil, Harris, and Tegmark. Their visions of the future of the human and the future of technology are controversial and are often dismissed as being concerned with science fiction. Yet it is interesting to make explicit and critically discuss their assumptions about human beings, technology, and society and ask how "fictional" the scenarios and arguments they present really are in the light of our current use of technologies—arguably a matter of primary concern for philosophers of technology. Should we enhance the human, changing not only our "software" but also our "hardware," as Max Tegmark puts it in his book *Life 3.0* (2017)? Are we already enhancing ourselves? And given that technology has increased our control and power over nature and the human, what future of the human, and hence of technology, do we want? What kind of (technological) society do we want? And one could add kind of planet?

The second section explores posthumanist thinking, which redefines the relation between humans and non-humans in ways that question the anthropocentric assumptions of traditional thinking about humans and non-humans and invites us to be more open to crossing ontological borders: between human and non-human (e.g., animals and machines), living and non-living, natural and artificial, mind and body, men and women, and so on. For example, are advanced intelligent machines capable of social communication *mere* machines, or can they be more? Should we be open to relationships with machines? How conceptually distinct are biological and artificial "systems" really, given that both seem to process information? And why do we care so much about distinguishing ourselves from machines in the first place? I will focus on Haraway and Latour, while acknowledging some posthumanist tendencies in contemporary philosophy of technology. Here too it is stressed that in spite of what may seem to be "extreme" or "exotic" positions on the human, their work makes us reflect on how we currently define ourselves (and on how we traditionally have defined the human) in relation to non-humans and to technology, and point to the need to reveal and critically discuss concepts and images we use when thinking about technologies—especially (and again) in the light of contemporary technologies. Will we become cyborgs, as Warwick proposed? Are we already cyborgs, and in what sense? And how dependent are we on the non-human for our thinking (about the human) and for our lives? The latter question (together with the question regarding the future of our planet in the previous section) will lead us into chapter 10 on the Anthropocene and technology.

9.2. Transhumanism and Human Enhancement

Transhumanists want to enhance human beings (individuals) and *the* human (the species) by means of technology. In the latter case, the aim is not just to enhance particular people but to bring humanity to a higher level. "Enhancement" is opposed to treatment and therapy: the idea is to improve the normal, healthy human capacities and features in such a way that they become better than human, or to add capacities and features that current humans do not have. This can include physical capacities such as running, cognitive capacities such as memory, emotional features such as mood, and even moral dispositions (Savulescu and Persson 2008). Many transhumanists endorse the aim to make humans live longer and fight disease. Some are on a quest for immortality. Nick Bostrom, a well-known transhumanist, tells the fable of a giant dragon that tyrannizes people and that demands sacrifices, creating endless suffering (2005). There are different responses to this situation: some argue that we should accept what is happening; others propose to fight and defeat the dragon (Bostrom 2005). Transhumanists such as Bostrom are on the side of the dragon fighters. Humanity should take its future in its own hands and change our species.

Moreover, the idea is that we *should* not only change ourselves but will *have to* anyway when there is a so-called **singularity** (or capitalized: "Singularity"): an intelligence explosion powered by new developments in artificial intelligence

FIGURE 9.2 Illustration of a transhuman head

that will lead to new, artificial entities that will surpass humans. Without enhancement, we would not be able to keep up. In *The Singularity Is Near* (2005), Ray Kurzweil argues that we will become cyborgs and upload ourselves, transcending our biological nature. John Harris (2007) speaks of enhancing evolution: human enhancement will replace Darwinian evolution. Max Tegmark thinks that it is likely that the development of AI, which already transforms our world, will lead to an intelligence explosion that will revolutionize life on earth. We will then be faced with questions such as who will and should be in control (machines or humans), whether artificial intelligences should be conscious, do we want to upload ourselves, and do we want life spreading in the cosmos. If we allow the latter, then the sky is no longer the limit, and life—which does not need to be biological—can flourish everywhere. Consciousness, he argues, is based on information processing and is substrate-independent; it can also be artificial. We'd better prepare to be humbled by ever smarter and possibly conscious machines. Today, we can start preparing our future by building safe AI (Tegmark 2017). Decades ago, Moravec (1990) already speculated about "a plausible, wonderful postbiological future and the ways our minds might participate in its unfolding" (abstract).

Views like this can be called a *radical* conception of human enhancement (Coeckelbergh 2013b) since in a more mundane or broader sense, we are already enhancing ourselves by means of technology and have always done so. From the use of simple tools and fire to modern medicine, the internet, and smartphones, we have always made things better for us humans, and in many ways we are now different from our ancient ancestors. Moreover, the therapy-versus-enhancement distinction gets blurred when we consider how we have already extended our lives through medical science and therapy; how we already improve cognitive functioning by means of stimulants such as caffeine; how some people already use prostheses that enable them to run better than normal; how surgery can give you better-than-normal vision; how military organizations are interested in "enhancing" the physical and mental-emotional capacities of soldiers; and how digital information technologies have, in a sense, also created new humans.

But even if one acknowledges these forms of enhancement, the radical, transhumanist version of human enhancement can be, and has been, criticized. Should we change human nature? For example, in response to visions of changing humans by means of biotechnology, it is said that we should not fiddle with nature (Kass 2003) and that we should reject the Promethean aspiration to change everything and remake (human) nature (Sandel 2002). Jürgen Habermas (2003) sees in biotechnology a threat to human dignity; Jean-Pierre Dupuy (2008) opposes the "rebellion" against the human condition; and Leon Kass (2003) argues that we should accept our finitude, which is the condition for many good things in life; we should criticize the dream of perfection.

Against these criticisms of genetic enhancement, one could argue that there is no fixed human nature, that human nature has always changed (Coeckelbergh 2013a). One could also reply that this kind of rebellion is part of what we are and do as humans, or that we have always dreamt of transforming ourselves to overcome our human limitations (Allhoff et al. 2010). Consider, for example, the myth of Icarus. But to say that human nature has always changed (also by means of technology) or that dreaming about overcoming our limitations belongs to human culture does not give us specific normative guidance about the particular changes proposed by the transhumanists. We need to discuss what changes we want (Coeckelbergh 2013a), about how and what should be changed. One could opt for a less radical version of enhancement; for instance, one that only tries to eradicate diseases rooted in genetic defects but not enhance bodily traits such as running or vision, or one that allows enhancement in medicine but not for military purposes. One could allow some enhancements but reject the vision of creating a new human being. (Of course in each case, such claims then need an argument for why the first is allowed or even mandatory whereas the latter is not.)

Moreover, we can also question some assumptions about human nature that are at the basis of many of the more informational, intelligence explosion views. Is intelligence the only value or trait we should aim for with regard to the future of humanity, as intelligence-oriented transhumanists such as Bostrom, Kurzweil, and Tegmark seem to assume? And is intelligence or consciousness a matter of information processing? Are humans basically information processing systems? Are they fundamentally informational at all? Is the nature of reality informational, as Floridi argues? There is at least the *danger* of a reductionist view, based on a version of scientism: the view that only science (here: natural science and computer science) can give us the answers, or the *only* true and meaningful answers, to such ultimate questions about the human and the nature of reality. Furthermore, against the vision of immortality, I have argued that even enhanced transhumans or "cyborgs" will necessarily be vulnerable and mortal (Coeckelbergh 2011). If this is true, then at least the goal of immortality seems mistaken. And Hauskeller (2011), interpreting Sandel (2007), has suggested that proponents of human enhancement, by focusing on perfection in the sense of enhancing traits, neglect issues concerning human flourishing, virtue, and the good life—a different and important project of perfection. In addition, with regard to genetic enhancement, one could add that there is a complex relation between nature and nurture, and hence that enhancement is not guaranteed. The outcome of editing the human genome is unsure and risky. And technologies such as mind uploading (scanning of the mental states of a biological brain and copying it to a computer, which then simulates the original brain and has consciousness) or artificial consciousness (consciousness that would arise in an engineered artifact) are entirely hypothetical and raise philosophical problems such as the mind–body problem. Proponents of uploading seem to assume a Platonic and Cartesian view of human beings, including the descriptive position that we can separate mind from body, which goes against all insights of contemporary cognitive science that understands mind as embodied. They also take the normative position that the body is only a source of limitations and problems and should and can be ignored and preferably be left and rejected. This kind of body-unfriendly transhumanism aims at creating what Moravec (1990) called "mind children," not "body children," let alone real children. It seems that for these transhumanists, real humans and their bodies are mainly a pain and a source of suffering. They are not smart. They are a disgrace, a bug, a glitch, and therefore they should be enhanced and overcome. Minds, not bodies or real people, are invited to participate in the wonderful unfolding of life and intelligence 3.0. Against this, one could invoke more positive views of the human body and embodiment.

Finally, it is unclear which implications transhumanism has for society. Transhumanism often has a blind spot when it comes to social and political questions. Transhumanists such as Bostrom study the risks of artificial intelligence for humanity as a whole, for instance, but the social and political dimension is largely neglected. Who is enhanced? Only the rich? Only people in the West? Which generation? What will the intelligence explosion, if it would happen at all, mean for the way we work and the way we live together? People such as Tegmark begin to discuss such issues, but when transhumanists do this, their discussions are usually not anchored in an intellectual background that relates to expertise from the social sciences or to philosophy that occupies itself with social and political questions. Their main background is often the natural sciences, computer sciences, etc., and philosophical approaches that do not engage with studies of the social in the humanities and the social sciences. This limitation is regrettable, since to answer such questions, knowledge from computer science, technical disciplines, natural sciences, mathematics, or abstract philosophical approaches is not sufficient. The humanities and social sciences are also needed. For example, in my book *Human Being @ Risk* (2013b), I have pointed to political issues and to political philosophy as one of the sources we can use to address these issues. In the case of genetic enhancement, for example, these issues include whether human enhancement should be free or compulsory, and more generally whether an authoritarian version can be avoided; whether it would be available only to the rich and, if so, whether this would be just and equal; whether it would lead to a world of brutal competition in which the unenhanced would be discriminated or even enslaved, or if it would be compatible with solidarity; whether there could be redistribution and, if so, what principle would govern it and what should be redistributed (genetic traits? money?—the former seems difficult to achieve;

Coeckelbergh 2013b). In the case of artificial entities, one could ask what the social position would be of humans (unenhanced or enhanced) and of artificial entities. Would a very smart AI get rights? Would *humans* still have rights if the AI takes over; and if so, would their rights be redefined? Is this the only scenario thinkable? Of course one may speculate about some scenarios based on some layperson knowledge of society, as Tegmark (2017) does in his book. But there are more ways of asking and answering the questions, based on long academic traditions and knowledge of society. Political philosophy and, more generally, the humanities and social sciences have a lot to ask and say, potentially, on these questions. Not only philosophy but also knowledge of the history of human culture and civilization may help: for example, knowledge of the history of how we treat animals, the history of slavery, and the history of technology use. The future of technology should not be left to computer scientists and physicists (nor should it be left to philosophers or historians). More interdisciplinary and transdisciplinary work seems to be needed.

Another dimension that is often neglected and insufficiently elaborated in discussions about transhumanism and human enhancement is the environmental and ecological dimension of technology use and development. The technological future is dependent on the resources of our planet. Transhumanists tend to ignore this earthly condition altogether or explicitly aim at escaping the planet, preparing for leaving the earth and going into the universe. The assumption seems to be that just as the body must be overcome by the mind, the earth must be overcome by going into space: as biological beings, we are now locked into our body and are imprisoned on this planet; but with technology, we can change that condition and escape both body and earth. This normative orientation and vision must be problematized. One could object that we may not even get to a near future of safe and ethically good AI on earth if we neglect problems related to environment, earth, and planet. Humans are earthly beings, and directly or indirectly, their technologies and enhancements and indeed their future are entirely dependent on what the earth provides. Thinking about technology, therefore, should be responsive to our ecological and terrestrial condition. In chapter 10, I will say more about these issues.

9.3. Posthumanism and Cyborgs

Like transhumanism, posthumanism questions humanism and exists in many versions. The term "posthuman" is often used in both discourses or as an umbrella term, which has led to confusion. Are these movements and approaches the same, and if not, what is the difference? Let me try to clear up the confusion.

First, their views differ. Both question what it means to be human in a technological age and in their answers reject traditional Western humanist conceptions of the human. However, transhumanists do so because they reject conceptions that see the human as unchangeable. They argue for the transformation of the human to a transhuman stage in the future by means of technology. Their view of the human that needs to be overcome, however, is still rooted in a Cartesian, dualist view, is focused on the human, and retains the idea that humans should be masters of the earth. Posthumanists, by contrast, focus on redefining the human itself in a non-anthropocentric, less dualist, and more relational way. They emphasize our relations with non-humans, and question boundaries between the human and the non-human: for example, animals or machines. Posthumanism "seeks to undermine the traditional boundaries between the human, the animal, and the technological" (Bolter 2016, 1) and rejects both Western humanism and Cartesian dualism.

Second, their approaches differ. As Stefan Sorgner correctly observes, the two movements tend to differ significantly in terms of approach, language, and background. Whereas transhumanists tend to embrace a naturalist understanding of human beings and focus on the evolutionary origin and technological future of the human being, posthumanists see the posthuman (e.g., the cyborg) as a result of a cultural process. And whereas transhumanism tends to have a background in the natural sciences and/or in Anglo-American philosophy such as utilitarianism (Sorgner 2017), posthumanists often have a background in the humanities and/or social sciences, including, for example, science and technology studies, literary studies, critical theory, sociology, communication studies (Bolter 2016), and anthropology. This background gives them a different orientation and different methods: "Transhumanists are linear thinkers, employ technical vocabulary, and have a scientific methodology, while posthumanists embrace a nonlinear way of thinking, use metaphors, and have a hermeneutic methodology" (Sorgner 2017, 1). For example, Donna Haraway has been concerned with literature and philosophy, Rosi Braidotti is a philosopher and women's studies and feminism scholar, and Bruno Latour started as an anthropologist and is now a key figure in science and technology studies. Sometimes posthumanism overlaps with **postmodernism** and poststructuralism—for instance, when it questions the unity of the humanist subject (Braidotti 2013)—although this is not always or necessarily the case. Posthumanists also argue that the humanities itself should be reconfigured, for example, in radically interdisciplinary ways. Once again, the focus is on crossing boundaries—including disciplinary ones. As a consequence of these different backgrounds and discourses, there has been little exchange between transhumanists and posthumanists (Sorgner 2017, 1).

In contemporary philosophy of technology, there are also posthumanist tendencies. Consider, for example, Floridi's non-anthropocentric philosophy of information (although in terms of approach, he is perhaps closer to transhumanist

FIGURE 9.3 Female cyborg removing her face showing machine structure underneath

and naturalist philosophers); Verbeek's view that artifacts have morality and that human subjectivity is always technologically mediated and constituted (although his approach is often engineering oriented and less informed by, e.g., the social sciences); or my attempts to arrive at a more relational approach (e.g., Coeckelbergh 2012, 2014a) and my claim that Western philosophical anthropology has always been a negative anthropology that is highly dependent on non-human others (see, e.g., Coeckelbergh 2013b, 2014b). However, in this section, I will focus on whom I regard as two foundational figures in the posthumanist discourse relevant to technology: Donna Haraway and Bruno Latour.

In her "A Cyborg Manifesto" ([1991] 2000), Haraway has famously questioned the boundaries between humans, machines, and animals by offering the cyborg metaphor. The cyborg is "a cybernetic organism, a hybrid of machine and organism, a creature of social reality as well as a creature of fiction" (Haraway [1991] 2000, 291). According to Haraway, the cyborg metaphor enables us to imagine a world in which people are no longer afraid of "their joint kinship with animals and machines" (295), a world in which we accept cultural monsters that subvert "the structure and modes of reproduction of 'Western' identity, of nature and culture, of mirror and eye, slave and master, body and mind" (312). While Haraway rejects narratives such as the restoration of the garden of Eden (293), she dreams of a goddess that breaks down barriers.

> **IN FOCUS:**
> **Donna Haraway**
>
> Donna Haraway was a professor at the University of California, Santa Cruz and is a prominent STS scholar who also influenced debates in philosophy and biology. She has been described as postmodernist, posthumanist, and (eco)feminist. In philosophy of technology and STS, she is best known for her "A Cyborg Manifesto" in which she uses the cyborg metaphor to reflect on human–machine relations; later, she focused more on human–animal relations.

This use of the cyborg metaphor was a direct response to the development of computing and the new, biotechnological possibilities to intervene and modify the human body. Haraway is right that, in this sense, there are already cyborgs. She gives an important role to *technology* in breaking down barriers. With regard to machines, she claims that

Late twentieth-century machines have made thoroughly ambiguous the difference between natural and artificial, mind and body, self-developing and artificially designed, and many other distinctions that used to apply to organisms and machines. Our machines are disturbingly lively, and we ourselves frighteningly inert. (Haraway [1991] 2000, 293–294)

And in the medical and therapeutic domain, there are already material and fleshly "couplings between organism and machine" (Haraway [1991] 2000, 292). Consider cochlear implants, prosthetic hands, and brain–computer interfaces. There are already many technologies that lead to an epistemic situation in which "mind, body and tool are on very intimate terms" (303) indeed. Haraway notes, for instance, that "severely handicapped people can have the most intense experiences of complex hybridization" (313). Consider, for example, computer technology that enables paralyzed people to communicate. And during the past decades, scientists such as Kevin Warwick and artists such as Stelarc have experimented with less familiar, more "monstrous" cyborg-like couplings and interactions. But one does not need to limit cyborgization to its more exceptional or "exotic" forms in frontier medicine or cutting-edge artistic work: today we are already so much connected with technologies such as the internet without any need for wires. *We are already cyborgs.* As Andy Clark puts it in his book *Natural-Born Cyborgs* (2003)

I incorporate no silicon chips, no retinal or cochlear implants, no pace-maker . . . but I am slowly becoming more and more a cyborg. So are you. Pretty soon, and still without the need for wires, surgery, or bodily alterations, we shall all be kin to the Terminator. . . . Perhaps we already are. For we shall be cyborgs not in the merely superficial sense of com-bining flesh and wires but in the more profound sense of being human-technology symbionts: thinking and reasoning systems whose minds and selves are spread across biological brain and nonbiological circuitry. (Clark 2003, 3)

IN FOCUS:
Stelarc

Stelarc is an artist who has explored themes such as enhancement, cyborgiza-tion, and human–machine interfaces in this work. For instance, in his project "Third Hand," a mechanical arm is attached to his body and controlled by the electric signals of his muscles. In his performance "Fractal Flesh," his body is wired into the internet and twitches as it is controlled by remote agents. He also imagines a body that "quivers and oscillates to the ebb and flow of net ac-tivity." These works invite us to reflect not only about the technological future but also about the present. For example, how much are we already moving and oscillating to the ebb and flow of the internet and its social media?

FIGURE 9.4 Stelarc performing "Re-wired/Re-mixed"

At the same time, Haraway's ([1991] 2000) metaphor was inspired by science fiction; remember that for her the cyborg is also "a creature of fiction" (291). In Haraway's view and that of many posthumanists, both are connected: borders that need to be crossed include those between reality and fiction, between reality and text, and between technology and culture. These posthumanists assume that technology is also always at the same time cultural and vice versa. Meaning does not stop at the border of text; other technologies and the material (and the "flesh") are also cultural and meaningful. Thus, we can use the cyborg metaphor to express our ongoing and perhaps increasing entanglement with technology; for example, in our daily use of computers and internet-connected smart devices. In that sense, we are all cyborgs. But we can also use the metaphor to express the blurring of, and the (desired) breaking down of, dichotomies such as technology/culture, material/culture, nature/society, and human/non-human. So cyborg thinking means more non dualist thinking and the questioning and crossing of traditional ontological borders.

Moreover, there is also a political, and in particular feminist, motive in Haraway's text. She argues against the "patriarchal capitalism" (Haraway [1991] 2000, 293) that initially produced cyborgs (e.g., in the military); instead she turns them into liberation machines that help us to question the "polarity and hierarchical domination" (293). Haraway's manifesto asks for recoupling but also for resistance (295). Her aim is revolution: the building of a new, monstrous political form that subverts the Western order. As such, it is also a response to, and contribution to, critical theory and feminism. Again technology plays a key role: as science and as fiction, the cyborg helps her to formulate the ideal of a nondualistic unity in which distinctions are "thoroughly blurred" (183). Like the 19th-century romantics and her fellow countercultural thinkers, she believes in the power of fiction and the power of the imagination: Haraway calls for "world-changing fiction" (291), for new myths (316)—albeit no myths that involve an "original symbiosis" (312).

Haraway's work still resonates in contemporary thinking about technology and in STS, posthumanist or not. The cyborg metaphor is a very powerful one; and for posthumanists and many feminists, Haraway is an obligatory source of reference. Her work has already dominated the debate for more than 25 years. My own response (in *New Romantic Cyborgs*; Coeckelbergh 2017) has been to use the metaphor to express how technology and humans are entangled (and have always been entangled), to criticize what turns out to be a more cultural and less material approach than she intended (i.e., to argue that she stayed close to her fellow postmodernists), to point to the romantic dimensions of her view, and to speculate about post-machines.

Another work that has been very influential in philosophy of technology and science and technology studies, which is also about crossing boundaries, is Bruno Latour's *We Have Never Been Modern* (1993).

IN FOCUS:
Bruno Latour

Bruno Latour is a contemporary French philosopher, anthropologist, and sociologist. He is very influential in STS but also in contemporary posthumanist philosophy of technology. He was professor at Sciences Po in Paris and at the London School of Economics. He is best known for his book *We Have Never Been Modern* (1993) and for his work on scientific practice. Together with Michel Callon and John Law, he developed the so-called actor–network theory (ANT), an approach to the social that sees networks

FIGURE 9.5 Bruno Latour in Taiwan

of relations between objects, discourse, and humans: there are also non-humans that participate in the social.

Latour also questions traditional ontological borders, but in contrast to Haraway, he rejects both modernism *and* postmodernism. He argues that we have never been modern in the sense that "modern" science has always produced hybrids that put into question the dichotomies on which it was supposed to rest, dichotomies such as society/nature and human/non-human. Modern science has tried to maintain distinct "ontological zones" (Latour 1993, 10) and has worked toward **purification**: it has tried to keep nature and culture apart, keep humans and non-humans apart, etc. But this project has failed. In contemporary science and society, subjects and objects mix and merge, as they have always done. We cannot be postmodern because we have never been modern in the first place: "we have never really left the old anthropological matrix behind" (Latour 1993, 47). In science and elsewhere, we have always lived and practiced in a non-modern way. Postmodernism thus reacted against a modernity that never really existed. And it was obsessed by signs and text. Latour is fed up with discourse, which postmodernists assumed to be "a world unto itself" (1993, 90). Not everything is **"sign and sign system"** (63). He sees the social as consisting of human actors and non-human *actants.* Discourse is also a population of such non-human actants, which mix with things and with societies (90). There is non-modern hybridity everywhere, not only in the laboratory. There is no Nature or Culture but rather natures-cultures (96). The human, then, is also a hybrid and can no longer be threatened by machines since "it has put itself into them" (137). The human is delegated, mediated, and distributed (138). And objects are also hybrid. They act. They have become quasi-subjects.

With regard to politics, Latour (1993) argues for including these hybrids and these actants into politics. He proposes a "Parliament of Things" (144) in which mediators speak in the name of citizens, societies, and natures. Discourse, also political discourse, is mixed with objects, nature, and society. In *Politics of Nature* (2004), Latour further develops this view. He claims that there are not even "nature-cultures"; there are only collectives. And there are no separate "things" and "persons"; to think so is a strange idea of us as Westerners (Latour 2004, 45). He imagines a social world in which there are "assemblages of humans and non-humans" (2004, 52). This also means that things cannot only act but also speak. They no longer belong to "the nature of mute things" (62) but are liberated and included in the collective. Speech, then, is no longer a specifically human property (65). Latour does not refer here to all kinds of machines that can speak (*if* their sound qualifies as "speech" at all) but rather to political speech. Like humans, whose speech is also always mediated, they may speak through technology and through spokespersons. For example, according to Latour, facts speak through the scientist and through the scientific instruments. Think, for instance, about climate change: in the political discussion, the facts speak through the scientists and the measurement instruments. In this way, Latour lets science and nature enter politics. Or, more precisely, the collective decides who and what can enter the collective. All the beings make proposals. Viruses say that they cause a deadly illness, consumers want their demands to be taken into account (Latour 2004, 168). We are not used to this way of speaking about politics. We are used to conceptualizing politics as being about humans. But in his reconceptualization of the social, Latour radically abolishes distinctions between nature and culture, human and non-human. The social and political question then becomes not "How can we humans live together?" but—as Latour puts it—"How can these contradictory beings be made to live together?" That is, how can subjects and objects, means and ends, humans and non-humans live together? Political ecology then becomes open and experimental: it becomes "experimental metaphysics" (Latour 2004, 235) in the sense that we no longer claim to know in advance who/what should be included in the collective and "what belongs to the kingdom of ends" (227).

For thinking about technology, Latour's posthumanist, more non-modern view implies that we reposition both the human and technology. Technology does no longer exclusively belong to the domain of things and nature; it also becomes political. Technology appears as "things," as non-humans that are part of the collectives (or want to become part of the collective) or as a means to let things speak. And humans seem to have to give up their hierarchical and separate position: they are assembled and mixed together with non-humans in the collective. They no longer occupy the privileged, exclusive, and central position in the social and political. They are part of a non-modern ecology in which hybridity and mediation, not purity and separation, is the rule. Things are not only there for humans; humans are also there for things, for example, when humans let things speak, through technology. Humans are not only responsible for other humans but also for non-humans. This responsibility is made possible by technologies of mediation. A new political constitution also seems to lead to a new moral constitution in which technology plays a key role: as things (artifacts) that may speak or as mediator for things (artifacts or facts) that may speak. The modern constitution, which separated humans and technology, is replaced by a social and political world in which humans are not the only political speakers and in which humans are not only speakers but also parts and participators, medium and mediators. It can hardly get more posthuman in such a non-modern world of assemblage and hybridity.

In response to posthumanism, one could defend traditional humanism. But few people will want to do this, at least if that would mean retaining a strong form of anthropocentrism. It is clear that after Copernicus, Darwin, Freud, and indeed the recent technological revolution (Floridi would say information revolution), we need to rethink our place in the universe. It is clear that in the light of ecological and environmental insights we need to question our anthropocentrism. And many will endorse the claim that we are relational beings. Some may also take on board claims about the decentering of the subject from 20th-century postmodernism. However, for various reasons, one may still not want to go "all the way" to a radical posthumanism. Retaining a (vague?) humanist intuition that there is still something special or distinct about humans, one could object that one needs to distinguish between more radical (or stronger) versions and more moderate (or weaker) versions of posthumanism, and claim that the latter are acceptable whereas the former are not. (Compare with the objection against transhumanism.) It is one thing to acknowledge that humans are relational beings; that the border between human and non-human is not very clear at all; that we are both mediated and mediators; and that we are constituted by human others, by non-humans, and by technology. It is another to claim that there are no distinctions at all, that there should be no borders, and that there is a total symmetry between humans and non-humans. More postmodern views such as Haraway's or Latour's (which indeed may well be more postmodern than Latour acknowledges) seem to tend toward such a blurring of all distinctions or a total symmetry. It might be possible to hold a more moderate position, which takes on board some insights from posthumanism but does not accept a total blurring or total symmetry.

However, this is a challenging project. Like in the case of transhumanism, the borders between more radical and more moderate positions are not very clear; it seems that the latter easily slips into the former. If one accepts that human nature *can* be changed, as *transhumanists* argue, then it seems that one at least should be open to ask normative questions about the human: What should the human be or become? In the current technological age, if not already earlier, it seems that philosophical anthropology becomes normative (Coeckelbergh 2013b). If one accepts that the human and the non-human (animals, technology, etc.) are very much related and entangled, as posthumanists argue, then it becomes difficult indeed, if not impossible, to speak of "the human" as if it had an essence and as if it was totally different from the non-human; then it seems reasonable to use another term such as "posthuman" to indicate this changed, more relational and decentered understanding. However, even if one accepted these positions (or one of them), then one could nevertheless reject *specific conceptions* of the transhuman or the posthuman. For instance, one may reject a Cartesian conception of the transhuman (as in the idea of uploading), or one may reject a postmodern conception of a totally decentered and fluid subject or a postmodern overemphasis on text and language. One may also reject a total symmetry between subjects and objects, a view many readers ascribe to Latour. Thus, one may accept that borders are blurred, as Haraway rightly points out; question a modern strict distinction between nature and the social, as Latour does; and endorse the claim that subjects and objects co-constitute one another, as, for example, Verbeek argues—but stay away from more radical postmodern claims.

Perhaps the most radical claims are that *there are no longer any distinctions* (or that we *should* aim for this) and that *there are no longer subjects and objects at all* (or that this is *desirable*). Such claims raise a lot of questions; but discussing them is an interesting philosophical exercise, which is also relevant to philosophy of technology. Do we need distinctions and dichotomies at all? And if so, which ones and what status do they have? To what extent is it *possible* and desirable to hold a radically nondualist view? Can we make sense of ourselves as humans if we shed all distinctions? Does a non-modern view, if desirable at all, require from us that we embrace a total nondualism and shed all distinctions? And if not, what *does* it require? Can we still retain the concept of the "human"? What, exactly, does the "post" mean in "posthuman"? Can we still use the term "person"? What are the more concrete and practical political implications of a non-modern view, as opposed those discussed in the more abstract Latourian discourse? Can politics be non-modern and democratic at the same time? What is politics anyway? To what extent is politics dependent on speech, and is that just a metaphor? And what kind of myths and narratives do we need today, if any? Are these necessarily meta-narratives, and what exactly is wrong with meta-narratives? As usual, philosophy of technology (and responding to technological developments) leads us into asking interesting and sometimes fundamental and perennial philosophical questions.

REVIEW QUESTIONS

1. What is transhumanism and human enhancement?
2. Review some problems transhumanist visions and enhancement technologies raise.
3. Give an example of a human enhancement technology and discuss the potential philosophical problems.
4. What is posthumanism, and how does it differ from transhumanism?
5. What are cyborgs?
6. Summarize Haraway's position in "A Cyborg Manifesto" ([1991] 2000). How does Haraway use the metaphor of the cyborg to intervene in the discourse on science and technology?
7. Summarize Latour's position in *We Have Never Been Modern* (1993). How does Latour respond to postmodernism?

DISCUSSION QUESTIONS

1. What do you think about the transhumanist view that humans, as a species, should enhance themselves? Argue for your response.
2. Is human enhancement acceptable to you? Why (not)?
3. What could be the political consequences of human enhancement? And do you think these are acceptable? Why (not)?
4. Do you find Haraway's cyborg politics attractive? Why (not)?
5. Do you agree with Bruno Latour's claim that we have never been modern? Should things be included into the social and into politics? Are they already included?
6. Are we cyborgs? If so, in what sense?
7. Is it possible to hold "moderate" or "weak" versions of transhumanism and posthumanism, or do they necessarily slip into more radical versions? What is your position (and defend it)?

RECOMMENDED READING

Coeckelbergh, Mark. 2013. *Human Being @ Risk: Enhancement, Technology, and the Evaluation of Vulnerability Transformations*. New York: Springer.
Haraway, Donna. (1991) 2000. "A Cyborg Manifesto." In *The Cybercultures Reader*, edited by D. Bell and B. M. Kennedy, 291–324. Reprint, London: Routledge.
Latour, Bruno. 1993. *We Have Never Been Modern*. Translated by Catherine Porter. Cambridge, MA: Harvard University Press.

KEY TERMS

Actants
Cyborg
Gene editing (or genome editing)

Genetic engineering (or genetic modification)
Genetically modified organisms (GMOs)
Human enhancement

Posthumanism
Postmodernism
Purification
Singularity
Transhumanism

10 FROM CLIMATE CHANGE AND GEOENGINEERING TO QUESTIONING "NATURE" AND THINKING IN AND ABOUT THE "ANTHROPOCENE"

CASE/TECHNOLOGY:
Solar Radiation Management as a Method
of Geoengineering

How can and should humanity respond to climate change? Some people argue that since in the short term, we cannot stop using fossil fuels, we should use more drastic, technological methods to counteract the problem of global warming and stabilize the climate. One method of so-called geoengineering (large-scale technological manipulation and control of the planetary environment) is to use technologies that reflect incoming solar radiation back to space. This could be done, so it is proposed, by sending into space giant mirrors (one big mirror or trillions of small mirrors) or a shielding cloud of dust to obscure the sun. Another slightly less science-fiction–like solution is releasing particles into the atmosphere, for example, so-called cloud whitening. The idea is to pump up sea water and spray it into the air and produce small salt aerosols that make whiter clouds, which reflect more sunlight. To have a global effect, this would have to be done on a huge scale. There are also other schemes (Ming et al. 2014). Geoengineering, also in the form of solar radiation management, is controversial. One objection is that there could be undesirable side effects, such as changes to weather patterns. More generally, one could question if it is wise to experiment with the climate and the planet. Isn't this part of the *problem* of climate change?

10.1. Introduction: Earth, We Have a Problem

Since the environmental movement called attention to environmental degradation and pollution in the 1960s and 1970s, there has been a growing awareness in the West that we are part of a natural and ecological whole, the earth's ecosystem, on which we, as individuals, societies, and civilization(s) depend. It has been increasingly recognized that we should not and cannot deplete natural resources if we want to continue to exist as a species, that our actions should be more sustainable. In the 1990s, environmentalists paid attention to global political issues such as global warming, acid rain, ozone depletion, and biodiversity. Ideas about sustainability

FIGURE 10.1 Dry landscape as an effect of climate change

became mainstream. In the beginning of the 21st century, the focus shifted to the term and phenomenon of **climate change**. While initially and scientifically this concept referred to statistical changes in (very) long-term weather patterns, without necessarily involving a discussion on what or whom may have caused the changes and with no attendant normative discussion, today climate change is often the main focus of public discussions on the environment. The phenomenon that receives most attention today is **global warming,** which is seen as a relatively recent problem caused by human activity (anthropogenic) as opposed to changes that seem to have resulted from the earth's natural processes, and which is feared to be largely irreversible and dangerous, not only for the environment but also for humans. Many scientists say that if we do not act soon, a tipping point will be crossed, or indeed has already been crossed. In particular, rising temperatures may lead to more environmental degradation and to food and water insecurity and economic decline in less developed countries, and hence to more migration and potential humanitarian crises (Warner et al. 2010). Another concept/phenomenon that is most widely discussed is the so-called **Anthropocene:** the idea that we are living in a new geological epoch due to the transformative and perhaps irreversible influence of human behavior on the earth. As Paul Crutzen (2006) puts it, human activities have grown to become a significant geological force. Seen in this light, climate change is part of our anthropocenic predicament.

In response to these problems, there have been many calls for producing, consuming, and living in more sustainable and less polluting ways—for example, to be more energy efficient and choose renewable power, eat more organic foods and less meat, consume less, opt for green ways of transportation and avoid long commutes, stop deforestation, etc. There have been international climate agreements such as the so-called Kyoto Protocol in the mid-1990s and the Paris agreement in 2015, which are related to the United Nations Framework Convention on Climate Change (UNFCCC), which aims to enhance collaboration among nations to limit global temperature increase and climate change. Many countries (but not all) have participated in such agreements and have adopted policies to reduce greenhouse gas emissions to safer levels, for instance by trying to shift their economies in ways that make them less dependent on the burning of fossil fuels such as coal, oil, and natural gas.

Technologies, including information technologies, are often seen as problematic (e.g., as enablers of industrial activities, oil and gas production, modern agriculture, mining, car transportation, deforestation) but may also be seen as part of the solution: they could help to reach the goals just mentioned. For instance, smart energy technologies may help to monitor energy consumption and produce sustainable energy, and intelligent electric cars might contribute to less fossil fuel consumption (depending on how the electricity is produced). But by far the most radical technological intervention that has been proposed is so-called climate engineering or **geoengineering**. The idea is that mitigation by means of the measures just mentioned is not enough to stop climate change, but more swift and effective action is needed since the tipping point has already been reached. Proponents of geoengineering argue that we need a large-scale intervention in the earth's climate system, for example, technologies to capture and remove carbon dioxide from the earth's atmosphere or so-called solar radiation management (see textbox "(Solar) Radiation Management as a Method of Geoengineering"). Methods range from the familiar such as reforestation to new technologies to remove CO_2 (so-called negative emission technologies) and more exotic ideas such as space-based mirrors or dust to obstruct solar radiation. These methods assume that we can have a "technological fix" for the problem. Opponents argue that geoengineering can also be used by so-called climate change deniers as an excuse not to reduce CO_2 emissions (Connolly 2017) and that such new and larger-scale interventions are very risky, and there is a lot of uncertainty about the side effects. It is also not clear how effective specific methods would be (climate change has many causes and effects), who might benefit (e.g., which countries and which people), and who would be responsible for the (good or bad) effects. Both the problem and the proposed solutions must be situated in a complex ecological and social whole, which renders the success of a "fix" implausible and may lead to even more problems. Moreover, one can also criticize the very idea of a "technological fix" at a more fundamental level (see the next sections). Is climate change just an "engineering problem," as Rex Tillerson, then US Secretary of

State, has claimed (Mooney 2016)? Finally, some argue that a combination of geoengineering and changes to our lifestyles and infrastructures is needed if we want to achieve, for instance, the goals of the Paris agreement (limit the temperature rise to 2 degrees or less).

Given that technology plays such a big role in the creation of, and responses to, environmental problems, it may surprise you that so far, most philosophers of technology have done little to respond to these environmental problems and the past and present discussions about how to address them, including the academic field of environmental philosophy. As Thompson (2017) shows, there are of course sources that are used by both fields (e.g., Heidegger and Jonas, or critical theory; more recently, Albert Borgmann's [1984] work), and there has been some interest in environmental matters by philosophers of technology from the empirical turn such as Evan Selinger (e.g., Seager et al. 2012) and Paul Thompson (e.g., Thompson 2010, 2017). There is also research in the empirically oriented philosophy of science on environmental and technological risk and health, for example by Kristin Shrader-Frechette (e.g., Schrader-Frechette & Westra 1997), Carl Cranor, and Steve Ove Hansson. There are more researchers who try to create bridges between philosophy of technology and environmental philosophy, such as Kaplan (2017) and myself (e.g., Coeckelbergh 2011, 2012, 2015, 2017b; Coeckelbergh and Gunkel 2014), sometimes also from a perspective of doing philosophy that is relevant to pressing societal issues (see work by Robert Frodeman and Adam Briggle, e.g., Briggle 2015). But these are exceptions; generally speaking, the fields of environmental philosophy and philosophy of technology are not very well connected.

In this chapter, I offer some further connections that can be made and, in some exceptional cases, *have* been made. One is a critical discussion of the notion of "nature," which is important in both fields (and of course in science) and which is often central in public discussions about environmental issues. Another is a discussion about how to address the Anthropocene as philosophers, especially as philosophers of technology. Like in the previous chapters, both discussions can be framed and understood as responses to technological and scientific developments; in this case, especially climate change science and geoengineering. They are motivated not just by a desire to contribute to theory but also by the feeling that in the "real world" outside academia, there are urgent technological and environmental issues that need to be addressed; and by the belief that philosophers of technology and environmental philosophers can help by doing some conceptual work. To continue the discussion about problems related to modernity (one of the themes in the theory chapters), the sections will focus on conceptual-philosophical interventions that question modern-technological thinking and modern-technological "fixes" as fundamental solutions to the problems at hand—and indeed that question even the modern-technological framing of these problems itself.

10.2. The Problem with "Nature": Modern Versus Non-Modern Approaches

Often environmental problems are discussed by using the term "nature." Scientists use the term, but also environmentalists and their opponents. It is said that we should protect nature, restore nature, use nature, and understand nature. But the

---

CASE/TECHNOLOGY:
Central Heating Versus Wood-Burning Stove

Central heating is easy. You don't have to do much: the technology produces the heat and a thermostat device maintains a constant temperature. The heat is continuously available. If you have a wood-burning stove and you are living in a remote place, however, a lot more effort and skill is required to produce heat. You have to gather and chop wood, and you have to stoke the fire. You have to focus on it. And maybe people have to help with these activities. That takes a lot more effort and time. So why would anyone deliberately not use central heating? The German-born American philosopher of technology (and environmental philosopher) Albert Borgmann argued in his book *Technology and the Character of Contemporary Life* (1984) that the stove implies more engagement and skill—there is bodily experience of the world and engagement with physical things and with other people such as family members and friends—and that therefore it is preferable to central heating and "devices" that are easy. In general, he defends "focal practices" that require skill, imply community life, and are more meaningful. Skillful engagement is a more intense way of dealing with the world and with others. And, one could add, a better, more engaged relation to the environment. The latter is the topic of this section and chapter: What is a good relation to the environment, and what role do and can technologies play in shaping such a relation?

FIGURE 10.2 Wood-burning stove

FIGURE 10.3 Portrait of Albert Borgmann

term "nature" is not neutral with regard to how we conceive of, and live, our relation to the environment. In environmental philosophy but also in philosophy of technology, we must question the very notion of "nature" (e.g., Ingold 2000; Coeckelbergh 2017a). Both environmentalists (e.g., climate activists) and their opponents (e.g., climate conservatives) seem to assume that there is a "nature" as opposed to "humans," "nature" as opposed to "technology," "nature" as opposed to "society," and so on. The same holds for scientists who want to regain control of nature by means of geoengineering: apparently there is a "nature" separate from us that we need to tame and control. But is this an adequate way of conceptualizing our environment?

A critical way to analyze and address this problem is to start from the claim that the notion of "nature" and the related dichotomies are typical modern dichotomies. They are linked to modern ways of perceiving and conceptualizing the environment, whether "objectivist-technoscientific" or "subjectivist-romantic" (Coeckelbergh 2017a). The first aims at understanding and controlling nature. It is assumed that, in Heidegger's words, nature is a "standing reserve" (Heidegger 1977). Here technology is an instrument to control, manipulate, and transform nature. When in today's discourse about the environment terms such as "natural resources," "natural capital," and "ecosystem services" are used, this way of perceiving nature is maintained. The environment is seen as a resource and service provider for humanity. Proposals to re-engineer "nature" and "the planet," and indeed the very idea of a "technological fix," fit this way of thinking. This attitude can and has been criticized from a romantic point of view. Against the objectivist domination of nature, the romantic expresses her love of nature, the importance of feeling, naturalness, harmony, authenticity, and so on. Again there is a separate "nature," but this time it is a recipient of our love, a source of authenticity, and perhaps a paradise lost: a place of harmony and goodness to which we would like to return. Today's environmental movement is still partly influenced by this romanticism, for example when people turn to the "wild" and to "nature" to find themselves and to restore harmony. We can also discern in Heidegger's later work a preference for pre-modern technologies that are supposed to respect nature, leave nature intact. In both modes of perceiving the environment, "nature" is seen as something external to the human—and to technology.

Against these modern dichotomies, which assume and preserve a "nature" separate from humans and technology, we could turn to a more non-modern view. As we have seen, Latour (1993, 2004) questions oppositions such as humans versus nature or technology versus nature and tries to construe a conception of the political and the collective that includes humans and non-humans. We can use this approach to point to various hybrids in the current discussion about climate change. That discussion is not only about science, nature, and objects but also at the same time about humans, society, and subjects. From this Latourian, non-modern perspective, it is not surprising that science becomes political or that politics becomes infused by science, since *science was always already political* and politics always mixed with matters that have to do with nature. It is also not surprising, then, that an institution such as the Intergovernmental Panel on Climate Change (IPCC), which acts as an authority in this area, is both scientific and political. It is a hybrid since what it is supposed to deal with is also hybrid. From a non-modern perspective, it could be argued that we need *more* hybrid institutions to deal with what is really a hybrid problem in the first place.

Latour's work is inspired by anthropology. To construct an alternative, non-modern view, one could also study how non-modern cultures relate(d) to the environment. In his influential book *The Perception of the Environment*, Tim Ingold (2000) criticizes the idea that there is first a "nature," which then gets transformed. Influenced by Heidegger but also grounded in anthropological research, he shows how hunter-gatherers perceive their environment very differently: they do not view nature as standing reserve, or something that we control, but as something that we do not and cannot entirely control—for example, when an animal reveals itself (or not)—and as something we actively relate to. The world of nature is not seen as separate from the world of humanity. Instead, these hunter-gatherers care for their environment "through a direct engagement with the constituents of the environment, not through a detached, hands-off approach" (Ingold 2000, 68). Instead of an alienated relation with an external "nature," which romantics then try to overcome, there is active engagement with, involvement in, and care for the environment.

In line with these non-modern directions, I have argued for a non-modern and non-romantic view of, and active relation to, the environment, and proposed the conception of "environmental skill" for this purpose (Coeckelbergh 2015). My starting point was the observation that although many people feel that they should live in more environmentally friendly ways and have more environmentally friendly policies, it is difficult to change their lives and our societies. My answer was that the problem lies in the kind of epistemic and practical relation we (Westerners) have to the environment: we know a lot of facts about the environment (e.g., statistical facts about climate change), and we have a romantic desire to return to "nature," but these kinds of knowledge and beliefs and the distance and alienation they create are actually part of the problem, not the solution: we lack a more engaged relation to the environment and we lack the required know-how and skill for making a real change. We need to move away from a dualistic and modern-romantic approach and toward less dualistic thinking and a more engaged relation to the environment. However, I also indicated that it is difficult to do this since it is difficult to move away from our modern form of life. Influenced by Heidegger and the later Wittgenstein, we could say that there is already a language and a "form of life," which constitute conditions of possibility that shape and constrain what we think and do (Coeckelbergh 2012, 2017c, 2017d). When we start thinking about the environment, there are already ways of talking about the environment, ways of living together, ways of relating to our body, ways of relating to technology, etc., that act as conditions of possibility that shape and constrain our practices and habits. Change is possible, but it is necessarily slow, and conceptual design is not sufficient. Perhaps making the change is itself a kind of craft, albeit one that we do not fully control. I use the metaphors of "growth" and "birth" to express this kind of change that is not fully under control (Coeckelbergh 2015).

For thinking about technology, this approach implies that the problem is not "modern technology," as Heidegger (1977) is said to have argued, but rather how we relate (and should relate) to the environment. This should be the normative focal point of an ethics of technology, which then becomes an ethics of relating to the environment (hence an environmental ethics) and an ethics of skill. Virtue is then not so much about theory, as the Aristotelian tradition has it, but about practice and responding to situations; about obtaining the necessary know-how; and about knowing how to relate to the environment and to others. We need technologies that shape and help us to find that better, more responsive, virtuous, skilled, careful, and engaged relation to our environment. Rejecting a romantic approach, I have stressed that in principle this may include new technologies and advanced technologies—a position that is different from Borgmann's (see textbox, "Case/Technology: Central Heating Versus Wood-Burning Stove"), which seems to suggest that we embrace older technologies. Even if currently they would fail to do this—but whether they do so or not is not so clear—we need to think about how they *could* contribute to environmental virtue and environmental skill and which changes need to be made in technology development to reach this goal. In this sense, reshaping human virtue and excellence also means reshaping technologies and our relations to technology (Coeckelbergh 2015, 190).

Since language is *part* of the problem, however, philosophers can contribute to and "accompany" the move toward a more engaged relation by means of critical discussion of key concepts and by trying to find a different, perhaps less modern language: a different language to speak about the environment, and of course also a different language to talk about technology. The latter is especially important for philosophers of technology. (See also chapter 11 in this book on philosophy of language and philosophy of technology.)

One way to reconceptualize the relations between "humans," "technology," and "nature" might be to adopt or at least critically discuss the term "Anthropocene." Let us look at another way of responding to the (discourse about) environmental problems, which is again not just about providing an answer to the problem—proposing or rejecting a "technological fix," for instance—but also about reframing the problem itself, about asking a different *question*.

10.3. The Anthropocene: Some Philosophical Responses

In the 19th century, it was already recognized that humankind's activities modify the earth; and in the early 20th century, Teilhard de Chardin and Vladimir Vernadsky coined the term "noosphere" to express that human thinking and technology shape the future and environment of humankind. Today some scientists and philosophers use the term "Anthropocene" to refer to the phenomenon that during the present geological epoch, and especially during the last two centuries (starting with the Industrial Revolution), humankind's activities "grew into a significant geological and morphological force" (Crutzen 2006, 13). Increase of the human population went hand in hand with a spectacular increase in urbanization and industrialization, use of fresh water, fishing and agriculture and hence fertilizers, transformations in the world's land surface (e.g., deforestation and disappearance of coastal wetlands), and the exploitation of the earth's resources. Crutzen writes, "In a few generations mankind is exhausting the fossil fuels that were generated over several hundred million years, resulting in large emissions of air pollutants" (14). Some point out that humans have already influenced the earth's system and ecology many thousands of years ago; others focus on the Industrial Revolution or point to changes since the mid-20th century (e.g., Ludwig and Steffen 2018). But there is agreement among Anthropocene researchers that the planet shifted into a new, problematic state characterized by significant changes in the earth's atmosphere and biosphere, and hence is presenting us with an urgent problem. If this is the case, then it seems that it should be of concern to philosophers of

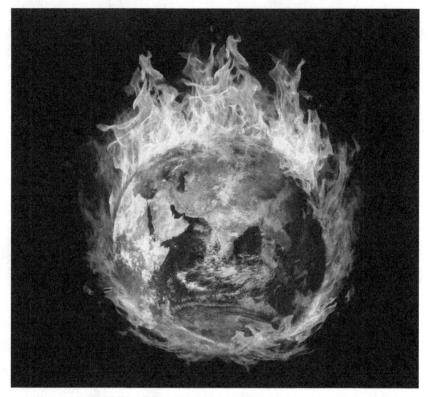

FIGURE 10.4 Illustration of Planet Earth burning

technology, since technology played and plays an important part in enabling these Anthropocenic changes. But also taking up our discussion in the previous section, is talking about the "Anthropocene" a good way of framing the problem?

Let us first see what happens if we reframe the problems regarding the environment and technology in terms of the problem of the Anthropocene. At first sight, use of the term "Anthropocene" is interesting from the point of view of deconstructing the humans-versus-nature and technology-versus-nature dichotomies, since it could be conceptualized as implying the entanglement of these terms: in the Anthropocene, there is a human/nature, human/earth, technology/nature, and there is a problem with this human/nature. The problem is hybrid. The term suggests asking a different question regarding the environment: the problem is no longer about "nature" but about nature and technology, nature and humans, at the same time. The collapse of these dichotomies, as defended by, for instance, Latour, can thus be seen as a feature of the Anthropocene itself. On the other hand, it could be argued that the idea that humans have become a geological force effectively assumes and maintains the human/nature and technology/nature dichotomy and is firmly rooted in the objectivist and technoscientific worldview mentioned previously. Moreover, in contrast to non-modern and ecological views, it seems also a very anthropocentric term. Should we use the term "Anthropocene" at all? And if so, what does the problem of the Anthropocene mean for doing philosophy of technology?

Let me further outline and review some ways philosophers, especially but not exclusively philosophers of technology, could respond or have responded to the discourse and question regarding the Anthropocene.

A first response is to criticize the way the problem is framed. This includes questioning the very term "Anthropocene." Langdon Winner (2017) has recently argued that the term is not only extremely anthropocentric and narcissistic but also does not ask the question of *who* is the source of all the changes and who has a stake in them. The term "Anthropocene" hides that there are many human beings "who over many centuries and to the present day have lived modestly with minimal impact on the local or global environs or the Earth's climate systems"; these people seem to be left out of the game. The focus on the human species as a whole "tends to overlook the actual social and economic institutions and activities that are clearly the primary cause of the massive effects in the biosphere evident today" (Winner 2017, 285). Some people (e.g., "Western" people, "capitalists") contribute far more to the problem than others. Use of the term "mankind" by some Anthropocene researchers is also sexist, and it is problematic to speak for many diverse populations of human beings and for many generations (287). Moreover, humans are seen as gods. Winner proposes to think more about the names we use and to return to the "Holocene" label, which is less problematic (293).

Other philosophers of technology nevertheless use the term and argue for taking the problem of the Anthropocene seriously. In a recent special issue of *Techné*, Lemmens et al. (2017) argue that a focus on the Anthropocene as the new terrestrial condition enables a much-needed critical response to the empirical turn in philosophy of technology since it offers a more macro-oriented and ontological approach. It encourages us to think of technology not just in terms of material artifacts but also in transcendental ways (Lemmens et al. 2017; Coeckelbergh 2018). The editors (Lemmens et al.) argue for a "terrestrial turn" in philosophy of technology. The latter should "start taking into account the earthly context and technological change as well as the fact that this earthly context is itself an increasingly technologized context" (Lemmens et al. 2017, 123). And with regard to philosophical anthropology, focusing on the Anthropocene question enables us to ask not so much what or who the human is but *where* the human is. For Sloterdijk and Stiegler, the question regarding the human has become a topological question, as Cera (2017) reminds us later in the special issue. Taking into account this earthly and planetary horizon (and more generally the place of the human being) then leads to questions about the relation(s) between earth and technology. What does it mean to say, for instance, that the earth has become more technological and technology more earthly? And what does it mean that humanity is threatened by its own technology "yet destined to start remedying this situation," as Blok (2015) has argued?

A second response, then, accepts the "Anthropocene" discourse and hence the way the problem is framed and focuses on this question regarding change. If "Anthropocene" is the problem, how can we address it? How can we bring about change? Or is this the wrong question?

If we reject the "technological fix" proposed by geoengineers and their support-ers, then we could argue that what is needed is that we—keeping in mind Winner's remark, "we" means here especially people who contribute more to the problem—change the way we live. But how can this be done, and does it really help with solving the "big" planetary problem? This question leads us to problems regarding knowledge, agency, and virtue in the Anthropocene. In line with some of my argu-ments presented previously (Coeckelbergh 2015), one could argue that there are significant barriers to making a change due to the way we epistemically relate to the problem and to the environment. I may have the statistical and scientific knowledge about changes in the planetary condition but doubt that my change in behavior would matter, or I may lack a less remote, more engaged kind of know-how and skill to change things. How are our "little" lives connected to the "big" Anthro-pocene problems? And what *can* I do anyway? What can *we* do, collectively, for example, as humanity or as a particular society? The problem is very challenging, and it is not clear who or what can and should act. There seem to be huge problems of individual but also collective action. There is a high level of complexity, and there are many agents involved, human and non-human, interconnected by technology-enabled networks (Jamieson and DiPaola 2016). As individuals, we may experi-ence powerlessness with regard to the Anthropocene. Or we may feel alienated from it. Our lives may seem disconnected to the larger whole(s) and its problems. The horizon is far away. We do not see the planet or the earth. Yet we know that we are involved in creating the problem. But what can we do? Paradoxically and ironi-cally, acknowledging the increase of agency of humanity as a whole, in the sense of its impact on the earth, goes hand in hand with a feeling that we as individuals or even as collectives are merely participants in, and victims of, the changes that "we" have caused and keep causing. We feel that we cannot do much, that we *lack* agency (with regard to changing things), and at the same time we realize that we are doing *too much* (and the wrong kind of things). Our moral frameworks tell us that we should make a change, that we are responsible. Thus, we feel helpless and guilty at the same time. Di Paola put the problem of agency in the Anthropocene thus:

> The irony is that after centuries of modernity and its contributions to human welfare and autonomy, we find ourselves at the portal of the Anthropocene with the widespread sense of a loss of agency. Together, we are remaking

the planet and undermining the conditions of our own existence, though no individual or collective decision was ever made to do so. Natural and human systems are being transformed not as a result of any rational plan, but rather because of the unintended effects of systemic, interlocking forces, and structures that have congealed and stratified in such a way that they seem to dominate our lives, our economies, and our politics. And even though responsibilities dissolve in the whirl of planetary complexity generated by the ever tighter codependency of human and natural systems, each of us is implicated, as a willing yet unintentional transmitter of spatiotemporally unbound harms and damages, in the configuration of a sorry fate for the global poor, future generations and nonhuman nature. (Di Paola 2018, 126)

How can we deal with this ironic and perhaps tragic situation? Congruent with my view in *Environmental Skill* (Coeckelbergh 2015), Di Paola points to virtue and the good life and argues for "rediscovering practices that favour agency retrieval" and that may "help us live more gracefully on this planet that we are so clumsily remaking" (Di Paola 2018, 126). This seems to imply that we can only regain our agency in practice. Theory does not necessarily lead to action, and the facts alone do not help; we need to develop practices in which we can retrieve agency. The challenge is then of course to say more about what kinds of practices we need for this. I suggest that the answer will have to do something with crafts and skill, and that theory may not be sufficient to understand its virtue and value: we need to experience it in practice. Especially craftwork seems very suitable, as it is a mode of skilled engagement with the environment and with others (Coeckelbergh 2015). Yet is it traditional crafts that may help, or can we also do new things with new technologies? I suggest in my (2015) book that the latter is also a possibility, and that our response need not be anti-technological; technologies can be part of such virtuous practices and part of living the good life.

Another, not necessarily incompatible, approach is to question the question of control itself. Di Paola still asks and addresses the question of agency and control. The challenge, according to him, is to regain agency. But maybe agency and control are part of the problem. With Heidegger, we may call for a different attitude altogether. With regard to the Anthropocene, one could interpret his term **Gelassenheit** or "releasement towards things" (Heidegger 1966) as follows: if we would focus less on control, then we disable the mechanism that promotes willing total control over everything and everyone, including the planet and its ecosystem and atmosphere. Instead of control and agency, Heidegger argued, we need a "releasement towards things" (Heidegger 1966, 55–56). With regard to technology, this means that we use technical devices but no longer see things only in a technical way and no longer let them dominate us (Heidegger 1966, 54). We may also call for more care, as Stiegler (2017) does. Influenced by Heidegger, he argues that the Anthropocene results from modern technology's domination of the earth and its current unfolding in a process of digital automation. This enframing (Heidegger 1977), Stiegler (2017) argues, undermines the possibility of thinking one should care for the present and hence take care of the Anthropocene and of technology. Again this argument is not against technology as such: with Stiegler, we can say that digital technology is toxic but can also be used as a **pharmakon** to move beyond the Anthropocene. It is however not so clear what this implies in practice. For example, does Stiegler mean the same technologies that cause the problems, or different technologies? In addition, taking up my earlier use of the term "tragic" when describing the paradox regarding agency in the Anthropocene, I suggest that one could use the concept of *tragedy* to illuminate the problem of the Anthropocene. Perhaps tragedy offers precisely the kind of understanding we need here: tragedy is all about humans wanting to (re)gain agency in the light of forces and events that overpower them but to which they have at the same time—often unintendedly and unknowingly—contributed. The Anthropocene, then, may well turn out to be a new face, form, and revelation of the tragic itself; that is, a new form of human existence, of what it means to be human.

These are merely suggestions for potential responses. It is not entirely clear yet how these proposed changes at the individual and human level, in terms of how we make changes to our lives and to our attitude, can solve the problem of the Anthropocene, which seems to be about much more than human experience and human action alone (although "solution" may be the wrong term, to the extent that it suggests there is an easy fix). In other words, we still have to face the paradox. Maybe this is part of the tragedy. For those interested in Heidegger's work, it must be noted that there is much more to say on how Heidegger could be used for thinking about the Anthropocene (see again the special issue mentioned; for instance, Zwier and Blok 2017). But the responses outlined here already help us to move on in the discussion: in contrast to views of the climate change deniers but also to the "technological fix" strategies of the geo engineers and their political accomplices, these approaches show how much more complex the problem of the Anthropocene is and how a response to the problem is not only about what "they" should do but about what we and I should do, with "we" not in the sense of humanity but in a more concrete, existential, and cultural sense: it is about attitude (e.g., the Western attitude of control), about *my* relation to technology, and about *our* culture and society—including perhaps its tragic condition. One could say, what is called the problem of "the Anthropocene" is about the planet and the earth: but it is also about *my* life and about *our* form of life.

That being said, this analysis shows that the Anthropocene discussion is still rather anthropocentric. It is "our problem" in the sense of "humanity's problem." Where are the non-humans? And do all humans face the agency problems in the same way? Are all equally involved in the tragedy? We may ask with Winner who the "I" and the "we" are that face the problems and who is excluded from consideration and from the discussion. Who is allowed to act and play along in this Anthropocene tragedy? Is the exclusion of the non-humans (next to the exclusion of many humans) perhaps the really tragic thing that is happening here?

Note that, as in section 10.2 on "nature," the issue of language turns out to be crucial when thinking about the Anthropocene and technology. As Winner pointed out, the terms we use in these discussions matter a lot. They relate to social, moral, and political meanings. They relate to how we view the world and ourselves, as humans and as persons. This encourages us to think more about all kinds of key terms we use in these discussions. For example, one should also reflect on the term "earth" as used in the Anthropocene discourse. What do people mean when they use the term "earth"? Does "earth" refer to a geological entity, or can we also understand earth in a more phenomenological (e.g., Heideggerian) sense as entangled with the lifeworld and experience of human beings? Is earth an ontic entity or is it a condition of possibility, a transcendental condition, a "grammar"? Is it a (big) thing or the grammar of our existence? Is our form of life made possible by earth as a condition of possibility, and should we hence speak of "the terrestrial transcendental"? Is it both, and if so, what is the relation between both meanings? One could do a similar exercise for the term "planet." What kind of point of view is implied when we use the term "planet"? Are we living on this planet, or are we viewing it as it were from a point of outer space? Is this point a view from nowhere? What are the (meta-)ethical implications of taking such a point of view? Asking about the "who" and the "where" of the Anthropocene-talkers/thinkers helps us to take some critical distance and ask interesting philosophical questions, including ethical and political questions. But this was facilitated by asking, which words are used? Which language is used? In chapter 11 on linking philosophy of technology to other philosophical (sub) disciplines, I will say more about how philosophy of technology could pay more attention to language and how it could connect to philosophy of language.

REVIEW QUESTIONS

1. What is climate change? Outline some ways in which we can respond to climate change.
2. What is geoengineering? Give some examples. What could be wrong with geoengineering?
3. Outline some modern and non-modern approaches to the environment, and explore what this means for thinking about technology.

4. What is wrong (or could be wrong) with the notion of "nature"? How is the notion of "nature" used in discussions about environmental problems? Critically discuss this notion in the light of work by Ingold and Latour.
5. What is the Anthropocene? Sketch some ways philosophers can respond to "the problem of the Anthropocene."
6. What is the paradox regarding agency in the Anthropocene?

DISCUSSION QUESTIONS

1. How should we respond to environmental problems and the Anthropocene? Do you think technology is the right answer? Why (not)? Discuss some criticisms of the technological "fix" and argue for your own response.
2. Should environmental philosophy and philosophy of technology remain entirely different fields? Should they talk more to one another? Should they merge?
3. Should we keep using the term "nature"? Why (not)? What language should we use to conceptualize our relation to the environment?
4. What do you think about non-modern approaches to environment and technology?
5. What do you think about Borgmann's view that we need focal practices?
6. What is the Anthropocene? Do you sympathize with this term? Why (not)?
7. What language should we use to talk about the "Anthropocene," if we should use the term at all?
8. How would you solve the paradox of agency in the Anthropocene? Can it be solved at all?
9. What can we learn about technology from the discussions about the Anthropocene?

RECOMMENDED READING

Coeckelbergh, Mark. 2015. *Environmental Skill: Motivation, Knowledge, and the Possibility of a Non-Romantic Environmental Ethics.* New York: Routledge.

Coeckelbergh, Mark. 2017. "Beyond 'Nature.' Towards More Engaged and Care-Full Ways of Relating to the Environment." In *Routledge Handbook of Environmental Anthropology*, edited by Helen Kopnina and Eleanor Shoreman-Ouimet, 105–116. Abingdon, UK: Earthscan/Routledge.

Special issue of *Techné* on the Anthropocene, especially the introduction by the editors: Lemmens, Pieter, Vincent Blok, and Jochem Zwier. 2017. "Guest Editors' Introduction: Toward a Terrestrial Turn in Philosophy of Technology." *Techné: Research in Philosophy and Technology* 21(2–3), Special issue on the Anthropocene: 114–126.

KEY TERMS

Anthropocene	*Gelassenheit*	Global warming
Climate change	Geoengineering	Pharmakon

4 THINKING ABOUT TECHNOLOGY BY GOING BEYOND PHILOSOPHY OF TECHNOLOGY (PHILOSOPHY OF TECHNOLOGY +)

PHILOSOPHY OF TECHNOLOGY AND OTHER PHILOSOPHY: (RE)CONNECTING WITH OTHER PHILOSOPHICAL SUBDISCIPLINES

CASE/TECHNOLOGY:
Social Media and Its Social Effects on Our Lives

In chapter 5, I already mentioned the case of social media. In the beginning of the 21st century, the internet evolved into a space of so-called social media, which facilitate the sharing and creation of content and communication between people. Services and platforms such as Facebook and Twitter, so-called Web 2.0. applications, enable users to easily generate and share content by posting and commenting, and facilitate online social networks by connecting user profiles. Compared to traditional media such as TV and newspapers, social media are far more interactive and immediate, and involve and immerse the user. This provides plenty of opportunities for information and communication.

FIGURE 11.1 People standing next to each other looking at their smartphones

However, there are also many criticisms of social media. Issues include privacy issues, information overload, bullying, distraction, addiction, the danger of narcissism and mere status-seeking, and even loneliness. Let us focus on these social effects now. A prominent researcher in this area is Sherry Turkle. Whereas in her earlier work she maintained that the internet can help us to explore identities, in *Alone Together* (2011) and more recently in *Reclaiming Conversation* (2015), Turkle has argued that we know how to connect but have forgotten how to talk to each other. Children are less empathic, family interaction is distracted, and we have an increasing need for constant stimulation. Few can resist the pull of the smartphone and its social media applications. The messages are waiting. Whether or not these effects are exaggerated and whether or not they are *only* due to our use of these media and technologies, it is clear that we need more research and reflection on these effects. One way to do that is to connect to philosophy, in particular ethics. Within ethics, one of the traditions is virtue ethics. What is the good life in the age of social media? Thinking about virtue and the good life as proposed by Vallor and others such as Brey and myself seems at least one meaningful way of addressing these issues about social media from a philosophical angle. For instance, self-control is a very ancient but still highly relevant issue in this context. However, it is also important to go beyond the personal level of analysis and consider more structural issues— that is, consider the societal and political contexts that may contribute to the effects mentioned. Consider again the analysis provided in chapter 5 on critical theory, which was focused on political economy. More generally, next to ethics, other fields of practical philosophy such as political philosophy may also be useful resources for philosophers of technology. (See also Coeckelbergh [2018b] on technology and the good society.) This chapter is about how philosophers of technology can draw on insights from other subfields in philosophy.

11.1. Introduction

Philosophers outside philosophy of technology are sometimes confused or skeptical about the nature and status of philosophy of technology. Is it a (sub)field on its own, or is it part of another field? And is it philosophical or theoretical enough? For example, some believe that philosophy of technology is a branch of **applied philosophy** or that it is a branch of philosophy of science. Others claim that it is more empirical than theoretical. Now there is some truth in this: sometimes philosophy of technology is done in that way. But this is not necessarily the case. For students and beginning researchers in the field, it is important to clarify some of these methodological issues. This is the topic of this and the next chapters.

Let me start with addressing the question concerning how empirical the field is and should be. While it is true that many philosophers concerned with technology do their thinking in a way that is sensitive to empirical and societal reality and that involves interdisciplinarity, there is more to it than that. How empirical a specific field in philosophy can and should be is a question that can and must be asked for all subfields in philosophy, and the view that philosophy of technology is always and necessarily applied is fundamentally flawed. There are many ways of doing philosophy of technology. Some conceptual work is abstract and remote from empirical work. Some start from theory and concepts and indeed apply these to issues concerning technology; others start from technology and work their way up to concepts that could guide technological practice. Sometimes philosophers of technology do both at the same time. Both methods can lead to more or less theoretical, or more or less abstract, work. There is much variety. Moreover, while some philosophers think about technology without relationships to other subfields, there are other ways of doing it. In my view, *philosophy of technology often does, and should, contribute to, interact with, overlap with, and learn from other philosophical subdisciplines*—including what are sometimes regarded as core subdisciplines (branches) such as epistemology and metaphysics—and the main philosophical traditions. This is where the strength of the field lies if it wants to grow as a *philosophical* project. For the continued growth of the field, it is important for researchers to not only focus on timely issues concerning technological development and engagement with society (see also chapters 12 and 13) and with the media (which is tempting if one gets a lot of media attention on fashionable issues) but also to remain connected to, and engaged with, philosophical work and philosophical traditions. So far in the development of the field, only a limited spectrum of theories and traditions have been used; there are more sources available. Finally, as has been argued throughout this textbook, philosophy of technology cannot be reduced to a subdivision of philosophy of science, even if some current philosophies have historical roots in that subdiscipline, or even if some representatives remain close to philosophy of science given their own philosophical backgrounds. Thinking about technology has its own specific focus in terms of problems, concepts, and theories.

In this chapter, I show some existing connections and crossovers between philosophy of technology and other subfields in philosophy. Particular attention will be given to (1) ethics and moral philosophy, (2) philosophical anthropology, and—a currently under-researched area in the field—(3) philosophy of language. This provides students with more examples of how to do philosophy of technology. The focus is on how to do philosophy of technology in a way that connects to other subdisciplines in philosophy: to major branches such as ethics and to areas of interest such as philosophy of science.

11.2. Ethics and Moral Philosophy: Thinking about Virtue and Thinking about Technology

One of the most popular areas, if not *the* most popular area, within philosophy of technology is *ethics* of technology. Sometimes there is also engagement with moral philosophy. The connection with practical philosophy is therefore the most obvious one to make. But there are many ways this can be done, some of which are more empirically oriented than others, and some hardly involve a cross-over between thinking about technology and thinking about ethics and morality elsewhere in philosophy. Let us consider some approaches.

First, with regard to the *empirical versus theoretical* question, we can observe that there is a wide variety of areas and approaches—even within a particular practical area. For instance, within **engineering ethics**, there are people who do something closer to applied ethics, such as when they create a list of ethical principles for a code of ethics that is meant to be applied by engineers, or when they think of the virtuous engineer by relying on traditional virtues. But there are also people who are more focused on engineering design and start from there to see what ethical issues could come up. Some people practice it as a form of applied ethics; others connect engineering ethics to philosophy of technology. Another example is that some ethicists of technology start from a particular ethical theory, say consequentialism or virtue ethics, and then apply this to issues concerning technology (in a similar way as other applied ethicists do—see, for instance, Vallor [2016] discussed following, although this goes further than a simple application); but there are also others who start from the phenomena and the material reality of the technology rather than (only) from theory and who do not make the link to normative theory or moral philosophy at all (see, e.g., the discussion between Verbeek and Peterson about whether technology can have moral agency (see section 4.4 in this book), which does not really link to work on agency in practical philosophy). And some manage to do philosophy of technology in a way that is both empirically sensitive *and* sound and interesting in terms of conceptual development, theory, and argument. Arguably the latter should be the preferred approach in the field and has been proven the most successful and influential.

Second, there is also variety in terms of the degree to which there is a *genuine crossover between thinking about technology and work in ethics and moral philosophy*. There is always the danger that good thinkers interested in technology, however original and daring their work may be in other ways, prefer to largely stay in the comfort zone of *either* the subfield of philosophy of technology *or* the subdisciplines of ethics and/or moral philosophy. This is understandable but misses the potential creation of spaces for mutual learning and interaction between the subfields. For instance, if a philosopher of technology proposes and uses a theory of responsibility or moral agency without engaging with theory of responsibility and moral agency developed in moral philosophy, then this is a missed opportunity. Or if someone doing applied ethics discusses a new technology without taking into consideration insights and theories about the non-instrumental nature of technology developed within philosophy of technology, then this is also a missed chance. More crossovers are needed, more work that leaves the comfort zones of either philosophy of technology (writ small) or ethics.

Let me give some examples. In chapter 7, I have shown that Floridi's information ethics not only is focused on understanding technology but is based on a position in metaphysics and engages with ethical theory. This can be the starting point for discussion that further crosses over to key discussions in ethics. For instance, Floridi (2013) argues against virtue ethics and for an environmental ethics: according to him, both are incompatible since virtue ethics is insufficiently patient-oriented—it is "me-oriented" (166–168). Against this, one could reply that it is possible to have an environmental virtue ethics, as several people have argued within environmental ethics (e.g., Van Wensveen 2000; Cafaro 2004 Sandler 2007;)—a direction of inquiry Floridi entirely ignores. Anyway, here there is sufficient crossover between thinking about technology and thinking about ethics to have this discussion in the first place. This is not just philosophy of technology; it is philosophy (here: ethics) *tout court*.

Another example of a crossover is my work on moral status ascription (e.g., Coeckelbergh 2012b), which I already mentioned in chapter 8 to show how technology is often the starting point for doing philosophy. It was initially meant to contribute to philosophy of technology (the status of robots), but it became a discussion that belongs to moral philosophy: it asks questions about the role of appearances with regard to moral status ascription and explores what it means to have a relational understanding of moral status and proposes a transcendental argument to show that how we think about moral status is itself shaped and made possible by conditions such as language and indeed (other) technologies. This approach can be applied beyond thinking about technology. For example, it can be argued that discussions about the moral status of particular animals are preconfigured by the ways we talk about that animal (e.g., in terms of food), which in turn are related to technological practices (e.g., meat production). Similar arguments can be made for how we talk about robots: it matters, for instance, if we name the robot or if we talk about "it" (Coeckelbergh 2017e). Another example is my book on environmental skill (Coeckelbergh 2015), which was meant to contribute to environmental ethics but also includes thinking about technology in relation to virtue and skill (see also Coeckelbergh 2011) and draws implications for thinking about technology.

The previous examples already referred to **virtue ethics**. A further example of a crossover from ethics to thinking about technology, which may still be labeled "applied ethics" but makes a serious and interesting effort in connecting a philosophical tradition with challenges posed by new and emerging technologies, and which is entirely focused on virtue, is Shannon Vallor's work on technology and the virtues (Vallor 2016). Let me discuss this at greater length.

Like Floridi's work and that of many other philosophies of technology, the starting point of Vallor's (2016) *Technology and the Virtues* is new technologies, in particular recent information and communication technologies (ICTs). But this time the main concern is not a metaphysical one but another, also very ancient, one: the problem of the good life. How can humans live well in a world shaped by emerging technologies? (See also Brey et al. 2012.) Vallor's starting motivation and intuition is that our moral character is already being shaped by the new technologies. Her answer is then that we need to cultivate what she calls "technomoral virtues" (Vallor 2016, 1): we need to cultivate "specific technomoral habits and virtues" (9) required to meet the problems. To work out what this means, she draws on the classical virtue traditions, which is not exclusively Western: Aristotelian, Confucian, and Buddhist ethics are interpreted as having shared commitments such as a commitment to the cultivation of character and a "thick" conception of human being as a relational being. She also discusses the question concerning ethics in a global world: how to deal with cultural difference.

However, here we are concerned with method. Vallor (2016) claims that she does applied ethics, but one with a very broad scope: since every applied ethics operates within a global context and in a context of technologies pervading all aspects of our everyday lives, it is an "applied ethic of contemporary life writ large" (34). This supports the point argued for in this chapter that doing philosophy of technology is always more than thinking about technology: it is also thinking about our lives, about ethics, about the human, and so on. Moreover, in my reading, Vallor goes beyond a simple application of virtue theory to technological contexts; it is also based on a more refined understanding of technologies. It is mainly an applied ethics, but it crosses the bridge to philosophy of technology to some extent.

This becomes especially clear when we get to Vallor's discussions of technomoral virtues. Transferring traditional virtues such as honesty, self-control, humility, and courage to the context of contemporary technosocial practices, she shows how contemporary ICTs present promises but also barriers to human flourishing and excellence, and more generally how starting from the virtue tradition we can ask urgent and pertinent questions about the good life in a technological age. For instance, what does honesty mean in the context of social media and related debates about privacy and transparency (Vallor 2016, 121)? (See also textbox "Social Media and Its Social Effects on Our Lives"). What is the difference between Quantified Self and an examined life (202)? How are we to exercise self-control and protect ourselves from "excessive and unproductive new media consumption"; or are we doomed to be (or remain) "viciously incontinent" given that "some new media habits pose an unusually strong challenge to our faculties of self-control"—not to say that we are addicted to them (167)? And how might robots used in care shape the goods internal to the practice of care and condition the social and emotional character of human beings (220; see also Coeckelbergh [2009] and other work on robots and the good life such as Coeckelbergh [2012a])? Clearly, the language of virtue ethics helps us to voice some concerns about how technologies transform our lives and help us to reflect on what it means to live well (or not) in the context of particular new technologies.

Bridging ethics and thinking about technology also implies letting debates in ethics and moral philosophy enter into philosophy of technology, and ideally vice versa (the latter is unfortunately rare). For instance, in this case, Vallor (2016) has to defend why a virtue ethics approach is better than others in moral theory. For example, one could object that virtue ethics is too self-centered (but not selfish) or "me-centered," as Floridi (2013, 166) puts it, since it has the center of moral concern in the self or in the person. It is questionable if such an approach scales to "very complex and open social contexts" (166). Moreover, even at the level of me–you relations, one could argue that virtue ethics is not sufficiently patient-oriented and/or does not do justice to the *otherness* of the other. (The latter concern may take inspiration from the work of Levinas, e.g.; see also chapter 8.) Furthermore, one could argue that Vallor's virtue approach to technology is too much focused on the individual level—and hence individual good—and fails to ask the question regarding the good society and politics (Coeckelbergh 2018b), questions that may be dealt with by, for instance, connecting to political philosophy. In the Aristotelian tradition Vallor draws on, the ethical and the political are firmly connected. Moreover, one could object that virtue ethics is too traditionally humanist in the sense that it is mainly about humans; non-humans such as animals do not seem to play a significant role. Counter-objections could then try to show that empathy is also one of the virtues (as Vallor argues) and argue that a virtue ethics is not *necessarily* limited in scope to humans. In response, the interlocutor could object that empathically responding to others does not fully respect their otherness, and that an account of the good of particular animals, for instance, is lacking, since virtue ethics is too much centered on human good. Once again, this discussion shows that doing philosophy of technology need not be isolated from other philosophical subdisciplines and that it is not necessarily any less philosophical than other subfields. Instead, doing philosophy of technology at its best (1) achieves a better understanding and evaluation of technologies *and* (2) contributes to philosophy writ large by engaging with perennial philosophical questions (here the question about the good life, but also environmental-philosophical and philosophical-anthropological questions) and by contributing to discussions about philosophical theories (here normative ethical theory, in particular, the discussion about virtue ethics). Let me now say more about how thinking about technology links to philosophical anthropology.

11.3. Philosophical Anthropology: Thinking about the Human and Thinking about Technology

Philosophical anthropology provides another interesting subfield for fruitful crossovers with philosophy of technology. The question regarding non-humans, for example, seems highly relevant to both fields. Whereas traditional definitions of the human tend to ignore technology since they assume a wide gap between humans (subjects) and everything else (objects) including technology, recognizing the non-instrumental roles of technology also poses the question if and how technology should somehow be included in thinking about the human. There are already answers to this question, some more radical than others. For instance, posthumanists fully embrace that there is no such thing as a pure human (or pure subject) and that non-humans such as animals and technologies are part of our hybrid nature. Transhumanists seek to use technology to enhance the human, to create a new, transhuman being. And most contemporary philosophers of technology, even if they do not endorse posthumanist or transhumanist views, would agree that technology (use) is at least one important dimension of human beings. Some would say that human beings are—among other things—technological beings. Let me give some examples of views on human beings that take into account technology. In all cases, it is once again new technological developments that inspire philosophers of technology and other philosophers to engage with the age-old philosophical question regarding the human. I already gave an overview of posthumanism and transhumanism; here the emphasis is on the anthropological question.

First, often technologies are used as metaphors for thinking about the human. For example, humans are seen as machines. Already in the past, new technologies inspired philosophers in their thinking about the human: to say what humans are or to say what humans are *not*. Often what I have called negative anthropologies have defined the human by saying what it is *not* (Coeckelbergh 2013, 195–196; see also Coeckelbergh 2014, 63–64, and elsewhere). Sometimes technology has been used for that purpose: it is said that the human is *not* an instrument, a thing, a tool, a machine, and so on. For instance, in early modern times, Descartes developed a negative anthropology in the form of what one could call a *machine anthropology*. Descartes relied on the machine to develop his famous mind–body distinction and human–animal distinction. In this view, animals are complex machines (today we might say robots); and like animals, humans also have a body; but in addition, humans have a soul (Descartes [1637] 1960). Hence, according to Descartes, we are not (mere) machines but more-than-machines: body-machines plus a soul. The machine was thus crucial in his definitional operation: it was a philosophical-anthropological tool in Descartes's techno-anthropology. Today some people insist that we are *not* robots, machines, artificial agents, and so on: again (new) technologies are used in negative anthropologies to define (and defend) the human.

FIGURE 11.2 Portrait of René Descartes

Second, **posthumanists** have criticized traditional humanist definitions of the human for assuming a far too wide gap between humans and non-humans and subjects and objects and have put more emphasis on non–humans such as animals, plants, and technological artifacts. Floridi's (2011) metaphysics, for instance, can be seen as a kind of posthumanism that links the human to the non-human world via the concept of information. Furthermore, the figure of the cyborg is often used to stress hybridity, in particular to blur the boundary between humans and machines. In this context, Donna Haraway's influential "A Cyborg Manifesto" must be mentioned again in which she defines the cyborg as "a hybrid of machine and organism" ([1991] 2000, 291) and embraces a world in which people are no longer afraid of their "joint kinship with animals and machines" (295). For Haraway, the cyborg is monstrous, but she sees this as something positive, since the confusion of boundaries helps to subvert all kinds of binaries of Western culture such as nature versus culture and body versus mind (312).

Haraway's manifesto was written before the internet and was inspired by personal computers; yet as I have argued (Coeckelbergh 2017c, 183), her cyborg is still rather cultural and ethereal. Today we encounter much more *material* cyborgs. There are, for instance, prosthetic devices that replace parts of the body like arms and legs, brain–computer interfaces, and neuroprosthetic devices such as cochlear implants (see textbox "Case/Technology: Cochlear Implants") that replace functions of the senses and nervous system. Here the cyborg is not a literary fiction used to support a postmodern and posthumanist program; it is part of reality and daily experience. And beyond prosthetics and therapy, some scientists and engineers *hope* for more integration between humans and machines. For instance, Kevin Warwick wants to "upgrade" himself by means of technology "to become a cyborg—part human, part machine" (Warwick 2004, 1) and imagines a future where we expand our senses and communicative abilities by means of connecting the human nervous system to machines.

CASE/TECHNOLOGY:
Cochlear Implants

A cochlear implant is an electronic device that helps persons who are deaf or have severe hearing problems. It receives and processes sound and sends this to the internal device, which stimulates the cochlear nerve with electric impulses. The nerve then sends signals to the brain. There is discussion in the scientific literature about how effective the devices are. Interestingly (from an ethics of technology point of view), there has also been resistance from the Deaf community: some people from this community have argued that cochlear implants threaten their (minority) culture, with the majority imposing their standards of normality on them and medicalizing them instead of respecting their unique language and culture (based on sign language). Others have argued that this does not need to be the case and that the device can be used to communicate between the two worlds and cultures. Hence, there is a tension between a medical and a sociocultural understanding of deafness; there are different models of deafness (Power 2005).

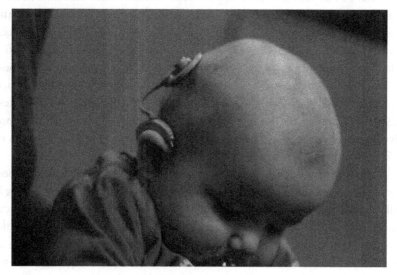

FIGURE 11.3 Infant with cochlear implant

Third, this brings us again to **transhumanists** and the discussion about **human enhancement**. The idea of human enhancement is that medical and other technologies now used for therapeutic and prosthetic purposes could also be used to give people more-than-human abilities. It is argued that the line is already blurred, that many people already use, for instance, drugs and mobile phones to support and enhance their cognitive functions. New and emerging technologies such as genetic engineering and gene therapy (including gene editing), nanomedicine, artificial intelligence, robotics, brain–computer interfaces, and so on, are then seen as offering the possibilities for not only enhancing particular humans but also enhancing the human species at large: what is needed, according to some, is a revolution rather than slow evolution. Transhumanists, in particular, assume this position. The human is seen as ready for improvement by means of technology. Transhumanists have argued that not to change human nature is a form of irrational conservatism, "status quo bias" (Bostrom and Ord 2006), and that it may even be a moral obligation to enhance (Harris 2007), including to enhance our moral dispositions (Savulescu and Persson 2008). And Ray Kurzweil (2005) has argued that with increasing computer power and artificial intelligence, we are on our way to a time (the Singularity) when machine intelligence will take over and when we will gradually be converted to non-biological, digital form. Many transhumanists hope for some form of immortality.

There are many ethical and political issues raised by such proposals (for an overview, see Coeckelbergh 2013 and 2017a). There are interesting overlaps here between thinking about technology and work in bioethics, for instance. But here my point is again that new technology inspires people to rethink the human or at least to discuss about human being and being human in the light of these new and emerging technologies: given these new technologies, what is the human, and what should the human be? What is human nature? Should we aim for human perfection or even immortality? Or should we rather ask what is a good and meaningful human life? What is the destiny of the human, or is it meaningless to ask that question? What is the relation between nature and nurture? How philosophically significant is the skin as a border (e.g., an ethical border)? Would transhumans still be vulnerable, and in what ways? Here philosophy of technology becomes philosophical anthropology and vice versa.

This is not to say that in practice there is always a serious effort on the part of those who think about new technologies (or put forward posthumanist or transhumanist ideas) to engage with *the tradition of philosophical anthropology as a subfield of philosophy*. There is still a lot of room for more genuine and substantial crossovers between the subfields philosophy of technology and philosophical anthropology. For instance, there could be more research on using Max Scheler, Helmuth Plessner, Arnold Gehlen, Hannah Arendt, Günter Anders, Paul Ricoeur, René Girard, Alasdair MacIntyre, Karl Marx, Sigmund Freud, Friedrich Nietzsche, and John Dewey—just to name a few thinkers known for their work in this area—for thinking about the relation between being human and *technology*. There are also potential bridges to work in anthropology, paleoanthropology, and archaeology—some of which already crosses over to philosophy: for instance, anthropological/philosophical work by Michael D. Jackson or Tim Ingold, which includes ethnographical methods. And within philosophy of technology, philosophers such as Bernard Stiegler, Don Ihde, and Bernhard Irrgang have an interest in paleoanthropology. (I will say more about interdisciplinarity and transdisciplinarity in chapter 12.)

11.4. Philosophy of Language: Thinking about Language and Thinking about Technology

In contrast to ethics and philosophical anthropology, crossing over to **philosophy of language** is a much less well-trodden path. After the empirical turn in philosophy of technology, much attention has been paid to artifacts, and language was largely neglected (Coeckelbergh 2017b). In response to this limitation (but not necessarily against the empirical turn as such), and to give more examples of interesting crossovers to other subfields in philosophy, let me consider work that concerns relations between *language and technology* and that uses philosophy of language as a rich source of inspiration. Here are two examples of how philosophy of language can be used in philosophy of technology, based on the work of John Searle and Ludwig Wittgenstein (for a more extended overview and discussion, see Coeckelbergh 2017e).

11.4.1. Using Searle for Thinking about Technology

Austin and Searle developed what they called **speech act** theory, which claims that speech is not only about representation—getting across propositional content—but also what Austin (1962) called "doing things with words." Later, Searle stressed that it is about creating social reality. In *The Construction of Social Reality* (1995) and in "Social Ontology" (2006), Searle is interested in explaining how there can be "social facts" such as money, property, marriage, and so on. His answer is that we collectively accept giving a certain status to a person or object, and that we do this by using language. He gives the example of paper money: a physical object like paper performs its social function not in virtue of its physical structure but in virtue of a collective intention, attitude, and agreement (Searle 2006, 17) This works via language, and in particular via a specific kind of grammatical form: declaration. We declare a particular object or person has a particular status. Searle calls this declaration a "status function" (18). For example, we agree and declare that "this piece of paper counts as money in the context of trade and exchange." In this way, social facts are made and social institutions take shape. And here language—in the form of speech acts—does not represent, but *does* something: in particular, it gives status to objects and persons and, more generally, constitutes social reality.

IN FOCUS:
John Searle

John Searle is an American analytic philosopher widely known for his views on mind, language, and the social. He was a professor at University of California, Berkeley. In his early work, he was influenced by Austin and Wittgenstein and wrote on speech acts. He is also known for his so-called Chinese room argument against strong artificial intelligence (the main point is that being able to translate by following rules and instructions does not entail understanding a language) and for his work in the area of social philosophy: in *The Construction of Social Reality* (1995), he explains social phenomena and institutions as arising out of collective intentionality through speech acts that

FIGURE 11.4 John Searle at the Faculty of Christ Church, Oxford, England, 2005

have the form of a declaration. (See the textbox "John Searle's Social Ontology" in chapter 6.) In 2017, he was sued for sexual harassment and in 2019 the university revoked his emeritus status.

Now one may critically discuss this view. For instance, one may object to Searle's dualist assumption that there is a strict distinction between the physical world and the social world. Is it possible to speak about the physical outside of the social? Is language a mere instrument or is it already connected to the social? Or one may question the contractarian basic assumption that there is first agreement and collective intentionality needed (in a kind of original position) and that this agreement and this use of language is necessary and sufficient for social institutions to be created. Against this assumption, one could argue that the social is not only a matter of agreement or collective intentionality, that the social does not need an explanation in the first place, or that language is only one tool in a social environment.

Yet whatever its problems may be, Searle's view could be used in philosophy of technology to deal with a particular problem: explaining how **virtual worlds**, computer games, and virtual objects within such a world can be socially meaningful.

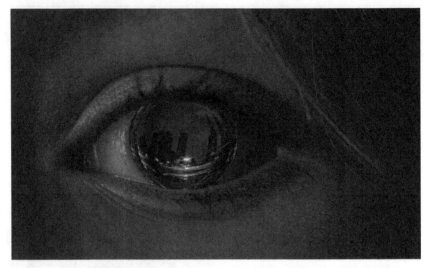

FIGURE 11.5 Virtual world mirroring in the iris of a woman

How, for instance, is it possible that some people in virtual worlds and games use **virtual money** and seem to attach real value to it, exchange it, and so on within their community and practices? Since for Searle, language alone does the trick of social status ascription—status functions work even without physical objects (Searle 2006, 22)—we can explain how, for instance, virtual money gets its value: if by collective intentionality and speech acts, we declare and agree that virtual object x has function f, then for all social purposes within the virtual world or game this suffices. It becomes a social reality, regardless of the virtual status of the object. The same could be said of money in digital form and **cryptocurrencies** like Bitcoin: these units have value if we declare and agree so. Thus, Searle's theory of status declaration and the distinction between physical and social reality enables philosophers of technology to make sense of what happens in virtual worlds and virtual game environments, and hence can and have been used by philosophers of technology (e.g., Brey 2003 and 2014; see also Søraker 2010), although not very often (yet).

11.4.2. Using Wittgenstein for Thinking about Technology

Wittgenstein is another philosopher whose work is not often used in philosophy of technology, apart from a few exceptions (e.g., Winner 1986; Nordmann 2002; Franssen and Koller 2016). Let me give an example of how the later Wittgenstein might be used for better understanding and evaluating technology by drawing on my recent work on this topic (Coeckelbergh 2017d and 2017e).

IN FOCUS:
Ludwig Wittgenstein

Ludwig Wittgenstein was a famous 20th-century, Austrian-British philosopher who is very well known for his original contributions to philosophy of language, philosophy of mind, epistemology, metaphysics, logic, and philosophy of mathematics. His teacher was Bertrand Russell. He was a professor at Cambridge University but also an engineer researcher in Manchester and a schoolteacher and gardener in Austria. He also helped design a house in Vienna. His best-known works are the *Tractatus Logico-Philosophicus* and the *Philosophical Investigations* ([1953] 2009), the latter of which appeared posthumously.

FIGURE 11.6 Portrait of Ludwig Wittgenstein

In the first book, written during World War I, he argued that thoughts and propositions are representations or pictures of reality, in particular of facts; propositions that cannot do that are nonsense. In the *Investigations*, Wittgenstein rejects this conception of meaning as representation and argues that the meaning of a word is its use in language. He compares words with tools that can have diverse functions, depending on use. That use is related to activities and what Wittgenstein calls "language-games" and a "form of life"; he also uses the term "grammar." These notions do not refer to technical instructions or syntax but to the context and culture that make a particular use possible and meaningful. At the same time, that context and culture should not be understood as something external or something that can be idealized. The grammar and the games only live in use. Wittgenstein is also known for his so-called private language argument, also to be found in the *Investigations*, which claims that for an utterance to be meaningful, it must be possible in principle to subject it to public standards of correctness of use. A language that can only be understood by one person is not meaningful.

Wittgenstein's view of language in the *Philosophical Investigations* is that meaning depends on use: the meaning of a word is not attached to the word-object we use, but depends on how we use it. For Wittgenstein, language is an instrument (Wittgenstein [1953] 2009, §569, 159e). He uses a technological metaphor:

> Think of the tools in a toolbox: there is a hammer, pliers, a saw, a screwdriver, a rule, a glue-pot, glue, nails and screws.—The functions of words are as diverse as the functions of these objects. (And in both cases there are similarities.) (Wittgenstein [1953] 2009, §11, 9e)

Furthermore, since meaning depends on use, we have to connect meaning to the contexts of that use, in particular to the activities our language is woven into (Wittgenstein [1953] 2009, §7, 8e) and to what Wittgenstein calls a **language game** (§7, 9e) or a **form of life** (§19, 11e). One could interpret this as saying that our language use is embedded in a "culture," although culture should then not be understood as a thing but as only existing and living in concrete use. Moreover, Wittgenstein is known for emphasizing rule following, but at the same time—for instance, in *On Certainty* (1969)—he also points to the implicit knowledge in our form(s) of life. Of course much more can be said and has been said about Wittgenstein's view of language and this interpretation; but for our purposes, this suffices as the working view we can start from in this illustration: it is a view of language that focuses on use, and that embeds this use within a larger whole— say, a culture.

This view of language can then be used in philosophy of technology; for instance, to attend to the use of language that often accompanies the use of tools (e.g., I use a hammer and I swear when something goes wrong), or to point to the phenomenon that today language is often entangled with the materiality of the technology. For example, my use of this computer to write a book is as much about language as it is about material technology: in use, matter and language seem to combine. This could be interesting for developing a more adequate ontology and phenomenology of technology, understood as technology use. It seems especially relevant for understanding recent ICTs such as computers, smartphones, and software, the use and ontology of which cannot be described without reference to language. For example, software is code, but in its use and functioning, it is always connected to the materiality of a device; it needs the materiality to perform its agency. Vice versa, the material artifact is "dead" without the code that gives it "life." Such artifacts hence seem to have a dual ontological nature: linguistic and material. And phenomenologically speaking, their use implies both experience of language use and experience of the use of a material artifact. My use of this computer now is experienced as the use of language (using words, making sentences, etc.) and at the same time the use of an artifact (computer as artifact).

Moreover, I have proposed that Wittgenstein's more holistic and contextual understanding of language use can also be transferred to thinking about technology: we can turn around Wittgenstein's metaphor and compare technology to language; in particular, apply Wittgenstein's view of language to *technology* (Coeckelbergh 2017d and 2017e). This then gives us a view of technology that is use-oriented (and is hence compatible with Franssen and Koller's [2016] proposal) and that, in line with Winner's (1986) suggestions on the topic, puts technology in the context of a form of life. For understanding technology, it implies that the meaning of technological artifacts must be related to their use and must be put in the context of particular *activities, games, and form of life*. For example, the meaning of a navigation device in a car can only be understood in the context of its use; that is, as being part of specific activities (driving, wayfinding), rules (e.g., traffic rules), and *the way we do things*—for example, drive—in a particular culture and society. Thus, there is already knowledge and know-how available within a given game and form of life; our technology use follows these lines. A form of life and a game are normative. I have argued that all this—one could call it a "grammar"—must be presupposed for our use to make sense: it makes possible our (meaningful) use of the technology. Technology might change the game, that is, a particular *use* of the technology might change the game, but not so much; there is always a game and a form of life that preexists our use, and in which our use—if it is to be useful and meaningful—must embed itself. In *Using Words and Things* (2017e) I have used transcendental (but not transcendent) language to express this: a particular use of a technology is *made possible* by a particular game and form of life; the form of life provides *conditions of possibility* for its use-meaning. One could also say the games and form of life pre-structure the use of technology.

This Wittgensteinian approach enables us to better understand technology: in response to the empirical turn, it helps us to articulate that technology is not only about artifacts as such (and what they do or how they change our perception) but also about what *we humans* do; that is, about our games and our form of life as human users. Furthermore, the proposed approach can also be used for ethics of technology since it points to the normativity that is at play in the games and lives in our form of life. This use of Wittgenstein thus enables us, when thinking about technology, to become aware of potentially problematic normative grammars that structure our use of the technology. For example, an analysis along the lines proposed may reveal that a specific gender bias that is already present in our society might shape the meaning and use of a specific technology. For instance, when discussing a particular robot, we may make, and critically discuss, a link between its gendered shape (e.g., female shape), its use, and the society in which it is developed (which may have a specific gender bias relating household tasks to females, for instance). Or we can discuss the question of whether an algorithm can be biased; and if so, if this bias is already there in the wider society, in the games and form of life a particular technology is embedded in. Hence, this approach provides a perspective that is not only hermeneutically interesting but can also assume a critical function.

More detailed work on this approach can be found in Coeckelbergh (2017d and 2017e); this summary was mainly meant as an illustration of what it could mean to use thinking about language for thinking about technology. Note also that of course other philosophies of language can and have been used in philosophy of technology; for instance, Ricoeur has been used to reflect on technology and narrativity (Coeckelbergh and Reijers 2016; Coeckelbergh 2017e); and Habermas's and Foucault's discourse theories have been discussed in relation to critical information systems research (Stahl 2004). Metaphor is also an interesting topic; I have written on using performance metaphors for thinking about technology (Coeckelbergh 2019).

11.5. Other Subfields: Some Examples

There are of course many other subfields that could afford interesting crossovers for philosophers of technology, including philosophy of science, epistemology, metaphysics, philosophy of action, history of philosophy, political philosophy, and so on. I have already shown, for instance, that Floridi engages with metaphysics. Let me offer some further examples.

An obvious candidate is *philosophy of science*, which has played an important role in the history of the discipline, but today philosophy of technology is often divorced from it. (An exception is Don Ihde's continuing work on philosophy of *technoscience*.) On the one hand, this development is part of the growth of philosophy of technology as a subdiscipline on its own, and issues in science are often different from issues in other fields where technology is used. But today there are also efforts to reconnect again with philosophy of science. And starting from *epistemology*, one can ask questions about knowledge in technological practices. For instance, one can ask about the nature of engineering knowledge and write about tacit knowledge and know-how in technological practices. For example, one can discuss the epistemology of innovation and invention: Is it a matter of design and/or scientific theory that is applied, or could it also be understood as a poetic process (Coeckelbergh 2018a)? An example of work that connects philosophy of science, epistemology, and thinking about technology is research on models in the engineering sciences (see, e.g., Boon and Knuuttila 2008). Other work on this intersection includes Ian Hacking (1983), who wrote on the instrumental mediation of knowledge (but, in contrast to Don Ihde, in a non-phenomenological, realist way), for example how a microscope is indispensable in cell biology; and more recently, Judith Simon (2010), who works on social epistemological issues in relation to information technologies, for example trust and knowledge on the web.

There are also crossovers between *philosophy of mind*, cognitive science, and philosophy of technology. For example, Andy Clark and David Chalmers (1998) famously argued for the so-called **extended mind thesis**, which sees no principled distinction between mind, body, and environment, and which understands technologies such as a notebook as extensions of the mind—in particular, as part of an extended cognitive system. For example, a notebook functions as an external memory. Clark (2003) is also known for his view that we are natural-born cyborgs: the human mind is naturally disposed to develop tools and incorporate them in our mind and existence; we think and feel through them. He thinks that today we are on our way to a human-machine merger.

In the context of the discussion about what machines can do (see Dreyfus's seminal work on this, especially 1972 and 1992) and using their backgrounds in sociology and philosophy, Harry Collins and Martin Kusch (1999) have done a *philosophy of action* type of intervention. Making a distinction between polymorphic actions, which vary with social context, and "mimeomorphic" actions (which do not vary), they have argued that machines, while not being able to act, can mimic mimeomorphic actions but not polymorphic ones, which cannot be automated (Collins and Kusch 1999). (Note that this is also an example of interdisciplinary work; see chapter 12.)

Furthermore, in the discussion about human enhancement and transhumanism, I have argued that one can use principles and arguments from *political philosophy* to raise and clarify problems regarding the politics of human enhancements, for instance, issues regarding fairness and equality. (Coeckelbergh 2013) For example, regarding the question of whether it is fair that only the rich might be able to buy themselves enhancements, and that hence there is a risk of a gap between rich and poor, one can ask what principle(s) of justice must be applied and what should be distributed, if anything. Answers to the first question can then take inspiration from relevant theory in political philosophy; for instance, Rawls's ([1971] 1999) principles of justice, in particular the difference principle. But answers are not limited to application of existing theory; answering the second question about what needs to be redistributed, if anything, requires, for example, engagement with the old nature/nurture question but in the light of new scientific insights (Coeckelbergh 2013).

A final example: some researchers draw on a particular figure from the *history of philosophy*, such as Wittgenstein (see previously), Kant, Hegel, Nietzsche, and so on. For instance, recently, Nolen Gertz has argued that Hegel's analysis of the struggle for recognition can be used to understand human–technology relations from a political perspective. In particular, Gertz has argued that technologies such as robots may serve roles in society that are functionally equivalent to the social roles of humans. Recognizing this then helps to take a critical and political perspective on specific cases (Gertz 2018).

11.6. Conclusions for Philosophers of Technology

In this chapter, I have shown that crossovers between philosophy of technology and other subfields of philosophy are fruitful, if not unavoidable and necessary if one wants to make progress in the discipline. I have also shown that such crossovers cannot be reduced to application of theories outside the field to problems of technology; rather, *thinking through technology also has implications for thinking through language, ethics, metaphysics, and so on.* It is time that philosophers from these other areas recognize the contributions made by philosophers of technology, and that both sides open up more to opportunities for meaningful dialogue and mutual learning. Moreover, while much of these efforts have been sensitive to empirical material, and while the empirical turn has been influential in the field, the general approach is often as conceptual, argumentative, and theoretical as that of other philosophical subdisciplines. Hence, there is no reason to limit philosophy of technology to the boundaries of an applied or empirical philosophy (especially if that would mean that there is less work on concepts, arguments, or theories) or to dismiss it as any less philosophical than other subdisciplines. Like in other subdisciplines, quality of work varies; but this can hardly be used as an argument for ignoring the field or for missing interesting opportunities for intellectual exchange between subfields.

REVIEW QUESTIONS

1. Give an example of a helpful crossover between philosophy of technology and another subfield in philosophy.
2. Give an example of a crossover between philosophy of technology and ethics.
3. Outline how Vallor uses the tradition of virtue ethics to think about new technologies.
4. Give an example of an issue in philosophy of technology that is relevant to philosophical anthropology.
5. Give an example of how to use philosophy of language in philosophy of technology.
6. How can Searle be used for philosophy of technology? Give an example of a technology and interpret/discuss by using Searle.
7. How can Wittgenstein be used for philosophy of technology? Give an example of a technology and interpret/discuss by using Wittgenstein.

DISCUSSION QUESTIONS

1. Should philosophers of technology use and engage with theory from other subfields of philosophy? And if so, how or to what extent?
2. Is and should philosophy of technology be a form of applied philosophy? Why (not), according to you?
3. Is and should philosophy of technology be a subdivision of philosophy of science? Why (not), according to you?
4. How empirical is and should philosophy of technology be, and what does and should "empirically oriented" mean?
5. How relevant is ethical theory to problems in the area of technology?
6. Is virtue ethics and talking about "the good life" helpful for understanding and evaluating technologies?
7. Should philosophy of technology learn from philosophical anthropology, and should the latter take into account thinking about technology? Why (not), and if so, how?
8. How technological is the human and how human is technology? Is it possible to define the human without technology (and vice versa)?
9. Should philosophers of technology use philosophy of language for thinking about technology?
10. Do you agree with the use of Searle for thinking about technology, as presented here? Why (not)?
11. Do you agree with the use of Wittgenstein for thinking about technology, as presented here? Why (not)?

RECOMMENDED READING

Coeckelbergh, Mark. 2017. "Technology Games: Using Wittgenstein for Understanding and Evaluating Technology." *Science and Engineering Ethics* 24(5): 1503–1519.
Coeckelbergh, Mark. 2017. *Using Words and Things: Language and Philosophy of Technology*. New York: Routledge. (Chapters on Wittgenstein and Searle.)
Haraway, Donna. (1991) 2000. "A Cyborg Manifesto." In *The Cybercultures Reader*, edited by David Bell and Barbara M. Kennedy, 291–324. London: Routledge.
Vallor, Shannon. 2016. *Technology and the Virtues*. New York: Oxford University Press.

KEY TERMS

Applied philosophy
Cryptocurrencies
Engineering ethics
Extended mind thesis
Human enhancement

Language game or form of life
Negative anthropology
Philosophical anthropology
Philosophy of language

Posthumanism
Speech act
Transhumanism
Virtual money
Virtual worlds
Virtue ethics

CASE/TECHNOLOGY:
Robotics and Interdisciplinarity

Technological innovation, development, and use—in academia and in industry—is often a matter of many disciplines working together or even merging to some extent. Consider, for example, robotics. Robotics is itself an interdisciplinary field: its development and use involves mechanical engineering but also electronics, computer science, and sometimes artificial intelligence, nanotechnology, or bioengineering. Robots are also a technology that consists of many different components such as actuators, computers, computer programs, and sensors, each of which are linked to their own disciplinary or interdisciplinary design and development (in different companies, universities, etc.). But today

FIGURE 12.1 Illustration of Robot with tools and talking on a smartphone

many projects in robotics also include social sciences such as psychology since there is more attention now to the interaction between robots and users, a topic that itself is interdisciplinary. Consider the field called human–robot interaction (HRI), which includes robotics, computer science, and engineering but also social sciences. Moreover, while usually the humanities are not included in robotics or HRI projects, this is changing today. This chapter includes examples of how even *philosophy* of technology, in particular but not limited to ethics of technology, can be connected to technological developments such as robotics.

12.1. Introduction

Whereas during most of the 20th century philosophy of technology stayed within philosophy as a discipline, after the empirical turn in the early 1990s, it became more common, especially in the United States and in the Netherlands but also in Germany, for instance, to connect to disciplines such as engineering, computer science, and science and technology studies. The rationale for doing so was that both understanding and evaluating technologies cannot be done without some perspective from "within" (a technical perspective) and if possible some influence on the actual development of technologies. Philosophers such as Ihde and Feenberg tried to bridge what Mitcham called "engineering" and "humanities" philosophy of technology (see chapter 2) by focusing on actual technological artifacts and by learning from the sciences, including the social sciences. This has delivered a body of work that renders philosophical reflection on technology relevant to use of everyday technologies. Encouraged (or forced) by institutional changes in universities toward more dependency on temporary external funding and the related project-oriented way of working, many philosophers of technology also started collaborating with all kinds of scientists in multidisciplinary and sometimes interdisciplinary and transdisciplinary research projects. In ethics of technology, sometimes these efforts are connected with, and justified by, a new approach to evaluating technologies: the vision that instead of reacting after technologies are already developed and used, it is better to think about technology and ethics in a proactive way and participate and intervene at the stage of innovation. The buzzword **responsible innovation** or responsible research and innovation (RRI) is one term that expresses this vision. For philosophers of technology who wish to contribute to it, collaboration with engineers and scientists is not optional but mandatory: one needs to connect directly to technology development, and together with the social sciences one can reflect on methodologies to, for instance, involve more stakeholders in the process of technology development, rendering it more participatory and democratic. At the same time, and partly because of similar institutional changes, engineers and scientists also became more interested in philosophy and ethics. Today some funding instruments, such as the Horizon2020 program of the European Commission, require some reflection on the potential ethical dimensions and impact of technologies.

There is also more interdisciplinarity and transdisciplinarity in technologies and in the sciences themselves. Consider, for instance, so-called **converging technologies**. It is often claimed that there is integration of nanotechnology, biotechnology, information technology, and cognitive science (so-called NBIC technologies). Robotics can be defined as "an interdisciplinary branch of engineering and science that includes mechanical engineering, electrical engineering, information engineering, computer science, and others" (Wikipedia).

And within the humanities, there have also been transformations toward more interdisciplinarity and even collaboration with technology-related sciences. A significant development that needs to be mentioned here but has received relatively little attention in empirical turn-oriented philosophy of technology today is the so-called **digital humanities**, which still asks traditional humanities questions but uses computational methods and digital resources in humanities disciplines such as literature, linguistics, history, and even philosophy to answer these questions—hence involving transdisciplinary research. (See later in this chapter.) And keeping in mind the non-neutrality of technology, perhaps even the questions will change, given the capacity of artificially intelligent systems to find their own patterns in data that humans did not think of. Some philosophers also interact with the sciences, for example the neurosciences and/or biology and biotechnology. The result of all these changes is more variety in approaches and methods to think about technology and a more complex research landscape.

Of course not everyone (fully) embraces these changes. Some philosophers of technology still work exclusively like many of their colleagues in "mainstream" philosophy: in a disciplinary way, using only the medium of text (today also presentation software) and talking only to fellow philosophers. Furthermore, I have argued in chapter 11 and elsewhere that even if one goes in a more empirical, transdisciplinary direction and even beyond academia (see chapter 13), one should remain connected to, engage with, and benefit from the philosophical traditions with their rich resources in terms of approaches, arguments, and themes. For example, in response to the empirical turn, I have argued that one should not entirely abandon the topic of language and related philosophical and humanities approaches (Coeckelbergh 2017a, 2017d). And placing technology in the context of cultural-material history is also important, as, for example, Ihde does when he makes claims about prehistorical use of technology; or as I did when showing how contemporary technology use must be understood in the context of romanticism and its history (Coeckelbergh 2017b). There is a lot more work to be done in connecting an empirical orientation with relevant work in the humanities. And other fields of philosophy remain and should remain important, including the history of philosophy. For example, contemporary philosophers of technology such as Bernard Stiegler or Pieter Lemmens, while not rejecting the empirical turn, remain inspired by the Heideggerian and Marxian traditions of thinking. That being said, on the whole, the more empirical and transdisciplinary directions have been, and remain, fruitful and influential for understanding and evaluating technology.

There are other reasons to be optimistic about the future of transdisciplinarity, in philosophy of technology and elsewhere. There have been very successful convergences of disciplines, for example the mentioned NBICs. If we look at the history of disciplinarity, we see that this is a relatively short and recent one. Historically speaking, knowledge has often been divided up; but academic disciplinarity in its strong, contemporary form and the related process of specialization has only existed since the 19th century, when there was a "scientification" of knowledge (Thompson Klein 1990, 21), scholarly activities became more institutionalized (the modern university), and a range of new technical-scientific and social sciences were invented to cope with the rapid industrialization and complexity of society. For example, industries demanded specialists and more sophisticated instrumentation was needed in the sciences (Thompson Klein 1990, 21). Throughout the 20th century until today, disciplinarity persists, and philosophy is no exception. And, as Foucault teaches us, disciplines also means *disciplining*. There is normativity and power in this creation and consolidation of disciplinary boundaries. There is resistance. But if there is work going on to protect boundaries (Thompson Klein 1996), then we can also do work to cross them.

If one chooses a transdisciplinary direction, however, one does not enter a ready-to-use, stable, and established field or range of methods and paradigms. It is not what Kuhn called "normal science" or what we could call "normal philosophy." And it is not a *discipline*. Philosophy is a discipline. While in principle questioning approaches is part of what philosophers do, and hence there never was full stability, in "mainstream" or disciplinary philosophy (analytic and continental), the general direction is usually more or less clear and accepted; there are various established areas of inquiry, schools, and methods. Few academic philosophers are very inventive when it comes to method; by and large, academic philosophers think within a familiar methodological world. This is not the case when one leaves the disciplinary comfort zone and moves toward interdisciplinarity and transdisciplinarity. Of course, there is *some* experience and know-how, there are philosophers who have done it and are doing it; but usually, and in practice, knowledge transfer in this area is limited. Usually this direction of research is not included in textbooks, for example. And when doing research in interdisciplinary and transdisciplinary projects, one has to start more or less from zero when it comes to methodology since the challenge is to find—to some extent at least—a *common* methodology. Hence, these projects are always challenging in two ways: one challenge is to reach the particular research aim of the project; another is the common method and hence *the collaboration itself*. This renders this kind of work both burdensome and interesting at the same time. Mainstream philosophers who do not know this kind of work usually underestimate the intellectual challenge and skill that it takes—if they recognize the *philosophical* relevance of dealing with this kind of problem at all.

In this chapter, I will outline some ways in which philosophers of technology can engage in interdisciplinary and transdisciplinary research. I offer examples of collaborations of philosophers of technology with (a) the natural sciences and engineering (engineering, computer science, robotics), (b) the social sciences (STS), and (c) the humanities (romanticism studies, digital humanities, and post-humanities). This will include some examples from my own research experience to show students what interdisciplinarity and transdisciplinary can mean in practice for philosophers of technology. Then I will briefly discuss some instruments that are at the same time barriers and tools when it comes to interdisciplinary and transdisciplinary collaboration. Connecting to recent work on transdisciplinarity in my group (Funk 2018), I will argue that transdisciplinarity is a technosocial problem that concerns finding (1) common technologies (tools, media) and objects, (2) communality between people, and (3) a common language (which is also a technology). Discussing these barriers is important for transdisciplinary research, but I will show that it is also at the same time philosophically interesting, and in particular for philosophers of technology. I offer some ways to address the problems.

A quick note on my use of the terms **transdisciplinarity** and **interdisciplinarity**. Transdisciplinarity and interdisciplinarity both cross the disciplinary boundaries. They thus go beyond multidisciplinarity, where there is collaboration between disciplines in a team, but where each member of a team stays within their own discipline. I assume for the remainder of the discussion that the difference between transdisciplinarity and interdisciplinarity is merely a matter of degree: transdisciplinarity is assumed to go further in crossing boundaries and in working together than interdisciplinarity, going more into the direction of merging disciplines. Typically, transdisciplinarity goes beyond academia. Since transdisciplinarity presents us with the biggest challenge, I shall focus on transdisciplinarity in section 12.3. But first, I give some examples of interdisciplinarity for and by philosophers of technology.

12.2. Some Examples of Interdisciplinary and Transdisciplinary Work for Philosophers of Technology

12.2.1. Natural Sciences and Engineering

Interdisciplinary collaboration of philosophers with engineering and sciences such as computing science has a history of many decades and is not limited to academia. This history includes initiatives from within the technical professions themselves. There is the field of **engineering ethics**, which grew out of efforts by the profession of engineering to respond to engineering failures and disasters (bridge failures, railroad disasters, the Space Shuttle **Challenger disaster**, the Bhopal disaster, Ford Pinto safety problems, etc.) but also involves philosophers (e.g., I started my career in thinking about technology with research on engineering ethics) and develops codes of engineering ethics and reflects on the ethical and societal responsibility of engineers and engineering. Another interdisciplinary field, which is especially relevant to thinking about digital technologies today, is **computer ethics**. It is specifically concerned with professionals and ethical problems raised by computing. Again here the initiative came from the scientists and engineers themselves: people such as Norbert Wiener and Jozeph Weizenbaum. Later philosophers published on computer ethics; for example, Terell Ward Bynum, James Moor (see, e.g., Moor's [1985] article), Deborah Johnson (see textbox "In Focus: Deborah Johnson"), Michael Davis, and Herman Tavani. There is also work on ethics in the context of various national and international professional organizations. For example, the Institute of Electrical and Electronics Engineers (IEEE), has a code of ethics; and there are recent initiatives on ethics in which philosophers play a key role, such as the IEEE Global Initiative on Ethics of Autonomous and Intelligent Systems, which argues for "ethically aligned design" (IEEE 2019). However, often there is, or has been, a gap between, on the one hand, work in the fields of practical and professional ethics and, on the other hand, work in philosophy of technology.

FIGURE 12.2 Space Shuttle Challenger exploding, January 28, 1986

IN FOCUS:
Deborah Johnson

Deborah Johnson is a philosopher and science and technology studies (STS) scholar and professor at the University of Virginia. She is known for her work in computer ethics, engineering ethics, and science and technology studies. In her writings, she tries to integrate insights from STS with (computer) ethics. She has been engaged in inter-disciplinary work for many years and wrote one of the first computer ethics textbooks.

FIGURE 12.3 Deborah Johnson

Today this has changed. After the empirical turn in philosophy of technology, which encouraged engagement with the natural sciences (e.g., Don Ihde's work on technosciences) but also engineering and design practices (many Dutch philosophers of technology), most philosophers of technology talk to engineers, computer scientists, and other people developing new technologies. They also interact with people from professional ethics. For example, I met with people from Honda, the car company, which also created the humanoid robot Asimo (see textbox "Humanoid Robots"), who invited me to talk about my research and present my vision on the future of robotics. I also visited technology companies such as Google and talked to robotics researchers in the United States and in Japan. I have also had many discussions with people from engineering ethics, computer ethics, and IEEE. Such visits and conversations are important for philosophers of technology to learn something about the technologies and about what those who develop the technology think about the technology, but also to have a conversation about the philosophical and ethical aspects of the technology. In the best case, there is some input from philosophers in the process of development and a good dialogue in which both sides learn from each other; in the worst case, philosophers at least learn something about the technology. Sometimes the initiative comes from the philosophers, but sometimes also from the company or the scientists and engineers who become increasingly aware of the need to address ethical issues and sometimes have a genuine interest in philosophy.

CASE/TECHNOLOGY:
Humanoid Robots

Asimo is a humanoid robot created by Honda in 2000. It could walk and was operated wirelessly. Other examples are Nao and Pepper (SoftBank). Humanoid robots are robots that have a body that looks like a human body, with arms, legs, and a face. Some of them are androids, built to also aesthetically resemble humans. Examples are Repliee, Geminoid, and Erica, designed by the Japanese scientist and engineer Hiroshi Ishiguro (Osaka University, Japan). His robots are made to resemble as closely as possible a live human being and to give a feeling of presence to the human spectator.

Some android robots raise the problem of the so-called uncanny valley, a concept that suggests that if humanoids appear almost like human beings, they create an uncanny feeling (strange and familiar at the same time) in the observers. Other examples of uncanny objects are lifelike dolls and human corpses. The phenomenon was identified by Japanese robotics professor Masahiro Mori in 1970, but the concept goes back to Jentsch and Freud, who in 1919 wrote an essay called "The Uncanny." Explanations and theories of the effect include mortality salience (subconscious fears of annihilation and death) and violation of human norms. It may appear to the observer that a border is crossed between human and non-human, life and death, and between what is acceptable/normal and unacceptable/abnormal. Many people, especially in the West, also feel that human distinctiveness and identity is threatened. Posthumanists, by contrast, question the value of maintaining such a fixed identity and encourage border crossings.

FIGURE 12.4 Hiroshi Ishiguro's robot "Geminoid F"

Ideally this interaction with technology development goes beyond occasional contacts and takes the form of a research collaboration. This can be in the form of a small project, like writing a paper together. For example, recently I wrote a paper together with two researchers from **music information retrieval** (MIR) technology about the ethics of MIR (Holzapfel et al. 2018). For me, this required getting a better understanding of what music information retrieval technology is and does, what the state of the art is in that field, and what kind of community it is. It meant conversations and correspondence to find some common ground to talk about ethics. But it can also be a larger, longer-term research project. For example, from 2014 to 2018, I have been involved in a large, relatively long (4.5 years) European research project called **DREAM**, which aimed at improving technology and child–robot interaction in robot-enhanced therapy for children with autism spectrum disorder (Esteban et al. 2017), and which included work on ethics of robotics and ethics of human–robot interaction (e.g. Coeckelbergh et al. 2016). Thinking about the ethics of this technology, therapy, and interaction was multidisciplinary and interdisciplinary, involving robotics, psychology, critical social science, and philosophy (ethics), among others. The idea was to integrate research and thinking about the ethics of the project rather than keeping it at a distance. This meant that philosophers like myself needed to try to understand more about the technological and psychological part of the project, and that technology and psychology researchers need to make an effort to understand what philosophy and ethics was about and could do in the project. Neither of these types of knowledge were fixed beforehand; instead, they developed during the project. Of course, the researchers knew what they were aiming at in terms of the technological and therapy goals, but they did not know beforehand if and how it would work in this project and how their work would relate to ethics. And the philosophers and social scientists had disciplinary knowledge and some experience with interdisciplinary collaboration, but they did not know beforehand what doing ethics would mean in (relation to) this particular research project. Interdisciplinary and transdisciplinary knowledge is always emergent and rather risky. One does not know beforehand if and how it will work. (This makes it rather difficult to create a successful funding proposal for an interdisciplinary project since high-risk projects are usually not funded.) It also means that as a philosopher of technology, one needs to leave the usual places (desk, office, seminar room, lecture room) and go to labs, to the places where the technology development takes place. For example, in this case, I visited the labs of robotics engineers (in Brussels, Belgium) and of psychotherapists (in Cluj, Romania). It means talking to people but also engaging with the technology in the lab, listening to technical papers, etc. It also means talking and listening to all kinds of stakeholders, such as parents with children with autism spectrum disorder. Philosophers of technology who take this interdisciplinary direction need to be prepared to leave the boundaries of philosophy and venture at least *some* way into other fields such as robotics and social sciences. This can take the form of learning some of these sciences or it can take the form of intense collaboration with people from these other disciplines. But also in the latter case, one needs to be prepared to stretch and (temporarily) leave the disciplinary boundary. This can be challenging, and it takes extra work

FIGURE 12.5   Robots from DREAM

and a lot of time. In this particular project, for example, it was good to have several years to develop the interdisciplinary collaboration on ethics of robotics.

Given this need for time and the challenges of interdisciplinary and transdisciplinary research, it is even better if there are institutional structures that support this kind of research. This can take the form of a research network or even a research center. For example, I am member of a Denmark-based international research network called TRANSOR, which is a platform for research exchange and joint research in the transdisciplinary area of "social robotics." It involves philosophers such as Johanna Seibt (initiator) and myself but also other disciplines: robotics, cognitive science, psychology, anthropology, educational science, linguistics, art and design studies, and communication and media studies. In 2018 I organized the third transdisciplinary **Robophilosophy** conference, which connects philosophy to social robotics. And I have been managing director of a research center now called 4TU.Ethics that brings together the philosophy departments from four technical universities in the Netherlands with the aim to stimulate and undertake interdisciplinary and applied research in the field of ethics of technology. Structural support can also mean that disciplinary departments make an extra effort to support interdisciplinary and transdisciplinary research that involves collaboration with the technical disciplines—for instance, by hiring researchers who can bridge between disciplines and by giving some seed funding to encourage developing this kind of project (often the development of an interdisciplinary or transdisciplinary proposal takes a lot more effort and time). Unfortunately, such institutional support is still rare, but it is happening; and given the influence technology has on our lives and on society, it will hopefully increase in the future.

12.2.2. Social Sciences

Another area for interdisciplinary and transdisciplinary work is collaboration with the social sciences, which itself already has an interdisciplinary field called science and technology studies or **science, technology, and society studies** (STS). STS studies investigate how society shapes innovation and how innovation in turn shapes society. Social scientists have been studying technology in its historical and social context, have been trying to influence science and technology policy or have even become activists, and have been setting up new interdisciplinary programs in higher education.

Historically, STS emerged from the sociology of science and scientific knowledge. Through the work of people such as Steve Woolgar, Trevor Pinch, and Wiebe Bijker, sociology took a technological and material turn. In their seminal publication in the 1980s (Pinch and Bijker 1984), Trevor Pinch and Wiebe Bijker launched a research program that focuses on the social construction of technology, in particular the social construction of artifacts. They argued that not only is science knowledge ("facts") socially constructed but also that the development of technology is subject to the same social processes. Focusing on technical innovation (instead of scientific discoveries), they argued that the success and shape of an artifact is not just the result of technical factors but is also the result of a social process. Initially, there is **interpretative flexibility** (Pinch and Bijker 1984, 409), and the technology can still take on all kinds of forms; but then there is "closure" due to social processes; that is, social groups that influenced the technology development. They give the example of the development of the bicycle: at the end of the 19th century, there were still different variants, but later only some survived (and arguably today there is one dominant form). The authors explain this by pointing to the role of social groups that shape the problems and the solutions. Hence, there is not just one best or "natural" design (428); next to technical possibilities and constraints, there is room for social processes to design and interpret technological artifacts. This work has initiated a lot of research on the social construction of technological artifacts. This social construction is not limited to looking at the social shaping of innovation; there is also co-construction by users. What the artifact becomes and means depends not only on the designers (and on the social groups influencing that design) but also on what users do with it. For example, Nelly Oudshoorn and Trevor Pinch (2003) have edited a volume on "how users consume, modify, domesticate, design, reconfigure, and resist technologies" (3). This work is interesting for philosophers of technology who wish to acknowledge or understand the social dimension of technology: technology can be understood in terms of artifacts that have a (design and use) history and whose meaning depends on use and social processes.

IN FOCUS:
Wiebe Bijker

Wiebe Bijker is a Dutch scholar in science and technology studies (STS) and a professor at Maastricht University, The Netherlands. He has an educational background in engineering and always did interdisciplinary research. Together with Trevor Pinch, he developed the new approach Social Construction of Technology (SCOT) in the 1980s, focusing on the social influences on the design and creation of artifacts. A paradigm case is their analysis of the development of the bicycle.

FIGURE 12.6 Wiebe Bijker

Bruno Latour's work should also be mentioned again with regard to social constructivist work in the social sciences and, more generally, as an example of interdisciplinarity. Here the roots are also rather in the study of the sciences, but his work is relevant to, and has been used by, both STS researchers and philosophers of technology. In the 1970s, Latour, who has a background in philosophy and anthropology, started to apply anthropological methods and thinking (in particular ethnography) to the sciences. Bringing anthropology home from the tropics, as he put it later, he and Steve Woolgar showed that scientific objects are socially and technologically constructed in the laboratory: there is always interpretation by humans, and the instruments used play a crucial role in the construction of knowledge (Latour and Woolgar 1979). In the 1980s, Michael Callon, Bruno Latour, and John Law developed what they called actor–network theory, an approach that studies social phenomena (such as knowledge creation in science) in terms of a network of human and non-human actors, including objects, humans, and discourse. In *We Have Never Been Modern* (1993), Latour further developed the view that the social is a hybrid realm that crosses the nature/society and human/non-human dichotomies. (See also chapters 9 and 10.) This provides an interesting and challenging perspective not only for those who want to understand science but also for thinking about technology. If technological artifacts are not mere tools, are they to be conceptualized as nonhuman "*actants*" (see earlier in this book) within the same network as humans? What does this mean? Latour's interdisciplinarity, which does not only include anthropology, philosophy, sociology, and STS but also linguistics, has led to interesting questions.

Philosophers of technology can be, and have been, inspired by this work in STS and related social sciences and have done work that interacts with the STS community. This is especially so for philosophers of the empirical turn. For example, as I mentioned in chapter 5 on critical theory, Langdon Winner has argued that technologies, understood as artifacts, are "political" in the sense that they embody power relations and are sometimes even directly related to a particular sociological and political systems. But, one may add, it is through their design and their materiality that they are political. He gave the example of a bridge on the Long Island Parkway, which he claimed was biased toward particular social categories of people since it did not enable busses to drive under it (Winner 1980). And as we have also seen in chapter 5, Andrew Feenberg has combined philosophical sources such as Marcuse and Heidegger with STS. By claiming in his instrumentalization theory that next to a rational and instrumental side to technology, there is also the functioning of the device in the social world and that hence one should also look at the realization and recontextualization of technology in a social context, Feenberg (2010) uses STS's insight that technology is an outcome of past social influences and choices: it "depends on social choices between alternative paths" with different consequences (3), which for him is part of what he calls "secondary instrumentalization" (72). Feenberg explicitly mentions constructivist sociology of technology as his source of inspiration (67). He argues that "technical codes are always biased to some extent by the values of the dominant actors" (68). He discusses concrete technologies such as the French Minitel to show how technology is shaped by social processes and how it can be transformed by users. And like Winner, Feenberg argues for a democratization of technology. Another interesting crossover to STS is offered by Deborah Johnson, whom I already mentioned in the context of computer ethics but who is also known for her STS-oriented approach to ethics of developing technologies. For example, her response to Floridi and others that computer systems are components in human moral action (Johnson 2006, already mentioned in chapter 8) is inspired by the STS-based view that these technologies are "components in socio-technical systems" and are hence "intertwined with the social practices and systems of meaning of human beings" (Johnson 2006, 195). She mentions explicitly STS and work by, for instance, Bijker and Law to argue that technology is not just a matter of physical or material objects but is instead part of a "'socio-technical system":

> Technology is a combination of artifacts, social practices, social relationships, and systems of knowledge. These combinations are sometimes referred to as socio-technical ensembles or socio-technical systems or networks. Artifacts (the products of human contrivance) do not exist without systems of knowledge, social practices, and human relationships. Artifacts are made, adopted, distributed, used and have meaning only in the context of human social activity.... Artifacts come into being through social activity, are distributed and used by human beings as part of social activity, and have meaning only in particular contexts in which they are recognized and used. When we conceptually separate an artifact from the contexts in which it was produced and used, we push the socio-technical system of which it is a part out of sight. (Johnson 2006, 197)

Another contemporary philosopher of technology who connects to the social sciences is Peter-Paul Verbeek, who used Latour in his Ihde-inspired, post-phenomenological work. In *What Things Do* (2005; see also chapter 4), he uses Latour to show how technological mediation is structured. For example, he uses Latour's term "translation" and gives the example of a gun, which can be seen as an *actant* that changes programs of action and translates, for example, the intention to take revenge into the program "killing a person" (Verbeek 2005, 156). And as already mentioned, he also uses Latour to support his posthumanist view, picking up Latour's non-modern approach and interpreting it as implying that things shape human subjects.

Of course this is a selection of relevant approaches; there is more work in STS and more generally in the social sciences that can be helpful in philosophy of technology. For example, in my book on financial technologies (Coeckelbergh 2015), I have attempted to take a transdisciplinary approach (10) and have drawn on social studies of finance and STS, anthropology of finance, and geography of finance. I have connected to work on globalization and space, Callon's STS work on markets, and social studies and anthropology of finance work by Knorr Cetina, Zaloom, Beunza and Stark, Hart, and Zelizer (among others) to say more on the material, social, geographical, and indeed human dimensions of the world of finance and its technologies. I argued that this placing, materializing, and humanizing global finance and financial technologies (Coeckelbergh 2015, 123)— consider also again Deborah Johnson's view that we should not forget the human and social side of technology—supports the development of a more refined phenomenology of financial technologies and hence also critical evaluations of these technologies and reflections on the future of finance. This shows also that taking a more empirically oriented approach or engaging *in* or (in this case) *with* interdisciplinary and transdisciplinary research does not render philosophy of technology less interesting or less normative. On the contrary, work in this area suggests that we *need* more empirical insights into technology if and before we want to improve our thinking about technology.

12.2.3. Humanities

Philosophers of technology may also connect to (other) humanities. Surprisingly, there is relatively little research in this direction, at least in philosophy of technology after the empirical turn. Of course philosophy is itself a humanities discipline, but philosophy of technology has often been divorced from other humanities disciplines. People such as Don Ihde turned away from a humanities that they felt was too much preoccupied with language; the new focus is and was on material artifacts. They chose what Mitcham called an "engineering" approach as opposed to a "humanities" philosophy of technology (see chapter 2 on history and landscape of the discipline). The result is that among many contemporary researchers influenced by this empirical turn, there is not much interest in the humanities—or in other humanities.

There are exceptions in the field. For example, Charles Ess, who has an educational background in languages and history of philosophy, has done research in interdisciplinary humanities, enabling him, for instance, to reflect on links between technology/media, culture, and religion. For example, he has written about what supports or hinders religious migration online (Ess et al. 2007). Today he is more focused on ethics. Furthermore, the mentioned TRANSOR network does not only reach out to the technical sciences but also aims to do "joint Humanities research." Moreover, I have recently argued that philosophers of technology should not neglect language (Coeckelbergh 2017a, 2017d); and in my book *New Romantic Cyborgs* (2017b), I have taken not only a philosophical but also an interdisciplinary humanities approach that included engagement with the history of technology, culture studies, media studies, literature, film, and so on. In these recent works, I argue that it is not enough for philosophers of technology to talk about specific artifacts, but that these artifacts must be placed within a wider cultural horizon and background, a "form of life" to use a Wittgensteinian term (Coeckelbergh 2017d). To reveal and critically study that form of life, it is not sufficient to do a "micro" phenomenology of artifacts; a "macro" perspective is also required: the artifacts need to be related to the activities, games, and form of life they are embedded in and help to constitute, and perhaps, and to some extent, change (Coeckelbergh 2017c). For this purpose, humanities research (and social science research) is not optional but necessary. Moreover, I have argued that this orientation does not necessarily render the inquiry less empirical or merely "culturally" oriented: the material aspect can and must be retained (including the hermeneutic, mediating role of artifacts) but should not be overemphasized to the neglect of language (which arguably is also a technology), for example, or the more structural forms and dimensions of technology-in-use and technology-in-society (technology as part of our form of life). Again, all this can and should be studied in collaboration with other disciplines.

Another way in which humanities research can and has been connected with technology is in the so-called digital humanities, which uses computational methods to do research in literature and history, for example. The focus is no longer reading and writing; this is "data-driven" research. As Adema and Hall put it (keeping in mind McLuhan), there is a transition "from the Gutenberg galaxy of reading and writing print texts that are published intermittently in codex book and journal form, to the Zuckerberg galaxy of fast-paced, high-volume, networked flows of digital writing, photography, film, video, sound, data, and hybrid combinations thereof" (Adema and Hall 2016). This can be an object of study for philosophers of science and technology: How could the new digital technologies and media change not only the natural sciences but also the social sciences and the humanities? And what would it mean for *philosophy* to use such methods? So far there are not many philosophers who use the techniques of the digital humanities. Is this to be regretted, or should philosophy and humanities resist this computational turn? Based on their own knowledge and expertise when it comes to thinking about how (new) technologies (in particular their insight that technologies are never mere instruments but also change our thinking), philosophers of technology could make their own, unique contribution to this debate rather than staying on the sideline.

Moreover, within the humanities there is also a movement to broaden its scope and focus more on non-human or hybrid elements. Here the so-called **posthumanities** must be mentioned: influenced by posthumanism, it aims to render the humanities less human-centric. This is how University of Minnesota Press presents its posthumanities book series, edited by posthumanist Cary Wolfe:

> Posthumanities situates itself at a crossroads: at the intersection of "the humanities" in its current academic configuration and the challenges it faces from "posthumanism" to move beyond its standard parameters and practices. Rather than simply reproducing established forms and methods of disciplinary knowledge, posthumanists confront how changes in society and culture require that scholars rethink what they do—theoretically, methodologically, and ethically. The "human" is enmeshed in the larger problem of what Jacques Derrida called "the living," and traditional humanism is no longer adequate to understand the human's entangled, complex relations with animals, the environment, and technology. (University of Minnesota Press)

What does this (critical) posthumanities imply? Does it mean a change of topics, or also a change in methods? What kind of methods? Is it the methods of the digital humanities, or others, such as the natural sciences? Would it get more "empirical"? And if so, what does that mean? For philosophers of technology, a "posthumanities" approach could mean that one studies the human in relation to technology and vice versa (and in relation to animals), that one takes a more posthumanist and relational perspective. But what does it mean for method? How should we study technology from a posthumanities perspective? What other disciplines are needed? Does it mean that thinking about technology gets closer to the natural sciences and/or computing sciences? Are there other ways? Furthermore, could the posthumanities also take us beyond academia? Could it mean that philosophers of technology would stop writing books and articles and instead engage in (other) creative practices, become what Adema and Hall call "hybridized, activist, practice-based researchers" (2016)?

In chapter 13, I further discuss what it might mean to go "beyond academia." But first, I offer a discussion of the challenges for transdisciplinary work.

12.3. Challenges for Transdisciplinary Work

Interdisciplinary research and especially transdisciplinary research, which aims at achieving a merging of disciplines, is hard to achieve. I will identify three kinds of challenges. My discussion of these challenges will at the same time suggest tools for addressing the challenges: some have to do with the technologies and media used, some with the people and the social interaction, and some with language and discourse. My focus will be on problems related to combining philosophy of technology (more generally humanities) with engineering (more generally technical disciplines), based on my own experience. I am aware that my discussion is too short and that further development of these arguments and avoidance of caricatures would require further discussion and empirical research—indeed, it would require a transdisciplinary project on its own. But this is what I can offer within the limits of this book. I think there are at least the following three kinds of challenges.

Language/words/discourse. A first challenge when trying to combine disciplines is to find a common language. In the natural sciences, this may be mathematical language; or in computer sciences, a particular coding language. But when it comes to combining humanities and technical disciplines, this solution is more problematic: the discourses in the humanities and the social sciences are often very different from those of the technical disciplines, and sometimes even actively opposed to the language of technical disciplines. Even if these different fields sometimes use the same words, the terms mean different things. For example, "autonomy" in robotics is a technical term that means that the robot can perform behaviors or tasks independent from direct human control; whereas in philosophy, the term "autonomy" belongs to moral and political philosophy and is connected with the idea to have control over one's life, to live one's life according to reasons, to follow one's own motives, to be respected as a person who wishes to make one's own decisions, and so on. "Ethics" is another example of a term that can have different meanings for different people, even within philosophy. When researchers from both disciplines talk to one another, they need to clarify the meaning of the words they use. But language is never just about language. Language use is connected to what Wittgenstein called a form of life. The words are connected to specific worldviews and epistemological perspectives, which may differ enormously. For example, most scientists are educated in a naturalist worldview; this may or may not be shared by philosophers. Some philosophers may have a more hermeneutic or constructivist view. Some philosophers are opposed to scientific language, or make a sharp distinction between culture and science, humans and nature, society and the environment, and so on. Moreover, these views are not isolated from the social practices to whom they belong. This takes us to the next point.

Community/people/social interaction/practices. Academia is not one monolithic culture; there are subcultures and different social practices. Some would say different tribes. There are different ways of doing. For example, for philosophers, discourse and argument is central to what they do. They discuss. And they write, often alone. This is part of their form of life, whether they are in an office or in a bar. Engineers, in my experience, tend to have a more collaborative attitude. Their aim is not to discuss but reach a common technical goal. And for them, writing is a by-product of what they do rather than a central activity. Whether or not they are in the lab, their goal is to make things work and achieve progress with regard to the technology. They are used to working in teams. In transdisciplinary collaboration, these different social practices need to come together somehow. Moreover, transdisciplinary collaboration is itself a specific social form: collaboration and cooperation. It requires not only that discourses and worldviews meet and get closer but also that concrete people meet and are able to work together. Here barriers could be the different subcultures, the different forms of life, but also simply different characters. Collaborative synergy depends on synergy between persons and personalities. Without this social glue, there is no transdisciplinary research. In my experience, this aspect is very important. For example, when you try to write a research proposal together and the disciplines differ significantly (e.g., philosophy and engineering), it really helps a lot if you get along with the other people. To get on the same wavelength with people from other disciplines in terms of content of the proposal, one first needs to get on the same wavelength socially and emotionally. Academics, believe it or not, are social and emotional beings just like everyone else (and like many other animals). If something goes wrong on this level, the collaboration and hence the transdisciplinary aim is endangered.

Things/technology and media/spaces, infrastructure, and architecture. A third challenge has to do with different technologies, media, and ways of organizing space. Philosophers and (other) humanities researchers mainly use writing technologies such as text processors and pens. Sometimes they use presentation software. And today they use social media like many people on the planet. But researchers in the natural sciences and engineering also use different kinds of technologies and media. For them, these instruments and media are not a minor matter; as philosophers and sociologists of science also know, their instruments are crucial for their work. (This is also the case for philosophers, but they are usually not aware of it.) This means that part of the scientists' and engineers' work is to discuss and tinker with the instruments they use. Today this often includes all kinds of digital technologies: software and hardware. Furthermore, the end result engineers aim at is a technological artifact (virtual or not), a thing such as a car, a robot, or an app. Philosophers also produce artifacts, such as articles and books, but they are usually not aware that they are doing that. They *aim* not at producing artifacts but rather at creating ideas, arguments, and other more abstract and more language-oriented entities. They don't see themselves as being busy with things (in spite of their heavy use of technology and their reliance on artifacts). Furthermore, various disciplines tend to have different ways of organizing space and different architectures. Philosophers in academia today (not in ancient times) tend to work at desks and "need" office space and a computer. Perhaps they work also in a bar or café, indoors. But scientists and engineers need a lab, connected to specialized infrastructure. They also go outdoors sometimes. The question for transdisciplinary research is then *where* is it going to take place, and which *media* and *technologies* will be used? What technologies, infrastructures, and architectures are appropriate for this kind of work? And if existing infrastructures are used, how can they be connected? Aiming at transdisciplinarity is not only about finding a common language and finding the right people to work with, but also about finding common spaces and common technologies (transdisciplinarity) or at least creating interfaces between spaces and technologies (interdisciplinarity).

Because of these challenges, transdisciplinarity (and already interdisciplinarity) are not the easiest paths to choose. Integrating discourses, collaborating, and finding technological interfaces is a lot of extra work and usually only partly succeeds. And even if we are prepared to do that, how can we address the challenges, as philosophers in general and as philosophers of technology in particular? Further reflection on the challenges, and taking into account lessons from philosophy of technology itself, suggests the following tools to handle the challenges.

First, for addressing the problem of finding a common language, it would help a lot if we, as philosophers and as philosophers of technology, thought more about language and its relation to technology (Coeckelbergh 2017d). In particular, here is my very specific proposal: it would help if we would adopt the philosophical position that language and its words and structures are also a technology, medium, and tool. Influenced by pragmatism (in my case Dewey—see, e.g., Steve Fesmire's excellent book on Dewey; Fesmire 2003), one could treat concepts not as a kind of "ends" or "things" that exist somewhere in a Platonic or Kantian noumenal sphere separated from the empirical world but rather as tools we use and craft to deal with problems: practical and social problems. The problem of transdisciplinarity as a *philosophical* problem, then, is a problem of crafting the adequate kind of concepts-tools that bring the disciplines together and (not to forget!) solve the problem for which the transdisciplinary research was necessary in the first place. If, on the one hand, philosophy, humanities, and social sciences take this more problem-oriented and pragmatist attitude toward concepts, arguments, and theories (and hence stop revering them as reified things or ends in themselves); and if, on the other hand, engineers and scientists take more seriously language and discourse and take a more critical attitude toward them (which can also be achieved by having them see language as a technology); then this could create a methodological space in which collaborative creative work on concepts-as-instruments and indeed on *the problem at hand* can take place. Then both philosophers and engineers, for example, are oriented toward solving a problem and then discuss what instruments (concepts and other technologies) they need, and need to craft, for solving these problems. If both sides see philosophy and science/technology development as crafts, then they can work together. It may still be the case that philosophers are better in working with language as a tool and engineers are better in working with artifacts and software, but this is then no longer a fundamental methodological gap since there no longer is the assumption of an ontological gap: words, artifacts, and software are all tools, technologies, and media. On this view, provided sufficient education and training takes place, engineers and computer scientists, for example, can in principle also take part in concept engineering (usually done by philosophers) and philosophers can also take part in artifact or software engineering (usually done by engineers and computer scientists). A problem-oriented and pragmatist approach thus takes away at least *this* (meta-)methodological barrier.

A second potential barrier is the risk of difficult social communication and the existence of different social practices. Here philosophy and theory can also help. Usually science, philosophy, and engineering are not seen as social and cultural practices; in and *by* theory, they are abstracted from these practices. They are supposed to be about truth, arguments, and creating technological solutions. They are not about people. But when, inspired by contemporary science and technology studies, we reveal and accept that it is human beings as social beings who do all this and that their activities constitute a social practice, if we indeed "humanize" and "socialize" the scientists (think again about Latour's work in the laboratory or social studies of finance) but also the engineers *and* the philosophers, then we open the door for solutions from the social sciences. If transdisciplinarity is also always a *social* problem, including a communication problem and a cultural problem, then we can learn from the theoretical and empirical social sciences and from social and political philosophy about how to deal with it. We can learn from psychologists and communication specialists how to create more synergy between people and how to facilitate cooperation and collaboration. We can also learn about the technologies, media, and spaces that are conducive for successful collaboration. (See also following.) We can learn from anthropologists and social and (inter/trans)cultural philosophers about problems and solutions with regard to bringing different cultures together: here, academic cultures. For example, we can solve part of the problem of different academic cultures by endorsing the insight that cultures are not like things or containers; instead, there is overlap and hybridity. For the case of philosophy and engineering, this could mean that we do not exaggerate the differences and focus on shared academic norms and practices. Engineers also discuss and argue, and philosophers are also often aiming at producing an artifact (e.g., a book) and use artifacts. And both disciplines share many academic values and practices such as blind peer review, honesty, recognition of the contributions of collaborators, etc. In sum, if we accept that science, philosophy, and academia in general is also always about people and about how to do things together, then we are already on our way to tackling the problem, because then we can think about what instruments we need to achieve transdisciplinarity, understood as a *social* project.

Finally, the previous two interventions then bring us to the third problem as the overarching problem that is of interest to philosophers of technology: Which *technologies* do we need for achieving transdisciplinarity? Which artifacts, infrastructures, and architectures can bring disciplines together? If artifacts were mere things, this question could not be one of the central questions. If architecture was merely about organizing space and about material things such as walls and a roof, it would seem disconnected from the present discussion. But we can learn from philosophy of technology (and architecture theory) that technologies are never mere means but also shape the ends. We can learn that technologies and media also shape our thinking. We can learn that architecture is not only about organizing space but also about organizing people and about shaping how we live. For science and philosophy, too, it *matters* what instruments we use. On the one hand, philosophers could learn this from scientists and engineers, and think more about the technologies and media and how they shape their work and their thinking. They could explore *different* media and technologies. (See also chapter 13: Would this be real transdisciplinarity? And would it be real "posthumanities"?) On the other hand, scientists and engineers could pay more attention to language, which they already use as an instrument but usually without giving it the same amount of attention as they give to other, more material instruments. For thinking about transdisciplinarity, finally, this approach means that the goal also depends on the instruments. What the goal of transdisciplinarity *means* depends on the means used: "transdisciplinarity" depends on the concepts and the discourse that are developed, it depends on the technologies for communication used, and it depends on the artifacts and spaces created. The means mean. Making sense of transdisciplinarity is done by means of technologies and is done in practice. It is not the case that we already know what transdisciplinarity is and then we can apply this concept to existing practices. Transdisciplinarity is about reinventing the practices themselves, and this is a problem that concerns language, the social, and technology, or rather language/ the social/technology: I have assumed here that language is a technology and that technology is always part of social practices. The question of transdisciplinarity, then, leads us back to philosophy of technology itself.

This discussion also shows that crossing over to other disciplines does not render philosophy of technology less "philosophical," at least if philosophy itself is reconceptualized in a more craft- and practice-oriented way. Transdisciplinarity also includes tinkering with concepts, and is thus philosophical. It can also lead to philosophical meta-reflections such as this one. But the difference with disciplinary philosophy is that it opens up the borders of this practice to other disciplines. Other disciplines, too, *already* work with concepts. This similarity should be recognized, even if these other disciplines should be encouraged to use concepts in a more critical way, to think more about the concepts and language they use. We all use concepts as tools. Furthermore, this approach invites *philosophers* to question their tools. They could explore working with different technologies and engaging in different practices within academia: for the purpose of achieving transdisciplinarity but also to achieve a more critical (and perhaps *gelassen*) relation to *their own instruments and technologies*. This is arguably an important discussion for philosophy of technology if it seeks to mature into a more self-critical subdiscipline, and an important issue for philosophy at large and any other academic discipline. The new technologies and media available today force us to at least ask the question about the technologies philosophers use and should use. Philosophers of technology, in collaboration with other disciplines, can help to ask and address that question. Normatively speaking, this discussion also suggests that both transdisciplinarity and thinking about technology should not just be optional but should be fostered as an academic and intellectual virtue, which needs more support from academic leadership than it currently gets.

But the (social) world is larger than academia. In chapter 13, I will discuss how philosophy of technology may also be understood in ways that take us *beyond* academia.

REVIEW QUESTIONS

1. How did interdisciplinary and transdisciplinary research emerge in the recent history of philosophy of technology?
2. What is responsible innovation?
3. Give an example of interdisciplinary or transdisciplinary research in contemporary philosophy of technology, involving (a) engineering and computer science, (b) social sciences, or (c) humanities.
4. What is posthumanities?
5. What are challenges for transdisciplinary research discussed in this chapter, and how can philosophers (of technology) deal with them, according to the author of this book and according to you?

DISCUSSION QUESTIONS

1. In the light of technological changes (the so-called digital revolution) and insights from posthumanist studies, should the humanities transform itself in terms of its focus and methods? And if so, in which direction? What does this mean for philosophy of technology?

2. This chapter offers a way to deal with the challenges of transdisciplinarity. What do you think about the proposed direction of thinking, which focuses on comparing, critically discussing, and perhaps bringing together the different technologies and media of the disciplines?
3. Is language a technology?
4. What technologies and media should philosophers use, according to you?

RECOMMENDED READING

Example of philosophy of technology and humanities research: Coeckelbergh, Mark. 2017. *New Romantic Cyborgs: Romanticism, Information Technology, and the End of the Machine*. Cambridge, MA: MIT Press.

Example of an interdisciplinary technical project including ethics: DREAM: Esteban, P. G., P. Baxter, P, T. Belpaeme, E. Billing, H. Cai, H.-L. Cao, M. Coeckelbergh, C. Costescu, D. David, A. De Beir, Y. Fang, Z. Ju, J. Kennedy, H. Liu, A. Mazel, A. Pandey, K. Richardson, E. Senft, S. Thill, G. Van de Perre, B. Vanderborght, D. Vernon, H. Yu, and T. Ziemke T. 2017. "How to Build a Supervised Autonomous System for Robot-Enhanced Therapy for Children with Autism Spectrum Disorder." *Paladyn, Journal of Behavioral Robotics* 8(1): 18–38.

KEY TERMS

Challenger disaster
Computer ethics
Converging technologies
Digital humanities
DREAM
Engineering ethics
Interdisciplinarity

Interpretative flexibility
Music information retrieval (MIR)
Posthumanities
Responsible innovation or responsible research and innovation (RRI)

Robophilosophy
Science, technology, and society studies (STS)
Transdisciplinarity

13 PHILOSOPHY OF TECHNOLOGY AND PRACTICES BEYOND ACADEMIA

CASE/TECHNOLOGY:
"Killer Drones" and Activism

New information technologies increasingly enable automated warfare. This raises ethical problems. For example, so-called unmanned aerial vehicles (UAVs), or drones, are used for surveillance but also for killing people. Is such killing at a distance permissible? And what if the killing is also automated? The use of such weapons is ethically highly problematic (for an overview of ethical issues and arguments against automated weapons, see Coeckelbergh [2018]). In the United States and elsewhere, there have been campaigns against so-called killer drones. For example, the international Campaign to Stop Killer Robots has called for a ban and has tried to influence governments and intergovernmental organizations to issue a ban. The leadership consists of people from non-governmental organizations (NGOs), but academics such as Peter Asaro and Noel Sharkey also play a key role in the campaign. They also co-chair the International

FIGURE 13.1 The MQ-9 Reaper, a combat drone, in flight

Committee for Robot Arms Control. This example shows that academics who think about new technologies can also take up the role of activists, next to or instead of doing only academic work. Such work has effects: for example, in 2018, the Belgian parliament adopted a ban on using fully autonomous weapons or "killer" robots (Cardone 2018). Earlier experts, including myself, provided arguments for such a ban in the relevant parliamentary commission. More generally, today many philosophers of technology engage with technology and innovation policy issues and express their opinions about political questions concerning technology in the media—traditional media such as the press and TV, but also social media. This chapter focuses on why and how philosophers of technology can go beyond academia.

13.1. Beyond Academia: Innovation, Policy, and Art

In this chapter, I raise the question of the role of philosophers of technology with regard to wider societal and public issues and practices beyond academia. Are they mainly academic experts, specialized in a subdiscipline of philosophy, or should they also take other roles? For example, should they be intellectuals, not in the sense of "having intellect" or "being smart" but in the sense of engaging in critical thinking about society and perhaps becoming *public* intellectuals who address social and political issues and participate in public discourse about these issues? Should they be activists and try to bring about social change? Should they connect with civil society? Should only experts be involved in discussions about technology, or many stakeholders and the general public? Should philosophers of technology promote this? Should philosophers of technology participate in policymaking and contribute to solving societal problems? Should they try to change innovation practices? Should they collaborate with artists?

My answer to these questions is positive: this chapter is motivated by the vision that philosophy of technology should not only include transdisciplinary research within the boundaries of academia but should also be open and responsive to what happens outside academia: to changes in society, to policy, and to non-academic practices that may also contribute to thinking about technology by exploring the possibilities and problems raised by new and emerging technology. However, the text presented here does not directly defend this vision; rather, it shows the reader a number of ways in which philosophers of technology *can* take this direction and *have already taken* this direction. I can only hope that students and beginning researchers in the field will conclude that engaging in these activities is not something optional but properly belongs to what philosophy of technology is about. But my main aim here is to show a number of possibilities for going beyond academia.

13.1.1. Responsible Innovation and Value-Sensitive Design

Many contemporary philosophers of technology share the vision just expressed and take up at least some of the roles mentioned in one or more areas. Let me start with the field of *innovation*. As mentioned in chapter 12, one way to work together with engineers and scientists is to participate in technical projects. Such projects may also include partners from outside academia, such as corporations and governmental and NGOs, and hence offer a chance to discuss and collaborate with them. For example, I have played a role as internal evaluator in the European project SATORI on ethics assessment (lead: Philip Brey), which included research ethics committees, corporations, and an intergovernmental organization (UNESCO). Thus, sometimes academia itself (and the relevant funding agencies) provides a bridge to the world outside academia.

Such collaborations with industry and other partners involved in innovation are sometimes driven by the vision that philosophers of technology should help people in industry and elsewhere to proactively think about the ethical and societal aspects of new technologies. As mentioned in chapter 12, an important concept in this context is **responsible innovation** or "responsible research and innovation" (RRI), which is an approach in research and innovation that aims to change these processes in such a way that ethical and societal impacts are taken into account, especially by involving stakeholders at an early stage (see, e.g., Owen et al. 2013; von Schomberg 2013). René von Schomberg from the European Commission has defined RRI:

> Responsible Research and Innovation is a transparent, interactive process by which societal actors and innovators become mutually responsive to each other with a view to the (ethical) acceptability, sustainability and societal desirability of the innovation process and its marketable products (in order to allow a proper embedding of scientific and technological advances in our society). (von Schomberg 2013, 63)

The idea is not only to achieve more ethically acceptable, sustainable, and socially desirable productions but also to change the *process* of innovation. In particular, the involvement of stakeholders is meant to lead to a precautionary and more inclusive and democratic-participative process whereby "technical innovators become responsive to societal needs and societal actors become co-responsible for the innovation process" (von Schomberg 2013, 65). Hence, the idea is that actors become mutually responsible. Moreover, it is recommended that there should be ongoing public debate about the technologies; for example, through the creation of "continuous public platforms" rather than one-off events (71). The RRI approach has been applied to various technologies, for instance information and communication technologies (Stahl et al. 2014), and has already been taken up by European policymakers. For example, it has been included in European funding programs such as the 7th Framework Programme and Horizon2020. Recently, some people in the United States have also called for responsible innovation in the tech sector.

RRI is compatible with **value-sensitive design** (see, e.g., van den Hoven 2007; Friedman et al. 2008), which is defined by Friedman et al. (2008 Friedman et al. 2008) as "a theoretically grounded approach to the design of technology that accounts for human values in a principled and comprehensive manner throughout the design process" (69). This approach is more design-and artifact-oriented, but it also includes the identification of stakeholders, identification of the relevant values, empirical investigations of the context of the artifact, and technical investigations of the properties of the technology and its relation to human values to achieve "proactive design of systems to support values identified in the conceptual investigation" (Friedman et al. 2008, 73). Applied to information technologies, for example, it means that it is acknowledged that these technologies are intentionally or unintentionally informed by the moral values of their makers—they are "value laden"—and that it is important to be aware of this and design in a way that operationalizes and incorporates values in the design of the technologies (van den Hoven 2007, 67) Jeroen van den Hoven (see textbox "In Focus: Jeroen van den Hoven") stresses that this can help to change the world:

> It assumes that human values, norms, moral considerations can be imparted to the things we make and use and it construes information technology (and other technologies for that matter) as a formidable force which can be used to make the world a better place, especially when we take the trouble of reflecting on its ethical aspects in advance. (van den Hoven 2007, 67)

For philosophers of technology, this means that they can or *should* contribute to the design of technologies and to innovation processes, rather than waiting until the technology is developed. I mentioned already the project that DREAM I contributed to as an example of how this can be done.

IN FOCUS:
Jeroen van den Hoven

Jeroen van den Hoven is a Dutch philosopher and professor at Delft University of Technology. He specializes in ethics of information technology and has written on responsible innovation. He was the founding director of the Dutch 3TU Centre for Ethics and Technology and has made advisory contributions to national and EU policy.

13.1.2. Policy, Public Engagement, and Activism

The same proactive approach can be applied to *policy* concerning new technologies: for policymakers; it is better to take into account ethics in policy instead of trying to remedy the bad effects afterward. And for philosophers of technology, it is better to get involved before the policy is there instead of complaining about it afterward. Since technology development is rapid and has wide-ranging consequences for the lives of people, this is an important and urgent task. Seen in this light, one could argue that philosophers of technology have a *duty* to help policymakers understand the issues and contribute to policymaking if they have a chance to do so.

Many philosophers of technology in fact contribute to policy, for instance, but not exclusively in American and European contexts. For example, Luciano Floridi has contributed to European Commission policy initiatives in the area of digital technologies and transformations (e.g., he chaired the Onlife Initiative project, which resulted in the Onlife Manifesto; Floridi [2015]) and is a member of Google's Advisory Board on the right to be forgotten. Next to her work as a professor, Shannon Vallor is a consulting AI ethicist helping Google Cloud AI. Another example is Patrick Lin, who talks to policymakers, governmental organizations (e.g., the US military), and businesses with regard to new and emerging technologies such as robotics and AI. I am currently advising the Austrian government on robotics policy as member of the national Austrican Council on Robotics and Artificial Intelligence and contribute to European policy on AI as a member of the "High-Level Expert Group on AI" appointed by the European Commission. Many philosophers of technology also engage with the wider public via social media (Facebook, Twitter, YouTube, etc.) and appearances in the media and public talks (e.g., TED talks). This is also a way of (indirectly) contributing to policy. It may include voicing strong opinions on technology policy or even forms of activism, such as the mentioned global campaigns against killer robots or the campaign against sex robots.

Indeed, some philosophers take up an explicitly activist role. This work can also be done at the local level. For example, at the nexus between environmental philosophy and philosophy of technology, Robert Frodeman and Adam Briggle have not only thought about interdisciplinarity (Frodeman et al. 2010) but have also stressed public outreach and even engaged in political activism. Briggle played a leading role in a campaign against fracking in his town, Denton, Texas; following Frodeman and others, he calls this **field philosophy** (Briggle 2015): philosophy that leaves the university buildings and is concerned with what happens near neighborhoods and playgrounds (in this case, drilling). This is not necessarily "unphilosophical"; on the contrary, Briggle interprets this as taking up a Socratic role:

> Like Socrates, field philosophers wander around questioning purported experts, trying to figure out what we really know and which choices we

should make. Rather than talk only to other academic philosophers, I talked to scientists, engineers, policy makers, citizens, and members of the industry. I also blogged, organized educational events, gave presentations at community rec centers, produced videos for YouTube, toured frack sites, spoke with concerned parents, wrote op-eds, and even had an uncanny visit from the FBI. (Briggle 2015, 2)

Instead of writing about innovation and technology from a distance, Briggle (2015) engaged with what happened in the real world around him, showing that philosophy can be more than an "inward-looking" professional academic discipline that confuses societal irrelevance with intellectual seriousness (11) but can help to question choices, conventions, and assumptions made in science and society. It can show, for example, that questions regarding technological risk and safety cannot be fully answered by science: whether something is safe also "depends on how one perceives and is situated in relation to the risks; everything is framed by, and interpreted through, values and worldviews" (Briggle 2015, 13). It can also try to influence political decisions. Sometimes activism succeeds, sometimes it fails; but often it has *some* influence on the decisions.

IN FOCUS:
Robert Frodeman

Robert Frodeman is an American professor at the University of North Texas, an expert in environmental ethics and public policy, and a promotor of interdisciplinarity research. He argues that philosophy can and should play a significant role in addressing, and engaging with, societal discussions and complex problems such as climate change. He supports doing "field philosophy": philosophers should work with scientists, engineers, and policymakers rather than just talking to other philosophers and writing. Frodeman has a background in philosophy and geology.

13.1.3. Art

Finally, art can help society and philosophy of technology to explore and address questions regarding technology. While there is discussion about why exactly this is so, and while there is always the danger of reducing art to its instrumental value, several philosophers—including philosophers of technology—have long recognized that art can be helpful with regard to thinking about technology. Dewey ([1934] 1980) wrote in *Art as Experience* that works of art embody possibilities "that are not elsewhere actualized" (268). Heidegger suggested that art opens up worlds and claimed that it is in the realm of art where "essential reflection upon technology and decisive confrontation with it must happen" (Heidegger 1977, 35). Furthermore, McLuhan argued that artists are "perception experts" or experts in perceiving and being sensitive to transformations of experience made possible by new media and technology (Coeckelbergh 2017d, 284–285). McLuhan wrote, "The serious artist is the only person able to encounter technology with impunity, just because he is an expert aware of the changes in sense perception" (McLuhan [1964] 2001, 19). According to McLuhan, this enables artists to pick up the challenges of technological transformations before their impact occurs (71) and thus both encounter the present (77) and prepare us for the future. For example, McLuhan thinks that art can liberate us from the "tyranny" of our "self-imposed environments" by presenting a "counter-environment" (226). Indeed, art can reveal something about our use of technology and about our society, for instance, by decontextualizing and recontextualizing artifacts, or by disrupting moral conventions. It can also open up new technological-experiential possibilities we did not see before.

Moreover, work on the intersection between art and technology is as old as Leonardo da Vinci, the Renaissance artist/scientist, if not older. Ancient

LEONARDO DA VINCI PITT. SCVL. E ARCHI
FIORENTINO

FIGURE 13.2 Leonardo da Vinci, head-and-shoulders portrait

craftspersons could also be seen in this light: what they did arguably preceded the very distinction between art and technology. Today many artists are active in this art/science field. In chapter 9, I mentioned Stelarc, who already in the 1980s and 1990s experimented with "cyborg" modes of perception and interaction. He was a pioneer, and today there seems to be a growing interest in this kind of combination: there are many artists who work with new and emerging technologies. Consider, for example, artwork shown at the Ars Electronica festivals—which focus on linking art, technology, and society and aim to improve human society—and various other art–science collaborations. By now, it is also relatively common that there are artists in residence at scientific institutions. Artists may use scientific instruments as a medium and engage in scientific practices. For example, bio-artist Anna Dumitriu uses bacteria in her work. Sometimes such art/science collaborations are supported by corporations or by policymakers. For instance, Steve Jobs (Apple) famously tried to bring together technology and the arts (including the humanities) in the design of new digital technology (smartphones and tablets—see textbox "Technology: Smartphones, Tablets, and Other Smart Devices"). He had computer scientists work together with artists and designers, and when he launched the iPad 2 in March 2011, he talked about marrying technology with the liberal arts, thus continuing the merger of tech culture and the romantic counterculture he was part of (Coeckelbergh 2017c). Today the European Commission's STARTS initiative funds projects that merge science, technology, and the arts: "it attempts to remove the boundaries between art and engineering to stimulate creativity and innovation" and tries to include artists in innovation projects (European Commission 2019). Some artists are also activists, and there are exchanges among artists, academics, and activists.

CASE/TECHNOLOGY:
Smartphones, Tablets, and Other Smart Devices

A contemporary textbook on philosophy of technology would be incomplete without at least mentioning one of the most influential and successful technologies of the beginning of the 21st century: the "mobile phone" or "cell phone" (US), and in particular the *smartphone*. While there were already handheld phones in the 1970s, in the 1990s, the small,

FIGURE 13.3 Drawing of a smartphone

handheld, mobile device and the required networks (GSM) became available and very popular. Smartphones—small personal computers that can connect to broadband cellular networks and Wi-Fi (and can still be used as phones) combined with software known as "apps," which connect the user to Web 2.0– type applications—became widely used in most countries only in the middle 2000s. In 2007, Apple launched the iPhone, featuring a touchscreen interface that spanned the front of the device—and an attractive design. In 2008, phones with Google's operating system (Android) became available. Windows followed later. In 2008 and 2009, app stores were launched, which enabled easy access and distribution and resulted in a huge variety of apps. In 2010, Apple released the iPad: a tablet, which is basically a larger version of the smartphone. The result of all these developments is that today many people find it difficult to imagine their lives without the smartphone. There are many ethical worries about the phones. Some researchers warn of addiction, sleep problems, and anxiety, or point to risks of accidents in traffic (e.g., when looking at the smartphone while crossing the street or while driving). One can also discuss how the smartphone has impacted social relations; for example, in the family or at work. Does the smartphone lead to fewer face-to-face interactions and fewer good relationships? Does it take away time from other, potentially more meaningful, activities? Or is the mediation provided by the device not necessarily a problem? Surprisingly, few philosophers of technology have done a lot of work on understanding and evaluating the smartphone in terms of its ethical and societal impact.

In response to these developments, philosophers of technology can do a number of things. Let me distinguish some options and give examples from my own activities in the past years to illustrate them. First, philosophers of technology can of course view, listen, touch, etc., art works on the intersection of art/technology. They can visit art exhibitions, performances, and art festivals. I focused on contemporary art, ranging from local concerts and performances to the 2017 Venice Biennale; but in principle, one can also include work from the history of art relevant to the theme technology (and art). Philosophers can then use this experience in thinking about technology. Second, they can write about the relation between art and technology. For example, I have written articles about the question of whether machines can create art (Coeckelbergh 2017b), and I have tried to conceptualize relations between art and innovation (Coeckelbergh 2017a). Third, philosophers of technology can get closer to the field and comment on, and enter in dialogue with, artists, curators, and indeed art/science collaborators. For example, in 2013 I talked at the Gogbot art and technology festival and in 2014 at the TEC ART festival in the Netherlands; and in 2017, I gave several talks at the Ars Electronica festival in Linz, Austria, which included a contribution to a panel that analyzed art and science collaborations. Third, philosophers can go further and *collaborate* with artists and curators. For example, I have worked with the Museum of Applied Arts (MAK) in Vienna in the context of the 2017 Vienna Biennale and co-organized a panel discussion for the art festival, The Future of Demonstration. Fourth, philosophers can leave their comfort zone and get involved in artistic or art/science collaborative practices in ways that may take them beyond the usual media and activities of philosophers, taking a truly transdisciplinary turn. For example, I am involved in a collaborative art project on robots and dance, which uses robots themselves as a medium next to dance, text, sound, and images, and I am involved in every stage and aspect of the creative process. I have also collaborated with sound artist and curator Martine-Nicole Rojina for an artwork (a quadrophonic soundscape) presented at the STARTS exhibition at the NET FUTURES 2017 conference. While for my part the latter collaboration still involved creating text (I wrote "inner thought monologues of future beings"), it was an artistic contribution (writing literary fiction), also involved the medium of sound and sound technology, and went already much further than the traditional detached role of the philosopher-commentator or philosopher-critic. Dance and robotics project shows that it is possible to use different media altogether and to engage more deeply in artistic practices.

Indeed, why should the role of philosophers be limited to reading, writing, and speaking? As I already suggested in chapter 12, we *can* also use different media and technologies and engage in different or transdisciplinary practices inside and outside academia, and this need *not* be seen as non-philosophical or as "something for your leisure time" but as potentially contributing to *philosophical* projects. For philosophy of technology, this could mean that we should at least consider the following possibility: that thinking about media and technologies may well be better if it is based on experiences with different media and technologies than text and word processors. If this is plausible, then such extra-academic activities and practices should be seen not as marginal but as central to philosophy of technology. Artistic practices (and art/science collaborations) can then be part of what it is to do philosophy of technology.

Today a number of philosophers are interested in blurring the boundaries between philosophy and art. For example, there are philosophers who try to cross the boundary between performance and philosophy: consider, for example, so-called **performance philosophy** research. Philosophers of technology could benefit from such boundary crossings and reflect more on what philosophy means, and at least consider, discuss, and open up to alternative views of what philosophy is and should be. For instance, Andrew Bowie has argued that

Figure 13.4 Novalis, steel engraving, 1845

practices that are usually not considered as philosophy can also be forms of sense-making that "reveal aspects of the world that are hidden by dominant practices and assumptions" and has suggested that "we may sometimes achieve more by thinking of some of our practices, particularly in the aesthetic domain, as manifestations of what philosophy might become, rather than just thinking of those practices as objects of philosophical analysis" (Bowie 2015, 51). This is not only a recent idea: in the 19th century, philosophers such as Schelling and Novalis thought about philosophy in much more transdisciplinary ways than many philosophers today. Schelling was interested in science, and Novalis ([1799] 1997) had the vision of a "community of all knowledge" (39); he wanted to merge philosophy and poetry, logical thinking and intuition, the rules and the wild. He argued that in the artist "living reflection comes into being" (Novalis 1997, 51). Such ideas may inspire those philosophers of technology interested in bringing together humanities, sciences, and art. And is not philosophy of technology all about reflection on media and technologies and what they may do to our experience, our thinking, and our lives? Again, is such a reflection good enough and grounded enough if it is not based on exploring different media and technologies and different technological practices? I suggest that we should at least seriously consider including this direction in new research programs in philosophy of technology.

13.2. Some Directions and Recommendations Concerning the Future of Research in Philosophy of Technology and Its Potential Implications for Education

These thoughts on the future of the field emerge from what is already happening today and from what I've been doing during the past years. I see two major and compatible challenges and directions for the field, which I believe may be of interest not only to researchers but also to students: I will highlight the implications for educational programs and beyond.

On the one hand, philosophy of technology needs to be better connected to, and anchored in, other philosophical work and the philosophical tradition. Like other small subfields in philosophy such as environmental philosophy, there is a danger that its discourse becomes too incestuous and isolated from what goes on in, for example, moral philosophy and ethics, political philosophy, epistemology, metaphysics, philosophy of language, philosophy of science, and so on—not to forget applied ethics and related fields. Also, in terms of academic community and social network, it is important that it remains open to, and interacts with, other philosophers. (Of course, these dangers also exist for other subfields in philosophy, but let me focus on philosophy of technology.) It is also important for its further development as a discipline that it remains sufficiently skilled in terms of philosophical methods and that it is firmly rooted in philosophical traditions (even if it is, hopefully, critical of these traditions). This includes some knowledge about the history of philosophy and indeed the history of philosophy of technology. If work becomes entirely divorced from such sources and lacks enough skill in critical thinking, there is the danger that it may become too dogmatic, insufficiently aware of its own roots, assumptions, problems, and possibilities. In sum, both "horizontally" (other subdisciplines) and "vertically" (history, traditions), but also in terms of community and networks, philosophy of technology needs to be sufficiently *relational* and open.

For students and educational programs, this means it is advisable that philosophy of technology is not entirely divorced from other education in philosophy, as is sometimes the case today, and that it is best if students acquire a broader background in philosophy before and next to their study of philosophy of technology. This ensures that they have greater freedom and abilities in working with the philosophical resources offered to them and in finding other resources.

On the other hand, relationality as a meta-methodological principle also implies at least some degree of transdisciplinarity, understood as connecting to, and to some extent merging with, disciplines outside philosophy and opening up to non-conventional technologies/media and practices outside academia such as innovation, policy, art, and activism. Here the idea is that one does not only "go horizontal" within philosophy but also stretches and questions the boundaries of the field itself. This can include working with engineers, doing public philosophy and trying to change policy, or collaborating with artists. These directions are not only interesting or even recommended for the reasons mentioned previously in this chapter, but as it turns out, also for philosophy and philosophy of technology itself. Transdisciplinarity is an interesting *philosophical* problem; and to the extent that it implies reflection on the use of different media and technology and their influence on thinking and practice, it is also an interesting problem for *philosophers of technology*.

For students and educational programs, this means that students should have not just one disciplinary background (e.g., philosophy or social science or engineering) but preferably two or more, that the problem of transdisciplinarity is part of the curriculum, and that students are encouraged to also engage in non-academic practices such as art or activism. Current study programs are usually isolated from practices outside the university seminar room; it is worth thinking about ways in which universities as institutions can be opened up and make more links not only to industry and business (which they already do) but also to artistic practices, activism, and so on.

When it comes to research, there is of course a lot of variation possible within these broad directions. This depends partly on personal preferences and inclinations. Some prefer to connect to ethics and other fields of practical philosophy, others to philosophy of science. Some prefer to talk to engineers and scientists; others feel more at home in policy networks or in artistic communities. Some, like myself, make several kinds of connections, such as recently philosophy of language and working with people in the art/technology world. It also depends on one's career development: on chance and opportunities, on the jobs one gets or creates, on the people one meets. For example, my path in thinking about technology began when, during and after my PhD, I landed jobs in a Belgian nuclear research center and in a department of mechanical engineering in England. Moreover, while I am making a normative point here—this is where I think the field *should* go—clearly many philosophers of technology have already been taking one or more of these directions for many years. And some, often the more successful ones, show that it is possible and fruitful to combine the two broad directions: to be a good philosopher and to include a transdisciplinarity angle at the same time. Achieving this combination and institutionalizing it remains a challenge for the future of the field.

When it comes to education, it seems important that students are given sufficient room and opportunities to develop in transdisciplinary directions. Of course now students are also free to follow their own inclinations when it comes to activities outside the university or when it comes to other programs. But this freedom is what political philosophers call a "negative" freedom: no one is stopping students from doing all this. This is insufficient: people need to be given real support for doing more than just disciplinary work or more than just following courses.

More generally, if the directions just outlined are desirable, then the question is how we can educate people in ways that give them the knowledge and skills to go in this direction. Now there are many programs in philosophy, and there are good programs in science and technology studies, but (a) there are very few specifically in *philosophy of technology* (one exception is the master's program at the University of Twente), (b) let alone programs that combine sufficient degrees of *both* disciplinarity and transdisciplinarity. It is recommended that more programs in this direction are initiated and institutionally supported and embedded. (More explicit reflection is needed on how to convince, e.g., other philosophers or leaders in higher education that such a project is important and urgent.)

But there is also an educational challenge in a broader sense, one that goes beyond worries about developing philosophy of technology as an academic (post?)discipline or transdiscipline or beyond issues concerning higher education: How can we ensure that more people, children and adults, become aware of the important role technology plays in their daily lives, and how can we give them the tools (conceptual and other) to critically reflect on the problems that this raises? And how can we enhance the quality of public debates about technology? Answering these questions requires reflection on university programs but also on the upbringing of children and on the educational and pedagogical programs for young children and for adults who do not go on to higher education. It requires reflection on how to reach people who are usually not included in higher education programs. It requires thinking about governmental and intergovernmental policies (e.g., UNESCO) but also about the role of civil society and NGOs. And ultimately it requires reflection on how children are raised and should be raised. The first encounters children have with advanced technologies is not at school or later in the workplace but in the family and in kindergarten. It is there that thinking about technology should start. It is there that we should begin with not only giving children a basic understanding and skills with regard to technologies, but also giving them the tools to, and helping them to develop the capacity to, critically reflect on the use of technology—by themselves and by others. This goal is not only relevant to students and researchers of philosophy of technology or other readers of this book; it should be seen as connected to the question of what it means to foster children's and adults' personal growth, virtue, and well-being in the context of a fast-changing and demanding technological society and culture.

Education is also important if we want to ensure that there is a good public debate about technology and that social change is possible with regard to how our societies deal with technology. Helping citizens to reflect on technology, starting at an early age, can be seen as part of what democracy requires—for example, if we apply Dewey's ideal of democracy. Dewey (1916) argued that our democracies are only nominally democratic; much more is needed to realize the democratic ideal: in particular, it requires changes in education. Moreover, according to Dewey (and before him Rousseau), education should not only be about the teacher giving instructions but should include experiential learning. I propose to add that democracy-supportive education should include experiential learning about new technologies, and it should take place not only in the classroom but also in the family. If it is true that learning happens in social contexts where "living together educates," as Dewey (1916, 7) put it, then democracy and social change, also with regard to technology, starts not only on in the university, on the street, in the bar, in the theater, or in the classic political institutions, but also at the kitchen table.

REVIEW QUESTIONS

1. In which ways can philosophy of technology go beyond academia? Give examples of concepts and/or practices from the spheres of innovation, policy, and art.
2. What is "responsible innovation"?
3. What is "value-sensitive design"?
4. What is "field philosophy"?
5. What directions should philosophy of technology take in the future, according to the author?
6. What does the vision articulated in this chapter imply for education, according to the author?

DISCUSSION QUESTIONS

1. Should philosophers of technology do research in transdisciplinary way(s), according to you, and why (not)? What do you think about the vision of a transdisciplinary philosophy of technology articulated by the author?
2. Do you like your current curriculum? Why (not)? What is the place of philosophy of technology in the curriculum? Does that make sense? Should educational programs be changed in a transdisciplinary direction, according to you? And, if so, in what direction precisely, and what concrete measures do you propose?

KEY TERMS

Field philosophy   Responsible innovation
Performance philosophy   Value-sensitive design

REFERENCES

Chapter 1: Introduction

Coeckelbergh, Mark. 2017. *Using Words and Things: Language and Philosophy of Technology*. New York: Routledge.

Heidegger, Martin. 1927. *Being and Time: A Translation of Sein und Zeit*. Translated by J. Stambaugh. Albany: State University of New York Press, 1996.

Heidegger, Martin. 1977. "The Question Concerning Technology." In *Martin Heidegger: The Question Concerning Technology and Other Essays*, translated by W. Lovitt, 3–35. New York: Harper Torchbooks.

Mitcham, Carl. 1994. *Thinking through Technology: The Path between Engineering and Philosophy*. Chicago: University of Chicago Press.

Chapter 2: History and Landscape

Bacon, Francis. (1620) 2000. *The New Organon*. Edited by L. Jardine and M. Silverthorne. Reprint, Cambridge, UK: Cambridge University Press.

Bacon, Francis. (1627) 2000. *The New Atlantis*. The Project Gutenberg EBook. Reprint, available at http://www.gutenberg.org/files/2434/2434-h/2434-h.htm

Benjamin, Walter. (1935) 1969. "The Work of Art in the Age of Mechanical Reproduction." In *Illuminations*, edited by H. Arendt, translated by H. Zohn, 217–251. Reprint, New York: Schocken Books.

Coeckelbergh, Mark. 2017. *New Romantic Cyborgs*. Cambridge, MA: MIT Press.

Ellul, Jacques. 1964. *The Technological Society*. Translated by J. Wilkinson. New York: Vintage Books.

Feuerbach, Ludwig. (1843) 1983. *Grundsätze einer Philosophie der Zukunft*. Reprint, Frankfurt, Germany: Vottorio Klostermann.

Heidegger, Martin. 1977. "The Question Concerning Technology." In *Martin Heidegger: The Question Concerning Technology and Other Essays*, translated by W. Lovitt, 3–35. New York: Harper Torchbooks.

Husserl, Edmund. (1936) 2012. *Die Krisis der europäischen Wissenschaften und die transzendentale Phänomenologie*. Reprint, Hamburg, Germany: Felix Meiner.

Jaspers, Karl. (1931) 2010. *Man in the Modern Age*. Translated by E. and C. Paul. Reprint, Abingdon, UK: Routledge.

Kapp, Ernst. (1877) 2015. *Grundlinien einer Philosophie der Technik*. Reprint, Hamburg, Germany: Felix Meiner Verlag.

Lowry, Martin J. C. 1979. *The World of Aldus Manutius: Business and Scholarship in Renaissance Venice*. Ithaca, NY: Cornell University Press.

McLuhan, Marshall. 1964. *Understanding Media: The Extensions of Man*. New York: McGraw-Hill.

Mitcham, Carl. 1994. *Thinking Through Technology: The Path between Engineering and Philosophy*. Chicago: University of Chicago Press.

Morris, William. 1884. *How We Live and How We Might Live*. Retrieved March 27, 2015, from https://www.marxists.org/archive/morris/works/1884/hwl/hwl.htm

Mumford, Lewis. 1934. *Technics and Civilization*. London: Routledge and Kegan Paul.

Ong, Walter. (1982) 2005. *Orality and Literacy*. Reprint, London: Routledge.

Plato. 1997. "Phaedrus." In *Plato, Complete Works*, edited by J. M. Cooper and D. S. Hutchinson, 506–556. Indianapolis: Hackett Publishing Company.

Plato. 1997. "Protagoras." In *Plato, Complete Works*, edited by J. M. Cooper and D. S. Hutchinson, 746–790. Indianapolis: Hackett Publishing Company.

Plessner, Helmuth. (1941) 2003. "Lachen und Weinen. Eine Untersuchung der Grenzen menschlichen Verhaltens." In *Ausdruck und menschliche Natur. Gesammelte Schriften VII*, 201–387. Reprint, Frankfurt, Germany: Suhrkamp.

Reydon, Thomas A. C. 2012. "Philosophy of Technology." *Internet Encyclopedia of Philosophy*. http://www.iep.utm.edu/technolo/

Rousseau, Jean-Jacques. (1750) 2011. *Discours sur les sciences et les arts*. Translated as *Discourse on the Science and the Arts*. In *The Basic Political Writings*, 2nd ed. Translated and edited by D. A. Cress, 1–26. Reprint, Indianapolis: Hackett Publishing Company.

Rousseau, Jean-Jacques. (1762) 1991. *Emile*, or *On Education*. Translated by A. Bloom. Reprint, London: Penguin.

Shelley, Mary. (1818) 1992. *Frankenstein; or, the Modern Prometheus*. Reprint, London: Penguin Books.

Simmel, Georg. (1903) 2002. "The Metropolis and Mental Life." In *The Blackwell City Reader*, 11–19. Reprint, Oxford, UK: Wiley-Blackwell.

Simmel, Georg. (1907) 2004. *The Philosophy of Money*, 3rd ed. Edited by D. Frisby. Translated by T. Bottomore and D. Frisby. Reprint, London: Routledge.

Stiegler, Bernard. 1998. *Technics and Time, 1: The Fault of Epimetheus*. Stanford, CA: Stanford University Press.

Stiegler, Bernard. 2004. *Philosopher par accident*. Paris: Éditions Galilée.

Weber, Max. (1905) 1992. *The Protestant Ethic and the Spirit of Capitalism*. Translated by T. Parsons. Reprint, London: Routledge.

Weber, Max. (1919) 2014. "Science and Vocation." In *From Max Weber: Essays in Sociology*, edited by H. H. Gerth and C. W. Mills, 129–156. London: Routledge.

Wittgenstein, Ludwig. (1953) 2009. *Philosophical Investigations*, rev. 4th ed., translated by G. E. M. Anscombe, P. M. S. Hacker, and J. Schulte. Reprint, Malden, MA: Wiley.

Chapter 3: Phenomenology and Hermeneutics: Heidegger, McLuhan, and Contemporary Work

Coeckelbergh, Mark. 2013. "Information Technology, Moral Anxiety, and the Implosion of the Public Sphere: A Preliminary Discussion of the McLuhanian Problem of Responsibility." In *Proceedings of "McLuhan's Philosophy of Media"—Centennial Conference*, edited by Y. Van Den Eede, J. Bauwens, J. Beyl, M. Van den Bossche, and K. Verstrynge. Contact Forum.

Coeckelbergh, Mark. 2015. *Environmental Skill: Motivation, Knowledge, and the Possibility of a Non-Romantic Environmental Ethics*. New York: Routledge.

Coeckelbergh, Mark. 2017. *Using Words and Things: Language and Philosophy of Technology*. New York: Routledge.

Coeckelbergh, Mark. 2018. "Skillful Coping with and through Technologies: Some Challenges and Avenues for a Dreyfus-inspired Philosophy of Technology." *AI & Society* 34(2): 269–287.

Deleuze, Gilles. 1992. "Postscript on the Societies of Control." *October* 59: 3–7.

De Preester, Helena. 2011. "Technology and the Body: The (Im)Possibilities of Re-embodiment." *Foundations of Science* 16(2–3): 119–137.

Dreyfus, Hubert L. 1972. *What Computers Can't Do: The Limits of Artificial Intelligence*. New York: MIT Press.

Dreyfus, Stuart, and Hubert L. Dreyfus. 1980. *A Five-Stage Model of the Mental Activities Involved in Directed Skill Acquisition*. University of California, Berkeley, Operations Research Center.

Feenberg, Andrew. 1999. *Questioning Technology*. London: Routledge.

Heidegger, Martin. (1927) 1996. *Being and Time: A Translation of Sein und Zeit*. Translated by J. Stambaugh. Reprint, Albany: State University of New York.

Heidegger, Martin. 1977. "The Question Concerning Technology." In *Martin Heidegger: The Question Concerning Technology and Other Essays*, translated by William Lovitt, 3–35. New York: Harper Torchbooks.

Ihde, Don. 1993. *Postphenomenology*. Evanston, IL: Northwestern University Press.

Irrgang, Bernhard. 2010. *Homo Faber: Arbeit, technische Lebensform und menschlicher Leib*. Würzburg, Germany: Königshausen & Neumann.

McLuhan, Marshall. (1964) 2001. *Understanding Media: The Extensions of Man*. Reprint, London: Routledge.

McLuhan, Marshall, and Eric McLuhan. 1988. *Laws of Media: The New Science*. Toronto: University of Toronto Press.

Merleau-Ponty, Maurice. (1945) 1962. *Phenomenology of Perception*. Translated by C. Smith. Reprint, New York: Routledge.

Nagel, Chris. 2010. "Exposure, Absorption, Subjection: Being-In-Media." In *Phenomenology beyond Philosophy*, edited by Lester Embree, Michael Barber, and Thomas J. Nenon. Bucharest, Romania: Zeta Books and Arghos-Diffusion.

Ong, Walter J. (1982) 2002. *Orality and Literacy: The Technologizing of the Word*. Reprint, London: Routledge.

Pattison, George. 2000. *The Later Heidegger*. London: Routledge.

Van Den Eede, Yoni. 2013. *Amor Technologiae: Marshall McLuhan as Philosopher of Technology*. Brussels, Belgium: VUB Press.

Van Den Eede, Yoni. 2015. "Exceeding Our Grasp: McLuhan's All-Metaphorical Outlook." In *Finding McLuhan: The Mind, the Man, the Message*, edited by Jacqueline McLeod Rogers, Tracy Whalen, and Catherine G. Taylor, 43–61. Regina, Canada: University of Regina Press.

Varela, Francisco J., Evan Thomson, and Eleanor Rosch. 1991. *The Embodied Mind: Cognitive Science and Human Experience*. Cambridge, MA: MIT Press.

Verbeek, Peter-Paul. 2005. *What Things Do: Philosophical Reflections on Technology, Agency, and Design*. University Park: Pennsylvania State University Press.

Zwier, Jochem, Vincent Blok, and Pieter Lemmens. 2016. "Phenomenology and the Empirical Turn: A Phenomenological Analysis of Postphenomenology." *Philosophy & Technology* 29(4): 313–333.

Chapter 4: Postphenomenology, Material Hermeneutics, and Mediation Theory

Achterhuis, Hans, ed. 2001. *American Philosophy of Technology: The Empirical Turn*. Bloomington: Indiana University Press.

Coeckelbergh, Mark. 2015. "Language and Technology: Maps, Bridges, and Pathways." *AI & Society* 32(2): 175–189.

Coeckelbergh, Mark. 2017a. "Technology Games: Using Wittgenstein for Understanding and Evaluating Technology." *Science and Engineering Ethics* 24(5): 1503–1519.

Coeckelbergh, Mark. 2017b. *Using Words and Things: Language and Philosophy of Technology*. New York: Routledge.

Coeckelbergh, Mark, and Wessel Reijers. 2016. "Narrative Technologies: A Philosophical Investigation of Narrative Capacities of Technologies by Using Ricoeur's Narrative Theory." *Human Studies* 39(3): 325–346.

De Preester, Helena. 2011. "Technology and the Body: The (Im)Possibilities of Re-embodiment." *Foundations of Science* 16(2–3): 119–137.

Hickman, Larry. 2015. "Science and Technology." In *The Bloomsbury Companion to Pragmatism*, edited by Sami Pihlström, 108–121. London: Bloomsbury.

Ihde, Don. 1990. *Technology and the Lifeworld: From Garden to Earth*. Bloomington: Indiana University Press.

Ihde, Don. 1998. *Expanding Hermeneutics: Visualism in Science*. Evanston, IL: Northwestern University Press.

Ihde, Don. 2009. "What Is Postphenomenology?" In *Postphenomenology and Technoscience: The Peking Lectures*, 5–24. Albany: State University of New York Press.

Kaplan, David M. 2006. "Paul Ricoeur and the Philosophy of Technology." *Journal of French and Francophone Philosophy* 16(1–2): 42–56.

Latour, Bruno. 1993. *We Have Never Been Modern*. Translated by Catherine Porter. Cambridge, MA: Harvard University Press.

Peterson, Martin, and Andreas Spahn. 2011. "Can Technological Artefacts be Moral Agents?" *Science and Engineering Ethics* 17(3): 411–424.

Reijers, Wessel, and Mark Coeckelbergh. 2016. "The Blockchain as a Narrative Technology: Investigating the Social Ontology and Normative Configurations of Cryptocurrencies." *Philosophy & Technology* 31(1): 103–130.

Sloterdijk, Peter. 1999. *Regeln für den Menschenpark*. Frankfurt, Germany: Suhrkamp.

Smith, Dominic. 2015. "Rewriting the Constitution: A Critique of Postphenomenology." *Philosophy & Technology* 28(4): 533–551.

Verbeek, Peter-Paul. 2005. *What Things Do: Philosophical Reflections on Technology, Agency, and Design*. University Park: Pennsylvania State University Press.

Verbeek, Peter-Paul. 2008a. "Cultivating Humanity: Towards a Non-Humanist Ethics of Technology." In *New Waves in Philosophy of Technology*, edited by Jan-Kyrre Berg Olsen, Evan Selinger, and Søren Riis, 241–266. Hampshire, UK: Palgrave MacMillan.

Verbeek, Peter-Paul. 2008b. "Obstetric Ultrasound and the Technological Mediation of Morality: A Postphenomenological Analysis." *Human Studies* 31(1): 11–26.

Verbeek, Peter-Paul. 2011. *Moralizing Technology: Understanding and Designing the Morality of Things*. Chicago: University of Chicago Press.

Verbeek, Peter-Paul. 2016. "The Struggle for Technology: Towards a Realistic Political Theory of Technology." *Foundations of Science* 22(2): 301–304.

Zwier, Jochem, Vincent Blok, and Pieter Lemmens. 2016. "Phenomenology and the Empirical Turn: A Phenomenological Analysis of Postphenomenology." *Philosophy & Technology* 29(4): 313–333.

Chapter 5: Critical Theory and Feminism

Adorno, Theodor and Max Horkheimer. (1944) 2002. *Dialectic of Enlightenment*. Translated by Edmund Jephcott. Reprint, Stanford, CA: Stanford University Press.

Butler, Judith. 1988. "Performative Acts and Gender Constitution: An Essay in Phenomenology and Feminist Theory." *Theatre Journal* 40(4): 519–531.

Coeckelbergh, Mark. 2012. "Hacking Feenberg." *Symploke, a Comparative Literature and Theory Journal* 20(1–2): 327–330.

Coeckelbergh, Mark. 2017a. "Technology Games: Using Wittgenstein for Understanding and Evaluating Technology." *Science and Engineering Ethics* 24(5): 1503–1519.

Coeckelbergh, Mark. 2017b. *Using Words and Things: Language and Philosophy of Technology*. New York: Routledge.

Dorrestijn, Steven. 2011. "Technical Mediation and Subjectivation: Tracing and Extending Foucault's Philosophy of Technology." *Philosophy & Technology* 25(2): 221–241.

Dusek, Val. 2006. "Women, Feminism, and Technology." In *Philosophy of Technology: An Introduction*, 136–155. Malden, MA: Blackwell.

Feenberg, Andrew. 2010. *Between Reason and Experience: Essays in Technology and Modernity*. Cambridge, MA: MIT Press.

Foucault, Michel. (1966) 1994. *The Order of Things: An Archeology of the Human Sciences*. A Translation of *Les mots et les choses*. Reprint, New York: Vintage Books/Random House.

Foucault, Michel. 1975. *Discipline and Punish: The Birth of the Prison*. New York: Random House.

Foucault, Michel. (1976) 1998. *The History of Sexuality, Vol. 1: The Will to Knowledge*. Translated by R. Hurley. Reprint, London: Penguin Books.

Foucault, Michel. 1980. *Power/Knowledge: Selected Interviews and Other Writings, 1972–1977*. Edited by Colin Gordon. Translated by C. Gordon and L. Marshall. New York: Pantheon Books.

Foucault, Michel. 1988. *Technologies of the Self: A Seminar with Michel Foucault*. Edited by Luther H. Martin, Huck Gutman, and Patrick H. Hutton. Amherst: University of Massachusetts Press.

Fuchs, Christian, Kees Boersma, Anders Albrechtslund, and Marisol Sandoval, eds. 2012. *Internet and Surveillance: The Challenges of Web 2.0 and Social Media*. New York: Routledge.

Fuchs, Christian. 2014. *Social Media: A Critical Introduction*. London: Sage.

Habermas, Jürgen. (1981) 1987. *Theory of Communicative Action, Volume Two: Lifeworld and System: A Critique of Functionalist Reason*. Translated by T. A. McCarthy. Boston: Beacon Press.

Haraway, Donna. (1991) 2000. "A Cyborg Manifesto." In *The Cybercultures Reader*, edited by David Bell and Barbara M. Kennedy, 291–324. London: Routledge.

Marcuse, Herbert. (1964) 2007. *One-Dimensional Man: Studies in the Ideology of Advanced Industrial Society*. Reprint, London: Routledge.

Marx, Karl. (1867) 1976. *Capital: A Critique of Political Economy*. Vol. 1. Translated by B. Fowkes. Reprint, London: Penguin. (Reprinted 1990.)

Pinch, Trevor, and Wiebe Bijker. 1989. "The Social Construction of Facts and Artifacts: Or How the Sociology of Science and Technology Might Benefit Each Other."

In *The Social Construction of Technological Systems*, edited by Wiebe Bijker, Thomas Hughes, and Trevor Pinch, 17–50. Cambridge, MA: MIT Press.

Verbeek, Peter-Paul. 2011. *Moralizing Technology: Understanding and Designing the Morality of Things*. Chicago: University of Chicago Press.

Wajcman, Judy. 2004. *TechnoFeminism*. Cambridge, UK: Polity Press.

Winner, Langdon. 1980. "Do Artifacts Have Politics?" *Daedalus* 109(1): 121–136.

Chapter 6: Pragmatism, Analytic Approaches, and Transcultural Philosophy

Aydin, Ciano. 2015. "The Artifactual Mind: Overcoming the 'Inside–Outside' Dualism in the Extended Mind Thesis and Recognizing the Technological Dimension of Cognition." *Phenomenology & the Cognitive Sciences* 14(1): 73–94.

Coeckelbergh, Mark. 2015. *Money Machines: Electronic Financial Technologies, Distancing, and Responsibility in Global Finance*. Farnham, Surrey, UK: Ashgate.

Coeckelbergh, Mark. 2017. *Using Words and Things: Language and Philosophy of Technology*. New York: Routledge.

Coeckelbergh, Mark, and Jessica Mesman. 2007. "With Hope and Imagination: Imaginative Moral Decision-Making in Neonatal Intensive Care Units." *Ethical Theory and Moral Practice* 10(1): 3–21.

Dewey, John. 1929. *Experience and Nature*. London: George Allen & Unwin.

Fesmire, Steven. 2003. *John Dewey and Moral Imagination: Pragmatism in Ethics*. Bloomington: Indiana University Press.

Flusser, Vilém. 1999. *The Shape of Things: A Philosophy of Design*. London: Reaktion Books.

Franssen, Maarten. 2009. "Analytic Philosophy of Technology." In *A Companion to the Philosophy of Technology*, edited by Jan K. B. Olsen, Stig A. Pedersen, and Vincent F. Hendricks, 184–188. Malden, MA: Wiley-Blackwell.

Hickman, Larry A. (1990) 1992. *John Dewey's Pragmatic Technology*. Reprint, Bloomington: Indiana University Press.

Hickman, Larry A. 2008. "Postphenomenology and Pragmatism: Closer Than You Might Think?" *Techné: Research in Philosophy and Technology* 12(2): 99–104.

Kroes, Peter. 2010. "Engineering and the Dual Nature of Technical Artefacts." *Cambridge Journal of Economics* 34(1): 51–62.

Kroes, Peter and Anthonie Meijers, eds. 2006. "The Dual Nature of Technical Artefacts." Special Issue of *Studies in History and Philosophy of Science* 37(1): 1–158.

Mills, Simon. 2016. *Gilbert Simondon: Information, Technology and Media*. London: Rowman & Littlefield.

Mitcham, Carl. 1994. *Thinking through Technology: The Path between Engineering and Philosophy*. Chicago: University of Chicago Press.

Pitt, Joseph. 2011. *Doing Philosophy of Technology: Essays in a Pragmatist Spirit*. Dordrecht, Netherlands: Springer.

Rorty, Richard. 1979. *Philosophy and the Mirror of Nature*. Princeton, NJ: Princeton University Press.

Searle, John R. 1995. *The Construction of Social Reality*. New York: Free Press.

Searle, John R. 2006. "Social Ontology." *Anthropological Theory* 6(1): 12–29.

Simondon, Gilbert. 2017. *On the Mode of Existence of Technical Objects*. Translated by C. Malaspina and J. Rogove. Minneapolis: Univocal.

van de Poel, Ibo. 2011. "Nuclear Energy as a Social Experiment." *Ethics, Policy, and Environment* 14(3): 285–290.

Vermaas, Pieter, Peter Kroes, Ibo van de Poel, Maarten Franssen, and Wybo Houkes. 2011. A *Philosophy of Technology: From Technical Artefacts to Sociotechnical Systems*. Synthesis Lectures on Engineers, Technology and Society, vol. 6. San Rafael, CA: Morgan & Claypool.

Wiener, Norbert. (1948) 1961. *Cybernetics: Or Control and Communication in the Animal and the Machine*. 2nd ed. Reprint, Cambridge, MA: MIT Press.

Wong, Pak-Hang. 2012. "Dao, Harmony, and Personhood: Towards a Confucian Ethics of Technology." *Philosophy & Technology* 25(1): 67–86.

Chapter 7: From Information Technologies to Philosophy and Ethics of Information

Brey, Philip. 2008. "Do We Have Moral Duties towards Information Objects?" *Ethics and Information Technology* 10(2–3): 109–114.

Capurro, Rafael. 2006. "Towards an Ontological Foundation of Information Ethics." *Ethics and Information Technology* 8(4): 175–186.

Capurro, Rafael, and Birger Hjørland. 2003. "The Concept of Information." *Annual Review of Information Science and Technology* 37(1): 343–411.

Coeckelbergh, Mark. 2012. *Growing Moral Relations: Critique of Moral Status Ascription*. Basingstoke, UK: Palgrave Macmillan.

Coeckelbergh, Mark. 2017. *Using Words and Things: Language and Philosophy of Technology*. New York: Routledge.

Ess, Charles. 2006. "Ethical Pluralism and Global Information Ethics." *Ethics and Information Technology* 8(4): 215–226.

Ess, Charles. 2008. "Luciano Floridi's Philosophy of Information and Information Ethics: Critical Reflections and the State of the Art." *Ethics and Information Technology* 10(2–3): 89–96.

Floridi, Luciano. 2011. *The Philosophy of Information*. Oxford, UK: Oxford University Press.

Floridi, Luciano. 2013. *The Ethics of Information*. Oxford, UK: Oxford University Press.

Floridi, Luciano. 2014. *The Fourth Revolution: How the Infosphere Is Reshaping Human Reality*. Oxford, UK: Oxford University Press.

Floridi, Luciano. 2016. "Tolerant Paternalism." *Science and Engineering Ethics* 22(6): 1669–1688.

Stahl, B. 2008. "Discourses on Information Ethics: The Claim to Universality." *Ethics and Information Technology* 10(2–3): 97–108.

Wiener, Norbert. (1948) 1961. *Cybernetics: Or Control and Communication in the Animal and the Machine.* 2nd ed. Reprint, Cambridge, MA: MIT Press.

Chapter 8: From Robotics and AI to Thinking about Moral Status and Human Relationships

Anderson, Michael, and Susan Leigth Anderson, eds. 2011. *Machine Ethics.* Cambridge, UK: Cambridge University Press.

Asimov, Isaac. 1942. "Runaround." *Astounding Science Fiction* 29(1): 94–103.

Breazeal, Cynthia L. 2002. *Designing Sociable Robots.* Cambridge, MA: MIT Press.

Bryson, Joanna. 2010. "Robots Should Be Slaves." In *Close Engagements with Artificial Companions: Key Social, Psychological, Ethical and Design Issues,* edited by Y. Wilks, 63–74. Amsterdam: John Benjamins.

Bryson, Joanna. 2016. "Patiency Is Not a Virtue: AI and the Design of Ethical Systems." AAAI Spring Symposium Series, Ethical and Moral Considerations in Non-Human Agents. http://www.aaai.org/ocs/index.php/SSS/SSS16/paper/view/12686

Clark, Roger. 2011. "Asimov's Laws of Robotics: Implications for Information Technology." In *Machine Ethics,* edited by Michael Anderson and Susan Leigth Anderson, 254–284. Cambridge, UK: Cambridge University Press.

Coeckelbergh, Mark. 2010a. "Moral Appearances: Emotions, Robots, and Human Morality." *Ethics and Information Technology* 12(3): 235–241.

Coeckelbergh, Mark. 2010b. "Robot Rights? Towards a Social-Relational Justification of Moral Consideration." *Ethics and Information Technology* 12(3): 209–221.

Coeckelbergh, Mark. 2011a. "Humans, Animals, and Robots: A Phenomenological Approach to Human-Robot Relations." *Philosophy & Technology* 24(3): 269–278.

Coeckelbergh, Mark. 2011b. "You, Robot: On the Linguistic Construction of Artificial Others." *AI & Society* 26(1): 61–69.

Coeckelbergh, Mark. 2012. *Growing Moral Relations: Critique of Moral Status Ascription.* Basingstoke, UK: Palgrave Macmillan.

Coeckelbergh, Mark. 2014. "The Moral Standing of Machines: Towards a Relational and Non-Cartesian Moral Hermeneutics." *Philosophy & Technology* 27(1): 61–77.

Coeckelbergh, Mark. 2017. *Using Words and Things: Language and Philosophy of Technology.* New York: Routledge.

Coeckelbergh, Mark, and David Gunkel. 2014. "Facing Animals: A Relational, Other-Oriented Approach to Moral Standing." *Journal of Agricultural and Environmental Ethics* 27(5): 715–733.

Darling, Kate. 2012. "Extending Legal Protection to Social Robots." *IEEE Spectrum,* September 10, 2012. Retrieved June 22, 2017, from http://spectrum.ieee.org/automaton/robotics/artificial-intelligence/extending-legal-protection-to-social-robots

Darling, Kate. 2017. "'Who's Johnny?' Anthropomorphic Framing in Human-Robot Interaction, Integration, and Policy." In *Robot Ethics 2.0*, edited by Patrick Lin, Keith Abney, and Ryan Jenkins, 173–192. New York: University Press.

Darling, Kate, Palash Nandy, and Cynthia Breazeal. 2015. "Empathic Concern and the Effect of Stories in Human-Robot Interaction." *Robot and Human Interactive Communication (RO-MAN), 2015 24th IEEE International Symposium*, 770–775. http://dx.doi.org/10.1109/ROMAN.2015.7333675

Floridi, Luciano, and J. W. Sanders. 2004. "On the Morality of Artificial Agents." *Minds and Machines* 14(3): 349–379.

Floridi, Luciano. 2013. *The Ethics of Information*. Oxford, UK: Oxford University Press.

Gunkel, David. 2012. *The Machine Question: Critical Perspectives on AI, Robots, and Ethics*. Cambridge, MA: MIT Press.

Gunkel, David. 2018. "The Other Question: Can and Should Robots Have Rights?" *Ethics and Information Technology* 20(2): 87–99.

Johnson, Deborah G. 2006. "Computer Systems: Moral Entities But Not Moral Agents." *Ethics and Information Technology* 8(4): 195–204.

Kant, Immanuel. 1997. *Lectures on Ethics*. Edited by P. Heath and J. B. Schneewind. Translated by P. Heath. Cambridge, UK: Cambridge University Press.

Kant, Immanuel. 2012. *Lectures on Anthropology*. Edited by A. W. Wood and R. B. Louden. Cambridge, UK: Cambridge University Press.

Levinas, Emmanuel. (1961) 1969. *Totality and Infinity: An Essay on Exteriority*. Translated by A. Lingis. Pittsburgh: Duquesne University.

Levy, David. 2007. *Love and Sex with Robots*. New York: Harper Collins.

Levy, David. 2012. "The Ethics of Robot Prostitutes." In *Robot Ethics: The Ethical and Social Implications of Robotics*, edited by Patrick Lin, Keith Abney, and George A. Bekey, 223–232. Cambridge, MA: MIT Press.

Moor, James H. 2006. "The Nature, Importance, and Difficult of Machine Ethics." *IEEE Intelligent Systems* 21(4): 18–21.

Richardson, Kathleen. 2016. "The Asymmetrical 'Relationship': Parallels Between Prostitution and the Development of Sex Robots." *ACM SIGCAS Computers and Society—Special Issue on Ethicomp* 45(3): 290–293.

Sullins, John. 2006. "When Is a Robot a Moral Agent?" *International Review of Information Ethics* 6(12): 23–30.

Sullins, John. 2012. "Robots, Love, and Sex: The Ethics of Building a Love Machine." *IEEE Transactions on Affective Computing* 3(4): 398–409.

Suzuki, Yutaka, Lisa Galli, Ayaka Ikeda, Shoji Itakura, and Michiteru Kitazaki. 2015. "Measuring Empathy for Human and Robot Hand Pain Using Electroencephalography." *Nature, Scientific Reports* 5, article 15924.

Wallach, Wendell, and Colin Allen. 2009. *Moral Machines: Teaching Robots Right from Wrong*. Oxford, UK: Oxford University Press.

Chapter 9: From Genetic Engineering and Cyborgs to Transhumanism and Posthumanism

Allhoff, Fritz, Patrick Lin, James Moor, and John Weckert. 2010. "Ethics of Human Enhancement: 25 Questions and Answers." *Studies in Ethics, Law, and Technology* 4(1): 1–39.

Bolter, Jay David. 2016. "Posthumanism." In *The International Encyclopedia of Communication Theory and Philosophy*, edited by Klaus Bruhn Jensen and Robert T. Craig, 1556–1563. Malden, MA: Wiley-Blackwell.

Bostrom, Nick. 2005. "The Fable of the Dragon Tyrant." *Journal of Medical Ethics* 31(5): 273–277.

Braidotti, Rosi. 2013. *The Posthuman*. Cambridge, UK: Polity Press.

Clark, Andy. 2003. *Natural-Born Cyborgs: Minds, Technologies, and the Future of Human Intelligence*. Oxford, UK: Oxford University Press.

Coeckelbergh, Mark. 2011. "Vulnerable Cyborgs: Learning to Live with Our Dragons." *Journal of Evolution and Technology* 22(1): 1–9.

Coeckelbergh, Mark. 2012. *Growing Moral Relations: Critique of Moral Status Ascription*. Basingstoke, UK: Palgrave Macmillan.

Coeckelbergh, Mark. 2013a. "Enhancement and the Vulnerable Body: Questioning Some Philosophical Assumptions." In *Beyond Therapy v. Enhancement?*, edited by Federica Lucivero and Anton Vedder, 15–26. Pisa, Italy: Pisa University Press.

Coeckelbergh, Mark. 2013b. *Human Being @ Risk: Enhancement, Technology, and the Evaluation of Vulnerability Transformations*. New York: Springer.

Coeckelbergh, Mark. 2014a. "The Moral Standing of Machines: Towards a Relational and Non-Cartesian Moral Hermeneutics." *Philosophy & Technology* 27(1): 61–77.

Coeckelbergh, Mark. 2014b. "Robotic Appearances and Forms of Life. A Phenomenological-Hermeneutical Approach to the Relation between Robotics and Culture." In *Robotics in Germany and Japan. Philosophical and Technical Perspectives*, edited by M. Funk and B. Irrgang. Dresden Philosophy of Technology Studies, 59–68. Dresden, Germany: Peter Lang.

Coeckelbergh, Mark. 2017. *New Romantic Cyborgs: Romanticism, Information Technology, and the End of the Machine*. Cambridge, MA: MIT Press.

Dupuy, Jean-Pierre. 2008. "Cybernetics Is an Antihumanism: Advanced Technologies and the Rebellion against the Human Condition." *The Global Spiral* 9 (3). Retrieved from https://www.metanexus.net/h-cybernetics-antihumanism-advanced-technologies-and-rebellion-against-human-condition/

Habermas, Jürgen. 2003. *The Future of Human Nature*. Translated by H. Beister and W. Rehg. London: Polity Press.

Haraway, Donna. (1991) 2000. "A Cyborg Manifesto." In *The Cybercultures Reader*, edited by D. Bell and B. M. Kennedy, 291–324. Reprint, London: Routledge.

Harris, John. 2007. *Enhancing Evolution: The Ethical Case for Making Better People.* Princeton, NJ: Princeton University Press.

Hauskeller, Michael. 2011. "Human Enhancement and the Giftedness of Life." *Philosophical Papers* 40(1): 55–79.

Kass, Leon R. 2003. "Ageless Bodies, Happy Souls: Biotechnology and Pursuit of Perfection." *The New Atlantis* 1(Spring): 9–28.

Kurzweil, Ray. 2005. *The Singularity is Near: When Humans Transcend Biology.* New York: Penguin.

Latour, Bruno. 1993. *We Have Never Been Modern.* Translated by Catherine Porter. Cambridge, MA: Harvard University Press.

Latour, Bruno. 2004. *Politics of Nature: How to Bring the Sciences into Democracy.* Translated by Catherine Porter. Cambridge, MA: Harvard University Press.

Moravec, Hans. 1990. *Mind Children: The Future of Robot and Human Intelligence.* Cambridge, MA: Harvard University Press.

Savulescu, Julian, and Ingmar Persson. 2008. "The Perils of Cognitive Enhancement and the Urgent Imperative to Enhance the Moral Character of Humanity." *Journal of Applied Philosophy* 25(3): 162–167.

Sandel, M. J. 2002. "What's Wrong with Enhancement." Working paper prepared for The President's Council on Bioethics. Available at https://bioethicsarchive.georgetown.edu/pcbe/background/sandelpaper.html

Sandel, Michael. 2007. *The Case Against Perfection.* Cambridge, MA: The Belknap Press of Harvard University Press.

Sorgner, Stefan. 2017. "Editor's Note." *Journal of Posthuman Studies* 1(1): 1–8.

Tegmark, Max. 2017. *Life 3.0: Being Human in the Age of Artificial Intelligence.* London: Allen Lane (Penguin Books).

Chapter 10: From Climate Change and Geoengineering to Questioning "Nature" and Thinking in and about the "Anthropocene"

Blok, Vincent. 2015. "The Human Glance, the Experience of Environmental Distress and the 'Affordance' of Nature: Toward a Phenomenology of the Ecological Crisis." *Journal of Agricultural and Environmental Ethics* 2(5): 925–938.

Borgmann, Albert. 1984. *Technology and the Character of Contemporary Life.* Chicago: University of Chicago Press.

Briggle, Adam. 2015. *A Field Philosopher's Guide to Fracking.* New York: Liveright.

Cera, Agostino. 2017. "The Technocene or Technology as (Neo)Environment." *Techné: Research in Philosophy and Technology* 21(2–3), Special issue on the Anthropocene: 243–281.

Coeckelbergh, Mark. 2011. "Environmental Virtue: Motivation, Skill, and (In)formation Technology." *Journal of Environmental Philosophy* 8(2): 141–170.

Coeckelbergh, Mark. 2012. *Growing Moral Relations: Critique of Moral Status Ascription*. Basingstoke, UK: Palgrave Macmillan.

Coeckelbergh, Mark. 2015. *Environmental Skill: Motivation, Knowledge, and the Possibility of a Non-Romantic Environmental Ethics*. New York: Routledge.

Coeckelbergh, Mark. 2017a. "Beyond 'Nature': Towards More Engaged and Care-Full Ways of Relating to the Environment." In *Routledge Handbook of Environmental Anthropology*, edited by Helen Kopnina and Eleanor Shoreman-Ouimet, 105–116. Abingdon, UK: Earthscan/Routledge.

Coeckelbergh, Mark. 2017b. "The Phenomenology of Environmental Health Risk: Vulnerability to Modern Technological Risk, Risk Alienation and Risk Politics." In *Ethics of Environmental Health*, edited by Friedo Zölzer and Gaston Meskens, 89–102. Routledge Studies in Environment and Health. Oxon, UK: Routledge.

Coeckelbergh, Mark. 2017c. "Technology Games: Using Wittgenstein for Understanding and Evaluating Technology." *Science and Engineering Ethics* 24(5): 1503–1519.

Coeckelbergh, Mark. 2017d. *Using Words and Things: Language and Philosophy of Technology*. New York: Routledge.

Coeckelbergh, Mark. 2018. "Technology, Language, Earth." (Talk in Nijmegen, Netherlands.)

Coeckelbergh, Mark, and David Gunkel. 2014. "Facing Animals: A Relational, Other-Oriented Approach to Moral Standing." *Journal of Agricultural and Environmental Ethics* 27(5): 715–733.

Connolly, Kate. 2017. "Geoengineering Is Not a Quick Fix for Climate Change, Experts Warn Trump." *The Guardian*, October 14, 2017. https://www.theguardian.com/environment/2017/oct/14/geoengineering-is-not-a-quick-fix-for-climate-change-experts-warn-trump

Crutzen Paul J. 2006. "The 'Anthropocene.'" In *Earth System Science in the Anthropocene*, edited by Eckkart Ehlers and Thomas Krafft, 13–18. Berlin: Springer.

Di Paola, Marcello. 2018. "Virtue." In *The Encyclopedia of the Anthropocene*, vol. 4, edited by Dominick A. DellaSala and Michael I. Goldstein, 119–126. Oxford, UK: Elsevier.

Heidegger, Martin. 1966. *Discourse on Thinking: A Translation of Gelassenheit*. Translated by J. M. Anderson and E. H. Freund. New York: Harper & Row.

Heidegger, Martin. 1977. "The Question Concerning Technology." In *Martin Heidegger: The Question Concerning Technology and Other Essays*, translated by William Lovitt, 3–35. New York: Harper Torchbooks.

Ingold, Tim. 2000. *The Perception of the Environment: Essays in Livelihood, Dwelling, and Skill*. London: Routledge.

Jamieson, D., and M. Di Paola. 2016. "Political Theory for the Anthropocene." In *Global Political Theory*, edited by D. Held and P. Maffettone. Cambridge, UK: Polity Press.

Kaplan, David M., ed. 2017. *Philosophy, Technology, and the Environment*. Cambridge, MA: MIT Press.

Latour, Bruno. 1993. *We Have Never Been Modern*. Translated by Catherine Porter. Cambridge, MA: Harvard University Press.

Latour, Bruno. 2004. *Politics of Nature: How to Bring the Sciences into Democracy*. Translated by Catherine Porter. Cambridge, MA: Harvard University Press.

Lemmens, Pieter, Vincent Blok, and Jochem Zwier. 2017. "Guest Editors' Introduction: Toward a Terrestrial Turn in Philosophy of Technology." *Techné: Research in Philosophy and Technology* 21(2–3), Special issue on the Anthropocene: 114–126.

Ludwig, Cornelia and Steffen, Will 2018. "The 1950s as the Beginning of the Anthropocene." In *The Encyclopedia of the Anthropocene*, vol. 2, edited by Dominick A. DellaSala and Michael I. Goldstein, 45–56. Oxford, UK: Elsevier.

Ming, Tingzhen, Renaud de Richter, Wei Liu, and Sylvain Caillol. 2014. "Fighting Global Warming by Climate Engineering." *Renewable and Sustainable Energy Reviews* 31: 792–834.

Mooney, Chris. 2016. "Rex Tillerson's View of Climate Change: It's Just an 'Engineering Problem.'" *Washington Post*, December 16, 2016. https://www. washingtonpost.com/news/energy-environment/wp/2016/12/13/rex-tillersons-view-of-climate-change-its-just-an-engineering-problem/?noredirect=on&utm_term=.14b5ab2c31c3

Schrader-Frechette, Kristin, and Laura Westra, eds. 1997. *Technology and Values*. Lanham, MD: Rowman & Littlefield.

Seager, Thomas, Evan Selinger, and Arnim Wiek. 2012. "Sustainable Engineering Science for Resolving Wicked Problems." *Journal of Agricultural and Environmental Ethics* 25(4): 467–484.

Stiegler, Bernard. 2017. "What is Called Caring? Beyond the Anthropocene." *Techné: Research in Philosophy and Technology* 21(2–3), Special issue on the Anthropocene: 386–404.

Thompson, Paul B. 2010. *Food Biotechnology in Ethical Perspective*. Rev. ed. Dordrecht, Netherlands: Springer.

Thompson, Paul B. 2017. "Philosophy of Technology and the Environment." In *The Oxford Handbook of Environmental Ethics*, edited by Stephen M. Gardiner and Allen Thompson. New York: Oxford University Press.

Warner, K., M. Hamza, A. Oliver-Smith, F. Renaud, and A. Julca. 2010. "Climate Change, Environmental Degradation and Migration." *Natural Hazards* 55(3): 689–715.

Winner, Langdon. 2017. "Rebranding the Anthropocene: A Rectification of Names." *Techné: Research in Philosophy and Technology* 21(2–3), Special issue on the Anthropocene: 282–294.

Zwier, Jochem, and Vincent Blok. 2017. "Saving Earth: Encountering Heidegger's Philosophy of Technology in the Anthropocene." *Techné: Research in Philosophy and Technology* 21(2–3), Special issue on the Anthropocene: 222–242.

Chapter 11: Philosophy of Technology and Other Philosophy: (Re)connecting with Other Philosophical Subdisciplines

Austin, J. L. 1962. *How to Do Things with Words: The William James Lectures Delivered at Harvard University in 1955.* Edited by J. O. Urmson and Marina Sbisà. Oxford, UK: Clarendon Press.

Boon, Mieke, and Tarja Knuuttila. 2008. "Models as Epistemic Tools in Engineering Sciences: A Pragmatic Approach." In *Handbook of the Philosophy of Science.* Edited by Dov M. Gabay, P. Thagard, and J. Woods. *Vol. 9, Philosophy of Technology and Engineering Sciences*, edited by A. Meijers. Amsterdam: Elsevier.

Bostrom, Nick, and Toby Ord. 2006. "The Reversal Test: Eliminating Status Quo Bias in Applied Ethics." *Ethics* 116(4): 656–679.

Brey, Philip A. E. 2003. "The Social Ontology of Virtual Environments." *American Journal of Economics and Sociology* 62(1): 269–282.

Brey, Philip A. E. 2014. "The Physical and Social Reality of Virtual Worlds." In *The Oxford Handbook of Virtual Reality*, edited by M. Grimshaw, 42–54. Oxford, UK: Oxford University Press.

Brey, Philip A. E., Adam Briggle, and Edward Spence, eds. 2012. *The Good Life in a Technological Age.* New York: Routledge.

Cafaro, Philip. 2004. *Thoreau's Living Ethics: Walden and the Pursuit of Virtue.* Athens: University of Georgia Press.

Clark, Andy. 2003. *Natural-Born Cyborgs: Minds, Technologies, and the Future of Human Intelligence.* Oxford, UK: Oxford University Press.

Clark, Andy, and David J. Chalmers. 1998. "The Extended Mind." *Analysis* 58(1): 7–19.

Coeckelbergh, Mark. 2009. "Personal Robots, Appearance, and Human Good: A Methodological Reflection on Roboethics." *International Journal of Social Robotics* 1(3): 217–221.

Coeckelbergh, M. 2011. "Environmental Virtue: Motivation, Skill, and (In)formation Technology." *Journal of Environmental Philosophy* 8(2): 141–170.

Coeckelbergh, Mark. 2012a. "Care Robots, Virtual Virtue, and the Best Possible Life." In *The Good Life in a Technological Age*, edited by P. Brey, A. Briggle, and E. Spence, 281–292. New York: Routledge.

Coeckelbergh, Mark. 2012b. *Growing Moral Relations: Critique of Moral Status Ascription.* Basingstoke, UK: Palgrave Macmillan.

Coeckelbergh, Mark. 2013. *Human Being @ Risk: Enhancement, Technology, and the Evaluation of Vulnerability Transformations.* New York: Springer.

Coeckelbergh, Mark. 2014. "Robotic Appearances and Forms of Life. A Phenomenological-Hermeneutical Approach to the Relation between Robotics and Culture." In *Robotics in Germany and Japan. Philosophical and Technical Perspectives*, edited by M. Funk and B. Irrgang. 59–68. Dresden, Germany: Peter Lang.

Coeckelbergh, Mark. 2015. *Environmental Skill: Motivation, Knowledge, and the Possibility of a Non-Romantic Environmental Ethics*. New York: Routledge.

Coeckelbergh, Mark. 2017a. "Cyborg Humanity and the Technologies of Human Enhancement." In *Philosophy: Technology*, edited by A. Beavers, 141–160. Farmington Hills, MI: Macmillan Reference USA/Gale, a Cengage Company.

Coeckelbergh, Mark. 2017b. "Language and Technology: Maps, Bridges, and Pathways." *AI & Society* 32(2): 175–189.

Coeckelbergh, Mark. 2017c. *New Romantic Cyborgs: Romanticism, Information Technology, and the End of the Machine*. Cambridge, MA: MIT Press.

Coeckelbergh, Mark. 2017d. "Technology Games: Using Wittgenstein for Understanding and Evaluating Technology." *Science and Engineering Ethics* 24(5): 1503–1519.

Coeckelbergh, Mark. 2017e. *Using Words and Things: Language and Philosophy of Technology*. New York: Routledge.

Coeckelbergh, Mark. 2018a. "The Art, Poetics, and Grammar of Technological Innovation as Practice, Process, and Performance." *AI & Society* 33(4): 501–510.

Coeckelbergh, Mark. 2018b. "Technology and the Good Society: A Polemical Essay on Social Ontology, Political Principles, and Responsibility for Technology." *Technology in Society* 52(February): 4–9.

Coeckelbergh, Mark. 2019. *Moved by Machines: Performance Metaphors and Philosophy of Technology*. New York: Routledge.

Coeckelbergh, Mark, and Wessel Reijers. 2016. "Narrative Technologies: A Philosophical Investigation of the Narrative Capacities of Technologies by Using Ricoeur's Narrative Theory." *Human Studies* 39(3): 325–346.

Collins, Harry, and Martin Kusch. 1999. *The Shape of Actions: What Humans and Machines Can Do*. Cambridge, MA: MIT Press.

Descartes, René. (1637) 1960. *Discours de la méthode* (Discourse on Method). Translated by L. J. Lafleur. In *Discourse on Method and Meditations*. Reprint, Indianapolis: Bobbs-Merrill.

Dreyfus, Hubert L. 1972. *What Computers Can't Do: The Limits of Artificial Reason*. New York: Harper and Row.

Dreyfus, Hubert L. 1992. *What Computers Still Can't Do: A Critique of Artificial Reason*. Cambridge, MA: MIT Press.

Floridi, Luciano. 2011. *The Philosophy of Information*. Oxford, UK: Oxford University Press.

Floridi, Luciano. 2013. *The Ethics of Information*. Oxford, UK: Oxford University Press.

Franssen, Maarten, and Stefan Koller. 2016. "Philosophy of Technology as a Serious Branch of Philosophy: The Empirical Turn as a Starting Point." In *Philosophy of Technology after the Empirical Turn*, edited by M. Franssen, P. E. Vermaas, P. Kroes, and A. W. M. Meijers, 31–61. Basel: Springer.

Gertz, Nolen. 2018. "Hegel, the Struggle for Recognition, and Robots." *Techné: Research in Philosophy and Technology* 22(2): 138–157.

Hacking, Ian. 1983. *Representing and Intervening*. Cambridge, UK: Cambridge University Press.

Haraway, Donna. (1991) 2000. "A Cyborg Manifesto." In *The Cybercultures Reader*, edited by David Bell and Barbara M. Kennedy, 291–324. Reprint, London: Routledge.

Harris, John. 2007. *Enhancing Evolution: The Ethical Case for Making Better People*. Princeton, NJ: Princeton University Press.

Kurzweil, Ray. 2005. *The Singularity Is Near: When Humans Transcend Biology*. New York: Viking.

Nordmann, Alfred. 2002. "Another New Wittgenstein: The Scientific and Engineering Background of the Tractatus." *Perspectives on Science* 10(3): 356–383.

Power, Des. 2005. "Models of Deafness." *Journal of Deaf Studies and Deaf Education* 10 (4): 451–459.

Rawls, John. (1971) 1999. *A Theory of Justice*, rev. ed. Cambridge, MA: Harvard University Press.

Sandler, Ronald. 2007. *Character and the Environment: A Virtue-Oriented Approach to Environmental Ethics*. New York: Columbia University Press.

Savulescu, Julian, and Ingmar Persson. 2008. "The Perils of Cognitive Enhancement and the Urgent Imperative to Enhance the Moral Character of Humanity." *Journal of Applied Philosophy* 25(3): 162–167.

Searle, John R. 1995. *The Construction of Social Reality*. New York: Free Press.

Searle, John R. 2006. "Social Ontology." *Anthropological Theory* 6(1): 12–29.

Simon, Judith. 2010. "The Entanglement of Trust and Knowledge on the We." *Ethics and Information Technology* 12(4): 343–355.

Søraker, Johnny Hartz. 2010. *The Value of Virtual Worlds: A Philosophical Analysis of Virtual Worlds and Their Potential Impact on Well-Being*. Dissertation, University of Twente, Netherlands.

Stahl, Bernd. 2004. "Whose Discourse? A Comparison of the Foucauldian and Habermasian Concepts of Discourse in Critical Information Systems Research." *Proceedings of the Tenth Americas Conference on Information Systems*, New York, August 2004.

Turkle, Sherry. 2011. *Alone Together: Why We Expect More from Technology and Less from Each Other*. New York: Basic Books.

Turkle, Sherry. 2015. *Reclaiming Conversation: The Power of Talk in a Digital Age*. New York: Penguin Press.

Vallor, Shannon. 2016. *Technology and the Virtues*. New York: Oxford University Press.

Van Wensveen, Louke. 2000. *Dirty Virtues: The Emergence of Ecological Virtue Ethics*. Amherst, NY: Prometheus Books.

Warwick, Kevin. 2004. *I, Cyborg*. Urbana: University of Illinois Press.

Winner, Langdon. 1986. *The Whale and the Reactor: A Search for Limits in an Age of High Technology*. Chicago: University of Chicago Press.

Wittgenstein, Ludwig. (1953) 2009. *Philosophische Untersuchungen* (*Philosophical Investigations*), rev. 4th ed. Translated by G. E. M. Anscombe, P. M. S. Hacker, and J. Schulte. Malden, MA: Wiley.

Wittgenstein, Ludwig. 1969. *On Certainty*. Translated by D. Paul and E. Anscombe. Oxford: Basil Blackwell.

Chapter 12: Philosophy of Technology and Other Academic Disciplines: Interdisciplinarity and Transdisciplinarity

Adema, Janneke, and Gary Hall. 2016. "Posthumanities: The Dark Side of 'The Dark Side of the Digital.'" *JEP: The Journal of Electronic Publishing* 19(2). *Disrupting the Humanities: Towards Posthumanities*. Available at: https://quod.lib.umich.edu/cgi/t/text/idx/j/jep/3336451.0019.201/--posthumanities-the-dark-side-of-the-dark-side-of-the-digital?rgn=main;view=fulltext

Coeckelbergh, Mark. 2015. *Money Machines: Electronic Financial Technologies, Distancing, and Responsibility in Global Finance*. Farnham, UK: Ashgate.

Coeckelbergh, Mark. 2017a. "Language and Technology: Maps, Bridges, and Pathways." *AI & Society* 32(2): 175–189. (Published online in 2015)

Coeckelbergh, Mark. 2017b. *New Romantic Cyborgs: Romanticism, Information Technology, and the End of the Machine*. Cambridge, MA: MIT Press.

Coeckelbergh, Mark. 2017c. "Technology Games: Using Wittgenstein for Understanding and Evaluating Technology." *Science and Engineering Ethics* 24(5): 1503–1519.

Coeckelbergh, Mark. 2017d. *Using Words and Things: Language and Philosophy of Technology*. New York: Routledge.

Coeckelbergh, Mark, Cristina Pop, Ramona Simut, Andreea Peca, Sebastian Pintea, Daniel David, and Bram Vanderborght. 2016. "A Survey of Expectations about the Role of Robots in Robot-Assisted Therapy for Children with ASD: Ethical Acceptability, Trust, Sociability, Appearance, and Attachment." *Science and Engineering Ethics* 22(1): 47–65.

Ess, Charles, Akira Kawabata, and Hiroyuki Kurosaki. 2007. "Cross-Cultural Perspectives on Religion and Computer-Mediated Communication." *Journal of Computer-Mediated Communication* 12(3): 939–955.

Esteban, Pablo G., Paul Baxter, Tony Belpaeme, Erik Billing, Haibin Cai, Hoang-Long Cao, Mark Coeckelbergh, Cristina Costescu, Daniel David, Albert De Beir, Yinfeng Fang, Zhaojie Ju, James Kennedy, Honghai Liu, Alexandre Mazel, Amit Pandey, Kathleen Richardson, Emmanuel Senft, Serge Thill, Greet Van de Perre, Bram Vanderborght, David Vernon, Hui Yu, and Tom Ziemke. 2017. "How to Build a Supervised Autonomous System for Robot-Enhanced Therapy for Children with Autism Spectrum Disorder." *Paladyn, Journal of Behavioral Robotics* 8(1): 18–38.

Feenberg, Andrew. 2010. *Between Reason and Experience: Essays in Technology and Modernity*. Cambridge, MA: MIT Press.

Fesmire, Steve. 2003. *John Dewey and Moral Imagination*. Bloomington: Indiana University Press.

Funk, Michael. 2018. Transcisiplinarity as Research Principle in the Philosophy of Technology. Talk in PhD seminar, Philosophy of Technology, Prof. Mark Coeckelbergh, University of Vienna, January 16, 2018.

Holzapfel, Andre, Bob L. Sturm, and Mark Coeckelbergh. 2018. "Ethical Dimensions of Music Information Retrieval Technology." *Transactions of the International Society for Music Information Retrieval* 1(1): 44–55.

IEEE. 2019. *Ethically Aligned Design: First Edition Overview*. https://standards.ieee.org/content/dam/ieee-standards/standards/web/documents/other/ead1e-overview.pdf

Johnson, Deborah G. 2006. "Computer Systems: Moral Entities But Not Moral Agents." *Ethics and Information Technology* 8(4): 195–204.

Latour, Bruno. 1993. *We Have Never Been Modern*. Translated by Catherine Porter. Cambridge, MA: Harvard University Press.

Latour, Bruno, and Steve Woolgar. 1979. *Laboratory Life: The Construction of Scientific Facts*. Beverly Hills, CA: Sage.

Moor, James H. 1985. "What Is Computer Ethics?" *Metaphilosophy* 16(4): 266–275.

Oudshoorn, Nelly, and Trevor Pinch, eds. 2003. *How Users Matter: The Co-Construction of Users and Technology*. Cambridge, MA: MIT Press.

Pinch, Trevor J., and Wiebe E. Bijker. 1984. "The Social Construction of Facts and Artefacts: Or How the Sociology of Science and the Sociology of Technology Might Benefit Each Other." *Social Studies of Science* 14(3): 399–441.

Thompson Klein, Julie. 1990. *Interdisciplinarity: History, Theory, and Practice*. Detroit: Wayne State University Press.

Thompson Klein, Julie. 1996. *Crossing Boundaries: Knowledge, Disciplinarities, and Interdisciplinarities*. Charlottesville: University Press of Virginia.

University of Minnesota Press. Posthumanities. https://www.upress.umn.edu/book-division/series/posthumanities

Verbeek, Peter-Paul. 2005. *What Things Do: Philosophical Reflections on Technology, Agency, and Design*. University Park: Pennsylvania State University Press.

Wikipedia. "Robotics." Last modified April 24, 2019. https://en.wikipedia.org/wiki/Robotics

Winner, Langdon. 1980. "Do Artifacts Have Politics?" *Daedalus* 109(1): 121–136.

Chapter 13: Philosophy of Technology and Practices beyond Academia

Bowie, Andrew. 2015. "The 'Philosophy of Performance' and the Performance of Philosophy." *Performance Philosophy* 1: 51–58.

Briggle, Adam. 2015. *A Field Philosopher's Guide to Fracking*. New York: Liveright.

Cardone, Nico. 2018. "België eerste land ter wereld om 'Killer Robots' te verbieden." VRT NWS, July 4, 2018. https://www.vrt.be/vrtnws/nl/2018/07/04/resolutie-killerrobots/

Coeckelbergh, Mark. 2017a. "The Art, Poetics, and Grammar of Technological Innovation as Practice, Process, and Performance." *AI & Society* 33(4): 501–510.

Coeckelbergh, Mark. 2017b. "Can Machines Create Art?" *Philosophy & Technology* 30(3): 285–303.

Coeckelbergh, Mark. 2017c. *New Romantic Cyborgs: Romanticism, Information Technology, and the End of the Machine.* Cambridge, MA: MIT Press.

Coeckelbergh, Mark. 2017d. *Using Words and Things: Language and Philosophy of Technology.* New York: Routledge.

Coeckelbergh, Mark. 2018. "Should We Ban Fully Autonomous Weapons?" Guest article in Uni:view Magazin, University of Vienna, January 12, 2018. https://medienportal.univie.ac.at/uniview/wissenschaft-gesellschaft/detailansicht/artikel/should-we-ban-fully-autonomous-weapons/

Dewey, John. 1916. *Democracy and Education.* New York: The Macmillan Company. Available at https://archive.org/stream/democracyandedu00dewegoog#page/n6/mode/2up

Dewey, John. (1934) 1980. *Art as Experience.* Reprint, New York: Perigee.

European Commission. 2019. "ICT and Art—the STARTS Initiative." Last updated February 14, 2019. https://ec.europa.eu/digital-single-market/en/ict-art-starts-platform

Floridi, Luciano, ed. 2015. *The Onlife Manifesto: Being Human in a Hyperconnected Era.* Heidelberg, Germany: Springer.

Friedman, Batya, Peter H. Kathn Jr., and Alan Borning. 2008. "Value Sensitive Design and Information Systems." In *The Handbook of Information and Computer Ethics*, edited by Kenneth Einar Himma and Herman T. Tavani, 69–101. Hoboken, NJ: John Wiley & Sons.

Frodeman, Robert, Julie Thompson Klein, and Carl Mitcham, eds. 2010. *The Oxford Handbook of Interdisciplinarity.* Oxford, UK: Oxford University Press.

Heidegger, Martin. 1977. "The Question Concerning Technology." In *Martin Heidegger: The Question Concerning Technology and Other Essays*, translated by William Lovitt, 3–35. New York: Harper Torchbooks.

McLuhan, Marshall. (1964) 2001. *Understanding Media: The Extensions of Man.* Reprint, London: Routledge.

Novalis. (1799) 1997. *Philosophical Writings.* Edited by Margaret Mahony Stoljar. Abany: State University of New York Press.

Owen, R., J. Stilgoe, P. Macnaghten, M. Gorman, E. Fisher, and D. Guston. 2013. "A Framework for Responsible Innovation." In *Responsible Innovation: Managing the Responsible Emergence of Science and Innovation in Society*, edited by Richard Owen, John Bessant, and Maggie Heintz. 27–50. Chichester, UK: John Wiley and Sons.

Stahl, Bernd Carsten, Grace Eden, Marina Jirotka, and Mark Coeckelbergh. 2014. "From Computer Ethics to Responsible Research and Innovation in ICT: The Transition of Reference Discourses Informing Ethics-Related Research in Information Systems." *Information & Management* 51(6): 810–818.

Van den Hoven, Jeroen. 2007. "ICT and Value Sensitive Design." In *IFIP International Federation for Information Processing*, Vol. 233: *The Information Society: Innovations, Legitimacy, Ethics and Democracy*, edited by P. Goujon, S. Lavelle, P. Duquenoy, K. Kimppa, and V. Laurent, 67–72. Boston: Springer.

Von Schomberg, René. 2013. "A Vision of Responsible Innovation." In *Responsible Innovation: Managing the Responsible Emergence of Science and Innovation in Society*, edited by Richard Owen, John Bessant, and Maggie Heintz, 51–74. London: John Wiley.

GLOSSARY

Actants Term coined by Latour to refer to non-human actors. According to Latour, things are also part of the social.

Alterity Concept used in philosophy and the social sciences (especially anthropology), for example, in the philosophy of Levinas: otherness.

Alternative modernity A term used by Feenberg to argue that we should not so much move beyond modernity but rather toward a different, alternative form of modernity in which technology is directed toward more democratic uses and processes.

Anthropocene The idea that we are living in a new geological epoch due to the transformative influence of human behavior on the earth; humans are seen as a significant "geological force" (Crutzen 2006).

Applied philosophy The application of principles, concepts, and theories from philosophy to practical problems and activities. For example, applied ethics uses principles from normative ethics to address problems in practices such as medicine and law.

Artifacts have politics Claim made by Winner to mean that artifacts are linked to social forms of organization and social structures and (hence) have political consequences. For example, political bias can enter the design of things.

Artificial agents Agents that are not natural but created by human beings. In the context of digital technologies, the term may refer to robots, artificially intelligent systems, bots on the internet, smart contracts, digital assistants, and so on.

Autonomous technology Technology that does things without direct human intervention (e.g., a robot) or technological development that takes its own course, without much control by human beings. The latter view is also called **technological determinism.**

Body schema Term used by Merleau-Ponty: Kinesthetic awareness of the position of the body (parts) in space, updated during body movement.

Capitalism Economic and political system based on private ownership of the means of production and free market competition, which according to Marx and other critics, leads to capital accumulation and power in the hands of a few and exploitation of workers.

Challenger disaster In January 1986, NASA Space Shuttle Challenger broke apart 73 seconds after take-off and exploded, killing all crew members. It was caused by the failure of an O-ring seal in a joint, which was not designed to handle unusually cold conditions. It can be seen as an engineering disaster, but also as a management and organizational problem: an investigation revealed that the problem was known but was not addressed by the managers, and that warnings about the cold temperatures by engineers were ignored.

Climate change Can refer to any change in climate during history of the Earth but is usually used as a synonym of the recent phenomenon of global warming (see **global warming**).

Co-construction of society and technology Term from **STS**, and against the idea that technology determines society or that society totally shapes technology. Rather, both shape one another, and there is no determinism or autonomy of either.

Computer ethics Field focused on ethical problems raised by computer technology.

Confucianism A philosophy, religion, or way of life that developed from the teachings of the Chinese philosopher Confucius (551–479 BCE). It emphasizes human relationships, family, and social harmony. These values manifest humanity's essence, compassion, or altruism, which is anchored in Heaven. Human beings are seen as good and perfectible through self-cultivation. Ethics is about knowing one's place in the social order, cultivating virtue, and acting in harmony with one's nature and the law of Heaven.

Converging technologies Existing technologies that merge into one form. For example, in the context of ICTs, typically several technologies come together in one device. It is claimed that information technology will increasingly be combined with, for example, biotechnology or nanotechnology.

Cryptocurrencies Digital currency and currency system that functions as a medium of exchange and uses cryptography to create units and to control transactions. It enables decentralized control of transactions as opposed to centralized control by banks and other financial institutions.

Cybernetics The science of communication and control systems. "Systems" is broadly defined. Norbert Wiener defined cybernetics as the scientific study of "control and communication in the animal and the machine" (Wiener [1948] 1961). Cybernetics influenced developments in computing, robotics, and artificial intelligence (among other fields).

Cyborg Can have various meanings, but here used (e.g., by Haraway) in the sense of a hybrid of biological organism and machine. The term can be used literally or metaphorically.

Dao (or Tao) Notion in traditional Chinese philosophies, meaning way, path, truth, principle, or natural order of the universe. In Confucian ethics, the way people should live; governing principle for human affairs. (For what this way is about, see **Confucianism.**)

Data commodity Data that are produced (e.g., on internet via social media) and bought and sold (e.g., to other companies).

Demiurge Ancient Greek notion (e.g., in Plato): maker or creator of the universe.

Democratic deliberation Pragmatists support democracy; for philosophy of technology, this implies the view that decisions about (the future of) technology should be a matter of democratic deliberation rather than left to technocratic and/or corporate control.

Digital humanities Use of digital resources (data) and application of tools from computer science to humanities fields such as literature, history, linguistics, and philosophy.

Disenchantment Term from Max Weber: the world becomes deprived of mystery, magic, and religion.

Dividuation Term from French philosopher Gilles Deleuze: the internal division of entities into measurable parameters that can then be modulated and controlled. In control societies, we are transformed into "dividuals" as we are mined for data. It impoverishes social connections.

DREAM Acronym of a research project in the area of robotics funded by the European Commission that is about robot-enhanced therapy for children with autism spectrum disorder (ASD).

Dual nature of artifacts thesis View in analytic philosophy of technology that sees artifacts as having a dual nature: physical properties, but also functional properties related to the intention of the designer.

Empirical turn in philosophy of technology: An approach in philosophy of technology that pays more attention to specific technological artifacts and their use as opposed to grand theories about (modern) technology at large and society at large.

Enactivism Approach in cognitive science that, inspired by phenomenology, argues that cognition arises, meaning is generated, and self emerges through the interaction between an acting organism and its environment. Experience is not a matter of passive reception; instead, worlds are enacted: experience is shaped by the actions of organisms.

Enframing, Modern technology as Heideggerian terminology: modern technology orders us as a "standing reserve": it reveals everything, including humans, as resources to use.

Engineering ethics Interdisciplinary fields consisting of engineers and philosophers that develop codes of ethics for engineers and reflect on the ethical and societal impact of engineering, values related to engineering design, and the responsibility of engineers. Sometimes also defined as a field of applied ethics that applies ethical principles to the practice of engineering.

Engineering philosophy of technology Thinking about technology focused on technological artifacts and using technological vocabulary, staying close to the engineering sciences.

Enlightenment Period in Western intellectual history in the 18th century in France, the early United States, and elsewhere when thinkers and movements valued reason, science, philosophy, liberty, and (other) progressive political values as opposed to monarchy, tradition, and religious dogma.

Entropy Term from physics (thermodynamics) but also used in a more general sense as meaning "lack of order."

Experience Learning from experience, also collectively, is key in Dewey's philosophy. Knowledge should not be divorced from experience.

Experimentation Important aspect of Dewey's philosophy. Technology can be seen as a kind of social experiment. For example, Ibo van de Poel has argued that nuclear technology is a social experiment (van de Poel 2011).

Extended mind thesis Term from philosophy of mind/cognitive science. View developed by Clark and Chalmers, according to which there is no principled distinction between mind, body, and environment (the are part of a coupled system). Technological artifacts can function as extensions of mind (or more precisely the cognitive system), for example, as an extension of memory.

Fake news False information spread by online social media.

False consciousness Term in Marxist theory denoting persons that do not perceive the true nature of their socioeconomic situation and the related exploitation and oppression.

False needs Term used by Marcuse to mean needs that are not necessary for survival but are imposed on persons by particular social interests to repress them, needs that perpetuate misery and injustice.

Feminism A range of social and political movements that share the goal of gender equality, often expressed in terms of women's rights or political, economic, and social equality.

Field philosophy Term used by Frodeman, Briggle, and others to argue for an activist form of philosophy that leaves the university office and goes into the world of industry, neighborhoods, and playgrounds to engage with real world issues.

Foundationalism In moral philosophy, it is the view that what mainly matters in morality is to have some solid foundations or principles, which can then guide and justify deliberation and be applied to concrete cases. In epistemology, it is the view that beliefs can be justified on the basis of basic or foundational beliefs. Pragmatists reject foundationalism.

Fourth revolution Term used by Floridi that refers to the revolution brought about by information technology, after the previous revolutions that displaced humans from the center of the universe: the Copernican, Darwinian, and Freudian.

Frankenstein Early 19th-century story by Mary Shelley about a scientist (Frankenstein) who creates a monster by means of technology. Still an important narrative that shapes contemporary discourse about technology.

Frankfurt School (*Frankfurter Schule*) Neo-Marxist school of social theory and philosophy founded in the interwar period at the Goethe University Frankfurt. Prominent members include Adorno, Horkheimer, Marcuse, Fromm, and (in more recent times) Habermas.

Functional morality Concept proposed by Wallach and Allen (2009): machines can have some capacity to deal with moral challenges but are not full moral agents.

Gelassenheit German word used by Heidegger to suggest an attitude of releasement, not wanting to control things. Used in opposition to the modern attitude of willing mastery and control, e.g., control over nature.

Gene editing (or **genome editing**) A type of **genetic engineering** in which DNA is inserted, deleted, modified, or replaced in the genome of a living organism. Today, a common method is the use of engineered nucleases (a kind of enzyme) also called "molecular scissors."

Genetic engineering (or **genetic modification**) Direct manipulation of the DNA in an organism's genome to alter one or more characteristics of an organism by using biotechnology.

Genetically modified organisms (GMOs) Organisms whose genetic material has been altered using **genetic engineering** techniques.

Geoengineering Responses to climate change that rely on technology and engineering, in particular, large-scale interventions in the earth's climate system such as methods to remove carbon dioxide from the earth's atmosphere or solar radiation management.

Global village Term from McLuhan: Technology has globalized our perception and society.

Global warming Scientifically the term refers to the observed rise in the average temperature of the climate system during the past 100 years. In 2013, the Intergovernmental Panel on Climate Change (IPCC) said in their report that it is "extremely likely" that humans have been the dominant cause of the rise in temperature since the mid-20th century, for example, through the emission of so-called greenhouse gasses. Effects of global warming include not only rise in temperature but also, for example, rising sea levels, changing rainfall, and more frequent extreme weather events. For humans, it could cause problems with food security and migration.

Google Corporation famous for its popular internet search engine (a program for finding information on the internet).

Habits Term in Dewey's philosophy. Next to novelty, experimentation, etc., there are also routines and habits. Pragmatists value both.

Hot and cool media Distinction made by McLuhan: Hot media, such as film, occupy one's senses completely but demand little engagement and interaction;

users are spoon-fed. Cool media, by contrast, require the person's active participation, for example, a phone conversation.

Human enhancement Improving the human or humans, for example, by genetic engineering or by means of technological implants. It can refer to improvement of the human species or to a single human. It is not clear what "enhancement" or "improving" means, and what the border is between therapy and enhancement. **Transhumanists** typically defend some form of human enhancement.

Humanities philosophy of technology Thinking about technology that focuses on humans, culture, and society rather than technological artifacts, and which uses vocabulary from the humanities and social sciences to study the effects of technology.

Human–technology relations Postphenomenology analyzes the various ways in which humans experience and engage with technologies and how technologies mediate our actions and experience of the world. (See also **technological mediation**.)

Hybris Ancient Greek concept: insult to the gods; doing more than humans are allowed to do.

ICTs Information and communication technologies.

Individuation Term used by Simondon to express that individuals are not the starting point but the outcome of a process.

Inforgs Term used by Floridi to say that human beings have an informational nature: we are "informationally embodied organisms" embedded in the infosphere.

Information ethics (IE) Ethics of information; can have various meanings. Conceptualized by Floridi as an ethics of the infosphere (see **Infosphere**), understood as an environmental ethics. Entities are seen as informational and as part of an informational environment and ecology, and the good is understood as what is good for informational entities and for the infosphere. Ethical principles aim at the avoidance of entropy in the infosphere. An alternative conceptualization of information ethics can be found in Capurro, who in contrast to Floridi stresses the body and its existential dimensions.

Information technologies Tools and processes that store, transmit, and manipulate information.

Infosphere Term used by Floridi to say that reality is the totality of information: all beings are informational and are part of an informational whole, an informational ecology.

Instrumental rationality A form of rationality that focuses on the means to achieve an end without reflecting on the value of that end.

Instrumentalism Here a specific, Deweyan view of knowledge. Knowledge is connected to experience and practice.

Instrumentalization (of humans) Term used by Marcuse denoting the use of humans as means and their consequent repression.

Instrumentalization theory Feenberg's theory according to which technologies have a functional and rational side but also an experiential side that concerns the context of use: users can co-shape the meaning and use of the technology; the technology becomes part of the lifeworld. The "world" or meaning of the technology has these two dimensions or stages.

Interdisciplinarity Going beyond the borders of one's discipline, rather than merely working together with other disciplines.

Interpretative flexibility Term used by Bijker and others in STS to mean that what a technological artifact becomes in an innovation process is initially open and only reaches closure after a process that involves various social actors with their interests and goals, which shape the design and the technological solutions (and even the problems).

Language game or **form of life** Terms used by Wittgenstein to argue that language is a matter of use and (according to the interpretation I propose here) that this use must always be put in the context of its use, since it is linked to activities, games, and ways of doing things in a wider social-cultural context.

Level of abstraction Method used by Floridi in his information ethics, inspired by theoretical computer science: only some variables are selected for the analysis (the most relevant ones). Applied to ethics and thinking about human beings, it implies, for example, that only information is considered; it is not human-centered (this is how Floridi uses the method).

Luddite movement A group of textile workers in 19th-century England (it started in Nottingham) who destroyed weaving machines as a way to protest against what they perceived as a threat to their skills and jobs. The term now often has a more general meaning: protest against technology in general (Neo-Luddism).

Machine ethics Term that can refer to ethics of machines, but also more narrowly to the project of building ethics into machines, in which case they have **machine morality**.

Machine morality Morality built into a machine. Could be similar to human morality or potentially also different.

Mass society Society of atomistic and alienated individuals, manipulated by capitalist and bureaucratic elites.

Material hermeneutics Term from Ihde. Interpretation, but not only interpretation of texts but also interpretation in other material engagements.

Micro-mechanisms of power Term used by Foucault to point to ways power is exercised and present in everyday relations and practices, not just in "macro" mechanisms of power used by the state (state power) or strong individuals.

Mindless morality Term used by Floridi to refer to a morality that is not based on mind or internal mental states of the moral agents or moral patients.

Minitel Minitel was an information system used in France that offered online services (e.g., online banking) via the telephone line, before the internet.

Moral agency vs. moral patiency Questions regarding moral agency concern the morality of what humans or non-humans do (the "giving" dimension), whereas moral patiency concerns the question of what is due to humans or non-humans, how they should be treated, and what moral status they have (the "receiving" dimension).

Moral mediation (sometimes also called the **morality of things**; see also **moral agency** of things) Terms from Verbeek (2011) to say that technological artifacts have moral consequences and influence and shape our moral decisions and actions.

Multistability Term used by Ihde and others to say that the meaning of a technology varies with use and (cultural and practical) context, even if the material artifact remains the same. Some uses may not have been intended by those who developed the technologies.

Music information retrieval (MIR) Interdisciplinary field that is concerned with retrieving information from music. It uses algorithms to analyze music and sometimes machine learning. It can be used to categorize, manipulate, and create music. For example, it can enable music services to determine users' preferences not only on the basis of their past and present behavior but also on the basis of the actual sound of the song, the audio signal. Machine learning could be used to predict listening preferences.

Narcissus Mythological figure (ancient Greece): Fell in love with his own reflection in the water. He stared at his image until he died.

Narrative technologies Term coined by Reijers and Coeckelbergh. According to this view, technologies shape and configure lived narrative time as they organize characters and events into a plot.

Naturalistic fallacy Term used by G.E. Moore to say that one should not explain good in terms of natural properties such as pleasant: one should not confuse moral with natural properties. But in this discussion, the term is used as synonymous with the so-called is-ought problem as introduced by David Hume, who famously pointed out that it is not obvious how one can move from claims about what *is* to claims about what *ought* to be.

Negative anthropology Term used by author of this book to refer to anthropologies that say what the human is not. The term has also been used (in a slightly different sense) by philosophers such as Günter Anders and the early *Frankfurter Schule*. According to Anders, humans have non-specificity and therefore we have to use technology to shape ourselves.

Occupy movement International political movement that protests against social and economic inequality (especially the concentration of wealth among a few) and the undermining of democracy. The movement started in the United States with the occupation of a park near Wall Street and received a lot of attention in 2011 and 2012.

Onlife Term used by Floridi and others to capture the experience that there is no longer a separate "online" sphere as opposed to an "offline" sphere in life; today the internet and related technologies pervade human lives. We live in an informational ecosystem.

Organ projection Term from Kapp: tools take the shape and function of human organs.

Panopticon Type of building designed by Jeremy Bentham that enables monitoring of prisoners such that they do not know whether they are being watched.

Patriarchy A system of social organization in which males hold the power and females are excluded from it.

Performance philosophy Interdisciplinary and pluralist research field that aims to connect philosophy and performance and reflects on the relationship between performance and philosophy.

Pharmakon Greek word meaning drug; in contemporary science, it can be any biologically active substance. The term is used by Stiegler to compare technology to a toxic substance (poison) that can at the same time be the remedy, the cure.

Philosophical anthropology Subfield of philosophy that asks (metaphysical and phenomenological) questions regarding the human. It has existed since ancient times, but only developed as a subdiscipline since the first half of the 20th century, first in German philosophy and then also in France and elsewhere.

Philosophy of language Subdiscipline in philosophy that focuses on language, including issues concerning meaning, interpretation, communication, the relation between language and reality, and the relation between language and truth.

Philosophy of technology A disciplined and systematic attempt to conceptually understand and evaluate technology and its implications for our lives and societies. It can be an academic discipline within philosophy, and it can take more disciplinary and academic or more public and transdisciplinary forms.

Phronesis Ancient Greek term found, for example, in Aristotle: practical wisdom (in ethics).

Pluralism As a normative stance, the view that there should be (or that one should tolerate) diversity of views, values, theories, or methods (e.g., in society or in a particular discipline) rather than one view, method, etc. Here, it is the view that philosophers of technology should use or tolerate more than one conceptualization of technology and/or more than one approach.

Political economy The study of production and trade and how these are organized in nation states. Here it is used in the sense of economics in the tradition of Marx and Engels, with a focus on theory concerning surplus value and class struggle.

Posthumanism Posthumanists reject the anthropocentrism of traditional humanist thinking and emphasize (our relations with) non-human entities such as animals, plants, and robots. They are also critical about ontological borders, for example, between nature and culture, or between humans and non-humans. Sometimes posthumanism is used as an umbrella term that includes transhumanism, but many (critical and cultural) posthumanists adopt a more relational and social thinking and reject the transhumanist focus on the human and the idea that humans should control the natural world.

Posthumanities Humanities research that takes posthumanist and interdisciplinary directions.

Postmodern identity Identity that is fluid and non-essentialist. Postmodern theorists also emphasize difference.

Postmodernism Umbrella term for 20th-century approaches and movements in philosophy and elsewhere (e.g., architecture) that question modernism. Often includes a relativist stance and questioning of modern meta-narratives about progress, Enlightenment rationality, and universalist notions of truth and morality. The term is often associated with Lyotard, Derrida, Foucault, and Rorty; but application of the term is usually controversial.

Postphenomenology Approach in philosophy of technology that is inspired by phenomenology and hermeneutics but is more empirically and materially oriented, studying the experiences, uses, and mediations of concrete technological artifacts.

Prima philosophia "First philosophy": ancient Greek notion. Aristotle argued that (what today is called) metaphysics is the first, most fundamental philosophy or science and should have priority. Later philosophers such as Thomas Aquinas and Descartes also used the term in their writings.

Problem of other minds Philosophical question: Given that I can only observe the behavior of others, how can I know that they have minds?

Prometheus Mythological figure in Plato's writings: a Titan who stole the mechanical arts (technology) from the gods and gave it to the humans.

Prosthetic beings Beings that lack something and have to compensate this with technology (humans).

Public deliberation Important for Dewey and Deweyan philosophers of technology (but also for authors in critical theory), who aim to render decisions in society, including decisions about technology, more participatory and democratic.

Purification Term used by Latour to express that modern ontology has tried to keep separate nature and culture, humans and non-humans, etc., whereas actually in practice, we have never lived in this way, done science in this way, and so forth. We have always been nonmoderns.

Representationalism Theory in epistemology and philosophy of mind that sees (gaining) knowledge as a matter of mentally representing or mirroring external reality. Pragmatists reject representationalism.

Responsible innovation or **responsible research and innovation (RRI)** The idea is to do research and innovation in a way that (or beforehand, proactively) takes into account the ethical, societal, and environmental impacts of the technology. In Europe, the European Commission has encouraged RRI in its recent funding programs.

Revealing or unconcealment, Technology as Heideggerian terminology: technology shapes how we perceive and experience the world.

Robophilosophy Transdisciplinary research and events (conferences) that bring together philosophers and other disciplines to discuss philosophy of robotics. So far, the focus has been on social robotics.

Robot prostitutes Robots used in prostitution, sometimes replacing human prostitutes.

Science, Technology, and Society studies or Science and Technology Studies (STS) Interdisciplinary field in the social sciences that studies how technology and society shape one another. It studies technological innovation in its social-historical context, assesses the societal and ethical impact of technologies, and studies (and sometimes influences) science and technology policy.

Semiotics The study of meaning-making and signs.

Sexism Bias and discrimination on the basis of sex, typically against women.

Singularity An intelligence explosion powered by new developments in artificial intelligence that will lead to new, artificial entities that will surpass humans (unless we enhance them and/or merge them with machines). Many **transhumanists** hold this belief.

Sisyphus Mythological figure (ancient Greece): was punished by being forced to roll a boulder up a hill and repeat this for eternity.

Social media Interactive digital technologies that enable the creation and sharing of information, with an emphasis on user-generated content and social networks (so-called Web 2.0).

Speech act Term from linguistics and philosophy of language: A speech act is an utterance that has a performative function in communication. Typical examples include promising and ordering. Speech acts are not about representing something but about doing something and influencing others (to do something).

Surplus value In Marxist theory, it denotes the increase in the value of capital, which equals the value created by workers in excess of the cost of their labor.

System and lifeworld Terms from critical theory to oppose or connect the world of rationality and technology to/with the experience of people.

Technofeminism Study of gender issues related to technology. Often used in a narrower sense as synonymous with Wajcman's approach, which focuses on the materiality of technology.

Technological mediation Term used by Ihde, Verbeek, and other philosophers from the postphenomenological school to say that technology is not a neutral instrument but shapes our perception of the world and our actions.

Technology Technology can have various meanings, including a tool, an instrument, an artifact, an infrastructure, a system, an activity, a will, or an idea. When doing philosophy of technology, it is always good to define what you mean by "technology."

Telematic society Term used by Flusser to argue that society and culture are becoming more immaterial, networked, informational, and symbolic—less dependent on material things.

Thamus Mythological figure in Plato's writings: god and king who argued against writing.

The good life Concept in Western ethics that is of ancient Greek origin (*eudaimonia*) and refers to ethics as concerned with the good way to live your life, rather than with right and wrong.

The medium is the message Famous phrase coined by McLuhan to say that media are more than a mere means for the message: they also shape the message, as they have effects on human consciousness and society.

Transdisciplinarity Going beyond the borders of one's discipline in the direction of a merging of disciplines and/or going beyond academia.

Transhumanism The belief that the human species can and should evolve beyond its present state by means of science and technology. Transhumanists usually defend **human enhancement**. It can also refer to the movement (or movements) and societies that hold this belief and (sometimes) actively take steps to realize it.

Trolley dilemma (or **trolley problem**) Thought experiment used by philosophers, especially consequentialist philosophers (e.g., utilitarians), to explore our moral intuitions and moral reasoning in dilemma situations. A typical story goes like this (but there are many variations): a runaway train is heading down a railway track. Five people are tied up against the track. You stand next to a lever; if you pull the lever, the train will be diverted to another track, where it will kill one person. What is the best moral choice: do nothing or pull the lever?

Value Sensitive Design An approach to technology design processes that systematically takes into account human values. The main idea is that design is already value laden, often unintentionally, and that once we become aware of this, we can and should try to proactively design in a way that also shapes this ethical dimension. Can be combined with **responsible innovation**.

Vampire Undead being in European folklore that feeds on the vital force (blood) of humans. Popular in 19th-century fiction and in the (later) horror genre.

Virtual worlds Computer-based simulated environment with multiple users; users can interact by means of an avatar (graphical representation of the user). Can be used for games but also for other applications.

Virtue ethics Normative theory in ethics centered on virtue and character rather than duties and rules (deontology) or consequences. In Western thinking, this approach has roots in Aristotle's ethics.

INDEX

Figures are indicated by "*f*" following the page number.